PHP & MySQL®

FOR

DUMMIES®

4TH EDITION

PHP & MySQL® FOR DUMMIES®

4TH EDITION

by Janet Valade

WILEY

Wiley Publishing, Inc.

PHP & MySQL® For Dummies,® 4th Edition

Published by
Wiley Publishing, Inc.
111 River Street
Hoboken, NJ 07030-5774

www.wiley.com

For general information on our other products and services, please contact our Customer Care Department within the U.S. at 877-762-2974, outside the U.S. at 317-572-3993, or fax 317-572-4002.

For technical support, please visit www.wiley.com/techsupport.

Wiley also publishes its books in a variety of electronic formats. Some content that appears in print may not be available in electronic books.

Library of Congress Control Number: 2009940274

ISBN: 978-0-470-52758-0

Manufactured in the United States of America

10 9 8 7 6 5 4 3 2

WILEY

About the Author

Janet Valade is the author of *PHP & MySQL Web Development All-in-One Desk Reference For Dummies, PHP 5 For Dummies, PHP & MySQL Everyday Apps For Dummies,* and *PHP & MySQL: Your visual blueprint for creating dynamic, database-driven Web sites,* as well as the first, second, and third editions of this book. In addition, Janet is the author of *Spring into Linux* and a coauthor of *Mastering Visually Dreamweaver 8 and Flash 8.*

Janet has twenty years of experience in the computing field. Most recently, she worked as a Web designer and programmer in an engineering firm for four years. Before that, Janet worked for thirteen years in a university environment, where she was a systems analyst. During her tenure, she supervised the installation and operation of computing resources, designed and developed a data archive, supported faculty and students in their computer usage, wrote numerous technical papers, and developed and presented seminars on a variety of technology topics.

To keep in touch, see `janetvalade.com`.

Author's Acknowledgments

First, I want to express my appreciation to the entire open source community. Without those who give their time and talent, there would be no cool PHP and MySQL for me to write about. Furthermore, I never would have learned this software without the lists, where people generously spend their time answering foolish questions from beginners.

I want to thank my mother for passing on a writing gene, along with many other things. And my children always for everything. My thanks to my friends Art, Dick, and Marge for responding to my last-minute call for help. I particularly want to thank Sammy, Dude, Spike, Lucky, Upanishad, Sadie, and E.B. for their important contributions.

And, of course, I want to thank the professionals who make it all possible. Without the people at Wiley, this book would not exist. Because they all do their jobs so well, I can contribute my part to this joint project.

Publisher's Acknowledgments

We're proud of this book; please send us your comments at http://dummies.custhelp.com. For other comments, please contact our Customer Care Department within the U.S. at 877-762-2974, outside the U.S. at 317-572-3993, or fax 317-572-4002.

Some of the people who helped bring this book to market include the following:

Acquisitions and Editorial

Project Editor: Rebecca Senninger
  (Previous Edition: Pat O'Brien)

Acquisitions Editor: Kyle Looper

Copy Editor: Virginia Sanders

Technical Editor: John Gosney

Editorial Manager: Leah Cameron

Editorial Assistant: Amanda Foxworth

Sr. Editorial Assistant: Cherie Case

Cartoons: Rich Tennant (www.the5thwave.com)

Composition Services

Project Coordinator: Kristie Rees

Layout and Graphics: Melissa K. Jester, Christine Williams

Proofreader: Toni Settle

Indexer: BIM Indexing & Proofreading

Publishing and Editorial for Technology Dummies

Richard Swadley, Vice President and Executive Group Publisher

Andy Cummings, Vice President and Publisher

Mary Bednarek, Executive Acquisitions Director

Mary C. Corder, Editorial Director

Publishing for Consumer Dummies

Diane Graves Steele, Vice President and Publisher

Composition Services

Debbie Stailey, Director of Composition Services

Contents at a Glance

Table of Contents

Introduction

*W*elcome to the exciting world of Web database applications. This book provides the basic techniques to build any Web database application, but I certainly recommend that you start with a simple one. In this book, I develop two sample applications, both chosen to represent two types of applications frequently encountered on the Web: product catalogs and customer- or member-only sites that require the user to register and log in with a password. The sample applications are complicated enough to require more than one program and to use a variety of data and data manipulation techniques, yet simple enough to be easily understood and adapted to a variety of Web sites. After you master the simple applications, you can expand the basic design to include all the functionality that you can think of.

About This Book

Think of this book as your friendly guide to building a Web database application. This book is designed as a reference, not as a tutorial, so you don't have to read it from cover to cover. You can start reading at any point — in Chapter 1, Chapter 9, wherever. I divide the task of building a Web database application into manageable chunks of information, so check out the table of contents and locate the topic that you're interested in. If you need to know information from another chapter to understand the chapter you're reading, I reference that chapter.

Here's a sample of the topics I discuss:

- ✔ Building and using a MySQL database
- ✔ Adding PHP to HTML files
- ✔ Using the features of the PHP language
- ✔ Using HTML forms to collect information from users
- ✔ Showing information from a database in a Web page
- ✔ Storing information in a database

Conventions Used in This Book

This book includes many examples of PHP programming statements, MySQL statements, and HTML. Such statements are shown in a different typeface, which looks like the following line:

```
A PHP program statement
```

In addition, snippets or key terms of PHP, MySQL, and HTML are sometimes shown in the text of a paragraph. When they are, the special text in the paragraph is also shown in the example typeface, different than the paragraph typeface. For instance, this text is an example of a PHP statement within the paragraph text.

In examples, you will often see some words in italic. Italicized words are general types that need to be replaced with the specific name appropriate for your data. For instance, when you see an example like the following:

```
SELECT field1,field2 FROM tablename
```

field1, field2, and tablename need to be replaced with real names because they are in italic. When you use this statement in your program, you might use it in the following form:

```
SELECT name,age FROM Customer
```

In addition, you might see three dots (...) following a list in an example line. You don't type the three dots. They just mean that you can have as many items in the list as you want. For instance, when you see

```
SELECT field1,field2,... FROM tablename
```

the three dots just mean that your list of fields can be longer than two. It means you can go on with field3, field4, and so forth. For example, your statement might be

```
SELECT name,age,height,shoesize FROM Customer
```

From time to time, you'll also see something in bold. Pay attention to these; they indicate something I want you to see or something you need to type.

What You're Not To Read

Some information in this book is flagged as *Technical Stuff* with an icon off to the left. Sometimes you'll see this technical stuff in a sidebar: Consider it information that you don't need to read to create a Web database application. This extra information might contain a further look under the hood or describe a technique that requires more technical knowledge to execute. Some readers may be interested in the extra technical information or techniques, but feel free to ignore them if you don't find them interesting or useful.

Foolish Assumptions

To write a focused book rather than an encyclopedia, I needed to assume some background for you, the reader. I assumed that you know HTML and CSS and have created Web sites with HTML and CSS. Consequently, although I use HTML/CSS in many examples, I do not explain the HTML/CSS. If you don't have an HTML background, this book will be more difficult to use. I suggest that you read an HTML book — such as *HTML, XHTML & CSS For Dummies* by Ed Tittel and Jeff Noble (Wiley) — and build some practice Web pages before you start this book. In particular, some background in HTML forms and tables is useful. However, if you're the impatient type, I won't tell you it's impossible to proceed without knowing HTML and CSS. You may be able to glean enough HTML and CSS from this book to build your particular Web site. If you choose to proceed without knowing HTML, I suggest that you have an HTML book by your side to assist you.

If you're proceeding without any experience with Web pages, you might not know some required basics. You must know how to create and save plain text files with an editor such as Notepad or save the file as plain text from your word processor (not in the word processor format). You also must know where to put the text files containing the code (HTML or PHP) for your Web pages so that the pages are available to all users with access to your Web site, and you must know how to move the files to the appropriate location.

You do *not* need to know how to design or create databases or how to program. All the information that you need to know about databases and programming is included in this book.

How This Book Is Organized

This book is divided into six parts, with several chapters in each part. The content ranges from an introduction to PHP and MySQL to installing to creating and using databases to writing PHP programs.

Part I: Developing a Web Database Application Using PHP and MySQL

Part I provides an overview of using PHP and MySQL to create a Web database application. It describes and gives the advantages of PHP, of MySQL, and of their use together. You find out how to get started, including what you need, how to get access to PHP and MySQL, and how to test your software. You then find out about the process of developing the application.

Part II: MySQL Database

In Part II you find out the details of working with MySQL databases. You create a database, change a database, and move data into and out of a database.

Part III: PHP

Part III provides the details of writing PHP programs that enable your Web pages to insert new information, update existing information, or remove information from a MySQL database. You find out how to use the PHP features that are used for database interaction and forms processing.

Part IV: Applications

Part IV describes the Web database application as a whole. You find out how to organize the PHP programs into a functioning application that interacts with the database. Two complete sample applications are provided, described, and explained.

Part V: The Part of Tens

Part V provides some useful lists of important things to do and not to do when developing a Web database application.

Part VI: Appendixes

The final part, Part VI, provides instructions for installing PHP and MySQL for those who need to install the software themselves. Appendix B discusses how to configure PHP.

Icons Used in This Book

This icon is a sticky note of sorts, highlighting information that's worth committing to memory.

This icon flags information and techniques that are more technical than other sections of the book. The information here can be interesting and helpful, but you don't need to understand it to use the information in the book.

Tips provide extra information for a specific purpose. Tips can save you time and effort, so they're worth checking out.

You should always read warnings. Warnings emphasize actions that you must take or must avoid to prevent dire consequences.

Where to Go from Here

This book is organized in the order in which things need to be done. If you're a newbie, you probably need to start with Part I, which describes how to get started, including how to design the pieces of your application and how the pieces will interact. When implementing your application, you need to create the MySQL database first, so I discuss MySQL before PHP. After you understand the details of MySQL and PHP, you need to put them together into a complete application, which I describe in Part IV. If you're already familiar with any part of the book, you can go directly to the part that you need. For instance, if you're familiar with database design, you can go directly to Part II, which describes how to implement the design in MySQL. Or if you know MySQL, you can just read about PHP in Part III.

And if you want even *more* information, check out the cheat sheet at www. dummies.com/cheatsheet/phpmysql.

Part I

Developing a Web Database Application Using PHP and MySQL

The 5th Wave

By Rich Tennant

In this part . . .

In this part, I provide an overview. I describe PHP and MySQL, how each one works, and how they work together to make your Web database application possible. After describing your tools, I show you how to set up your working environment. I present your options for accessing PHP and MySQL and point out what to look for in each environment.

After describing your tools and your options for your development environment, I provide an overview of the development process. I discuss planning, design, and building your application.

Chapter 1

Introduction to PHP and MySQL

S o you need to develop an interactive Web site. Perhaps your boss just put you in charge of the company's online product catalog. Or you want to develop your own Web business. Or your sister wants to sell her paintings online. Or you volunteered to put up a Web site open only to members of your circus acrobats' association. Whatever your motivation might be, you can see that the application needs to store information (such as information about products or member passwords), thus requiring a database. You can see also that the application needs to interact *dynamically* with the user; for instance, the user selects a product to view or enters membership information. This type of Web site is a *Web database application*.

I assume that you've created static Web pages before, using HTML (HyperText Markup Language), but creating an interactive Web site is a new challenge, as is designing a database. You asked three computer gurus you know what you should do. They said a lot of things you didn't understand, but among the technical jargon, you heard "quick" and "easy," and "free" mentioned in the same sentence as PHP and MySQL. Now you want to know more about using PHP and MySQL to develop the Web site that you need.

PHP and MySQL work together very well; it's a dynamic partnership. In this chapter, you find out the advantages of each, how each one works, and how they work together to produce a dynamic Web database application.

What Is a Web Database Application?

An *application* is a program or a group of programs designed for use by an *end user* (for example, customers, members, or circus acrobats). If the end user interacts with the application via a Web browser, the application is a

Web based or *Web application.* If the Web application requires the long-term storage of information using a database, it's a *Web database application.* This book provides you with the information that you need to develop a Web database application that can be accessed with Web browsers such as Internet Explorer and Firefox.

A Web database application is designed to help a user accomplish a task. It can be a simple application that displays information in a browser window (for example, current job openings when the user selects a job title) or a complicated program with extended functionality (for example, the book-ordering application at Amazon.com or the bidding application at eBay).

A Web database application consists of just two pieces:

- ✔ **Database:** The *database* is the long-term memory of your Web database application. The application can't fulfill its purpose without the database. However, the database alone is not enough.

- ✔ **Application:** The *application* piece is the program or group of programs that performs the tasks. Programs create the display that the user sees in the browser window; they make your application interactive by accepting and processing information that the user types in the browser window; and they store information in the database and get information out of the database. (The database is useless unless you can move data in and out.)

The Web pages that you've previously created with HTML alone are *static,* meaning the user can't interact with the Web page. All users see the same Web page. *Dynamic* Web pages, on the other hand, allow the user to interact with the Web page. Different users might see different Web pages. For instance, one user looking at a furniture store's online product catalog might choose to view information about the sofas, whereas another user might choose to view information about coffee tables. To create dynamic Web pages, you must use another language in addition to HTML.

One language widely used to make Web pages dynamic is JavaScript. JavaScript is useful for several purposes, such as *mouse-overs* (for example, to highlight a navigation button when the user moves the mouse pointer over it) or accepting and validating information that users type into a Web form. However, it's not useful for interacting with a database. You wouldn't use JavaScript to move the information from the Web form into a database. PHP, however, is a language particularly well suited to interacting with databases. PHP can accept and validate the information that users type into a Web form and can also move the information into a database. The programs in this book are written with PHP.

The database: Storing data

The core of a Web database application is the *database*, which is the long-term memory (I hope more efficient than my long-term memory) that stores information for the application. A database is an electronic file cabinet that stores information in an organized manner so that you can find it when you need it. After all, storing information is pointless if you can't find it. A database can be small, with a simple structure — for example, a database containing the titles and authors' names of all the books that you own. Or a database can be huge, with an extremely complex structure — such as the database that Amazon.com has to hold all its information.

The information that you store in the database comes in many varieties. A company's online catalog requires a database to store information about all the company's products. A membership Web site requires a database to store information about members. An employment Web site requires a database (or perhaps two databases) to store information about job openings and information from résumés. The information that you plan to store could be similar to information that's stored by Web sites all over the Internet — or information that's unique to your application.

The term *database* refers to the file or group of files that holds the actual data. The data is accessed by using a set of programs called a DBMS (Database Management System). Almost all DBMSs these days are RDBMSs (Relational Database Management Systems), in which data is organized and stored in a set of related tables.

In this book, MySQL is the RDBMS used because it's particularly well suited for Web sites. MySQL and its advantages are discussed in the section, "MySQL, My Database," later in this chapter. You can find out how to organize and design a MySQL database in Chapter 3.

The application: Moving data in and out of the database

For a database to be useful, you need to be able to move data into and out of it. Programs are your tools for this because they interact with the database to store and retrieve data. A program connects to the database and makes a request: "Take this data and store it in the specified location." Another program makes the request: "Find the specified data and give it to me." The application programs that interact with the database run when the user interacts with the Web page. For instance, when the user clicks the submit button after filling in a Web form, a program processes the information in the form and stores it in a database.

E-mail discussion lists

Good technical support is available from *e-mail discussion lists,* which are groups of people discussing specific topics through e-mail. E-mail lists are available for pretty much any subject you can think of: Powerball, ancient philosophy, cooking, The Beatles, Scottish terriers, politics, and so on. The *list manager* maintains a distribution list of e-mail addresses for anyone who wants to join the discussion. When you send a message to the discussion list, your message is sent to the entire list so that everyone can see it. Thus, the discussion is a group effort, and anyone can respond to any message that interests him or her.

E-mail discussion lists are supported by various sponsors. Any individual or organization can run a list. Most software vendors run one or more lists devoted to their software. Universities run many lists for educational subjects. In addition, some Web sites manage discussion lists, such as Yahoo! Groups and Topica. Users can create a new list or join an existing list through the Web application.

Software-related e-mail lists are a treasure trove of technical support. Anywhere from a hundred to several thousand users of the software subscribe to the list. Often the developers, programmers, and technical support staff for the software vendor are on the list. You're unlikely to be the first person to ever experience your problem. Whatever your question or problem, someone on the list probably knows the answer or the solution. When you post a question to an e-mail list, the answer usually appears in your inbox within minutes. In addition, most lists maintain an archive of previous discussions so that you can search for answers. When you're new to any software, you can find out a great deal simply by joining the discussion list and reading the messages for a few days.

PHP and MySQL have e-mail discussion lists. Actually, each has several discussion lists for special topics, such as *databases and PHP*. You can find the names of the mailing lists and instructions for joining them on the PHP (www. php.net) and MySQL (www.mysql.com) Web sites.

MySQL, My Database

MySQL is a fast, easy-to-use RDBMS used on many Web sites. Speed was the developers' main focus from the beginning. In the interest of speed, they made the decision to offer fewer features than their major competitors (such as Oracle and Sybase). However, even though MySQL is less full-featured than its commercial competitors, it has all the features needed by the majority of database developers. It's easier to install and use than its commercial competitors, and the difference in price is strongly in favor of MySQL.

MySQL was developed originally by a Swedish company but is now developed, marketed, and supported by Sun Microsystems. The company licenses it in two ways:

 ✔ **MySQL Community Server:** A freely downloadable, open source edition of MySQL, released early and often with the most advanced features. Anyone who can meet the requirements of the GPL can use the software for free. If you're using MySQL as a database on a Web site (the subject of this book), you can use MySQL for free, even if you're making money with your Web site.

✔ **MySQL Enterprise Subscription:** A comprehensive offering of production support, monitoring tools, and MySQL database software. For a subscription fee paid per year per server, monthly software updates, consulting services, technical support, and other services are available. You can choose the level of services you want for the fee that you want to pay.

Finding technical support for MySQL Community Server is not a problem. You can join one of several e-mail discussion lists offered on the MySQL Web site at www.mysql.com. You can even search the e-mail list archives, which contain a large archive of MySQL questions and answers.

Advantages of MySQL

MySQL is a popular database with Web developers. Its speed and small size make it ideal for a Web site. Add to that the fact that it's open source, which means free, and you have the foundation of its popularity. Here's a rundown of some of its advantages:

✔ **It's fast.** The main goal of the folks who developed MySQL was speed. Thus, the software was designed from the beginning with speed in mind.

✔ **It's inexpensive.** MySQL is free under the open source GPL license, and the fee for a commercial license is reasonable.

✔ **It's easy to use.** You can build and interact with a MySQL database by using a few simple statements in the SQL language, which is the standard language for communicating with RDBMSs. Check out Chapter 4 for the lowdown on the SQL language.

✔ **It can run on many operating systems.** MySQL runs on many operating systems — Windows, Linux, Mac OS, most varieties of Unix (including Solaris and AIX), FreeBSD, OS/2, Irix, and others.

✔ **It's available on almost all Web hosts.** If you're going to run your Web site on a Web hosting company, MySQL is widely available without extra cost. Using MySQL on a Web host is discussed in more detail in Chapter 2.

✔ **Technical support is widely available.** A large base of users provides free support through mailing lists. The MySQL developers also participate in the e-mail lists.

✔ **It's secure.** MySQL's flexible system of authorization allows some or all database privileges (such as the privilege to create a database or delete data) to specific users or groups of users. Passwords are encrypted.

✔ **It supports large databases.** MySQL handles databases up to 50 million rows or more. The default file size limit for a table is 4GB, but you can increase this (if your operating system can handle it) to a theoretical limit of 8 million terabytes (TB).

✔ **It's customizable.** The open source GPL license allows programmers to modify the MySQL software to fit their own specific environments.

How MySQL works

The MySQL software consists of the MySQL server, several utility programs that assist in the administration of MySQL databases, and some supporting software that the MySQL server needs (but you don't need to know about). The heart of the system is the MySQL server.

The MySQL server is the manager of the database system. It handles all your database instructions. For instance, if you want to create a new database, you send a message to the MySQL server that says "create a new database and call it newdata." The MySQL server then creates a subdirectory in its data directory, names the new subdirectory `newdata`, and puts the necessary files with the required format into the `newdata` subdirectory. In the same manner, to add data to that database, you send a message to the MySQL server, giving it the data and telling it where you want the data to be added. You find out how to write and send messages to MySQL in Part II.

Before you can pass instructions to the MySQL server, it must be running and waiting for requests. The MySQL server is usually set up so that it starts when the computer starts and continues running all the time. This is the usual setup for a Web site. However, it's not necessary to set it up to start when the computer starts. If you need to, you can start it manually whenever you want to access a database. When it's running, the MySQL server listens continuously for messages that are directed to it.

Communicating with the MySQL server

All your interaction with the database is accomplished by passing messages to the MySQL server. You can send messages to the MySQL server several ways, but this book focuses on sending messages using PHP. The PHP software has specific statements that you use to send instructions to the MySQL server.

The MySQL server must be able to understand the instructions that you send it. You communicate by using *SQL (Structured Query Language),* which is a standard language understood by many RDBMSs. The MySQL server understands SQL. PHP doesn't understand SQL, but it doesn't need to: PHP just establishes a connection with the MySQL server and sends the SQL message over the connection. The MySQL server interprets the SQL message and follows the instructions. The MySQL server sends a return message, stating its status and what it did (or reporting an error if it was unable to understand or follow the instructions).

Software designed specifically to interact with MySQL database is also discussed in this book. You can use this software, called phpMyAdmin, on your own computer to communicate with your MySQL databases. PhpMyAdmin is also available on almost all Web hosts.

For the lowdown on how to write and send SQL messages to MySQL, check out Part II.

PHP, a Data Mover

PHP, a scripting language designed specifically for use on the Web, is your tool for creating dynamic Web pages. Rich in features that make Web design and programming easier, PHP is in use on more than 20 million domains (according to the Netcraft survey at `www.php.net/usage.php`). Its popularity continues to grow, so it must be fulfilling its function pretty well.

PHP stands for *PHP: HyperText Preprocessor.* In its early development by a guy named Rasmus Lerdorf, it was called *Personal Home Page tools.* When it developed into a full-blown language, the name was changed to be more in line with its expanded functionality.

The syntax of the PHP language is similar to the syntax of C, so if you have experience with C, you'll be comfortable with PHP. PHP is actually simpler than C because it doesn't use some of the more difficult concepts of C. PHP also doesn't include the low-level programming capabilities of C because PHP is designed to program Web sites and doesn't require the capabilities required by C.

PHP is particularly strong in its ability to interact with databases. It supports pretty much every database you've ever heard of (and some you haven't). PHP handles connecting to the database and communicating with it. You don't need to know the technical details for connecting to a database or for exchanging messages with it. You tell PHP the name of the database and where it is, and PHP handles the details. It connects to the database, passes your instructions to the database, and returns the database response to you.

Technical support is available for PHP. You can join one of several e-mail discussion lists offered on the PHP Web site (`www.php.net`), including a list for *databases and PHP.* In addition, a Web interface to the discussion lists is available at `http://news.php.net`, where you can browse or search the messages.

Advantages of PHP

The popularity of PHP is growing rapidly because of its many advantages:

- ✔ **It's fast.** Because it is embedded in HTML code, the response time is short.

- ✔ **It's inexpensive — free, in fact.** PHP is proof that free lunches do exist and that you can get more than you paid for.

- ✔ **It's easy to use.** PHP contains many special features and functions needed to create dynamic Web pages. The PHP language is designed to be included easily in an HTML file.

- ✔ **It can run on many operating systems.** It runs on a variety of operating systems — Windows, Linux, Mac OS, and most varieties of Unix.

- ✔ **It's available on almost all Web hosts.** If you are going to publish your Web site on a Web host, you will find PHP installed on almost all Web hosts for free.

- ✔ **Technical support is widely available.** A large base of users provides free support through e-mail discussion lists.

- ✔ **It's secure.** The user does not see the PHP code.

- ✔ **It's designed to support databases.** PHP includes functionality designed to interact with specific databases. It relieves you of the need to know the technical details required to communicate with a database.

- ✔ **It's customizable.** The open source license allows programmers to modify the PHP software, adding or modifying features as needed to fit their own specific environments.

How PHP works

PHP is an embedded scripting language when used in Web pages. This means that PHP code is embedded in HTML code. You use HTML tags to enclose the PHP language that you embed in your HTML file — the same way that you would use other HTML tags. You create and edit Web pages containing PHP the same way that you create and edit regular HTML pages.

The PHP software works with the Web server. The Web server is the software that delivers Web pages to the world. When you type a URL into your Web browser, you're sending a message to the Web server at that URL, asking it to send you an HTML file. The Web server responds by sending the requested file. Your browser reads the HTML file and displays the Web page. You also request the Web server to send you a file when you click a link in a Web page. In addition, the Web server processes a file when you click a Web page button that submits a form.

When PHP is installed, the Web server is configured to expect certain file extensions to contain PHP language statements. Often the extension is `.php` or `.phtml`, but any extension can be used. When the Web server gets a request for a file with the designated extension, it sends the HTML statements as is, but PHP statements are processed by the PHP software before they're sent to the requester.

When PHP language statements are processed, only the output is sent by the Web server to the Web browser. The PHP language statements are not included in the output sent to the browser, so the PHP code is secure and transparent to the user. For instance, in this simple PHP statement:

```
<?php echo "<p>Hello World</p>"; ?>
```
HTML

`<?php` is the PHP opening tag, and `?>` is the closing tag. `echo` is a PHP instruction that tells PHP to output the upcoming text. The PHP software processes the PHP statement and outputs this:

```
<p>Hello World</p>
```

which is a regular HTML statement. This HTML statement is delivered to the user's browser. The browser interprets the statement as HTML code and displays a Web page with one paragraph — Hello World. The PHP statement is not delivered to the browser, so the user never sees any PHP statements. PHP and the Web server must work closely together.

PHP is not integrated with all Web servers but does work with many of the popular Web servers. PHP is developed as a project of the Apache Software Foundation — thus, it works best with Apache. PHP also works with Microsoft IIS/PWS, iPlanet (formerly Netscape Enterprise Server), and others.

Although PHP works with several Web servers, it works best with Apache. If you can select or influence the selection of the Web server used in your organization, select Apache. By itself, Apache is a good choice. It's free, open source, stable, and popular. It currently powers more than 60 percent of all Web sites, according to the Web server survey at `www.netcraft.com`. It runs on Windows, Linux, Mac OS, and most flavors of Unix.

MySQL and PHP, the Perfect Pair

MySQL and PHP are frequently used together. They're often called the *dynamic duo*. MySQL provides the database part, and PHP provides the application part of your Web database application.

Advantages of the relationship

MySQL and PHP as a pair have several advantages:

- ✔ **They're free.** It's hard to beat free for cost-effectiveness.
- ✔ **They're Web oriented.** Both were designed specifically for use on Web sites. Both have a set of features focused on building dynamic Web sites.
- ✔ **They're easy to use.** Both were designed to get a Web site up quickly.
- ✔ **They're fast.** Both were designed with speed as a major goal. Together they provide one of the fastest ways to deliver dynamic Web pages to users.
- ✔ **They communicate well with one another.** PHP has built-in features for communicating with MySQL. You don't need to know the technical details; just leave it to PHP.

How MySQL and PHP work together

PHP provides the application part, and MySQL provides the database part of a Web database application. You use the PHP language to write the programs that perform the application tasks. PHP can be used for simple tasks (such as displaying a Web page) or for complicated tasks (such as accepting and veri-fying data that a user typed into an HTML form). One of the tasks that your application must do is move data into and out of the database — and PHP has built-in features to use when writing programs that move data into and out of a MySQL database.

PHP statements are embedded in your HTML files with PHP tags. When the task to be performed by the application requires storing or retrieving data, you use specific PHP statements designed to interact with a MySQL database. You use one PHP statement to connect to the correct database, telling PHP where the database is located, its name, and the password needed to connect to it. The database doesn't need to be on the same machine as your Web site; PHP can communicate with a database across a network. You use another PHP statement to send an SQL message to MySQL, giving MySQL instructions for the task you want to accomplish. MySQL returns a status message that shows whether it successfully performed the task. If a problem came up, it returns an error message. If your SQL message asked to retrieve some data, MySQL sends the data that you asked for, and PHP stores it in a temporary location where it's available to you.

You then use one or more PHP statements to complete the application task. For instance, you can use PHP statements to display data that you retrieved. Or you might use PHP statements to display a status message in the browser, informing the user that the data was saved.

As an RDBMS, MySQL can store complex information. As a scripting language, PHP can perform complicated manipulations of data, on either data that you need to modify before saving it in the database or data that you retrieved from the database and need to modify before displaying or using it for another task. Together, PHP and MySQL can be used to build a sophisticated and complicated Web database application.

Keeping Up with PHP and MySQL Changes

PHP and MySQL are open source software. If you've used only software from major software publishers — such as Microsoft, Macromedia, or Adobe — you'll find that open source software is an entirely different species. It's developed by a group of programmers who write the code in their spare time, for fun and for free. There's no corporate office.

Open source software changes frequently, rather than once every year or two like commercial software does. It changes when the developers feel that it's ready. It also changes quickly in response to problems. When a serious problem is found — such as a security hole — a new version that fixes the problem can be released in days. You don't receive glossy brochures or see splashy magazine ads for a year before a new version is released. Thus, if you don't make the effort to stay informed, you could miss the release of a new version or be unaware of a serious problem with your current version.

Visit the PHP and MySQL Web sites often. You need to know the information that's published there. Join the mailing lists, which often are high in traffic. When you first get acquainted with PHP and MySQL, the large number of mail messages on the discussion lists brings valuable information into your e-mail inbox; you can pick up a lot by reading those messages. And soon, you might be able to help others based on your own experience. At the very least, subscribe to the announcement mailing list, which delivers e-mail only occasionally. Any important problems or new versions are announced here. The e-mail that you receive from the announcement list contains information you need to know. So, right now, before you forget, hop over to the PHP and MySQL Web sites and sign up for a list or two at `www.php.net/mailing-lists.php` and `lists.mysql.com`.

PHP versions

The current version of PHP is PHP 5. Some existing applications still run PHP 4, but because you're building your first PHP application, you should be using PHP 5.

PHP 6 is due to be released soon. Perhaps it has already been released by the time you're reading this book. When PHP changes from version 5 to version 6, the following important changes will occur:

- ✔ The setting for `register_globals` will no longer exist.
- ✔ The setting for magic quotes will no longer exist.
- ✔ The long arrays, such as `HTTP_POST_VARS`, will no longer exist. These arrays were commonly used in PHP 4.

If you're ever converting scripts that ran under PHP 4 or 5 to run under PHP 6, you may need to make changes to the scripts, based on the preceding changes, before the scripts will run correctly under PHP 6. I explain these changes throughout the book where they apply to the techniques and procedures.

MySQL versions

MySQL 5.1 is the current version, as of this writing. MySQL 5.0 is also available. The examples and scripts in this book run equally well under either version. Some of the more advanced features of 5.1 may not be available on sites running 5.0, but none of those advanced features are discussed in this book.

MySQL 6 is also available for download on the MySQL Web site. However, at the time of this writing, version 6.0 is an alpha release and not suitable for working Web sites or for beginning developers.

You may occasionally find a Web site running MySQL 4.3.1. The examples and scripts in this book can execute properly on these sites as well. It is not wise to run a Web site using MySQL 4.3.0 or earlier.

Chapter 2

Setting Up Your Work Environment

• •

In This Chapter

▶ Accessing PHP and MySQL through company Web sites and Web hosting companies

▶ Building your own Web site from scratch

▶ Testing PHP and MySQL

• •

*N*ow that you've decided to use PHP and MySQL to build your interactive Web site, you can begin working on the site. Your first task is to set up the environment in which you're going to build the site. This chapter describes how to set up your Web site environment with all the tools you need to build your Web database application.

Anatomy of a Web Site

Because you most likely have created simple Web sites before, you know what a Web site is. It's a collection of text files that contain the HTML code that the browser reads to display the Web pages. The computer space where the files are stored is the physical location of your Web site.

Web users often talk about Web site visitors, but the term *visitors* is technically misleading. Visitors don't actually visit a Web site. When a person types the address (called a URL or Uniform Resource Locator) of a Web site into a Web browser, the browser sends a request over the Internet, asking to view the Web page at that address. Software at the Web site, called a Web server, receives the request and responds by sending the requested Web page. The browser receives the Web page file and displays the Web page in the browser window.

To make your Web site available to the public, you place the text files containing HTML code on the Web site where users can access them. A Web database application is similar. The difference is that the files contain PHP code, as well as HTML code.

To provide the dynamic Web database applications discussed in this book, your Web site must have the following software:

✔ **A Web server:** The software that delivers your Web pages to the world

✔ **MySQL:** The RDBMS (Relational Database Management System) that will store information for your Web database application

✔ **PHP:** The scripting language that you'll use to write the programs that provide the dynamic functionality for your Web site

I describe these three tools in detail in Chapter 1.

Building a Web Site

As discussed in the previous section, a Web site is a collection of text files placed on a computer in a location where users can access them. Placing the Web site files where they can be accessed by the public is called *publishing* the Web site. However, this is the final step of building the Web site, not the first step. You don't want to publish the Web site until it's finished — a perfect Web site ready for public viewing.

To prevent the public from seeing your half-finished Web site, warts and all, you need to develop your Web site in a location that isn't available to the public. While developing your Web site, you'll be testing things and trouble-shooting problems. You need to do this work in private.

Because you need to build your Web site in private and hold off on making it public until it's finished and perfect, your work environment needs two sites:

✔ **Your Web site:** The site where your published Web site is located. The location where the public views your Web site.

✔ **Your development site:** The location where you develop your Web pages. When your pages are complete, you then move them to your Web site.

Your Web site publishes your Web pages to the world. Your development site shouldn't be available for the world to see your errors and half-done Web pages. Your development site needs to be hidden from the world. Never publish your Web pages until they are complete and perfect.

You need to decide where you're going to publish your Web site and where you're going to develop it. The information you need to make these decisions is provided in the next few sections of this chapter.

Deciding Where to Publish Your Web Site

One of your first decisions is where to publish your Web site. You need to publish it on a computer that's connected to the World Wide Web. The computer should also provide the tools you need, as discussed earlier: a Web server, PHP, and MySQL. The most common locations for publishing your Web site are

- ✔ **A Web site hosted by a Web hosting company:** The Web site is located on the Web hosting company's computer. The Web hosting company installs and maintains the Web site software and provides space on its computer where you can install the files for the Web site.

- ✔ **A Web site put up by a company on its own computer:** The company — usually the company's IT (Information Technology) department — installs and administers the Web site software. Your job, for the purposes of this book, is to program the Web site, either as an employee of the company or as a contractor.

- ✔ **A Web site that you set up yourself:** You plan to install and maintain the Web site software yourself. It could be a Web site of your own that you're building on your own computer, or it might be a Web site that you're installing for a client on the client's computer.

You'll most likely publish your Web site on one of the first two options. For these options, you don't need to know much about the administration and operation of the Web site software. The Web server, PHP, and MySQL are already installed, and the information you need to access them is provided by the company responsible for the Web site.

The third option requires that you install, set up, administer, and maintain the Web site software yourself. This option requires much more technical knowledge of computer software than the first two options, where others provide the software for you. However, the advantage of this option is that you have more control. You can set up the Web site software with the settings that you prefer.

In the next three sections, I describe the publishing options in more detail and provide the information you need to decide where to publish your Web site.

Using a Web hosting company

A *Web hosting company* provides everything that you need to put up a Web site, including the computer space and all the Web site software. You just create the files for your Web pages and move them to a location specified by the Web hosting company. Most small-to-medium-sized Web sites are hosted by Web hosting companies.

About a gazillion companies offer Web hosting services. Most charge a monthly fee (often quite small), and some are even free. (Most, but not all, of the free ones require you to display advertising.) Usually, the monthly fee varies depending on the resources provided for your Web site. For instance, a Web site with 2MB of disk space for your Web page files costs less than a Web site with 10MB of disk space.

When looking for a place to host your Web site, make sure that the Web hosting company offers the following:

✔ **PHP and MySQL:** Not all companies provide these tools. You might have to pay more for a site with access to PHP and MySQL; sometimes you have to pay an additional fee for MySQL databases.

✔ **A recent version of PHP:** Sometimes the PHP versions offered aren't the most recent versions. As of this writing, PHP 6 is close to being released.

Until PHP 6 is released, two versions of PHP are generally available — PHP 4 and PHP 5. Even though PHP 5 has been out for several years, many Web sites still run PHP 4. PHP 4 is still supported because existing PHP 4 code does not always run perfectly under PHP 5. Many developers have not yet converted their code to run under PHP 5. However, the demise of PHP 4 is looming. Support for PHP 4 stopped at the end of 2007. There will be no more releases of PHP 4, and critical security fixes ended in late 2008. There is no reason for anyone developing new code to use PHP 4.

Look for a Web hosting company that provides PHP 5. Some Web hosts provide both PHP 4 and PHP 5, but they use PHP 4 as the default. You may need to talk to technical support at the Web hosting company to find out how to get PHP 5 on your Web site, rather than PHP 4.

✔ **A recent version of MySQL:** The current preferred version of MySQL is MySQL 5.1. However, using an older version of MySQL is not as much of a problem as using older versions of PHP. The techniques in this book work with older versions of MySQL. In the future, you may learn more advanced MySQL features and may need a newer version of MySQL. However, even older versions provide a feature set that allows quite sophisticated dynamic Web sites.

✔ **Ability to change PHP settings:** Changing PHP settings can affect some of PHP's behavior. Web hosts vary in the amount of access to PHP settings that you, as their customer, are given. More access to PHP settings gives you more control over your Web site functionality.

A text file named `php.ini` contains the PHP settings. Your Web host will not give you access to the general `php.ini` file for the host's system, but some hosts allow you to use a local `php.ini` file that affects only your Web site. This is a useful feature to look for because it's an easy way to change the settings.

Another way to change PHP settings is using an `.htaccess` file. This is a file that the Apache Web server reads that can contain some PHP settings. Many Web hosts allow you to store an `.htaccess` file on your Web site, which changes settings for your Web site only.

When you select a Web host, be sure the hosting company allows you to use either a local `php.ini` file or an `.htaccess` file. It's important that you be able to change the PHP settings for your Web site.

✔ **PhpMyAdmin:** To create and use MySQL databases, you need specific software. Any Web host that provides MySQL needs to provide software to communicate with MySQL databases. Most Web hosts provide phpMyAdmin, a Web application written in PHP and designed specifically for managing MySQL databases. Other software also works, but this book assumes you have access to phpMyAdmin.

Other considerations when choosing a Web hosting company are

✔ **Reliability:** You need a Web hosting company that you can depend on — one that won't go broke and disappear tomorrow, and one that isn't running on old computers, held together by chewing gum and baling wire, with more downtime than uptime.

✔ **Speed:** Web pages that download slowly are a problem because users will get impatient and go elsewhere. Slow pages could be a result of a Web hosting company that started its business on a shoestring and has a shortage of good equipment — or the Web hosting company might be so successful that its equipment is overwhelmed by new customers. Either way, Web hosting companies that deliver Web pages too slowly are unacceptable.

✔ **Technical support:** Some Web hosting companies have no one available to answer questions or troubleshoot problems. Technical support is often provided only through e-mail, which can be very good if the response time is short. Sometimes you can test the quality of the company's support by calling the tech support number, or test the e-mail response time by sending an e-mail.

✔ **The domain name:** Each Web site has a domain name that Web browsers use to find the site on the Web. Each domain name is registered for a small yearly fee so that only one Web site can use it. Some Web hosting companies allow you to use a domain name that you have registered independently of the Web hosting company, some assist you in registering and using a new domain name, and some require that you use their domain name. For instance, suppose that your name is Lola Designer and you want your Web site to be named LolaDesigner. Some Web hosting companies allow your Web site to be `LolaDesigner.com`, but some require that your Web site be named `LolaDesigner.webhosting companyname.com`, or `webhostingcompanyname.com/~Lola Designer`, or something similar. In general, your Web site looks more professional if you use your own domain name.

✔ **Backups:** *Backups* are copies of your Web page files and your database that are stored in case your files or database are lost or damaged. You want to be sure that the company makes regular, frequent backup copies of your application. You also want to know how long it would take for backups to be put in place to restore your Web site to working order after a problem.

✔ **Features:** Select features based on the purpose of your Web site. Usually a hosting company bundles features together into plans — more features equal a higher cost. Some features to consider are

- *Disk space:* How many MB or GB of disk space will your Web site require? Media files, such as graphics or music files, can be quite large.

- *Data transfer:* Some hosting companies charge you for sending Web pages to users. If you expect to have a lot of traffic on your Web site, this cost should be a consideration.

- *E-mail addresses:* Most hosting companies provide you with one or more e-mail addresses for your Web site. For instance, if your Web site is `LolaDesigner.com`, you could allow users to send you e-mail at `me@LolaDesigner.com`.

- *Software:* Hosting companies offer access to a variety of software for Web development. PHP and MySQL are the software that I discuss in this book. Some hosting companies might offer other databases, and some might offer other development tools such as FrontPage extensions, shopping cart software, and credit card validation.

- *Statistics:* Often you can get statistics regarding your Web traffic, such as the number of users, time of access, access by Web page, and so on.

Domain names

Every Web site needs a unique address on the Web. The unique address used by computers to locate a Web site is the *IP address,* which is a series of four numbers between 0 and 255, separated by dots — for example, 172.17.204.2 or 192.163.2.33.

Because IP addresses are made up of numbers and dots, they're not easy to remember. Fortunately, most IP addresses have an associated name that's much easier to remember, such as amazon.com, www.irs.gov, or mycompany.com. A name that's an address for a Web site is a *domain name.* A *domain* can be one computer or many connected computers. When a domain refers to several computers, each computer in the domain can have its own name. A name that includes an individual computer name, such as thor.my company.com, identifies a *subdomain.*

Each domain name must be unique in order to serve as an address. Consequently, a system of registering domain names ensures that no two locations use the same domain name. Anyone can register any domain name as long as the name isn't already taken. You can register a domain name on the Web. First, you test your potential domain name to find out whether it's available. If it's available, you register it in your name or a company name and pay the fee. The name is then yours to use, and no one else can use it. The standard fee for domain name registration is $35 per year. You should never pay more, but bargains are often available.

Many Web sites provide the ability to register a domain name, including many Web hosting companies. A search at Google (www.google.com) for *register domain name* results in more than 85 million hits. Shop around to be sure that you find the lowest price. Also, many Web sites allow you to enter a domain name and see whom it is registered to. These Web sites do a domain name database search using a tool called *whois.* A search at Google for *domain name whois* results in more than 17 million hits. A couple of places where you can do a whois search are Allwhois.com (www.allwhois.com) and BetterWhois.com (www.betterwhois.com).

Researching Web hosting companies from a standing start is pretty difficult — a search at Google.com for *"Web hosting"* results in almost 400 million hits. The best way to research Web hosting companies is to ask for recommendations from people who have experience with those companies. People who have used a hosting company can warn you if the service is slow or the computers are down often. After you gather a few names of Web hosting companies from satisfied customers, you can narrow the list to the one that's best suited to your purposes and the most cost effective.

The following is a list of Web hosts that offer the tools needed, including PHP 5, MySQL, phpMyAdmin, .htaccess files, and good technical support:

- ✔ Host Gator, www.hostgator.com
- ✔ HostMonster, www.hostmonster.com
- ✔ WebHostingBuzz (WHB), www.webhostingbuzz.com
- ✔ midPhase, www.midphase.com
- ✔ BlueHost, www.bluehost.com

Please bear in mind that this list is based solely on the Web site of the hosting company and reviews found on Web sites that review Web hosts — not on personal experience.

Using a company Web site

When the Web site is run by the company, you don't need to understand the installation and administration of the Web site software at all. The company is responsible for the operation of the Web site, so that burden is off your shoulders. In most cases, the Web site already exists, and your job is to add to, modify, or redesign the existing Web site. In a few cases, the company might be installing its first Web site, and your job is to design the Web site. In either case, your responsibility is to write and install the HTML files for the Web site.

You access the Web site software through the company's IT department. The name of this department can vary in different companies, but its function is the same: It keeps the company's computers running and up-to-date.

If PHP or MySQL or both aren't available on the company's Web site, IT needs to install them and make them available to you. PHP and MySQL have many options, but IT might not understand the best options — and might have options set in ways that aren't well suited for your purposes. If you need PHP or MySQL options changed, you need to request that IT make the change; you won't be able to make the change yourself. For instance, PHP must be installed with MySQL support enabled, so if PHP isn't communicating correctly with MySQL, IT might have to reinstall PHP with MySQL support enabled.

You will interact with the IT folks frequently as needs arise. For example, you might need options changed, you might need information to help you interpret an error message, or you might need to report a problem with the Web site software. So a good relationship with the IT folks will make your life much easier. Bring them tasty cookies and doughnuts often.

Setting up your own server

If you're setting up your own Web server from scratch, to publish your own Web site, you need to understand the Web site software fairly well. You have to make several decisions regarding hardware and software. You have to install a Web server, PHP, and MySQL — as well as maintain, administer, and update the system yourself. Taking this route, rather than using a Web site provided by others, requires more work and more knowledge. Don't attempt this unless you are pretty knowledgeable about the Web, legal restrictions, security concerns, and other relevant issues. The advantage is that you have total control over the Web development environment.

Here are the general steps that lead to your dynamic Web site:

1. **Set up the computer.**

   While you can set up your existing computer that you use for all your other computer work to be the Web server that delivers a Web site, it's not wise. If your Web site receives much traffic, it may not have enough resources and may bog down. It's much better to set up a new machine to be your Web server.

2. **Install the Web server.**

   After you set up the computer, you need to install Web server software. In most cases, you want to install Apache. It's free, popular, reliable, secure, and runs on most operating systems. Apache is automatically installed with the operating system on Macs and Linux. Currently, Apache powers about 60 percent of Web sites. You can find information about installing Apache at http://httpd.apache.org.

3. **Install MySQL.**

   To run your Web database application, you need to install MySQL. Many Mac and Linux computers arrive with MySQL already installed, although they still may need to be upgraded to the most recent version. You can download and install MySQL from www.mysql.com.

4. **Install PHP.**

   After you install MySQL and Apache, you're ready to install PHP. Some versions of Mac and Linux arrive with PHP already installed. You can find software to download and install, as well as thorough documentation, at www.php.net.

Install XAMPP is better option!

Deciding Where to Develop Your Web Site

As discussed previously, you need to develop your Web site in a different location from where you publish your Web site. You need a location where you can write the Web page files free from public view. You don't want your experiments and error-filled first-tries to be public.

The most common place to develop your Web site is on your local computer. If you can't develop on your computer, you have to have a private area of someone else's computer, such as your Web host's computer, where you can develop your Web site.

On your own computer

You can develop your Web site on your local computer and upload the files to your Web site when your Web site is finished and ready for the world to see. In most cases, this work process is the best solution.

When you develop on your own computer, you need to test the Web page files, including the PHP programs, that you are writing. To test your work, you need to install the software on your local computer. If you can't test your work on your development site, you will have to upload the files to your Web site to test them, and you will then have the same problem of half-done, untested files available for the public to see.

Your development site on your local computer needs to include Apache, PHP, and MySQL. If your computer doesn't have this software installed, you can easily install it. I discuss installing the software later in this chapter.

In addition to this software, you need software for editing the text files that make up your Web site. Your computer comes with text editing software, such as Notepad or WordPad on Windows. However, you may want to install software designed specifically for program editing, with features that are helpful when you're writing programs. I discuss software you can use for editing your files later in this chapter.

On another computer

If you have a very unusual situation that prevents you from developing your Web site on your local computer, you can develop your Web site on another computer, such as your Web hosting company computer or your company computer. However, you need a separate, private location on the computer.

On your Web host, you can create a subdirectory (folder) in your Web hosting account where you can develop your Web page files. You don't need to install any extra software, because PHP and MySQL are already installed. However, you do need to protect the subdirectory from public view. You can do this by adding a directive to an `.htaccess` file. I explain how to do this later in this chapter.

On your company Web site, IT needs to set up a separate location, which is not available to the public, where you can develop your Web page files. You need to talk to IT about setting up such a location for you and allowing file transfer between that location and your Web site location.

Setting Up Your Web Site

After you decide where to publish your Web site, your next step is to set up your Web site. The following sections tell you what you need to know.

With a Web hosting company

You set up an account with a Web hosting company on its Web site. Most of them offer more than one type of account, with varying resources, for varying prices. You obtain an account by filling out a form on the Web site and providing a credit card number. The Web host provides you with the information you need to use your new account, usually by sending you an e-mail.

If you have trouble with the procedure for obtaining an account, you should be able to contact Technical Support at the Web hosting company. Some provide a phone number, some an e-mail address, and some provide support via instant messaging. Some provide all three. If they are unable to answer your questions or take a long time to answer, perhaps this is not the best Web host for you.

When you have your new account, it may take a day or two for the URL to connect to your Web site. When the URL points to your Web site, your Web site is public. Anything you put there can be seen by the entire world.

Your new account provides a control panel that you use to manage your account. Many Web hosts provide a control panel called cPanel. Others provide other control panels, such as a control panel specific to the Web host, but the control panels have similar functionality, such as setting up e-mail accounts. You use the control panel to access software that allows you to create new MySQL databases and add/change MySQL accounts and passwords. You also have access to phpMyAdmin for managing your MySQL databases. Managing your MySQL accounts and databases is discussed in detail in Chapters 4 and 5.

As discussed previously, the Web page files stored on your Web hosting account can be seen by the world. Therefore, you want to develop and perfect the files on your development site and then move them to this Web site. The preferred arrangement for most developers is to use software on your local computer to edit and upload your Web site files. On your local computer, you can install software that assists you with organizing and transferring your files. I discuss this software in the section, "Setting Up Your Development Environment."

If, for some reason, you can't upload from your development environment, you can upload your files from the control panel provided by your Web host. For example, to upload a file using cPanel, find the section labeled Files and click the File Manager icon. The page that opens allows you to manage your files, including upload and download files and backup your files. If you click the upload link, you can browse to the file on your local computer that you want to upload.

The file manager page also provides the option for you to edit your files directly on your Web site. This is rarely a good idea. The most useful structure for your work environment consists of two complete Web sites — one is the development site and one is the Web site. You develop the files on your development site and transfer only the complete files to your Web site. Thus, you have two complete Web sites, and your local development site can serve as a backup if something happens to your Web site. For this reason, you want your local site to look exactly like your Web site, including the same subdirectories and files. Thus, if a mysterious disaster occurs and your Web site files disappear, you can quickly upload your development site and be back in business in minutes.

On a company Web site

When you set up your Web site on a company computer, you need to work with the company IT staff. It's up to them to set up your Web site and provide you with access to the location where you need to place your Web site files. You need to coordinate everything through them. You need to make sure they know exactly what you need.

Which tasks you can perform independently and which tasks must be done by the IT staff depends on the company policies. Some companies allow you a fair amount of access to the Web site software and its settings, whereas other companies don't want you to touch anything. For example, one company might allow you to edit the main PHP configuration file (php.ini), but another company might require you to request setting changes that the IT staff will make. Whatever your level of access, you need to work closely with the company IT department.

✓ Information you need

Whether you're setting up with a Web hosting company or on a company Web site, you need some information to get the job done. When you sign up for an account on a Web hosting company, the Web host needs to provide you with the information you need to use the Web software tools and build your dynamic Web site. You usually receive an e-mail from the Web host that provides the needed information. If you're publishing your Web site on a company Web site, the IT department needs to provide you with the necessary information.

Be sure to get the following information from your host:

check with ISP

- ✓ **The location of the Web site:** You need to know where to put the files for the Web pages. The Web host or IT department needs to provide you with the name and location of the directory where the files should be installed. Also, you need to know how to install the files — copy them, FTP them, or use other methods. If you are using a Web hosting company, you need a user ID and password to install the files. On your company Web site, you may or may not need an ID and password.

- ✓ **The default filename:** When users point their browsers at a URL, a file is sent to them. The Web server is set up to send a file with a specific name when the URL points to a directory. The file that is automatically sent is the *default file*. Very often the default file is named `index.htm` or `index.html`, but sometimes other names are used, such as `default.htm`. You need to know what you should name your default file.

- ✓ **A MySQL account:** Access to MySQL databases is controlled through a system of account names and passwords. Your host sets up a MySQL account for you that has the appropriate permissions and also gives you the MySQL account name and password. (I explain MySQL accounts in detail in Chapter 5.)

- ✓ **The location of the MySQL databases:** When you access a MySQL database from a PHP script, you need to specify where the MySQL server is located. If it's on the same server as PHP, you can specify *localhost*. However, MySQL databases need not be located on the same computer as the Web site. If the MySQL databases are located on a computer other than that of the Web site, you need to know the *hostname* (for example, `thor.companyname.com`) where the databases can be found.

- ✓ **The PHP file extension:** When PHP is installed, the Web server is instructed to expect PHP statements in files with specific extensions. Frequently, the extensions used are `.php` or `.phtml`, but other extensions can be used. PHP statements in files that don't have the correct extension won't be processed. Ask which extension to use for your PHP programs.

Setting Up Your Development Environment

Your development site is the location where you write and test your Web files before uploading the finished files to your Web site. You need to be able to edit files and test them in your development environment.

Your own computer

The most common location for your development site is your own local computer. You can create the files on your computer and upload them to your Web site.

Installing the Web development software

To test the PHP programs that you write, you need Apache, PHP, and MySQL installed in your development site. You can install the software on your machine using one of two methods:

✔ **Install from an all-in-one package.** Installing the software from an all-in-one package is the faster, easier method. I prefer a free package called XAMPP. XAMPP is not recommended for Web servers where the public accesses the files, but it's very suitable for a development Web site.

XAMPP installs Apache, PHP, and MySQL in one easy procedure. It also installs phpMyAdmin. XAMPP is available for Windows, Mac, Linux, and Solaris. Detailed instructions for downloading and installing XAMPP can be found in Appendix A.

✔ **Install each software package individually.** You can install the software individually. The software can be downloaded and installed without charge. It's available for most operating systems, including Windows and Mac. Apache, MySQL, and phpMyAdmin provide an installer that you run to install the software. PHP also provides an installer, but I prefer to install it from the Zip file.

Instructions for installing the software are available on the official Web sites, as follows:

• *Apache:* http://httpd.apache.org/docs/2.2/install.html

• *PHP:* www.php.net/manual/en/install.php

• *MySQL:* http://dev.mysql.com/doc/refman/5.1/en/installing.html

• *phpMyAdmin:* www.phpmyadmin.net

Writing the files

In addition to the software for testing your programs, you need software to write the programs. Because PHP programs are just text files, like HTML files are just text files, you can use your favorite text editor (such as WordPad or NotePad on Windows) to write PHP programs. However, there are tools that offer features that make program writing much easier.

It's worthwhile to check out programming editors and integrated development environments (IDEs) before writing your programs.

Programming editors and IDEs offer features that can save you enormous amounts of time during development. Download some demos, try the software, and select the one that suits you best. You can take a vacation later on the time you save.

Programming editors

Programming editors offer many features specifically for writing programs. The following features are offered by most programming editors:

- **Color highlighting:** The editor highlights parts of the program — such as HTML tags, text strings, keywords, and comments — in different colors so they're easy to identify.

- **Indentation:** The editor automatically indents inside parentheses and curly braces to make programs easier to read.

- **Line numbers:** The editor adds temporary line numbers. This is important because PHP error messages specify the line where the error was encountered. It would be cumbersome to have to count 872 lines from the top of the file to the line that PHP says is a problem.

- **Multiple files:** You can have more than one file open at once.

- **Easy code insertion:** The editor offers buttons for inserting code, such as HTML tags or PHP statements or functions.

- **Code library:** You can save snippets of your own code that you can insert by clicking a button.

Many programming editors are available on the Internet for free or for a low price. Some of the more popular editors include the following:

- **Arachnophilia:** (www.arachnoid.com/arachnophilia) This multi-platform editor is written in Java. It's freeware. It's oriented to HTML and Web page development.

- **BBEdit:** (www.barebones.com/products/bbedit/index.shtml) This is the most popular editor for the Mac. BBEdit sells for $125.00.

- **EditPlus:** (www.editplus.com) This editor is designed for use on Windows machines. It highlights HTML, PHP, and other languages. It costs $35.00.

✔ **Emacs:** (www.gnu.org/software/emacs/emacs.html) Emacs works with Windows, Mac, and several flavors of Linux and Unix. It's free.

✔ **HTML-Kit:** (www.chami.com/html-kit) This is a full-featured free editor for HTML, XHTML, XML, CSS, JavaScript, PHP and other text files. A popular editor available for Windows.

✔ **TextWrangler:** (www.barebones.com/products/textwrangler) This editor is provided by the same people who make BBEdit. It's sort of BBEdit lite, also for the Mac. It's free.

Integrated development environment (IDE)

An IDE is an entire workspace for developing applications. It includes a programming editor as well as other features. The following are some features included by most IDEs:

✔ **Debugging:** Has built-in debugging features.

✔ **Previewing:** Displays the Web page output by the program.

✔ **Testing:** Has built-in testing features for your programs.

✔ **FTP:** Has built-in ability to connect and upload/download via FTP (File Transfer Protocol). Keeps track of which files belong in which Web site and keeps the Web site up-to-date.

✔ **Project management:** Organizes programs into projects; manages the files in the project; and includes file checkout and checkin features.

✔ **Backups:** Makes automatic backups of your Web site at periodic intervals.

IDEs are more difficult to learn that programming editors. Some are fairly expensive, but their wealth of features can be worth it. IDEs are particularly useful when several people will be writing programs for the same application. An IDE can make project coordination much simpler and make the code more compatible.

The following are popular IDEs:

✔ **Dreamweaver:** (www.adobe.com/products/dreamweaver) This IDE is available for the Windows and Mac platforms. It provides visual layout tools so you can create a Web page by dragging elements around and clicking buttons to insert elements. Dreamweaver can write the HTML code for you. It also supports PHP. The current version is CS4, which costs $399.00. You can also get Dreamweaver in a suite with other Adobe products.

✔ **Komodo:** (www.activestate.com/komodo) Komodo is offered for Linux and Windows. It supports HTML, JavaScript, CSS, and XML, as well as PHP and other open source languages, such as PERL and Python. It costs $295.00.

✔ **PHPEdit:** (www.phpedit.com) PHPEdit is available for Windows. It has several different versions, with different features and different prices.

[Handwritten margin note: For Windows use Microsoft Expression Web 4]

Uploading your files to your Web site

When your Web page files are complete and ready for the public, you need to transfer them to your Web site. In most cases, you upload them from your local machine using FTP. You can install FTP software on your computer that makes uploading the files an easy process.

If you use an IDE, as I suggest earlier, you have a built-in FTP feature. For instance, if you're using Dreamweaver, when you first set up your Dreamweaver project, you set up a remote site that's connected to your Web site. Whenever you want to upload or download a file, you just highlight it and click a Dreamweaver button. Also, Dreamweaver keeps track of the versions, letting you know whether you're about to replace a newer file with one that has an older date.

Some programming editors also have built in FTP features. For instance, HTML-Kit has a built-in FTP feature that makes uploading your files easy.

If your editor does not include an FTP feature, you can install FTP software on your local computer. This software usually organizes file views similarly to Windows Explorer. It has two panels: one showing the files in the current directory on your local computer and one showing the files on a remote location — your Web site. You then just highlight and move files from one location to the other.

One software package you can use to transfer files is Filezilla (http://filezilla-project.org). It's free software that you can download and install. If you install your Web software using XAMPP, Filezilla is automatically installed at the same time. Some other FTP software is:

- ✔ **FTP Voyager:** (www.ftpvoyager.com) A powerful, secure FTP client for Windows. It has many features, including drag-and-drop file transfer. It costs $39.95.

- ✔ **WS_FTP:** (www.ipswitchft.com) A full-featured FTP client for Windows. It costs $54.95. The same company also sells Fetch, an FTP client for the Mac.

- ✔ **SmartFTP:** (www.smartftp.com) A popular FTP client with many features, especially features oriented toward communication with a Web hosting company. The home version is $36.95, and the professional version is $49.95.

Web hosting company

If you have a reason why you must develop on your Web hosting account, you need a private location for the development files. You can obtain a second account from the Web host for development, and you can transfer the files to your Web site when they're done. Or, you can create a subdirectory on your Web site that you use only for development, transferring the files to the main Web site directory when they're completed.

Whichever way you do it, you need to set up a couple of things. You need to be sure the development area is private, not available to the public. And you need to make sure that the development area is not indexed by search engines. If search engines run across the same Web pages in two different locations, it can lower your search engine results quite a bit.

Keeping it private

You need to set up a directory in your Web hosting account to serve as your development site. You can make the directory private, with no public access with your .htaccess file. To block access to your development directory:

1. **Create a file named .htaccess in the directory you want to protect.**

   That is, if you created a subdirectory named devel to be your development site, create the .htaccess file inside the devel directory. And, yes, that's a dot at the beginning of the filename.

2. **Add a line to the .htaccess file.**

   The line should read as follows:

   ```
   Deny from all
   ```

The Deny directive in the .htaccess file prevents anyone from accessing any files in the directory where the .htaccess file is located.

Keeping out the search engines

You can instruct search engines not to index any files in a directory with a robots.txt file. Create this file with the following contents:

```
##############################
#
# robots.txt file for this website
#
# addresses all robots by using wild card *
#
User-agent: *
# list folders robots are not allowed to index
Disallow: /
#
```

```
# list specific files robots are not allowed to index
#
#Disallow: /tutorials/meta_tags.html
#Disallow: /tutorials/custom_error_page.html
#
# End of robots.txt file
#
###############################
```

The line that begin with number signs (#) are comments, which are ignored. Notice that only two lines are not comments. The first line is

```
User-agent: *
```

This line specifies that all search engines should follow the directions in this file. The second line is

```
Disallow: /
```

This line specifies that the search engines should ignore all files in this directory, including subdirectories.

A company computer

If your development site is located on a company computer, your company IT department is responsible for setting up the site and making is private. You need to communicate your needs to your IT department. You need to be able to transfer the completed files from the development site to the Web site. Your IT department should tell you how to do that. Also, your IT department needs to make a text file editor available for your use and provide documentation or instructions on how to use the editor.

Testing, Testing, 1,2,3

Suppose you believe that PHP and MySQL are available for you to use, for one or more of the following reasons:

- ✔ The IT department at your company or your client company gave you all the information that you asked for and told you that you're good to go.

- ✔ The Web hosting company gave you all the information that you need and told you that you're good to go.

- ✔ You followed all the instructions and installed PHP and MySQL yourself on your local computer.

Now you need to test to make sure that PHP and MySQL are working correctly.

Understanding PHP/MySQL functions

PHP can communicate with any version of MySQL. However, PHP needs to be installed differently, depending on which version of MySQL you're using. PHP provides one set of functions (mysql functions) that communicate with MySQL 4.0 or earlier and a different set of functions (mysqli functions) that communicate with MySQL 4.1 or later. The mysql functions, which communicate with earlier versions of MySQL, can also communicate with the later versions of MySQL, but you may not be able to use some of the newer, advanced features that were added to MySQL in the later versions. The mysqli functions, which can take advantage of all the MySQL features, are available only with PHP 5 or later.

The programs in this book, including the test programs in this section, use MySQL 5.0 and the mysqli functions. If you're using PHP 4, you need to change the programs to use the mysql functions, rather than the mysqli functions. The functions are similar, but some have slight changes in syntax. Chapter 8 provides a table (Table 8-1) showing the differences between the functions used in this book. Versions of the programs that run with PHP 4 are available for download at my Web site (www.janetvalade.com).

If you do use the wrong function, you might see an error message similar to the following:

```
Fatal error: Call to undefined function mysql_connect()
```

The message means that you're using a mysql function in your program, but the mysql functions are not enabled. MySQL support might not be enabled at all or mysqli support might be enabled instead of mysql support. Enabling MySQL support is explained in Appendix B.

Functions are explained later in the book, and the PHP functions that communicate with MySQL are discussed at the beginning of Chapter 8. I mention them briefly here just in case you're using PHP 4, because the test programs that follow this section don't run correctly with PHP 4.

Testing PHP

You need to test that PHP is installed and working in both your development site and your Web site.

On your local computer

To test whether PHP is installed and working, follow these steps:

1. **Find the directory in which your PHP programs need to be saved.**

   This directory and the subdirectories under it are your *Web space.* Apache calls this directory the *document root.* Here's where you can find your directory:

   • If you installed PHP from XAMPP, the default Web space is `c:\xampp\htdocs` on Windows and `Applications/xampp/htdocs` on Mac.

   • If you installed PHP and Apache yourself, individually, the default Web space is the subdirectory `htdocs` in the directory where Apache is installed.

   • If you're using IIS as your Web server, it's `Inetpub\wwwroot`.

   • In Linux, it might be `/var/www/html`.

   You can set the Web space to a different directory by configuring the Web server (see Appendix B).

2. **Create the following file somewhere in your Web space with the name `test.php`.**

   ```
   <html>
   <head><title>PHP Test</title></head>
   <body>
   <p>This is an HTML line</p>
   <?php
       echo "<p>This is a PHP line</p>";
       phpinfo();
   ?>
   </body></html>
   ```

   The file must be saved in your Web space for the Web server to find it.

3. **Execute the `test.php` file created in Step 2.**

   To run a file on your own computer, you can access the default Web space by using the name localhost. Therefore, to execute the file, type **localhost/test.php** into your browser address window.

   For the file to be processed by PHP, you need to access the file through the Web server — not by choosing File➪Open from your Web browser menu.

   You should see the following in the Web browser:

   ```
   This is an HTML line
   This is a PHP line
   ```

Below these lines, you should see a large table that shows information associated with PHP on your system. It shows PHP information, pathnames and filenames, variable values, and the status of various options. The table is produced by the `phpinfo()` line in the test script. Anytime you have a question about the settings for PHP, you can use the `phpinfo()` statement to display this table and check a setting.

 4. Check the PHP values for the settings you need.

For instance, you need MySQL support enabled. Looking through the listing, find the section for MySQL and make sure that MySQL support is On.

Also, at the top of the output, you'll see the version number of the PHP you're running. Be sure you are running PHP 5, not PHP 4.

 5. Change values if necessary.

The general settings for PHP are stored in a file named `php.ini`. You can change the settings to change PHP's behavior. Various PHP settings are discussed throughout the book in the appropriate sections. Appendix B discusses how you can change PHP settings.

On a Web hosting company

If your Web site is hosted at a Web hosting company, you need to test that PHP is working and see what the settings are. In the previous section, in Step 2, you created a test PHP program. In this test, you upload this file to your Web site and make sure it runs correctly.

 1. Locate the test file.

 2. Upload the test file to your Web site.

 3. Execute the test PHP file on your Web site by typing its address into your browser address window.

That is, type your domain name with the filename included, such as **www.myfinecompany.com/test.php**.

If the file runs successfully, you see a long listing on a Web page, similar to the output you saw when you executed this file on your local computer.

 4. Check the PHP values for the settings you need.

Check to make sure that your Web site is running PHP 5, not PHP 4. Also, make sure that MySQL support is activated.

 5. Change values if necessary.

On your Web site, you can't change the settings in the general `php.ini` file. However, you can change PHP settings on a Web hosting account in other ways. Changing the settings is described in Appendix B.

Testing your local PHP configuration file

PHP has many configuration settings that you may want to change. The settings are stored in a text file named php.ini. Your Web host will certainly not provide you with access to the general php.ini file that affects the PHP settings of all users, but some hosts allow you to use a local php.ini file in your own Web site that affects only your PHP settings.

If you can use a local php.ini file, writing your PHP programs is much easier. You should test to see whether your Web host allows a local php.ini file. Here's how to do it:

1. **Create an empty text file named php.ini and upload the empty file to your Web site main directory.**

2. **Execute the program, test.php, that you previously created on your Web site.**

3. **Examine the list of settings the program outputs.**

   Close to the top is a setting called Loaded Configuration File. This setting shows the path to the php.ini file that is currently in effect. If your host allows a local php.ini file, the setting shows the path to the empty file that you just uploaded.

If the path to your uploaded file is not the path to your local php.ini file, your host probably doesn't allow local php.ini files. However, it can't hurt to ask. Perhaps one of you, you or your host, has to do something extra to set it up. Or perhaps if enough people ask for it, your host will change its policies.

Testing MySQL

After you know that PHP is running okay, you can test whether you can access MySQL by using PHP. The following test should be run on both your development environment and your Web site. First run the test on your development site and then upload the file to your Web site and run the test there. Just follow these steps:

1. **Create the following file somewhere in your Web space with the name mysql_test.php.**

   On your Web site, you can run it in the main directory or in a subdirectory.

TIP

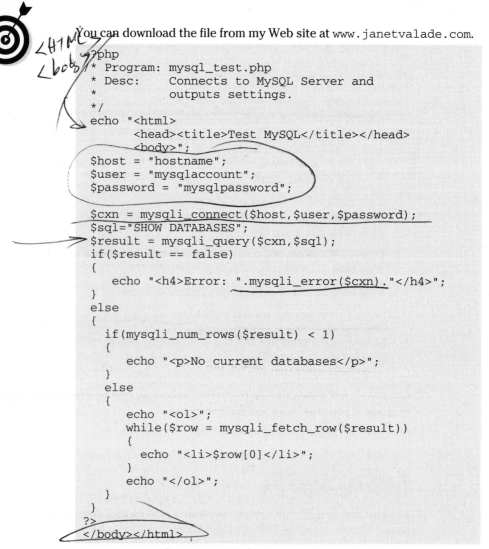

You can download the file from my Web site at www.janetvalade.com.

```php
<?php
/* Program: mysql_test.php
 * Desc:    Connects to MySQL Server and
 *          outputs settings.
 */
echo "<html>
        <head><title>Test MySQL</title></head>
        <body>";
$host = "hostname";
$user = "mysqlaccount";
$password = "mysqlpassword";

$cxn = mysqli_connect($host,$user,$password);
$sql="SHOW DATABASES";
$result = mysqli_query($cxn,$sql);
if($result == false)
{
    echo "<h4>Error: ".mysqli_error($cxn)."</h4>";
}
else
{
  if(mysqli_num_rows($result) < 1)
  {
      echo "<p>No current databases</p>";
  }
  else
  {
      echo "<ol>";
      while($row = mysqli_fetch_row($result))
      {
        echo "<li>$row[0]</li>";
      }
      echo "</ol>";
  }
}
?>
</body></html>
```

2. **Change lines 9, 10, and 11 of the program:**

   ```
   $host="hostname";            "localhost"
   $user="mysqlaccount";        "root"
   $password="mysqlpassword";   " "
   ```

   On your local computer, change "hostname" to "localhost". If
   your Web site is located at a Web hosting company, you may need to
   use "localhost" or you may need to use your domain name, such as
   myfinecompany.com. Some Web hosts use other designations for the
   hostname. The information needed should be included in the information you received from your host when you signed up. If you can't figure
   it out, contact tech support at your Web host and ask them what to use
   for the hostname in a PHP program. On a company computer, you need
   to get the hostname from your IT department.

Change *mysqlaccount* and *mysqlpassword* to the appropriate values. On your local machine, an account named root is installed when MySQL is installed, which may or may not have a password. (I discuss MySQL accounts and passwords in Chapter 5.) If your MySQL account doesn't require a password, type nothing between the quotes, as follows:

```
$password="";
```

On your Web host account, the MySQL account name and password should be included in the information your host sent you when you signed up. On a company computer, you need to get this information from the IT department.

3. **Execute mysql_test.php.**

   You should see a list of database names. You don't want to see an error message or a warning message. If no error or warning message is displayed, MySQL is working fine. If you see an error or a warning message, you need to fix the problem that's causing the message.

The following is a common error message:

```
MySQL Connection Failed: Access denied for user: 'user73@
           localhost' (Using password: YES)
```

This message means that MySQL did not accept your MySQL account number or your MySQL password. Notice that the message reads YES for Using password but doesn't show the actual password that you tried for security reasons. If you tried with a blank password, the message would read NO.

If you receive an error message, double-check your account number and password. Remember that this is your MySQL account number — not your account number to log on to the computer or on to your Web host account. If you can't connect with the account number and password that you have, contact the IT department or the Web hosting company that gave you the account number. (For a further discussion of MySQL accounts and passwords, see Chapter 5.)

Chapter 3

Developing a Web Database Application

Developing a Web database application involves more than just storing data in MySQL databases and typing in PHP programs. Development has to start with planning. Building the application pieces comes after planning. The development steps are

1. Develop a plan, listing the tasks that your application will perform.

2. Design the database needed to support your application tasks.

3. Build the MySQL database, based on the database design.

4. Write the PHP programs that perform the application tasks.

I discuss these steps in detail in this chapter.

Planning Your Web Database Application

Before you ever put finger to keyboard to write a PHP program, you need to plan your Web database application. This is possibly the most important step in developing your application. It's painful to discover, especially just after you finish the last program for your application, that you left something out and have to start over from the beginning. It's also hard on your computer (and your foot) when you take out your frustrations by drop-kicking it across the room.

Good planning prevents such painful backtracking. In addition, it keeps you focused on the functionality of your application, thus preventing you from writing pieces for the application that do really cool things but turn out to have no real purpose in the finished application. And if more than one person is working on your application, planning ensures that all the pieces will fit together in the end.

Identifying what you want from the application

The first step in the planning phase is to identify exactly why you're developing your application and what you want from it. For example, your main purpose might be to

✔ Collect names and addresses from users so that you can develop a customer list.

✔ Deliver information about your products to users, as in a customer catalog.

✔ Sell products online.

✔ Provide technical support to people who already own your product.

After you clearly identify the general purpose of your application, make a list of exactly what you want that application to do. For instance, if your goal is to develop a database of customer names and addresses for marketing purposes, the application's list of required tasks is fairly short:

✔ Provide a form for customers to fill out.

✔ Store the customer information in a database.

If your goal is to sell products online, the list is a little longer:

✔ Provide information about your products to the customer.

✔ Motivate the customer to buy the product.

✔ Provide a way for the customer to order the product online.

✔ Provide a method for the customer to pay for the product online.

✔ Validate the payment so you know that you'll actually get the money.

✔ Send the order to the person responsible for filling the order and sending the product to the customer.

At this point in the planning process, the tasks that you want your application to perform are still pretty general. You can accomplish each of these tasks in many different ways. So now you need to examine the tasks closely and detail exactly how the application will accomplish them. For instance, if your goal is to sell products online, you might expand the preceding list like this:

✔ **Provide information about products to the customer.**

- Display a list of product categories. Each category is a link.

- When the customer clicks a category link, the list of products in that category is displayed. Each product name is a link.

- When a customer clicks a product link, the description of the product is displayed.

✔ **Motivate the customer to buy the product.**

- Provide well-written descriptions of the products that communicate their obviously superior qualities.

- Use flattering pictures of the products.

- Make color product brochures available online.

- Offer quantity discounts.

✔ **Provide a way for customers to order the product online.**

- Provide a button that customers can click to indicate their intention to buy the product.

- Provide a form that collects necessary information about the product the customer is ordering, such as size and color.

- Provide forms for customers to enter shipping and billing addresses.

- Compute and display the total cost for all items in the order.

- Compute and display the shipping costs.

- Compute and display the sales tax.

✔ **Provide a method for customers to pay for the product online.**

- Provide a button that customers can click to pay with a credit card.

- Display a form that collects customers' credit card information.

✔ **Validate the payment so you know that you'll actually get the money.**

The usual method is to send the customer's credit card information to a credit card processing service.

✔ **Send the order to the person responsible for filling the order and sending the product to the customer.**

E-mailing order information to the shipping department should do it.

At this point, you should have a fairly clear idea of what you want from your Web database application. However, this doesn't mean that your goals can't change. In fact, your goals are likely to change as you develop your Web database application and discover new possibilities. At the onset of the project, start with as comprehensive a plan as possible to stay focused.

Taking the user into consideration

Identifying what *you* want your Web database application to do is only one aspect of planning. You must also consider what your users will want from it. For example, say your goal is to gather a list of names and addresses for marketing purposes. Will customers be willing to give up that information?

Your application needs to fulfill a purpose for the users as well as for you. Otherwise, they'll just ignore it. Before users will be willing to give you their names and addresses, for example, they need to perceive that they will benefit from giving you this information. Here are a few examples of why users might be willing to register their names and addresses at your site:

- ✔ **To receive a newsletter:** To be perceived as valuable, the newsletter should cover an industry related to your products. It should offer news and spot trends — and not just serve as marketing material about your products.

- ✔ **To enter a sweepstakes for a nice prize:** Who can turn down a chance to win an all-expense-paid vacation to Hawaii or a brand-new SUV?

- ✔ **To receive special discounts:** For example, you can periodically e-mail special discount opportunities to customers.

- ✔ **To be notified about new products or product upgrades when they become available:** For example, customers might be interested in being notified when a software update is available for downloading.

- ✔ **To get access to valuable information:** For instance, many magazines and newspapers require that you register at their sites to gain access to their articles online.

Now add the customer tasks to your list of tasks that you want the application to perform. For example, consider this list of tasks that you identified for setting up an online retailer:

- ✔ Provide a form for customers to fill out.
- ✔ Store the customer information in a database.

If you take the customer's viewpoint into account, the list expands a bit:

- ✔ Present a description of the advantages customers receive by registering with the site.

✔ Provide a form for customers to fill out.

✔ Add customers' e-mail addresses to the newsletter distribution list.

✔ Store the customer information in a database.

After you have a list of tasks that you want and tasks that your users want, you have a plan for a Web application that's worth your time to develop and worth your users' time to use.

Making the site easy to use

In addition to planning what your Web application is going to do, you need to consider how it's going to do it. Making your application easy to use is important: If customers can't find your products, they aren't going to buy them. And if customers can't find the information they need in a short time, they will look elsewhere. On the Web, customers can easily go elsewhere.

Making your application easy to use is *usability engineering*. Web usability includes such issues as

✔ **Navigation:** What's on your site and where it's located should be immediately obvious to a user.

✔ **Graphics:** Graphics make your site attractive, but graphic files can be slow to display.

✔ **Access:** Some design decisions can make your application accessible or not accessible to users who have disabilities such as impaired vision.

✔ **Browsers:** Different browsers (even different versions of the same browser) can display the same HTML file differently.

Web usability is a large and important subject, and delving into the topic more deeply is beyond the scope of this book. But fear not; you can find lots of helpful information about Web usability on — you guessed it — the Web. Be sure to check out the Web sites of usability experts Jakob Nielsen (www.useit.com) and Jared Spool (www.uie.com). Vincent Flanders also has a fun site full of helpful information about Web design at http://webpagesthatsuck.com. And books on the subject can be very helpful, such as *Web Design For Dummies* by Lisa Lopuck (Wiley).

Leaving room for expansion

One certainty about your Web application is that it will change over time. Down the line, you might think of new functions for it or just simply want to change something about it. Or maybe Web site software improves so that your Web application can do things that it couldn't do when you first put it up. Whatever the reason, your Web site will change. When you plan your application, you need to keep future changes in mind.

You can design your application in steps, taking planned changes into account. You can develop a plan in which you build an application today that meets your most immediate needs and make it available as soon as it's ready. Your plan can include adding functions to the application as quickly as you can develop them. For example, you can build a product catalog and publish it on your Web site as soon as it's ready. You can then begin work on an online ordering function for the Web site, which you will add when it's ready.

You can't necessarily foresee all the functions that you might want in your application. For instance, you might design your travel Web site with sections for all possible destinations today, but the future could surprise you. Trips to Mars? Alpha Centauri? An alternate universe? Plan your application with the flexibility needed to add functionality in the future.

Writing it down

Write down your plan. You'll get this often from me. I speak from the painful experience of not writing it down. When you develop your plan, it's foremost in your mind and perfectly clear. But in a few short weeks, you'll be astonished to discover that it has gone absolutely hazy while your attention was on other pressing issues. Or you'll want to make some changes in the application a year from now and won't remember exactly how the application was designed. Or you're working with a partner to develop an application and you discover that your partner misunderstood your verbal explanation and developed functions for the application that don't fit in your plan. You can avoid these types of problems by writing down everything.

Presenting the Two Running Examples in This Book

In the next two sections, I introduce the two example Web database applications that I created for this book. I refer to these examples throughout the book to demonstrate aspects of application design and development.

Stuff for Sale

The first example is an online product catalog. You're the owner of a pet store, and you want your catalog to provide customers with information about the pets for sale. Selling the pets online is not feasible, although you're toying with the idea of allowing customers to reserve pets online — that is, before they come into the store to purchase them. Currently, the application is simply an online catalog. Customers can look through the catalog online and then come into the store to buy the pet. The information about all the pets is stored in a database, and customers can search the database for information on specific pets or types of pets.

Here's your plan for this application:

✔ **Allow customers to select which pet information they want to see.**

Offer two selection methods:

- *Selecting from a list of links:* Display a list of links that are pet categories (dog, cat, dinosaur, and so on). When the customer clicks a category link, a list of pets is displayed. Each pet in the list is a link to a description of the pet.

- *Typing search terms:* Display a search form in which customers can type words that describe the type of pet they're looking for. The application searches the database for matching words and displays the pet information for pets that match the search words. For example, a customer can type **cat** to see a list of all available cats. Each cat in the list is a link to a description of that cat.

✔ **Display a description of the pet when the customer clicks the link.**

The description is stored in a database.

Members Only

The second example Web database application is related to the preceding pet store example. In addition to the online catalog, you also want to put up a section on your pet store Web site that's for members only. To access this area of the site, customers have to register — providing their names and addresses. In this Members Only section, customers can order pet food at a discount, find out about pets that are on order but haven't arrived yet, and gain access to articles with news and information about pets and pet care.

This is your plan for this application:

✔ **Display a description of what special features and information are available in the Members Only section.**

✔ **Provide an area where customers can register for the Members Only section.**

- *Provide a link to the registration area.*

- *Display a form in the registration area where customers can type their registration information.*

The form should include space for a user login name and password as well as the information that you want to collect.

- *Validate the information that the user entered.*

  For example, verify that the zip code is the correct length and that the e-mail address is in the correct format.

- *Store the information in the database.*

✔ **Provide a login section for customers who are already registered for the Members Only section.**

- *Display a login form that asks for the customer's username and password.*

- *Compare the username and password that are entered with the usernames and passwords in the database.*

  If no match is found, display an error message.

✔ **Display the Members Only Web page after the customer has successfully logged in.**

Designing the Database

After you determine exactly what the Web database application is going to do (see the beginning part of this chapter if you haven't done this yet), you're ready to design the database that holds the information needed by the application. Designing the database includes identifying the data that you need and organizing the data in the way required by the database software.

Choosing the data

First, you must identify what information belongs in your database. Look at the list of tasks that you want the application to perform and determine what information you need to complete each of those tasks.

Here are a few examples:

✔ An online catalog needs a database containing product information.

✔ An online order application needs a database that can hold customer information and order information.

✔ A travel Web site needs a database with information on destinations, reservations, fares, schedules, and so on.

In many cases, your application might include a task that collects information from the user. You'll have to balance your urge to collect all the potentially useful information that you can think of against your users' reluctance to give out personal information — as well as their avoidance of forms that look too time-consuming. One compromise is to ask for some optional information. Users who don't mind can enter it, but users who object can leave it blank. Another possibility is to offer an incentive: The longer the form, the stronger the incentive that you'll need to offer to motivate the user to fill out the form. A user might be willing to fill out a short form to enter a sweepstakes that offers two sneak-preview movie tickets for a prize. But if the form is long and complicated, the prize needs to be more valuable, such as a free trip to California and a tour of a Hollywood movie studio.

In the Pet Catalog application, your customers search the online catalog for information on pets that they might want to buy. You want customers to see information that will motivate them to buy a pet. The information that you want to have available in the database for the customer to see is as follows:

- ✔ The name of the pet (for example, poodle or unicorn)
- ✔ A description of the pet
- ✔ A picture of the pet
- ✔ The cost of the pet

In the second example application, the Members Only section, you want to store information about registered members. The information that you want to store in the database is as follows:

- ✔ Member name
- ✔ Member address
- ✔ Member phone number
- ✔ Member fax number
- ✔ Member e-mail address

Take the time to develop a comprehensive list of the information you need to store in your database. Although you can change and add information to your database after it's developed, including the information from the beginning is easier. Also, if you add information to the database later — after it's in use — the first users in the database will have incomplete information. For example, if you change your form so that it now asks for the user's age, you won't have the age for the people who have already filled out the form and are already in the database.

Organizing the data

MySQL is an RDBMS (Relational Database Management System), which means that the data is organized into tables. (See Chapter 1 for more on MySQL.) You can establish relationships between the tables in the database.

Organizing data in tables

RDBMS tables are organized like other tables that you're used to — in rows and columns, as shown in Figure 3-1. The place where a particular row and column intersect, the individual cell, is a *field*.

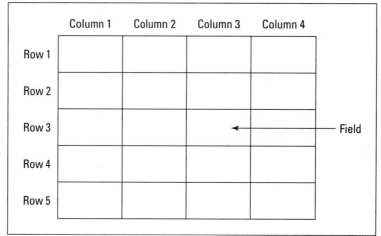

Figure 3-1:
MySQL data
is organized
into tables.

The focus of each table is an *object* (a thing) that you want to store information about. Here are some examples of objects:

Customers	Products
Companies	Animals
Cities	Rooms
Books	Computers
Shapes	Documents
Projects	Weeks

You create a table for each object. The table name should clearly identify the objects that it contains with a descriptive word or term. The name must be a character string, containing letters, numbers, underscores, or dollar signs, with no spaces in it. It's customary to name the table in the singular. Thus, a name for a table of customers might be `Customer`, and a table containing customer orders might be named `CustomerOrder`.

Uppercase and lowercase are significant on Linux and Unix but not on Windows: `CustomerOrder` and `Customerorder` are the same to Windows — but not to Linux or Unix.

In database talk, an object is an *entity,* and an entity has *attributes.* In the table, each row represents an entity, and the columns contain the attributes of each entity. For example, in a table of customers, each row contains information for a single customer. Some of the attributes contained in the columns might be first name, last name, phone number, and age.

Here are the steps for organizing your data into tables:

1. **Name your database.**

   Assign a name to the database for your application. For instance, a database containing information about households in a neighborhood might be named `HouseholdDirectory`.

2. **Identify the objects.**

   Look at the list of information that you want to store in the database (as discussed in the section, "Choosing the data," earlier in this chapter). Analyze your list and identify the objects. For instance, the `HouseholdDirectory` database might need to store the following:

   - Name of each family member

   - Address of the house

   - Phone number

   - Age of each household member

   - Favorite breakfast cereal of each household member

   When you analyze this list carefully, you realize that you're storing information about two objects: the household and the household members. That is, the address and phone number are for the household in general, but the name, age, and favorite cereal are for a particular household member.

3. **Define and name a table for each object.**

   For instance, the `HouseholdDirectory` database needs a table called `Household` and a table called `HouseholdMember`.

4. **Identify the attributes for each object.**

   Analyze your information list and identify the attributes you need to store for each object. Break the information to be stored into its smallest reasonable pieces. For example, when storing the name of a person in a table, you can break the name into first name and last name. Doing this enables you to sort by the last name, which would be more difficult if the first and last name were stored together. You can even break down the name into first name, middle name, and last name, although not many applications need to use the middle name separately.

5. **Define and name columns for each separate attribute that you identified in Step 4.**

Give each column a name that clearly identifies the information in that column. The column names should be one word, with no spaces. For example, you might have columns named `firstName` and `lastName` or `first_name` and `last_name`.

Some words are reserved by MySQL and SQL for their own use and can't be used as column names. The words are currently used in SQL statements or are reserved for future use. For example, `ADD`, `ALL`, `AND`, `CREATE`, `DROP`, `GROUP`, `ORDER`, `RETURN`, `SELECT`, `SET`, `TABLE`, `USE`, `WHERE`, and many, many more can't be used as column names. For a complete list of reserved words, see the online MySQL manual at www.mysql.com/doc/en/Reserved_words.html.

6. **Identify the primary key.**

Each row in a table needs a unique identifier. No two rows in a table should be exactly the same. When you design your table, you decide which column holds the unique identifier, called the *primary key*. The primary key can be more than one column combined. In many cases, your object attributes will not have a unique identifier. For example, a customer table might not have a unique identifier because two customers can have the same name. When there's no unique identifier column, you need to add a column specifically to be the primary key. Frequently, a column with a sequence number is used for this purpose. For example, in Figure 3-2, the primary key is the `cust_id` field because each customer has a unique ID number.

cust_id	first_name	last_name	phone
27895	John	Smith	555-5555
44555	Joe	Lopez	555-5553
23695	Judy	Chang	555-5552
27822	Jubal	Tudor	555-5556
29844	Joan	Smythe	555-5559

Figure 3-2: A sample from the Customer table.

7. **Define the defaults.**

   You can define a default that MySQL will assign to a field when no data is entered into the field. A default is not required but is often useful. For example, if your application stores an address that includes a country, you can specify US as the default. If the user does not type a country, US will be entered.

8. **Identify columns that require data.**

   You can specify that certain columns are not allowed to be empty (also called NULL). For instance, the column containing your primary key can't be empty. That means that MySQL will not create the row and will return an error message if no value is stored in the column. The value can be a blank space or an empty string (for example, " "), but some value must be stored in the column. Other columns, in addition to the primary key, can be set to require data.

Well-designed databases store each piece of information in only one place. Storing it in more than one place is inefficient and creates problems if information needs to be changed. If you change information in one place but forget to change it in another place, your database can have serious problems.

If you find that you're storing the same data in several rows, you probably need to reorganize your tables. For example, suppose you're storing data about books, including the publisher's address. When you enter the data, you realize that you're entering the same publisher's address in many rows. A more efficient way to store this data would be to store the book information in one table and the book publisher information in a separate table. You can define two tables: Book and BookPublisher. In the Book table, you would have the columns title, author, pub_date, and price. In the BookPublisher table, you would have columns such as name, street Address, and city.

Creating relationships between tables

Some tables in a database are related. Most often, a row in one table is related to several rows in another table. A column is needed to connect the related rows in different tables. In many cases, you include a column in one table to hold data that matches data in the primary key column of another table.

A common application that needs a database with two related tables is a customer order application. For example, one table contains the customer information, such as name, address, and phone number. Each customer can have from zero to many orders. You could store the order information in the table with the customer information, but a new row would be created each time that the customer placed an order, and each new row would contain all the customer's information. It would be much more efficient to store the orders in a separate table, named perhaps CustomerOrder. (You can't name the table

Order because that's a reserved word.) The CustomerOrder table would have a column that contains the primary key from a row in the Customer table so that the order is related to the correct row of the Customer table. The relationship is shown in the tables in Figures 3-2 and 3-3.

The Customer table in this example looks like Figure 3-2 (see the preceding section). Notice the unique cust_id for each customer. The related CustomerOrder table is shown in Figure 3-3. Notice that it has the same cust_id column that appears in the Customer table. In this way, the order information in the CustomerOrder table is connected to the related customer's name and phone number in the Customer table.

Order_no	cust_id	item_num	cost
87-222	27895	cat-3	200.00
87-223	27895	cat-4	225.00
87-224	44555	horse-1	550.00
87-225	44555	dog-27	210.00
87-226	27895	bird-1	50.00

Figure 3-3: A sample from the Customer Order table.

In this example, the columns that relate the Customer table and the CustomerOrder table have the same name. They could have different names as long as the data in the columns is the same.

Designing the Sample Databases

In the following two sections, I design the two databases for the two example applications used in this book.

Pet Catalog design process

You want to display the following list of information when customers search your pet catalog:

✔ The name of the pet (for example, poodle or unicorn)

✔ A description of the pet

✔ A picture of the pet

✔ The cost of the pet

In the Pet Catalog plan, a list of pet categories is displayed. This requires that each pet be classified into a pet category and that the pet category be stored in the database.

You design the `PetCatalog` database by following the steps presented in the "Organizing data in tables" section, earlier in this chapter:

1. **Name your database.**

   The name for the Pet Catalog database is `PetCatalog`.

2. **Identify the objects.**

   The information list is

   - The name of the pet (poodle, unicorn, and so on)

   - A description of the pet

   - A picture of the pet

   - The cost of the pet

   - The category for the pet

   All this information is about pets, so the only object for this list is `Pet`.

3. **Define and name a table for each object.**

   The Pet Catalog application needs a table called `Pet`.

4. **Identify the attributes for each object.**

   Now you look at the information in detail:

   - *Name of the pet:* A single attribute (for example, poodle or unicorn). However, it seems likely that your pet shop might have more than one poodle for sale at a time. Therefore, your table needs a unique identifier to serve as the primary key.

- *Pet identification number:* A sequence number assigned to each pet when it's added to the table. This number is the primary key.

- *Description of the pet:* Two attributes — the written description of the pet as it would appear in print and the color of the pet.

- *Picture of the pet:* A path name to a graphic file containing a beautiful picture of the pet.

- *Cost of the pet:* The dollar amount that the store is asking for the pet.

- *Category for the pet:* Two attributes: a category name that includes the pet — for example, dog, horse, dragon — and a description of the category.

It would be inefficient to include two types of information in the Pet table:

- *Category description:* The category information includes a description of the category. Because each category can include several pets, including the category description in the Pet table would result in the same description appearing in several rows. It's more efficient to define the pet category as an object with its own table.

- *Pet color:* If the pet comes in several colors, all the pet information will be repeated in a separate row for each color. It's more efficient to define the pet color as an object with its own table.

The added tables are named PetType and PetColor.

5. **Define and name columns.**

The Pet table has one row for each pet. The columns for the Pet table are

- petID: Unique sequence number assigned to each pet.

- petName: Name of the pet.

- petType: The category name. This is the column that connects the pet to the correct row in the PetType table.

- petDescription: The description of the pet.

- price: The price of the pet.

- pix: The filename of a file that contains a picture of the pet.

The PetType table has one row for each pet category. It has the following columns:

- petType: The category name of a type of pet. This is the primary key for this table. Notice that the Pet table has a column with the same name. These columns link this table with the Pet table.

- typeDescription: The description of the pet type.

The `PetColor` table has one row for each pet color. It has the following columns:

- `petName`: The name of the pet. This is the column that connects the color row to the correct row in the `Pet` table.
- `petColor`: The color of the pet.
- `pix`: The filename of a file that contains a picture of the pet of the specified color.

6. **Identify the primary key.**

- The primary key of the `Pet` table is `petID`.
- The primary key of the `PetType` table is `petType`.
- The primary key of the `PetColor` table is `petName` and `petColor` together.

7. **Define the defaults.**

No defaults are defined for any of the tables.

8. **Identify columns with required data.**

The following columns should never be allowed to be empty:

- `petID`
- `petName`
- `petColor`
- `petType`

These columns are the primary key columns. A row without these values should never be allowed in the tables.

Members Only design process

You create the following list of information that you want to store when customers register for the Members Only section of your Web site:

- ✔ Member name
- ✔ Member address
- ✔ Member phone number
- ✔ Member fax number
- ✔ Member e-mail address

In addition, you would like to collect the date when the member registers and track how often the member goes into the Members Only section.

You design the Members Only database by following the steps presented in the "Organizing data in tables" section, earlier in this chapter:

1. **Name your database.**

   The name for the Members Only database is `MemberDirectory`.

2. **Identify the objects.**

   The information list is

   - Member name
   - Member address
   - Member phone number
   - Member fax number
   - Member e-mail address
   - Member registration date
   - Member logins

   All this information pertains to members, so the only object for this list is `member`.

3. **Define and name a table for each object.**

   The `MemberDirectory` database needs a table called `Member`.

4. **Identify the attributes for each object.**

   Look at the information list in detail:

   - *Member name:* Two attributes: first name and last name.
   - *Member address:* Four attributes: street address, city, state, and zip code. Currently, you have pet stores only in the United States, so you can assume that the member address is an address in the U.S. mailing address format.
   - *Member phone number:* One attribute.
   - *Member fax number:* One attribute.
   - *Member e-mail address:* One attribute.
   - *Member registration date:* One attribute.

   Several pieces of information are related to member logins:

   - *User info:* Logging in to the Members Only section requires a login name and a password. These two items need to be stored in the database.

- *Date and time:* The easiest way to keep track of member logins is to store the date and time when the user logged in to the Members Only section.

Because each member can have many logins, many dates and times for logins need to be stored. Therefore, rather than defining the login time as an attribute of the member, define login as an object, related to the member but requiring its own table.

The added table is named `Login`. The attribute of a login object is its login time (the time includes the date).

5. **Define and name the columns.**

The `Member` table has one row for each member. The columns for the `Member` table are

loginName	city
password	state
createDate	zip
firstName	email
lastName	phone
street	fax

The `Login` table has one row for each *login:* that is, each time a member logs into the Members Only section. It has the following columns:

- `loginName`: The login name of the member who logged in. This is the column that links this table to the `Member` table. This value is unique in the `Member` table but not unique in this table.
- `loginTime`: The date and time of login.

6. **Identify the primary key.**

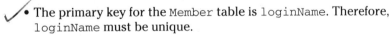

- The primary key for the `Member` table is `loginName`. Therefore, `loginName` must be unique.
- The primary key for the `Login` table is `loginName` and `login Time` together.

7. **Define the defaults.**

No defaults are defined for either table.

8. **Identify columns with required data.**

The following columns should never be allowed to be empty:

- `loginName`
- `password`
- `loginTime`

These columns are the primary key columns. A row without these values should never be allowed in the tables.

Types of Data

MySQL stores information in different formats based on the type of information that you tell MySQL to expect. MySQL allows different types of data to be used in different ways. The main types of data are character, numerical, and date and time data.

Character data

The most common type of data is *character* data — data that is stored as strings of characters and can be manipulated only in strings. Most of the information that you store will be character data, such as customer name, address, phone, and pet description. Character data can be moved and printed. Two character strings can be put together *(concatenated),* a substring can be selected from a longer string, and one string can be substituted for another.

Character data can be stored in one of two formats:

- ✔ **Fixed-length:** In this format, MySQL reserves a fixed space for the data. If the data is longer than the fixed length, only the characters that fit are stored — the remaining characters on the end are not stored. If the string is shorter than the fixed length, the extra spaces are left empty and wasted.

- ✔ **Variable-length:** In this format, MySQL stores the string in a field that is the same length as the string. You specify a string length, but if the string is shorter than the specified length, MySQL uses only the space required rather than leaving the extra space empty. If the string is longer than the space specified, the extra characters are not stored.

If a character string length varies only a little, use the fixed-length format. For example, a length of 10 works for all zip codes, including those with the zip+4 number. If the zip code does not include the zip+4 number, only five spaces are left empty. However, most strings are more variable, so in most cases use a variable-length format. For example, your pet description might be *Small bat* or might run to several lines of description. It would be better to store this description in a variable-length format.

Numerical data

Another common type of data is *numerical* data — data that's stored as a number. Decimal numbers (for example, 10.5, 2.34567, 23456.7) can be stored as well as integers (for example, 1, 2, 248). When data is stored as a number, it can be used in numerical operations, such as adding, subtracting, and squaring.

If data isn't used for numerical operations, however, storing it as a character string is better because the programmer will be using it as a character string. No conversion is required. For example, you probably won't want to add the digits in the users' phone numbers, so phone numbers should be stored as character strings.

MySQL stores positive and negative numbers, but you can tell MySQL to store only positive numbers. If your data is never negative, store the data as *unsigned* (without using a + or – sign before the number). For example, a city population or the number of pages in a document can never be negative.

MySQL provides a specific type of numeric column called an auto-increment column. This type of column is automatically filled with a sequential number when no specific number is provided. For example, when a table row is added with 5 in the auto-increment column, the next row is automatically assigned 6 in the column, unless a different number is specified. Auto-increment columns are useful when unique numbers are needed, such as a product number or an order number.

Date and time data

A third common type of data is date and time data. Data stored as a date can be displayed in a variety of date formats. It can also be used to determine the length of time between two dates or two times — or between a specific date or time and some arbitrary date or time.

Enumeration data

Sometimes data can have only a limited number of values. For example, the only possible values for a column might be yes or no. MySQL provides a data type called *enumeration* for use with this type of data. You tell MySQL what values can be stored in the column (for example, yes, no), and MySQL will not store any other values in the column.

MySQL data type names

When you create a database, you tell MySQL what kind of data to expect in a particular column by using the MySQL names for data types. Table 3-1 shows the MySQL data types used most often in Web database applications.

Table 3-1	MySQL Data Types
MySQL Data Type	**Description**
CHAR(*length*)	Fixed-length character string.
VARCHAR(*length*)	Variable-length character string. The longest string that can be stored is *length*, which must be between 1 and 255.
TEXT	Variable-length character string with a maximum length of 64K of text.
INT(*length*)	Integer with a range from –2147483648 to +2147483647. The number that can be displayed is limited by *length*. For example, if *length* is 4, only numbers from –999 to 9999 can be displayed, even though higher numbers are stored.
INT(*length*) UNSIGNED	Integer with a range from 0 to 4294967295. *length* is the size of the number that can be displayed. For example, if *length* is 4, only numbers up to 9999 can be displayed, even though higher numbers are stored.
BIGINT	A large integer. The signed range is –9223372036854775808 to 9223372036854775807. The unsigned range is 0 to 18446744073709551615.
DECIMAL(*length*,*dec*)	Decimal number where *length* is the number of characters that can be used to display the number, including decimal points, signs, and exponents, and *dec* is the maximum number of decimal places allowed. For example, 12.34 has a *length* of 5 and a *dec* of 2.
DATE	Date value with year, month, and date. Displays the value as YYYY-MM-DD (for example, 2009-09-03).
TIME	Time value with hour, minute, and second. Displays as HH:MM:SS.
DATETIME	Date and time are stored together. Displays as YYYY-MM-DD HH:MM:SS.
ENUM ("*val1*","*val2*"...)	Only the values listed can be stored. A maximum of 65,535 values can be listed.
SERIAL	A shortcut name for BIGINT UNSIGNED NOT NULL AUTO_INCREMENT.

Note that the data type SERIAL is available only in MySQL 5.0 or later. Also, you can't set the data type SERIAL using phpMyAdmin. You must use SQL to set the data type SERIAL, as explained in Chapter 4.

MySQL allows many other data types, but they're needed less frequently. For a description of all the available data types, see the MySQL online manual at http://dev.mysql.com/doc/refman/5.1/en/data-types.html.

Writing it down

Here's my usual nagging: *Write it down.* You probably spent substantial time making the design decisions for your database. At this point, the decisions are firmly fixed in your mind. You don't believe that you can forget them. However, suppose that a crisis intervenes; you don't get back to this project for two months. You'll have to analyze your data and make all the design decisions again. You can avoid this by writing down the decisions now.

Document the organization of the tables, the column names, and all other design decisions. A good format is a document that describes each table in table format, with a row for each column and a column for each design decision. For example, your columns would be *column name, data type,* and *description.*

Taking a Look at the Sample Database Designs

This section contains the database designs for the two example Web database applications.

Stuff for Sale database tables

The database design for the Pet Catalog application includes three tables: Pet, PetType, and PetColor. Tables 3-2 through 3-4 show the organization of these tables. The table definition isn't set in concrete; MySQL allows you to change tables pretty easily. For example, if you set the data type for a variable to CHAR(20) and find that isn't long enough, you can easily change the data type. The database design follows.

Table 3-2	PetCatalog Database Table 1: Pet	
Column Name	*Type*	*Description*
petID	SERIAL	Sequence number for pet (primary key)
petName	VARCHAR(25)	Name of pet
petType	VARCHAR(15)	Category of pet
petDescription	VARCHAR(255)	Description of pet
price	DECIMAL(9,2)	Price of pet
pix	VARCHAR(15)	Path name to graphic file containing picture of pet

Table 3-3	PetCatalog Database Table 2: PetType	
Column Name	*Type*	*Description*
petType	VARCHAR(15)	Name of pet category (primary key)
typeDescription	VARCHAR(255)	Description of category

Table 3-4	PetCatalog Database Table 3: PetColor	
Column Name	*Type*	*Description*
petName	VARCHAR(25)	Name of pet (primary key 1)
petColor	VARCHAR(15)	Color name (primary key 2)
pix	VARCHAR(15)	Path name to graphic file containing picture of pet

Members Only database tables

The database design for the Members Only application includes two tables — Member and Login. Tables 3-5 and 3-6 document the organization of these tables. The table definition isn't set in concrete; MySQL allows you to change tables pretty easily. If you set the data type for a variable to CHAR(5) and find that it isn't long enough, it's easy to change the data type.

The database design follows.

Table 3-5   MemberDirectory Database Table 1: Member

Column Name	Type	Description
loginName	VARCHAR(20)	User-specified login name (primary key)
password	VARCHAR(255)	User-specified password
createDate	DATE	Date member registered and created login account
lastName	VARCHAR(50)	Member's last name
firstName	VARCHAR(40)	Member's first name
street	VARCHAR(50)	Member's street address
city	VARCHAR(50)	Member's city
state	CHAR(2)	Member's state
zip	CHAR(10)	Member's zip code
email	VARCHAR(50)	Member's e-mail address
phone	VARCHAR(15)	Member's phone number
fax	VARCHAR(15)	Member's fax number

Table 3-6   MemberDirectory Database Table 2: Login

Column Name	Type	Description
loginName	VARCHAR(20)	Login name specified by user (primary key 1)
loginTime	DATETIME	Date and time of login (primary key 2)

Developing the Application

After you develop a plan listing the tasks that your application will perform and you develop a database design, you're ready to create your application. First you build the database and then you write your PHP programs. You're moments away from a working Web database application. Well, perhaps that's an exaggeration. But you are making progress.

Use phpMyAdmin to create database

REMEMBER

Building the database

Building the database means turning the paper database design into a working database. Building the database is independent of the PHP programs that your application uses to interact with the database. The database can be accessed using programming languages other than PHP, such as Perl, C, or Java. The database stands on its own to hold the data.

You should build the database before writing the PHP programs. The PHP programs are written to move data in and out of the database, so you can't develop and test them until the database is available.

The database design names the database and defines the tables that make up the database. To build the database, you communicate with MySQL by using the SQL language. You tell MySQL to create the database and to add tables to the database. You tell MySQL how to organize the data tables and what format to use to store the data. Detailed instructions for building the database are provided in Chapter 4.

Writing the programs

Your programs perform the tasks for your Web database application. They create the display that the user sees in the browser window. They make your application interactive by accepting and processing information typed in the browser window by the user. They store information in the database and get information out of the database. The database is useless unless you can move data in and out of it.

The plan that you develop (as I discuss in the earlier sections in this chapter) outlines the programs that you need to write. In general, each task in your plan calls for a program. If your plan says that your application will display a form, you need a program that displays a form. If your plan says that your application will store the data from a form, you need a program that gets the data from the form and puts it in the database.

The PHP language was developed specifically to write interactive Web applications. It has the built-in functionality needed to make writing application programs as painless as possible. Methods were included in the language specifically to access data from forms, to put data into a MySQL database, and to get data from a MySQL database. You can find detailed instructions for writing PHP programs in Part III.

Part II
MySQL Database

The 5th Wave — By Rich Tennant

"Great goulash, Stan. That reminds me, are you still scripting your own Web page?"

In this part . . .

This part provides the details of working with a MySQL database. You find out how to use SQL (Structured Query Language) to communicate with MySQL. In addition, you discover how to create a database, change a database, and move data into and out of a database.

Chapter 4

Building the Database

*A*fter completing your database design (see Chapter 3 if you haven't done this yet), you're ready to turn it into a working database. In this chapter, you find out how to build a database based on your design — and how to move data into and out of it.

The database design names the database and defines the tables that make up the database. To build the database, you must communicate with MySQL, providing the database name and the table structure. Later, you must communicate with MySQL to add data to (or request information from) the database. The language that you use to communicate with MySQL is SQL. In this chapter, I explain how to create SQL queries and use them to build new databases and interact with existing databases.

Communicating with MySQL

The MySQL server is the manager of your database:

✔ It creates new databases.

✔ It knows where the databases are stored.

✔ It stores and retrieves information, guided by the requests, or *queries,* that it receives.

To make a request that MySQL can understand, you build an SQL query and send it to the MySQL server. (For a more complete description of the MySQL server, see Chapter 1.) The next two sections detail how to do this.

Building SQL queries

SQL (Structured Query Language) is the computer language that you use to communicate with MySQL. SQL is almost English; it's made up largely of English words, put together into strings of words that sound similar to English sentences. In general (fortunately), you don't need to understand any arcane technical language to write SQL queries that work.

The first word of each query is its name, which is an action word (a verb) that tells MySQL what you want to do. The queries that I discuss in this chapter are CREATE, DROP, ALTER, SHOW, INSERT, LOAD, SELECT, UPDATE, and DELETE. This basic vocabulary is sufficient to create — and interact with — databases on Web sites.

The query name is followed by words and phrases — some required and some optional — that tell MySQL how to perform the action. For instance, you always need to tell MySQL what to create, and you always need to tell it which table to insert data into or to select data from.

The following is a typical SQL query. As you can see, it uses English words:

```
SELECT lastName FROM Member
```

This query retrieves all the last names stored in the table named Member. More complicated queries, such as the following, are less English-like:

```
SELECT lastName,firstName FROM Member WHERE state="CA" AND
        city="Fresno" ORDER BY lastName
```

This query retrieves all the last names and first names of members who live in Fresno California and then puts them in alphabetical order by last name. This query is less English-like but still pretty clear.

Here are some general points to keep in mind when constructing an SQL query, as illustrated in the preceding sample query:

- ✔ **Capitalization:** In this book, I put SQL language words in all caps; items of variable information (such as column names) are usually given labels that are all or mostly lowercase letters. I did this to make it easier for you to read — not because MySQL needs this format. The case of the

SQL words doesn't matter; for example, select is the same as SELECT, and from is the same as FROM, as far as MySQL is concerned. On the other hand, the case of the table names, column names, and other variable information does matter if your operating system is Unix or Linux. When using Unix or Linux, MySQL needs to match the column names exactly, so the case for the column names has to be correct — for example, lastname is not the same as lastName. Windows, however, isn't as picky as Unix and Linux; from its point of view, lastname and lastName are the same.

✔ **Spacing:** SQL words must be separated by one or more spaces. It doesn't matter how many spaces you use; you could just as well use 20 spaces or just 1 space. SQL also doesn't pay any attention to the end of the line. You can start a new line at any point in the SQL statement or write the entire statement on one line.

✔ **Quotes:** Notice that CA and Fresno are enclosed in double quotes (") in the preceding query. CA and Fresno are series of characters called _text strings,_ or _character strings._ (I explain strings in detail later in this chapter.) You're asking MySQL to compare the text strings in the SQL query with the text strings already stored in the database. When you compare numbers (such as integers) stored in numeric columns, you don't enclose the numbers in quotes. (In Chapter 3, I explain the types of data that you can store in a MySQL database.)

Sending SQL queries

When building a Web database application, two common ways to send SQL queries to the MySQL server are

✔ **phpMyAdmin:** phpMyAdmin is software developed specifically for the purpose of managing MySQL databases. It's written in PHP and runs in a browser. It provides a user interface that greatly simplifies your interactions with MySQL.

✔ **PHP scripts:** The PHP language contains features developed specifically for the purpose of sending SQL queries to MySQL databases and receiving information from the databases.

Using phpMyAdmin

The phpMyAdmin software page provides an interface for interacting with the MySQL server. To open the main phpMyAdmin page, type **localhost/ phpmyadmin/** into the address field in your browser. If you're using XAMPP, you can also open phpMyAdmin from the XAMPP main page by clicking the phpMyAdmin link located toward the bottom of the left orange pane.

The phpMyAdmin main page is shown in Figure 4-1.

Home Help

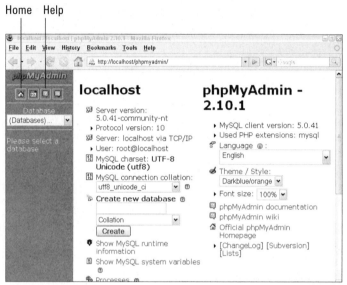

Figure 4-1:
The
phpMyAdmin
main page.

Notice the pane on the left of the page. The top of the pane shows some small icons. The first icon on the left is the icon for home. Any time you click that icon, you will return to this main page.

Another icon is a question mark. When you click the question mark icon, a new window opens with documentation for phpMyAdmin.

You can use phpMyAdmin to administer your databases in one of two ways:

- ✔ **Write SQL queries.** You can write your own SQL query and use the SQL feature of phpMyAdmin to send your query to the MySQL server.

- ✔ **Click links and buttons in the phpMyAdmin interface.** The interface provides many features that make MySQL interaction easy. For instance, the interface has features for browsing the data, searching the data, inserting data, removing data, importing data, and many other features.

Sending your own SQL queries using the phpMyAdmin query sender

You can write your own SQL query and send the query to the MySQL query using phpMyAdmin. To send the query, follow these steps:

1. **Open the main phpMyAdmin page.**

2. **Click the SQL icon at the top of the left panel.**

   The following page opens, as shown in Figure 4-2. This page is a smaller page that opens on top of the main page.

Figure 4-2:
The phpMyAdmin SQL query page.

3. **Type the SQL query into the top panel of the page.**

4. **Click the Go button.**

   The SQL query executes and the response is displayed on the main page. The small screen remains open so that you can type another query if desired.

Using this method, you can write any SQL query that you want and send it. The response is displayed on the main page.

Using the phpMyAdmin interface

The phpMyAdmin software provides an interface you can use to manage your databases. It contains buttons, links, and fields that perform the tasks you need to perform, such as create a database, insert data, browse the data, search for data, remove data, and so forth.

When you use the interface to perform a task, phpMyAdmin actually creates the SQL query needed to tell MySQL what you want to do and sends the query to the MySQL server. If the query returns any information, such as retrieves some data, the information returned is displayed on the phpMyAdmin page. The results page also shows you the query that was executed.

The most common operations you need to perform on your data are discussed in the remainder of this chapter. You find out how you perform these actions, including how to perform the tasks with phpMyAdmin.

A quicker way to send SQL queries to the MySQL server

In some situations, you can't use phpMyAdmin to administer or modify your database. And writing an entire PHP script for a simple database task is a waste of time. This sidebar explains a simple, quick method for sending SQL queries to the MySQL server.

When MySQL is installed, a simple, text-based program called `mysql` (or sometimes the *terminal monitor* or the *monitor*) is also installed. Programs that communicate with servers are *client software;* because this program communicates with the MySQL server, it's a client. When you enter SQL queries in this client, the response is returned to the client and displayed onscreen. The monitor program can send queries across a network; it doesn't have to be running on the machine where the database is stored.

To send SQL queries to MySQL by using the `mysql` client, follow these steps:

1. **Locate the `mysql` client.**

   By default, the `mysql` client program is installed in the subdirectory `bin` under the directory where MySQL is installed. In Unix/Linux, the default is `/usr/local/mysql/bin` or `/usr/local/bin`. In Windows, the default is `c:\Program Files\MySQL\MySQL Server 5.0\bin`. However, the client might be installed in a different directory. Or, if you're not the MySQL administrator, you might not have access to the `mysql` client. If you don't know where MySQL is installed or can't run the client, ask the MySQL administrator to put the client somewhere where you can run it or to give you a copy that you can put on your own computer.

2. **Start the client.**

   In Unix and Linux, type the path/filename (for example, `/usr/local/mysql/bin/mysql`). In Windows, open a command prompt window and then type the path\filename (for example, `c:\ Program Files\MySQL\MySQL Server 5.0\bin\mysql`). This command starts the client if you don't need to use an account name or a password. If you need to enter an account or a password or both, use the following parameters:

   `-u` *user: user* is your MySQL account name.

   `-p`: This parameter prompts you for the password for your MySQL account.

   For instance, if you're in the directory where the `mysql` client is located, the command might look like this:

   ```
   mysql -u root -p
   ```

3. **If you're starting the `mysql` client to access a database across the network, use the following parameter after the `mysql` command:**

   -h *host*: *host* is the name of the machine where MySQL is located.

   For instance, if you're in the directory where the `mysql` client is located, the command might look like this:

   ```
   mysql -h mysqlhost.mycompany.com -u root -p
   ```

   Press Enter after typing the command.

4. **Enter your password when prompted for it.**

   The `mysql` client starts, and you see something similar to this:

   ```
   Welcome to the MySQL monitor. Commands end with ; or
   \g.
   Your MySQL connection id is 459 to server version:
   5.0.15
   Type 'help;' or '\h' for help. Type '\c' to clear the
   buffer.
   mysql>
   ```

5. **Select the database that you want to use.**

   At the `mysql` prompt, type the following:

   ```
   use databasename
   ```

   Use the name of the database that you want to query.

6. **At the `mysql` prompt, type your SQL query followed by a semicolon (;) and then press Enter.**

   The `mysql` client continues to prompt for input and does not execute the query until you enter a semicolon. The response to the query is displayed onscreen.

7. **To leave the `mysql` client, type** quit **at the prompt and then press Enter.**

Using PHP scripts

Because this book is about PHP and MySQL, the focus is on accessing MySQL databases from PHP scripts. PHP and MySQL work well together. PHP provides built-in functions to interact with MySQL. You don't need to know the details of interacting with the database because the functions handle all the details. You just need to know how to use the functions.

PHP functions connect to the MySQL server, select the correct database, send a query, and receive any data that the query retrieves from the database. I explain using PHP functions to interact with your MySQL database in detail in Chapter 8.

Building a Database

A database has two parts: a structure to hold the data and the data itself. In the following few sections, I explain how to create the database structure. First you create an empty database with no structure at all, and then you add tables to it.

Rarely do you create your database from a PHP script. Generally, the database needs to exist before your Web application can perform its tasks — display data from the database, store data in the database, or both. Perhaps an application might require you to create a new table for each customer, such as create a new picture gallery or product information table for each individual. In this case, an application might need to create a new table while it is running. But it's unusual for an application to create a database or a table while running.

Creating a new database

You can create your new, empty database using phpMyAdmin. After you create a new database, you can add tables to it. Adding tables is explained later in this chapter.

In this section, I explain how to create your new database on your local computer and on a Web hosting account.

On your local computer

To create a new empty database, take these steps:

1. **Open the phpMyAdmin main page in a browser.**

   The phpMyAdmin page opens. (Refer to Figure 4-1.)

2. **Scroll down to the Create New Database heading.**

   The heading is located in the left column of the main panel.

3. **Type the name of the database you want to create into the blank field.**

4. **Click Create.**

When you create the new database, a new phpMyAdmin page is displayed, as shown in Figure 4-3.

Notice that the new database name — Customer — is now shown in the left pane. Customer is the named I typed in the field to name the new database. The 0 after the database name means that there are, as yet, no tables in the database.

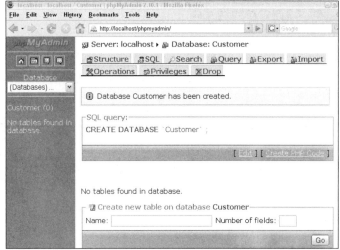

Figure 4-3:
The
phpMyAdmin
new data-
base page.

In the main panel, the following is displayed

```
Database Customer has been created
```

Showing that the database was successfully created. It also shows the SQL query that phpMyAdmin sent to create the database, which was:

```
CREATE DATABASE 'Customer'
```

Below the SQL statement, the page shows that no tables have been created and provides a section where you can proceed to create tables. I discuss creating tables later in this chapter.

On your Web hosting account

Most Web hosts provide phpMyAdmin for your use. So, in some cases, you may be able to use the same procedure described in the preceding section to create a new database. However, many Web hosts do not allow you to create a new database in phpMyAdmin. When you scroll down the phpMyAdmin main page to the Create New Database section, you may not see the field and Create button needed to create the new database. Instead, you may see a message similar to the following:

```
No Privileges
```

This may mean that you must use another procedure to create a new database. Or it may mean that you're not allowed to create a new database at all. You may be allowed only one database to use with MySQL, and you can create tables in only this one database. You can try requesting another database, but you need a good reason. MySQL and PHP don't care that all your tables are in one database instead of organized into databases with meaningful names. It's just easier for humans to keep track of projects when they're organized.

If you're allowed to create a new database but not allowed to create it in phpMyAdmin, the Web hosting company provides a way for you to create a database from your Web account control panel. Many Web hosting companies provide cPanel to manage your account. Other companies provide a different, but similar, control panel. The following steps show how to create a new database using cPanel. You should find a similar procedure on other control panels. If you can't figure it out, you need to ask the tech support staff at your Web hosting company.

1. **Open the control panel for your Web hosting account.**

2. **Find and click the icon for MySQL databases.**

   In cPanel, the icon is located in the section labeled Databases. The icon says MySQL Databases.

   A page opens so that you can create a new database, shown in Figure 4-4.

   The page lists your current databases, if you have any.

3. **Type the name of the database you want to create into the blank field labeled New Database.**

4. **Click the Create Database button.**

   A page displays informing you that the database was created successfully. From this page, you can go back to the control panel and then to phpMyAdmin. You can see the new database listed on the phpMyAdmin main page, in the left pane.

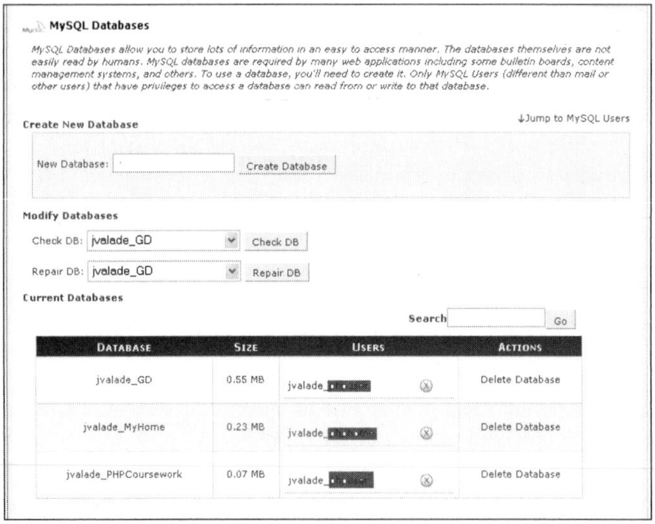

Figure 4-4:
The page where you create a new database.

Viewing the databases

You can see a list of the names of your current databases at any time by opening the main phpMyAdmin page. The names are shown in the left pane of the page. The list includes a number after the database name. This number represents the number of tables currently defined for the database.

The SQL query that displays a list of database names is

```
SHOW DATABASES
```

After you create an empty database, you can add tables to it. (Adding tables to a database is described later in this chapter.)

Deleting a database

You can delete a database on your local computer using phpMyAdmin, as follows:

1. **Open the phpMyAdmin main page.**

2. **Click the name of the database you want to delete.**

   The names of all your databases appear in the left pane. You may need to choose your database from a drop-down list.

   A page opens and displays the name and structure of the database. The page displays a set of tabs across the top of the page, shown in Figure 4-5.

3. **Click Drop.**

   A panel asks you to verify that you want to destroy the database.

4. **Click Okay.**

   A page opens with a message letting you know that the database has been dropped. It also shows you the SQL query that was executed:

```
DROP DATABASE databasename
```

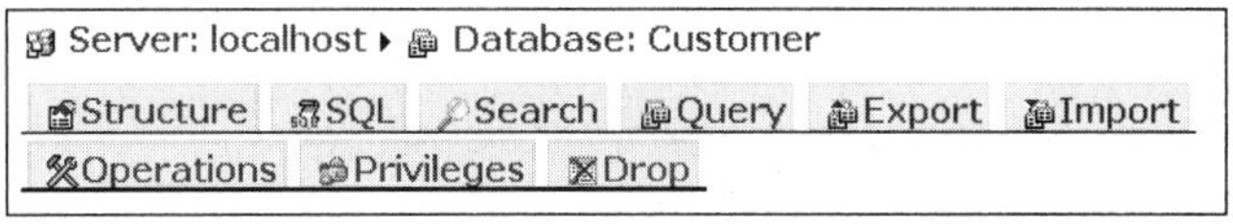

Figure 4-5:
Tabs at the top of the phpMyAdmin page.

> Server: localhost ▸ Database: Customer
>
> Structure | SQL | Search | Query | Export | Import
> Operations | Privileges | Drop

Use DROP carefully because it's irreversible. After a database is dropped, it's gone forever. And any data that was in it is gone as well.

To delete a database on your Web hosting account, you use a specific procedure provided by the Web hosting company. For example, in cPanel, you use the same page that you used to create the database. As shown earlier in Figure 4-4, the page lists all your existing databases in a table. The table includes a column named Actions with a link for each database to Delete Database. Click the Delete Database link to remove the database. However, remember, after you delete the database, it's gone forever.

Adding tables to a database

You can add tables to any database, whether it's a new, empty database that you just created or an existing database that already has tables and data in it. In most cases, you create the tables in the database before the PHP script(s) access the database. Therefore, in most cases, you use phpMyAdmin to add the tables.

In the sample database designs that I introduce in Chapter 3, the PetCatalog database is designed with three tables: Pet, PetType, and PetColor. The MemberDirectory database is designed with two tables: Member and Login.

The definition of the table, Pet, is shown in Table 4-1. The table shows a list of the column names and data types. It also specifies which column is the primary key for the table.

Table 4-1	PetCatalog Database Table 1: Pet	
Column Name	*Type*	*Description*
petID	SERIAL	Sequence number for pet (primary key)
petName	VARCHAR(25)	Name of pet
petType	VARCHAR(15)	Category of pet
petDescription	VARCHAR(255)	Description of pet
price	DECIMAL(9,2)	Price of pet
pix	VARCHAR(15)	Path name to graphic file containing picture of pet

Data type is not the only characteristic you can apply to a field. Here are some common definitions that you can use:

✔ NOT NULL: This column must have a value; it can't be empty.

✔ DEFAULT *value*: This value is stored in the column when the row is created if no other value is given for this column.

✔ AUTO_INCREMENT: You use this definition to create a sequence number. As each row is added, the value of this field increases by one integer from the last row entered. You can override the auto number by assigning a specific value to the field.

✔ UNSIGNED: You use this definition to indicate that the values for this numeric field will never be negative numbers.

You can create a table in phpMyAdmin, either using the interface or with an SQL query.

Using the phpMyAdmin interface

PhpMyAdmin provides an interface page for adding a new table to a database, as follows:

1. **Open the main phpMyAdmin page.**

2. **Click the name of the database you want to add a table to.**

   The database name is displayed in the left pane.

   The Database Page opens. The page lists the tables currently in the database or states that no tables are found in the database. The page also displays a section labeled Create New Table on database. The section contains a field labeled Name.

3. **Type the name of the table into the field.**

4. **Type the number of fields you want in the table into the field labeled Number of fields.**

   Don't worry about making a mistake. Nothing is set in stone. You can change the table structure easily if you need to.

   For example, for the Pet table defined in Table 4-1, you type **6** into the field because the table contains six fields: petID, petName, petType, petDescription, price, and pix.

5. **Click Go.**

   The page that opens allows you to define each column, or *field*. The page provides a table, which is quite wide, where you can define the fields. Figure 4-6 shows the left half of the page, and Figure 4-7 shows the right half.

6. Enter the definitions for all the fields.

Figure 4-6 shows the left side of the table definition with its cells filled in. Type the field name in the first column.

In the second column, select the data type from a drop-down list. The data type for the first field is SERIAL. If you don't find SERIAL in the drop-down list, select BIGINT for the field.

In the third column, type the length or values for the field. For instance, for VARCHAR data types, enter the number of characters, such as **15**.

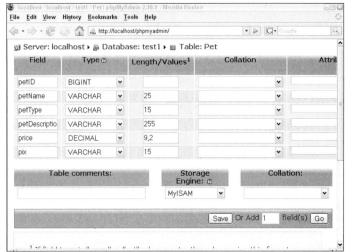

Figure 4-6: The table definition page (left half).

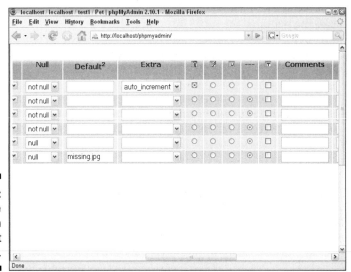

Figure 4-7: The table definition page (right half).

Figure 4-7 shows the right side of the table definition. The column called `Null` specifies whether the field can be blank or not. The default is `Not Null`, but you can change it to `Null` with the drop-down list.

In the column named `Default`, you can specify a default value for the field. MySQL will insert this value when no value is stored in the field.

The column named `Extra` allows you to define the field as `auto_increment` from the drop-down list.

The next column includes several radio buttons. The only one you need to worry about is the first one. Select the first radio button to define a column as the primary key. The other radio buttons are used for more advanced features of MySQL that are not covered in this book.

7. Click Save.

A new phpMyAdmin page opens with a message stating that the table has been created. The new page also shows the SQL query that was used to create the table.

You can view the tables in a database and their structure any time by going to the database page. That is, you can open the main phpMyAdmin page and click the name of the database. The page that opens lists the tables currently in the database.

Each table is displayed in a row, beginning with the table name. Next, the row shows several icons. The second icon is the structure icon. If you click this icon, the structure of the table is displayed, showing the field names and definitions.

Another icon shown in the listing for the table is a large red X. If you click this icon, the table is dropped, removed completely.

Writing an SQL query

You can also create a table by writing your own SQL query and sending it to the MySQL server. In some cases, it's faster to just write the query.

The `CREATE TABLE` query creates a new table. The name is followed by the names and definitions of all the fields, separated by commas, with parentheses around the entire set of definitions. For instance, the query you would use to create the `Pet` table is

```
CREATE TABLE Pet (
   petID           SERIAL,
   petName         VARCHAR(25)   NOT NULL,
   petType         VARCHAR(15)   NOT NULL,
   petDescription  VARCHAR(255)  NOT NULL,
   price           DECIMAL(9,2)  NULL,
   pix             VARCHAR(15)   DEFAULT "missing.jpg",
)
```

You can also define the first field using the following:

```
PetID  BIGINT NOT NULL UNSIGNED AUTO_INCREMENT PRIMARY KEY
```

If you're using a combination of columns as the primary key, include `PRIMARY KEY` in the definition for all the columns that are part of the primary key. Or, you can use a `PRIMARY KEY` statement at the end of the `CREATE TABLE` query. For instance, you can define a `Login` table (refer to Table 3-6 in Chapter 3) with the following query:

```
CREATE TABLE Login (
   loginName      VARCHAR(20) NOT NULL,
   loginTime      DATETIME NOT NULL,
PRIMARY KEY (loginName,loginTime) )
```

Do not use any MySQL reserved words for column names, as I discuss in Chapter 3. If you do, MySQL gives you an error message that looks like this:

```
You have an error in your SQL syntax near 'order var(20))'
             at line 1
```

Note that this message shows the column definition that it didn't like and the line where it found the offending definition. However, the message doesn't tell you much about what the problem is. The `error in your SQL syntax` that it refers to is the use of the MySQL reserved word `order` as a column name.

After a table has been created, you can query to see it, review its structure, or remove it.

- ✔ **To see the tables you've added to a database, use this query:**

  ```
  SHOW TABLES
  ```

- ✔ **To see the structure of a table, use this query:**

  ```
  EXPLAIN tablename
  ```

- ✔ **To remove any table, use this query:**

  ```
  DROP TABLE tablename
  ```

Use `DROP` carefully because it's irreversible. After a table is dropped, it's gone forever, and any data that was in it is gone as well.

Changing the database structure

Your database isn't written in stone. You can change the name of the table; add, drop, or rename a column; or change the data type or other attributes of the column. You can change the structure even after the table contains data, as long as you do not change the definition of a field to a definition that's incompatible with the data currently in the column.

Changing a database is not a rare occurrence. You might want to change your database for many reasons. For example, suppose that you defined the column lastName with VARCHAR(20) in the Member table of the MemberDirectory database. At the time, 20 characters seemed sufficient for a last name. But now you just received a memo announcing the new CEO, John Schwartzheimer-Losertman. Oops. MySQL will truncate his name to the first 20 letters, a less-than-desirable new name for the boss. So you need to make the column wider — pronto.

Using phpMyAdmin

To change the structure in phpMyAdmin, follow these steps:

1. **Open the main phpMyAdmin page.**

2. **Click the name of the database that contains the table to be modified.**

   A page opens listing the tables that are in the database. Each table is listed in a separate row on the page.

3. **In the row for the table to be modified, click the second icon (the structure icon).**

   The page that opens shows the structure of the table. Each field is listed in a row on the page.

4. **Click the pencil icon for the field you want to modify.**

   The pencil icon is in a column named Action, which contains several icons. The pencil icon is the second icon.

   A page opens where you can change any definition for the field. In this page, you can change the data type for the field lastName from VARCHAR(20) to VARCHAR(30).

   The page that lists the table structure also provides a red X icon that you can use to drop a field. And a section below the list of fields that you can use to add a field.

5. **After making changes to the field definition, click Save.**

6. **Repeat Steps 4 and 5 until you've modified all the fields you want to change.**

Writing your own SQL query

You can change the table structure with the ALTER query. The basic format for this query is ALTER TABLE *tablename*, followed by the specified changes. Table 4-2 shows the changes that you can make.

Table 4-2	Changes You Can Make with the ALTER Query
Change	*Description*
ADD *columnname* *definition*	Adds a column; *definition* includes the data type and optional definitions.
ALTER *columnname* SET DEFAULT *value*	Changes the default value for a column.
ALTER *columnname* DROP DEFAULT	Removes the default value for a column.
CHANGE *columnname* *new-columnname* *definition*	Changes the definition of a column and renames the column; *definition* includes the data type and optional definitions.
DROP *columnname*	Deletes a column, including all the data in the column. The data cannot be recovered.
MODIFY *columnname* *definition*	Changes the definition of a column; *definition* includes the data type and optional definitions.
RENAME *newtablename*	Renames a table.

You can make the lastName field wider by sending this query to change the column in a second:

```
ALTER TABLE Member MODIFY lastName VARCHAR(50)
```

Moving Data Into and Out of the Database

An empty database is like an empty cookie jar — it's not much fun. And searching an empty database is no more interesting or fruitful than searching an empty cookie jar. A database is useful only with respect to the information that it holds.

A database needs to be able to receive information for storage and to deliver information on request. For instance, the MemberDirectory database needs to be able to receive the member information, and it also needs to be able to deliver its stored information when you request it. If you want to know the address of a particular member, for example, the database needs to deliver that information when you request it.

You're likely to perform four types of task on your database:

- ✔ **Adding information:** Adding a row to a table.
- ✔ **Updating information:** Changing information in an existing row. This includes adding data to a blank field in an existing row.
- ✔ **Retrieving information:** Looking at the data. This request does not remove data from the database.
- ✔ **Removing information:** Deleting data from the database.

Sometimes your question requires information from more than one table. For instance, the question, "How much does a green dragon cost?" requires information from the Pet table and from the Color table. You can ask this question easily in a single SELECT query by combining the tables.

In the following sections, I discuss how to receive and deliver information as well as how to combine tables.

Adding information

Every database needs data. For example, you might want to add data to your database so that your users can look at it — an example of this is the Pet Catalog that I introduce in Chapter 3. Or you might want to create an empty database for users to put data into, making the data available for your eyes only — an example of this is the Member Directory. In either scenario, data will be added to the database.

If your data is still on paper, you can enter it directly into a MySQL database, one row at a time, typing it in. However, if you have a lot of data, this process could be tedious and involve a lot of typing. Suppose that you have information on 1,000 products that must be added to your database. Assuming that you're greased lightening on a keyboard and can enter a row per minute, that's 16 hours of rapid typing — well, rapid editing, anyway. Doable, but not fun. On the other hand, suppose that you need to enter 5,000 members of an organization into a database and that it takes 5 minutes to enter each member. Now you're looking at more than 400 hours of typing — who has time for that?

If you have a large amount of data to enter, consider some alternatives. Sometimes scanning in the data is an option. Or perhaps you need to beg, borrow, or hire some help. In many cases, it could be faster to enter the data into a big text file than to enter each row manually.

With phpMyAdmin, you can read data from a big text file (or even a small text file). So, if your data is already in a computer file, you can work with that file; you don't need to retype all the data. Even if the data is in a format other than a text file (for example, in an Excel, Access, or Oracle file), you can usually convert the file to a big text file, which can then be read into your MySQL database. If the data isn't yet in a computer file and there's a lot of data, it might be faster to enter that data into the computer in a big text file and transfer it into MySQL as a second step.

Most text files can be read into MySQL, but some formats are easier than others. If you're planning to enter the data into a big text file, read the "Adding a bunch of data" section to find the best format. Of course, if the data is already on the computer, you have to work with the file as it is.

Adding one row at a time with an SQL query

It's common to want your PHP script to store data in your database. For instance, when you sell a product, the customer enters her name, address, product she wants to buy, and other information into forms on the Web page. Your PHP script needs to add this data to your database. You use an SQL query in the script to add the data to the database.

You use the INSERT query to add a row to a database. This query tells MySQL which table to add the row to and what the values are for the fields in the row. The general form of the query is

```
INSERT INTO tablename (columnname, columnname,...,columnname)
     VALUES (value, value,...,value)
```

The following rules apply to the INSERT query:

- ✔ **Values must be listed in the same order in which the column names are listed.** The first value in the value list is inserted into the column that's named first in the column list; the second value in the value list is inserted into the column that's named second; and so on.

- ✔ **A partial column list is allowed.** You don't need to list all the columns. Columns that are not listed are given their default value or left blank if no default value is defined.

- ✔ **A column list is not required.** If you're entering values for all the columns, you don't need to list the columns at all. If no columns are listed, MySQL looks for values for all the columns, in the order in which they appear in the table.

- ✔ **The column list and value list must be the same length.** If the list of columns is longer or shorter than the list of values, you get an error message like this: Column count doesn't match value count.

The following INSERT query adds a row to the Member table:

```
INSERT INTO Member (loginName,createDate,password,lastName,
                    street,city,state,zip,email,phone,fax)
      VALUES ("bigguy","2001-Dec-2","secret","Smith",
              "1234 Happy St","Las Vegas","NV","88888",
              "gsmith@GSmithCompany.com","(555) 555-5555","")
```

Notice that firstName is not listed in the column name list. No value is entered into the firstName field. If firstName were defined as NOT NULL, MySQL would not allow this. Also, if the definition for firstName included a default, the default value would be entered, but because it doesn't, the field is left empty. Notice that the value stored for fax is an empty string.

Adding one row at a time with phpMyAdmin

Many Web database applications include a database of information that you display on the Web page. For instance, a product catalog contains product information that the application displays when the customer wants to view it. In this type of application, you add the information to the database outside the application. You can create the catalog using phpMyAdmin.

To add data to the database table using phpMyAdmin, follow these steps:

1. **Open the main phpMyAdmin page.**

   Figure 4-1, which appears earlier in the chapter, shows the main page.

2. **Click a database name.**

3. **Click the insert icon.**

   In the action column, in the row for the table, the insert icon is the fourth icon.

   The page shown in Figure 4-8 opens where you can enter the data for a row.

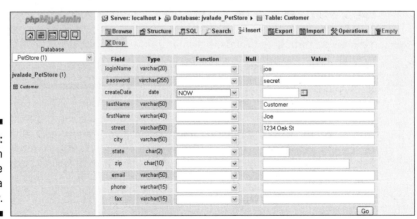

Figure 4-8: phpMyAdmin page where you enter a row.

4. **Add your data to each row.**

   You enter the values in the column named Values. Notice that there is also a column named Function, which contains a drop-down list of MySQL functions that you can use to enter the data. For instance, in this case, the function NOW is specified for the date. The function NOW enters the current date.

5. **Click Go.**

   A new page opens, showing that the data was inserted and showing the SQL query that was used.

Adding a bunch of data

If you have a large amount of data to enter and it's already in a computer file, you can transfer the data from the existing computer file to your MySQL database using phpMyAdmin.

Because data in a database is organized in rows and columns, the text file being read must indicate where the data for each column begins and ends and where the end of a row is. To indicate columns, a specific character separates the data for each column. By default, MySQL looks for a tab character to separate the fields. However, if a tab doesn't work for your data file, you can choose a different character to separate the fields and tell MySQL in the query that a different character than the tab separates the fields. Also by default, the end of a line is expected to be the end of a row — although you can choose a character to indicate the end of a line if you need to. A data file for the Pet table might look like this:

```
Unicorn<TAB>horse<TAB>Spiral horn<Tab>5000.00<Tab>/pix/unicorn.jpg
Pegasus<TAB>horse<TAB>Winged<Tab>8000.00<Tab>/pix/pegasus.jpg
Lion<TAB>cat<TAB>Large; Mane on neck<Tab>2000.00<Tab>/pix/lion.jpg
```

A data file with tabs between the fields is a *tab-delimited* file. Another common format is a *comma-delimited* file, where commas separate the fields. If your data is in another file format, you need to convert it into a delimited file.

To convert data in another file format into a delimited file, check the manual for that software or talk to your local expert who understands the data's current format. Many programs, such as Excel, Access, and Oracle, allow you to output the data into a delimited file. For a text file, you might be able to convert it to delimited format by using the search-and-replace function of an editor or word processor. For a truly troublesome file, you might need to seek the help of an expert or a programmer.

To insert data into your database table with phpMyAdmin, follow these steps:

1. **Open the main phpMyAdmin page.**

   Figure 4-1, earlier in this chapter, shows the main page.

2. **Click a database name.**

3. **Click the table name.**

   The table names are listed in the left pane of the page.

4. **Click the Import tab at the top of the page.**

   The phpMyAdmin Import page opens, as shown in Figure 4-9.

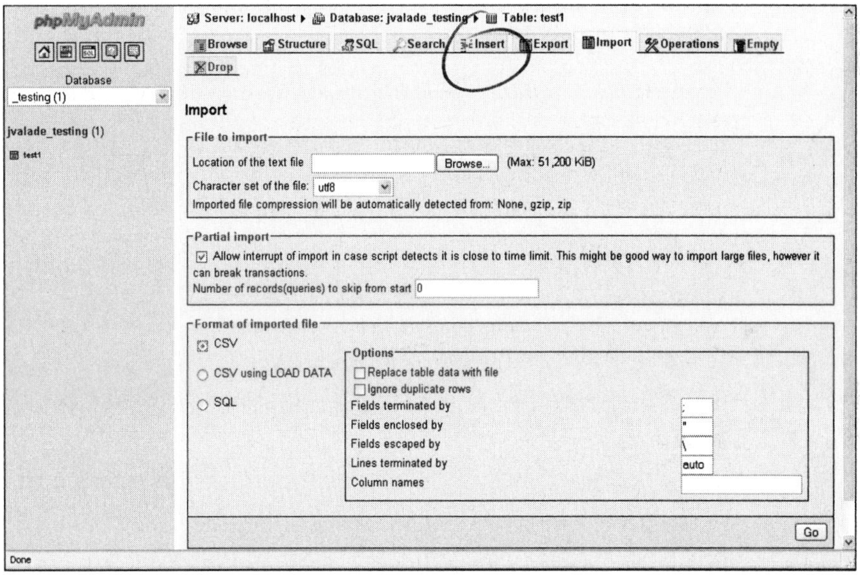

Figure 4-9:
phpMyAdmin import page where you can import a file of data.

5. **Click the Browse button.**

6. **Navigate to the file that contains the data to be imported.**

7. **Select the CSV or the CSV Using LOAD DATA option.**

   The CSV option imports each row using a separate INSERT statement for each row. The CSV Using LOAD DATA option uses a LOAD DATA query. The LOAD DATA query is faster when you have a really huge file of data to import, but you must have certain settings in order to use the LOAD DATA query. CSV always works. I recommend trying the CSV Using LOAD DATA option for large data files. If the settings are incorrect, the import fails, but you can then use the CSV option.

When you click either option, a set of options appears. You need to set the options to match your data file.

8. **Enter the correct character for the Fields Terminated By field.**

   The default is a semicolon (;). You can change that to any character. For instance, change it to a comma if you use a comma to separate your fields. If your fields are separated by a tab, use \t in the field.

9. **Enter the correct character for the Fields Enclosed By field.**

   The default is double quotes. If your values are enclosed by single quotes, you can change it to a single quote. If your values are not enclosed by anything, just separated by a comma or other character, you can remove the value from the field and leave it blank.

10. **Enter the correct character for the Lines Terminated By field.**

    The default is auto, which means the row ends at the end of the line in the data file. If you separated your rows of data by a character, instead of at the end of the line, you can enter this character.

11. **Click Go.**

    A page displays, telling you that your data was successfully imported. It also shows the SQL queries used.

If you used the CSV option, the results page shows a series of INSERT queries. If you used the CSV Using LOAD DATA option, the SQL query looks something like this:

```
LOAD DATA LOCAL INFILE '/tmp/phpPqqfOm' INTO TABLE `test1`
          FIELDS TERMINATED BY ',' ESCAPED BY '\\' LINES
          TERMINATED BY '\r\n'
```

To use the LOAD DATA INFILE query, the MySQL account must have the FILE privilege on the server host. I discuss the MySQL account privileges in Chapter 5.

Viewing information

You can browse the data in a database table at any time. You may want to be sure that the data you entered is correct. Or, you may want to see what type of data customers are entering into the forms in your application.

To look at the information in a table, you can do this:

1. **Open the main phpMyAdmin page.**

   Refer to Figure 4-1 to see the main page.

2. **Click a database name.**

A page opens that lists the tables currently in the database.

3. **Click the browse icon.**

   In the action column, in the row for the table, the browse icon is the first icon.

Retrieving information

The only purpose in storing information is to have it available when you need it. A database lives to answer questions. What pets are for sale? Who are the members? How many members live in Arkansas? Do you have an alligator for sale? How much does a dragon cost? What is Goliath Smith's phone number? And on and on. Your application may need to display the answers to any one of these questions. To query the database from your application, you use an SQL query.

You use the SELECT query to ask the database questions. The simplest, most basic SELECT query is

```
SELECT * FROM tablename
```

This query retrieves all the information from the table. The asterisk (*) is a wildcard meaning *all the columns*.

The SELECT query can be much more selective. SQL words and phrases in the SELECT query can pinpoint the information needed to answer your question. You can specify which information you want, how you want it organized, and the source of the information.

  ✔ **You can request only the information (the columns) that you need to answer your question.** For instance, you can request only the first and last names to create a list of members.

  ✔ **You can request the information in a particular order.** For instance, you can request that the information be sorted in alphabetical order.

  ✔ **You can request information from selected objects (the rows) in your table.** (See Chapter 3 for an explanation of database objects.) For instance, you can request the first and last names for only those members whose addresses are in Florida.

In MySQL 4.1, MySQL added the ability to nest a SELECT query inside another query. The nested query is called a *subquery*. You can use a subquery in SELECT, INSERT, UPDATE, or DELETE queries or in SET clauses. A subquery can return a single value, a single row or column, or a table, which is used in the outer query. All the features of SELECT queries can be used in subqueries. See the MySQL online manual at http://dev.mysql.com/doc/refman/5.1/en/subqueries.html for detailed information on using subqueries.

Retrieving specific information

To retrieve specific information, list the columns containing the information you want. For example:

```
SELECT columnname,columnname,columnname,... FROM tablename
```

This query retrieves the values from all the rows for the indicated column(s). For instance, the following query retrieves all the last names and first names stored in the Member table:

```
SELECT lastName,firstName FROM Member
```

You can perform mathematical operations on columns when you select them. For example, you can use the following SELECT query to add two columns:

```
SELECT col1+col2 FROM tablename
```

Or you could use the following query:

```
SELECT price,price*1.08 FROM Pet
```

The result is the price and the price with the sales tax of 8 percent added. You can change the name of a column when selecting it, as follows:

```
SELECT price,price*1.08 AS priceWithTax FROM Pet
```

The AS clause tells MySQL to give the name priceWithTax to the second column retrieved. Thus, the query retrieves two columns of data: price and priceWithTax.

In some cases, you don't want to see the values in a column, but you want to know something about the column. For instance, you might want to know the lowest value in the column or the highest value in the column. Table 4-3 lists some of the information that is available about a column.

Table 4-3	Information That Can Be Selected
SQL Format	*Description of Information*
AVG(columnname)	Returns the average of all the values in columnname
COUNT(columnname)	Returns the number of rows in which columnname is not blank
MAX(columnname)	Returns the largest value in columnname
MIN(columnname)	Returns the smallest value in columnname
SUM(columnname)	Returns the sum of all the values in columnname

For example, the query to find out the highest price in the `Pet` table is

```
SELECT MAX(price) FROM Pet
```

SQL words that look like `MAX()` and `SUM()`, with parentheses following the name, are *functions*. SQL provides many functions in addition to those in Table 4-3. Some functions, like those in Table 4-3, provide information about a column. Other functions change each value selected. For example, `SQRT()` returns the square root of each value in the column, and `DAYNAME()` returns the name of the day of the week for each value in a date column, rather than the actual date stored in the column. More than 100 functions are available for use in a `SELECT` query. For descriptions of all the functions, see the MySQL online manual at `http://dev.mysql.com/doc/refman/5.0/en/ functions.html`.

Retrieving data in a specific order

You might want to retrieve data in a particular order. For instance, in the `Member` table, you might want members organized in alphabetical order by last name. Or, in the `Pet` table, you might want the pets grouped by type of pet.

In a `SELECT` query, `ORDER BY` and `GROUP BY` affect the order in which the data is delivered to you:

✔ `ORDER BY`: To sort information, use the phrase

```
ORDER BY columnname
```

The data is sorted by *columnname* in ascending order. For instance, if *columnname* is `lastName`, the data is delivered to you in alphabetical order by the last name.

You can sort in descending order by adding the word `DESC` before the column name. For example:

```
SELECT * FROM Member ORDER BY DESC lastName
```

✔ `GROUP BY`: To group information, use the following phrase:

```
GROUP BY columnname
```

The rows that have the same value of *columnname* are grouped together. For example, use this query to group the rows that have the same value as `petType`:

```
SELECT * FROM Pet GROUP BY petType
```

You can use `GROUP BY` and `ORDER BY` in the same query.

Retrieving data from a specific source

Frequently, you don't want all the information from a table. You want information from selected database objects, that is, *rows*. Three SQL words are frequently used to specify the source of the information:

✔ WHERE: Allows you to request information from database objects with certain characteristics. For instance, you can request the names of members who live in California, or you can list only pets that are cats.

✔ LIMIT: Allows you to limit the number of rows from which information is retrieved. For instance, you can request all the information from the first three rows in the table.

✔ DISTINCT: Allows you to request information from only one row of identical rows. For instance, in the Login table, you can request loginName but specify no duplicate names, thus limiting the response to one record for each member. This would answer the question, "Has the member ever logged in?" rather than the question "How many times has the member logged in?"

The WHERE clause of the SELECT query enables you to make complicated selections. For instance, suppose your boss asks for a list of all members whose last names begin with *B,* who live in Santa Barbara, and who have an 8 in either their phone or fax number. I'm sure there are many uses for such a list. You can get this list for your boss with a SELECT query by using a WHERE clause.

The basic format of the WHERE clause is

```
WHERE expression AND|OR expression AND|OR expression ...
```

expression specifies a value to compare with the values stored in the database. Only the rows containing a match for the expression are selected. You can use as many expressions as needed, each one separated by AND or OR. When you use AND, both of the expressions connected by the AND (that is, both the expression before the AND *and* the expression after the AND) must be true in order for the row to be selected. When you use OR, only one of the expressions connected by the OR must be true for the row to be selected.

Some common expressions are shown in Table 4-4.

Table 4-4	Expressions for the WHERE Clause	
Expression	*Example*	*Result*
`column = value`	`zip="12345"`	Selects only the rows where 12345 is stored in the column named `zip`
`column > value`	`zip > "50000"`	Selects only the rows where the zip code is 50001 or higher
`column >= value`	`zip >= "50000"`	Selects only the rows where the zip code is 50000 or higher
`column < value`	`zip < "50000"`	Selects only the rows where the zip code is 49999 or lower
`column <= value`	`zip <= "50000"`	Selects only the rows where the zip code is 50000 or lower
`column BETWEEN value1 AND value2`	`zip BETWEEN "20000" AND "30000"`	Selects only the rows where the zip code is greater than 19999 but less 30001
`column IN (value1,value2,…)`	`zip IN ("90001","30044")`	Selects only the rows where the zip code is 90001 or 30044
`column NOT IN (value1,value2,…)`	`zip NOT IN ("90001","30044")`	Selects only the rows where the zip code is any zip code except 90001 or 30044
`column LIKE value` — *value* can contain the wildcards % (which matches any string) and _ (which matches any character)	`zip LIKE "9%"`	Selects all rows where the zip code begins with 9
`column NOT LIKE value` — *value* can contain the wildcards % (which matches any string) and _ (which matches any character)	`zip NOT LIKE "9%"`	Selects all rows where the zip code does not begin with 9

You can combine any of the expressions in Table 4-4 with ANDs and ORs. In some cases, you need to use parentheses to clarify the selection criteria. For instance, you can use the following query to answer your boss's urgent need to find all people in the Member Directory whose names begin with *B,* who live in Santa Barbara, and who have an 8 in either their phone or fax number:

```
SELECT lastName,firstName FROM Member
    WHERE lastName LIKE "B%"
        AND city = "Santa Barbara"
        AND (phone LIKE "%8%" OR fax LIKE "%8%")
```

Notice the parentheses in the last line. You would not get the results that your boss asked for without the parentheses. Without the parentheses, each connector would be processed in order from the first to the last, resulting in a list that includes all members whose names begin with *B* and who live in Santa Barbara and whose phone numbers have an 8 in them *and* all members whose fax numbers have an 8 in them, whether or not they live in Santa Barbara and whether or not their name begins with a *B.* When the last OR is processed, members are selected whose characteristics match the expression before the OR *or* the expression after the OR. The expression before the OR is connected to previous expressions by the previous ANDs and so does not stand alone, but the expression after the OR does stand alone, resulting in the selection of all members with an 8 in their fax number.

LIMIT specifies how many rows can be returned. The form for LIMIT is

```
LIMIT startnumber,numberofrows
```

The first row that you want to retrieve is *startnumber,* and the number of rows to retrieve is *numberofrows.* If *startnumber* is not specified, 1 is assumed. To select only the first three members who live in Texas, use this query:

```
SELECT * FROM Member WHERE state="TX" LIMIT 3
```

 Some SELECT queries will find identical records, but in this example, you want to see only one — not all — of the identical records. To prevent the query from returning all identical records, add the word DISTINCT immediately after SELECT.

Combining information from tables

In previous sections of this chapter, I assume that all the information you want is in a single table. However, you might want to combine information from different tables. You can do this easily in a single query.

You can use two words in a SELECT query to combine information from two or more tables:

✔ UNION: Rows are retrieved from one or more tables and stored together, one after the other, in a single result. For example, if your query selected 6 rows from one table and 5 rows from another table, the result would contain 11 rows.

✔ Join: The tables are combined side by side, and the information is retrieved from both tables.

UNION

UNION is used to combine the results from two or more SELECT queries. The results from each query are added to the result set following the results of the previous query. The format of the UNION query is as follows:

```
SELECT query UNION ALL SELECT query ...
```

You can combine as many SELECT queries as you need. A SELECT query can include any valid SELECT format, including WHERE clauses, LIMIT clauses, and so on. The rules for the queries are

✔ All the SELECT queries must select the same number of columns.

✔ The columns selected in the queries must contain the same type of data.

The result set will contain all the rows from the first query followed by all the rows from the second query and so on. The column names used in the result set are the column names from the first SELECT query.

The series of SELECT queries can select different columns from the same table, but situations in which you want a new table with one column in a table followed by another column from the same table are unusual. It's much more likely that you want to combine columns from different tables. For example, you might have a table of members who have resigned from the club and a separate table of current members. You can get a list of all members, both current and resigned, with the following query:

```
SELECT lastName,firstName FROM Member UNION ALL
    SELECT lastName,firstName FROM OldMember
```

The result of this query is the last and first names of all current members, followed by the last and first names of all the members who have resigned.

Depending on how you organized your data, you might have duplicate names. For instance, perhaps a member resigned, and his name is in the OldMember table — but he joined again, so his name is added to the Member table. If you don't want duplicates, don't include the word ALL. If ALL is not included, duplicate lines are not added to the result.

You can use ORDER BY with each SELECT query, as I discuss in the previous section, or you can use ORDER BY with a UNION query to sort all the rows in the result set. If you want ORDER BY to apply to the entire result set, rather than just to the query that it follows, use parentheses as follows:

```
(SELECT lastName FROM Member UNION ALL
    SELECT lastName FROM OldMember) ORDER BY lastName
```

WARNING!

The UNION statement was introduced in MySQL 4.0. It is not available in MySQL 3.

Join

Combining tables side by side is a *join*. Tables are combined by matching data in a column — the column that they have in common. The combined results table produced by a join contains all the columns from both tables. For instance, if one table has two columns (memberID and height), and the second table has two columns (memberID and weight), a join results in a table with four columns: memberID (from the first table), height, memberID (from the second table), and weight.

The two common types of joins are an *inner join* and an *outer join*. The difference between an inner and outer join is in the number of rows included in the results table. The results table produced by an inner join contains only rows that existed in both tables. The combined table produced by an outer join contains all rows that existed in one table with blanks in the columns for the rows that did not exist in the second table. For instance, if table1 contains a row for Joe and a row for Sally, and table2 contains only a row for Sally, an inner join would contain only one row: the row for Sally. However, an outer join would contain two rows — a row for Joe and a row for Sally — even though the row for Joe would have a blank field for weight.

The results table for the outer join contains all the rows for one table. If any of the rows for that table don't exist in the second table, the columns for the second table are empty. Clearly, the contents of the results table are determined by which table contributes all its rows, requiring the second table to match it. Two kinds of outer joins control which table sets the rows and which match: a LEFT JOIN and a RIGHT JOIN.

You use different SELECT queries for an inner join and the two types of outer joins. The following query is an inner join:

```
SELECT columnnamelist FROM table1,table2
                WHERE table1.col2 = table2.col2
```

inner join

And these queries are outer joins:

outer join

```
SELECT columnnamelist FROM table1 LEFT JOIN table2
       ON table1.col1=table2.col2
```

```
SELECT columnnamelist FROM table1 RIGHT JOIN table2
       ON table1.col1=table2.col2
```

In all three queries, `table1` and `table2` are the tables to be joined. You can join more than two tables. In both queries, `col1` and `col2` are the names of the columns being matched to join the tables. The tables are matched based on the data in these columns. These two columns can have the same name or different names. The two columns must contain the same type of data.

As an example of inner and outer joins, consider a short form of the `Pet Catalog`. One table is `Pet`, with the two columns `petName` and `petType` holding the following data:

petName	petType
Unicorn	Horse
Pegasus	Horse
Lion	Cat

The second table is `Color`, with two columns `petName` and `petColor` holding the following data:

petName	petColor
Unicorn	white
Unicorn	silver
Fish	Gold

You need to ask a question that requires information from both tables. If you do an inner join with the following query:

```
SELECT * FROM Pet,Color WHERE Pet.petName = Color.petName
```

you get the following results table with four columns: `petName` (from `Pet`), `petType`, `petName` (from `Color`), and `petColor`.

petName	petType	petName	petColor
Unicorn	Horse	Unicorn	white
Unicorn	Horse	Unicorn	silver

Notice that only `Unicorn` appears in the results table — because only `Unicorn` was in both of the original tables, before the join. On the other hand, suppose you do a left outer join with the following query:

```
SELECT * FROM Pet LEFT JOIN Color
       ON Pet.petName=Color.petName
```

You get the following results table, with the same four columns — petName (from Pet), petType, petName (from Color), and petColor — but with different rows:

petName	petType	petName	petColor
Unicorn	Horse	Unicorn	white
Unicorn	Horse	Unicorn	silver
Pegasus	Horse	<NULL>	<NULL>
Lion	Cat	<NULL>	<NULL>

This table has four rows. It has the same first two rows as the inner join, but it has two additional rows — rows that are in the PetType table on the left but not in the Color table. Notice that the columns from the table Color are blank for the last two rows.

And, on the third hand, suppose that you do a right outer join with the following query:

```
SELECT * FROM Pet RIGHT JOIN Color
        ON Pet.petName=Color.petName
```

You get the following results table, with the same four columns, but with still different rows:

petName	petType	petName	petColor
Unicorn	Horse	Unicorn	white
Unicorn	Horse	Unicorn	silver
<NULL>	<NULL>	Fish	Gold

Notice that these results contain all the rows for the Color table on the right but not for the Pet table. Notice the blanks in the columns for the Pet table, which doesn't have a row for Fish.

The joins that I've talked about so far find matching entries in tables. Sometimes it's useful to find out which rows in a table have no matching entries in another table. For example, suppose that you want to know who has never logged into your Members Only section. Because you have one table with the member's login name and another table with the login dates, you can ask this question by using the two tables. You can find out which login names do not have an entry in the Login table with the following query:

```
SELECT loginName from Member LEFT JOIN Login
        ON Member.loginName=Login.loginName
        WHERE Login.loginName IS NULL
```

This query gives you a list of all the login names in Member that are not in the Login table.

Updating information

Changing information in an existing row is *updating* the information. For instance, you might need to change the address of a member because she has moved, or you might need to change the price of a product in your catalog.

If you're updating database information from an application, you use an SQL query. The UPDATE query is straightforward:

```
UPDATE tablename SET column=value,column=value,...
        WHERE clause
```

In the SET clause, you list the columns to be updated and the new values to be inserted. List all the columns that you want to change in one query. Without a WHERE clause, the values of the column(s) would be changed in all rows. But with the WHERE clause, you can specify which rows to update. For instance, to update an address in the Member table, use this query:

```
UPDATE Member SET street="3333 Giant St",
              phone="555-555-5555"
            WHERE loginName="bigguy"
```

You can also update your data using phpMyAdmin, such as when you need to change a product price in your catalog. To change the data in your database, here's what you do:

1. **Open the main phpMyAdmin page. (Refer to Figure 4-1.)**

2. **Click a database name.**

3. **Click the browse icon.**

   In the action column, in the row for the table, the browse icon is the first icon.

   A page opens that displays all the data in the table. At the beginning of each row, a pencil (edit) icon and a red X (delete) icon are displayed.

4. **Click the edit icon (the pencil).**

   A page opens that allows you to change any of the values in the row of data. Figure 4-8, which appears earlier, shows the page.

5. **Change the data that needs updating in the Values column.**

6. **Click Go.**

   A page opens that shows the UPDATE query that was used.

Removing information

Keep the information in your database up to date by deleting obsolete information. If you need to remove data from an application, you can use an SQL query. You can remove a row from a table with the DELETE query:

```
DELETE FROM tablename WHERE clause
```

Be extremely careful when using DELETE. If you use a DELETE query without a WHERE clause, it will delete all the data in the table. I mean *all the data.* I repeat, *all the data.* The data cannot be recovered. This function of the DELETE query is right at the top of my don't-try-this-at-home list.

You can delete a column from a table by using the ALTER query:

```
ALTER TABLE tablename DROP columnname
```

Or you could remove the whole thing and start over again with

```
DROP TABLE tablename
```

or

```
DROP DATABASE databasename
```

You can also remove data from the database with phpMyAdmin:

1. **Open the main phpMyAdmin page (shown earlier in Figure 4-1).**

2. **Click a database name.**

3. **Click the browse icon for the table which has data you want to delete.**

   In the action column, in the row for the table, the browse icon is the first icon.

   A page opens that displays all the data in the table. At the beginning of each row, a pencil (edit) icon and a red X (delete) icon are displayed.

4. **Click the delete icon (the red X).**

   The page redisplays, showing the data without the deleted row.

You can delete a column by changing the table structure as described earlier in this chapter.

You can remove an entire table by clicking the Drop button at the top of the page when the table page is open or remove an entire database by clicking the Drop button at the top of the page when the database page is open.

Chapter 5

Protecting Your Data

* *

* *

*Y*our data is essential to your Web database application. You have spent valuable time developing your database, and it contains important information entered by you or by your users. You need to protect it. In this chapter, I show you how.

Controlling Access to Your Data

You need to control access to the information in your database. You need to decide who can see the data and who can change it. Imagine what would happen if your competitors could change the information in your online product catalog or copy your list of customers — you'd be out of business in no time flat. Clearly, you need to guard your data.

MySQL provides a security system for protecting your data. No one can access the data in your database without an account. Each MySQL account has the following attributes:

✔ A name

✔ A *hostname* — the machine from which the account can access the MySQL server

✔ A password

✔ A set of privileges

To access your data, someone must use a valid account name and know the password associated with that account. In addition, that person must be connecting from a computer that's permitted to connect to your database via that specific account.

After the user is granted access to the database, what he or she can do to the data depends on what privileges have been set for the account. Each account is either allowed or not allowed to perform an operation in your database, such as SELECT, DELETE, INSERT, CREATE, or DROP. The settings that specify what an account can do are *privileges, or permissions.* You can set up an account with all privileges, no privileges, or anything in between. For instance, for an online product catalog, you want the customer to be able to see the information in the catalog but not be able to change it.

When a user attempts to connect to MySQL and execute a query, MySQL controls access to the data in two stages:

- ✔ **Connection verification:** MySQL checks the validity of the account name and password and checks whether the connection is coming from a host that's allowed to connect to the MySQL server by using the specified account. If everything checks out, MySQL accepts the connection.

- ✔ **Request verification:** After MySQL accepts the connection, it checks whether the account has the necessary privileges to execute the specified query. If it does, MySQL executes the query.

Any query that you send to MySQL can fail either because the connection is rejected in the first step or because the query is not permitted in the second step. An error message is returned to help you identify the source of the problem.

In the following few sections, I describe accounts and privileges in detail.

Understanding account names and hostnames

Together, the account name and *hostname* (the name of the computer that is authorized to connect to the database) identify a unique account. Two accounts with the same name but different hostnames can exist and can have different passwords and privileges. However, you *cannot* have two accounts with the same name *and* the same hostname.

The MySQL account name is completely unrelated in any way to the Unix, Linux, or Windows username (also sometimes called the *login name*). If you're using an administrative MySQL account named root, it is not related to the Unix or Linux root login name. Changing the MySQL login name does not affect the Unix, Linux, or Windows login name, and vice versa.

MySQL account names and hostnames are defined as follows:

✔ **An account name can be up to 16 characters long.** You can use special characters in account names, such as a space or a hyphen (–). However, you cannot use wildcards in the account name.

✔ **An account name can be blank.** If an account exists in MySQL with a blank account name, any account name will be valid for that account. A user could use any account name to connect to your database, given that the user is connecting from a hostname that's allowed to connect to the blank account name and uses the correct password, if required. You can use an account with a blank name to allow anonymous users to connect to your database.

✔ **The hostname can be a name or an IP address.** For example, it can be a name such as `thor.mycompany.com` or an IP (Internet protocol) address such as `192.163.2.33`. The machine on which the MySQL server is installed is `localhost`. The hostname can contain a wildcard, such as `%`, which means any host, or can be blank, which also allows the account to connect from any host.

 When MySQL is installed with XAMPP, it automatically installs an account `root@localhost`. Thus, you can access your MySQL server from the computer on which it's installed, and from no other computer. This account is okay for a development account on your local computer.

When you open an account with a Web hosting company, the name and hostname of your database is provided to you. The hostname you use to access the database from your Web site is often `localhost`, but it might be something else. If you don't receive this information, you need to ask for it.

Finding out about passwords

A password is set up for every account. If no password is provided for the account, the password is blank, which means that no password is required. MySQL doesn't have any limit for the length of a password, but sometimes other software on your system limits the length to eight characters. If so, any characters after eight are dropped.

For extra security, MySQL encrypts passwords before it stores them. That means passwords are not stored in the recognizable characters that you entered. This security measure ensures that no one can look at the stored passwords and see what they are.

Unfortunately, some bad people out there might try to access your data by guessing your password. They use software that tries to connect rapidly in succession using different passwords — a practice called *cracking*. The following are some recommendations for choosing a password that is as difficult to crack as possible:

✔ Use six to eight characters.

✔ Include one or more of each of the following — uppercase letter, lower-case letter, number, and punctuation mark.

✔ Do not use your account name or any variation of your account name.

✔ Do not include any word in a dictionary, including foreign language dictionaries.

✔ Do not include a name.

✔ Do not use a word that might be easily identified as related to you, such as a pet's name, the street you live on, and so forth.

✔ Do not use a phone number or a date.

A good password is hard to guess and easy to remember. If it's too hard to remember, you might need to write it down, which defeats the purpose of having a password. One way to create a good password is to use the first characters of a favorite phrase. For instance, you could use the phrase "All for one! One for all!" to make this password:

```
Afo!Ofa!
```

This password doesn't include any numbers, but you can fix that by using the numeral *4* instead of the letter *f.* Then your password is

```
A4o!O4a!
```

Or you could use the number *1* instead of the letter *o* to represent one. Then the password is

```
A41!14a!
```

This password is definitely hard to guess. Other ways to incorporate numbers into your passwords include substituting *1* (one) for the letter *l* or substituting *0* (zero) for the letter *o.*

When MySQL is installed with XAMPP, the `root@localhost` account is installed with no password, meaning that no password is required to access the database using this account. Because no one can access the database from any other machine, having no password is probably fine. However, if others have access to your local computer, you might want to add a password to this account.

When you obtain your Web hosting account, you're provided with a MySQL account and password. This information should be provided to you at that time.

Taking a look at account privileges

MySQL uses account privileges to specify who can do what. Anyone using a valid account can connect to the MySQL server, but he or she can do only the things that are allowed by the privileges for the account. For example, an account might be set up so that users can select data but cannot insert or update data.

Privileges can be granted for particular databases, tables, or columns. For instance, an account can be set up that allows the user to select data from all the tables in the database, but insert data into only one table and update only a single column in a specific table.

Privileges can be granted or removed individually or all at once. Table 5-1 lists some privileges that you might want to assign or remove.

Table 5-1	MySQL Account Privileges
Privilege	*Description*
ALL	All privileges
ALTER	Can alter the structure of tables
CREATE	Can create new databases or tables
DELETE	Can delete rows in tables
DROP	Can drop databases or tables
FILE	Can read and write files on the server
GRANT	Can change the privileges on a MySQL account
INSERT	Can insert new rows into tables
SELECT	Can read data from tables
SHUTDOWN	Can shut down the MySQL server
UPDATE	Can change data in a table
USAGE	No privileges

Granting ALL is not a good idea because it includes privileges for administrative operations, such as shutting down the MySQL server. You're unlikely to want anyone other than yourself to have such sweeping privileges.

Setting Up MySQL Accounts

An *account* is identified by the account name and the name of the computer allowed to access MySQL using this account. You have one account that you can use to administer your MySQL databases. This account is shown on the phpMyAdmin main page. On your local computer, it's probably `root@localhost`. This is the only account you need for your development site because no one needs to access it from the outside — only from your computer.

On your Web hosting account, the account may be `domain@localhost` or something else. Web hosting companies use different naming conventions. However, you don't need to worry about the hostname. Your Web host handles that. You can see the account and hostname on the phpMyAdmin main page. If you're using a company Web site, your company IT staff provides you with an account name and hostname.

In this book, you're discovering how to write PHP scripts that interact with your database. The script might retrieve data from the database to display on a Web page or store data from a form into the database or both. The script uses a MySQL account in a code statement to access the database. For security reasons, you don't want the account used by the script to have any more privileges than necessary. If the account used by the script has only `SELECT` privileges, you don't have to worry about a bad guy using the script to delete or change data or for other unintended purposes.

You need to create at least one account with limited privileges to use on your Web site in PHP scripts that access the database. When you create a new account, you can specify a password when you create the account or you can add a password later. You can set up privileges when you create the account or add/remove privileges later.

You don't need to create a restricted account for your PHP scripts on your local computer, where no one can access the scripts from outside. You need to create only the new account for the PHP scripts that are accessed by visitors to your Web site.

The following sections describe how to create accounts, add or change passwords, and add/remove account privileges on your Web hosting account. If your Web site is hosted on a company Web site, you need to discuss adding accounts with the IT staff at your company.

Adding accounts

The preferred way to access MySQL from PHP is to set up an account specifically for this purpose with only the privileges that are needed. Some Web hosts don't allow you to create a new account. If you can't create a new account on your Web hosting account, perhaps your Web host will create a new account for you, with limited privileges.

One way to create accounts is to send SQL queries, such as INSERT or UPDATE, directly to the mysql database that stores the account information. This is a database that's created when MySQL is installed. However, most Web hosts do not give you access to this database, either to send direct SQL queries to affect this database or through your phpMyAdmin interface. Efforts to interact with the mysql database generally produce error messages, such as

```
Access denied for user 'me'@'localhost' to database
           'mysql'
```

Instead of allowing you access to the mysql database directly, most Web hosts provide a page specifically for the purpose of creating and managing accounts. You need to look at your control panel icons to find the icon for creating new MySQL accounts. Because they are MySQL accounts, the icon is probably in the database section of your control panel. It may be the same icon you use to create a new MySQL database. If you can't figure out where it is, read the documentation provided by your Web host or ask tech support at your Web hosting company.

The following steps show how to create a new account on cPanel, a popular control panel used by many Web hosting companies:

1. **Open cPanel on your Web hosting account.**

2. **Find and click the icon for MySQL databases.**

   In cPanel, the icon is located in the section labeled Databases. The icon says MySQL Databases.

   A MySQL databases page opens. Notice that the page lists all the current databases, along with the account names of the accounts allowed to access the database.

3. **Click Jump to MySQL Users in the upper-right corner or scroll down to the MySQL Users section.**

   Figure 5-1 shows the MySQL Users section of the page. The section lists all the current accounts.

4. Type the new account name into the Username field.

5. Type a password into the Password field.

Notice the field underneath the password labeled Password Strength. A bar in the field shows how strong the password is. This password isn't very strong, less than 50 percent. Factors that add to password strength are length; making sure it's not a word in the dictionary; and using characters, numbers, and punctuation.

Notice the Generate Password button. I guarantee the password generated by clicking the button will be 100 percent strong, but I also guarantee that it will be impossible to remember.

6. Type the same password into the Password (Again) field.

This repetition is to ensure you typed the password correctly.

7. Click the Create User button.

A page displays, showing your new account and password.

8. Click Go Back to return to the MySQL database page.

The new account you just created is now listed on the MySQL page as one of the current users. However, if you scroll up to the list of databases, you won't see the new account listed for any of the databases. At this point, the account exists but can't access any databases. You must specifically allow it to access one or more databases, as shown in the next section.

Allowing access to a database

If you use the procedure described in the preceding section, no account has automatic access to any database. You must specifically give the account access to each database. You can give the account access to as many databases as you want the account to use.

To allow access, follow these steps:

1. **Go to the MySQL User section of the MySQL database page.**

   You can see this section in Figure 5-1, shown earlier.

   The list of users should contain all your accounts, including any new account you just created.

2. **In the Add User to Database section, select a user from the User drop-down list.**

   The drop-down list contains all your existing accounts.

3. **Select a database from the Database drop-down list.**

   All your current databases are included in the drop-down list.

4. **Click the Add button.**

   The selected user is given access to the selected database.

   The Manage User Privileges page opens showing the privileges given the account for the selected database. Because you're just giving this account access to the database for the first time, the account currently has no privileges. You undoubtedly want to select some privileges, if only SELECT.

5. **Select the check boxes next to the privileges you want for this account on this database.**

   Figure 5-2 shows the Manage User Privileges page after you have selected some privileges. You can change the privileges at any time, as shown in the next section.

Figure 5-2:
The Manage
User
Privileges
page.

6. **Click the Make Changes button.**

   A page displays showing that the changes were successful.

7. **Return to the Database page.**

   The account is now listed next to the database name in the list of data-bases, showing that the account now has access to the database.

Changing privileges

The privileges that you can give an account on a database are listed and explained earlier in this chapter. Accounts should be given only the privileges needed. The previous section explained how to set privileges when creating a new account. In this section, you see how to change the privileges for an existing account.

To change an account's privileges, follow these steps:

1. **Open cPanel on your Web hosting account.**

2. **Find and click the icon for MySQL databases.**

   The MySQL databases page opens.

3. **Scroll down to the Current Databases section of the page.**

   You can see a list of your current MySQL databases, as shown in Figure 5-3.

DATABASE	SIZE	USERS		ACTIONS
_GD	0.55 MB	_phpuser	⊗	Delete Database
_MyHome	0.23 MB	_phphome	⊗	Delete Database
		_phpuser	⊗	
_PHPCoursework	0.07 MB	_phpuser	⊗	Delete Database
_PetStore	0.03 MB	_phpuser	⊗	Delete Database
_testing	0.03 MB			Delete Database

Figure 5-3:
The list of your MySQL databases.

In the database list, each database name starts a row. The third column contains the account names that are allowed to access the database. More than one account can access a database.

4. **Find the row for the database you want to change privileges for.**

   If the account you want to modify is not listed as able to access the database, you must first add it to the list of accounts that are allowed to access this database. To add the account, follow the instructions in the previous section, "Allowing access to a database."

5. **Click the name of the account you want to modify in the row for the database you want to change privileges for.**

   The Manage Account Privileges page opens, as shown earlier in Figure 5-2. The page shows the current privileges that this account has for the database.

6. **Select the check boxes for the privileges you want to add or remove.**

7. **Click the Make Changes button.**

   If you don't click this button, the changes won't be saved.

   A results page displays, showing that the privileges were updated.

Adding and changing passwords

When you create an account, you can add a password or not. You can change a password or add a password to an existing account; you don't need to add the password when the account is created.

To change the password, add the account again. That is, use the same steps you used to create the account. In the Add New User section, type the account name that you want to change the password for and type the new password into the Password and Password (Again) fields. Click the Add User button. The account is added again with the new password. Any existing privileges for any databases remain the same.

In addition, MySQL provides an SQL query specifically for creating a password that looks like this:

```
SET PASSWORD FOR username@hostname = PASSWORD('password')
```

However, most Web hosts do not allow you to use this SQL query. You see the access denied error message, such as

```
Access denied for user 'me'@'localhost' to database
          'mysql'
```

Removing accounts

When you look at the list of usernames on the database page, you see a column named Delete and a red x displayed for each username. To remove any account, click the red x by the account name.

If you look at the list of databases, you see a red x by each username in the User Name column. You can remove access to the database for any username by clicking the red x by the username. The database is not affected, but the username removed can no longer access the specified database. However, the username can still access any other databases for which it has access.

Backing Up Your Data

You need to have at least one copy of your valuable database. Disasters occur rarely, but they do occur. The computer where your database is stored can break down and lose your data, the computer file can become corrupted, the building can burn down, and so on. Backup copies of your database guard against data loss from such disasters.

If your Web site is housed at a Web hosting company or on your company computer, other people are responsible for backing up the Web site, including the database. The administrators of the computers will have backup procedures in place. At least, you can assume they have such procedures. However, it's best to be sure. Talk to your Web hosting company staff or your company IT department about its backup procedures. Be sure it performs backups that make you feel secure about your data and that allow rapid replacement of a damaged database.

Even if you're happy with the backup procedures in place at your Web hosting company, you probably want to back up your database to your local computer. By doing so, you make doubly sure that you have a backup and speed up the process of replacing a damaged file. You can back up your database as often as you consider necessary.

In addition, if your Web site collects data from users, you can install the backup from your Web site on your local computer. Thus, when you're developing and testing on your local development site, you're using the actual database, making your testing more reliable.

In general, you need to have two backup copies of your data: one copy in a handy location where it can be quickly replaced and another copy in a different physical location from the Web site location for that remote chance that the building burns down. The Web host probably stores the backups on a different computer than the computer that hosts the Web site and/or database. The Web host may also store a copy of its backups offsite. If you back up the database regularly to your local computer, your backup is both convenient and offsite.

You should not copy the actual data files from one computer, such as the Web host computer, to another computer, such as your local computer, exactly as they are. However, you can move the data using features of phpMyAdmin. In the following sections, I use the example of backing up (moving) the data from your Web host to your local computer as an example. You can use the same procedure to move the data from any MySQL database to another.

First, you export the database from your Web host. The export procedure saves a text file on your local computer that contains all the SQL queries needed to re-create your database. Then you use the import feature of phpMyAdmin on your local computer to execute the SQL queries in the text file, which builds the database.

Exporting your data with phpMyAdmin

Follow these steps to make a backup copy of the database on your Web hosting company using phpMyAdmin.

1. **Open the main phpMyAdmin page.**

2. **Select a database from the list in the left section of the page.**

   The Database page for the selected database appears, as shown in Figure 5-4.

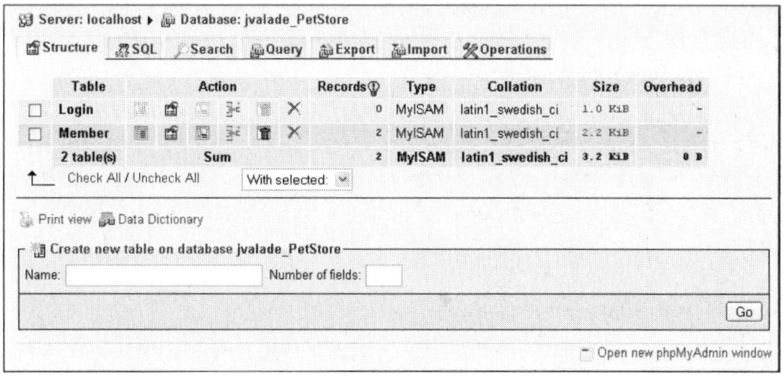

Figure 5-4: The phpMyAdmin Database page.

The Database page lists the tables in the database. In this case, the database contains two tables: Member and Login.

3. **Click the Export tab at the top of the page.**

   The Export page opens, as shown in Figure 5-5.

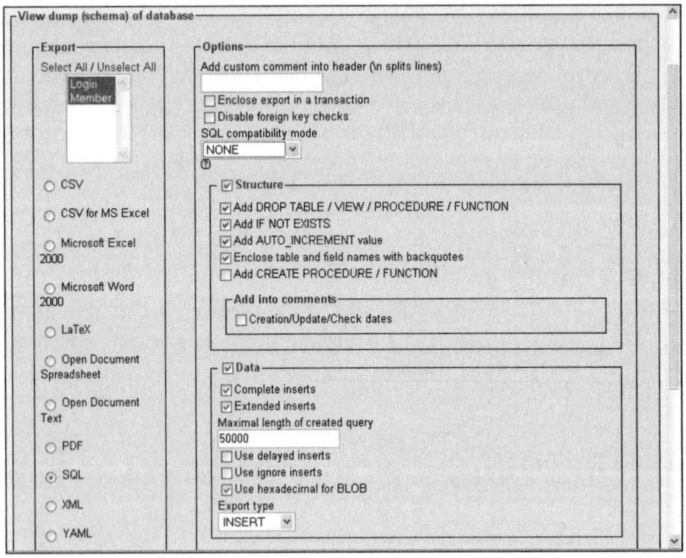

View dump (schema) of database

Export

Select All / Unselect All

Login
Member

○ CSV

○ CSV for MS Excel

○ Microsoft Excel 2000

○ Microsoft Word 2000

○ LaTeX

○ Open Document Spreadsheet

○ Open Document Text

○ PDF

⊙ SQL

○ XML

○ YAML

Options

Add custom comment into header (\n splits lines)

☐ Enclose export in a transaction
☐ Disable foreign key checks
SQL compatibility mode
NONE

☑ Structure
☑ Add DROP TABLE / VIEW / PROCEDURE / FUNCTION
☑ Add IF NOT EXISTS
☑ Add AUTO_INCREMENT value
☑ Enclose table and field names with backquotes
☐ Add CREATE PROCEDURE / FUNCTION

Add into comments
☐ Creation/Update/Check dates

☑ Data
☑ Complete inserts
☑ Extended inserts
Maximal length of created query
50000
☐ Use delayed inserts
☐ Use ignore inserts
☑ Use hexadecimal for BLOB
Export type
INSERT

Figure 5-5:
The phpMyAdmin Export page.

---

4. **In the Export section on the left pane of the main panel, in the top list box, select the tables you want to export.**

5. **In the Export section, select the SQL radio button.**

6. **Select the Structure check box and the four check boxes at the top of the Structure section if they aren't already selected.**

7. **Select the Data check box and the Use Hexadecimal for Binary Data check box (or Use Hexadecimal for BLOB check box) if they aren't already selected.**

8. **Scroll down to the File section (see Figure 5-6).**

Figure 5-6:
The phpMyAdmin Save as File section of the export page.

☑ Save as file
File name template (*): __DB__-%Y%m%d   { ☑ remember template }
Compression: ⊙ None ○ "zipped" ○ "gzipped"
                                                                    Go

9. **Select the Save As File check box.**

10. **Specify the filename.**

    The File Name Template field contains __DB__, which saves the file with the database name. You can add text or special characters to the filename to make a more meaningful filename. In this case, I added %Y%m%d, which adds the current date to the filename of the exported file.

11. **Select the Remember Template check box.**

12. **Next to Compression, select the None radio button.**

13. **Click Go.**

    Your browser's Save File window opens. You see the name of the file being saved.

14. **Select the option to save your file to disk and click OK.**

    The file is saved where your browser saves files. If you have your browser set to ask you where to save files, a window opens, and you can navigate to the directory where you want to save the file.

    In this example, a file named `jvalade_PetStore-20090520` is saved on my local computer.

Now you have a backup copy of your database. You can save the text file on your Web host, on your local computer, on your neighbor's computer, and as many other places that make you feel that your data is safe. You can then re-create your database easily from this file on any computer that has MySQL installed.

Viewing the Export file

The file exported by the phpMyAdmin Export feature is a text file that contains the SQL queries needed to re-create the database, exactly as it was when you exported it. It contains a CREATE query for each table in the database. It contains INSERT queries for every row of data in the tables.

The following is the export file that contains the queries needed to re-create two tables: Member and Login.

```
-- phpMyAdmin SQL Dump
-- version 2.11.9.5
-- http://www.phpmyadmin.net
--
-- Host: localhost
-- Generation Time: May 22, 2009 at 03:28 PM
-- Server version: 5.1.30
-- PHP Version: 5.2.5
```

```
SET SQL_MODE="NO_AUTO_VALUE_ON_ZERO";

--
-- Database: `jvalade_PetStore`
--

-- ------------------------------------------------------------

--
-- Table structure for table `Login`
--

DROP TABLE IF EXISTS `Login`;
CREATE TABLE IF NOT EXISTS `Login` (
  `loginName` varchar(20) NOT NULL,
  `loginTime` datetime NOT NULL
) ENGINE=MyISAM DEFAULT CHARSET=latin1;

--
-- Dumping data for table `Login`
--

-- ------------------------------------------------------------

--
-- Table structure for table `Member`
--

DROP TABLE IF EXISTS `Member`;
CREATE TABLE IF NOT EXISTS `Member` (
  `loginName` varchar(20) NOT NULL,
  `password` varchar(255) NOT NULL,
  `createDate` date NOT NULL,
  `lastName` varchar(50) NOT NULL,
  `firstName` varchar(40) NOT NULL,
  `street` varchar(50) NOT NULL,
  `city` varchar(50) NOT NULL,
  `state` char(2) NOT NULL,
  `zip` char(10) NOT NULL,
  `email` varchar(50) NOT NULL,
  `phone` varchar(15) NOT NULL,
  `fax` varchar(15) NOT NULL,
  PRIMARY KEY (`loginName`)
) ENGINE=MyISAM DEFAULT CHARSET=latin1;

--
-- Dumping data for table `Member`
--
```

```
INSERT INTO `Member` (`loginName`, `password`,
        `createDate`, `lastName`, `firstName`,
        `street`, `city`, `state`, `zip`, `email`,
        `phone`, `fax`) VALUES
('joey', 'secret', '2009-05-12', 'Customer', 'Joe', '1234
        Oak St', 'Here', 'CA', '12345-1234', 'me@home.
        com', '888-888-8888', ''),
('sammy', 'secret', '2009-05-22', 'Customer', 'Sam', '123
        Pine St', 'New York', 'NY', '54321-4321', 'sam@
        customer.com', '888-888-8888', '');
```

Notice the final section for each table is `Dumping data for table tablename`. For the first table, `Login`, this section contains no `INSERT` queries because the table is empty. For the `Member` table, the dump section contains an `INSERT` query that inserts three rows.

If for some reason you're unable to use phpMyAdmin to back up your database, you can create the same text file using the mysqldump program. The mysqldump program was installed automatically when MySQL was installed. Instructions for using the mysqldump program are provided in the MySQL online documentation, such as `http://dev.mysql.com/doc/refman/5.1/en/mysqldump.html` for MySQL 5.1.

Restoring Your Data

In the preceding section, you find out how to create a backup copy of your database. You saved the SQL queries necessary to re-create your database into a text file. You can re-create your database on any computer that has MySQL installed from the backup file you saved. You can replace your database or move your database onto a new computer where it doesn't currently exist.

You may want to replace a database because a table has become damaged and unusable. It's unusual, but it happens. For instance, a hardware problem or an unexpected shutdown of the computer can cause corrupted tables. Sometimes an anomaly in the data that confuses MySQL can cause corrupt tables. In some cases, a corrupt table can cause your MySQL server to shut down.

Here's a typical error message that signals a corrupted table:

```
Incorrect key file for table: 'tablename'.
```

You can replace the corrupted table(s) with the data stored in a backup copy. In some cases, the database might be lost completely. For instance, if the computer where your database resides breaks down and can't be fixed, your current database is lost, but your data isn't gone forever. You can replace the broken computer with a new computer and restore your database from a backup copy.

You may want to re-create the database on a different computer where it doesn't currently exist. For instance, you may want to copy the database from one Web host account to another if you're changing hosting companies. Or, you may want to replace the database on your local development computer with the most recent database from your Web hosting account, so that you're testing your scripts on the latest customer data.

You can use the text file that you created in the preceding section to re-create the database. However, as described previously, you build a database by creating the database and then adding tables to the database. The backup file contains all the SQL statements necessary to rebuild the tables, but it does not contain the statements needed to create the database. Your database must exist before you can re-create the tables from the backup file.

You can re-create the database from the backup file with the IMPORT feature of phpMyAdmin by following these steps:

1. **Open the main phpMyAdmin page.**

2. **Click the name of the database you want to re-create.**

   If the database doesn't exist, you need to create it before proceeding. Creating an empty database is described earlier in this chapter.

   The Database page opens, as shown earlier in Figure 5-4.

3. **Click the Import tab at the top of the page.**

   The Import page opens, as shown in Figure 5-7.

4. **Click the Browse button and navigate to the file that you exported.**

5. **In the Format section, select the SQL radio button if it isn't already selected.**

6. **Click the Go button.**

   A new page appears with a message stating that your import was successful.

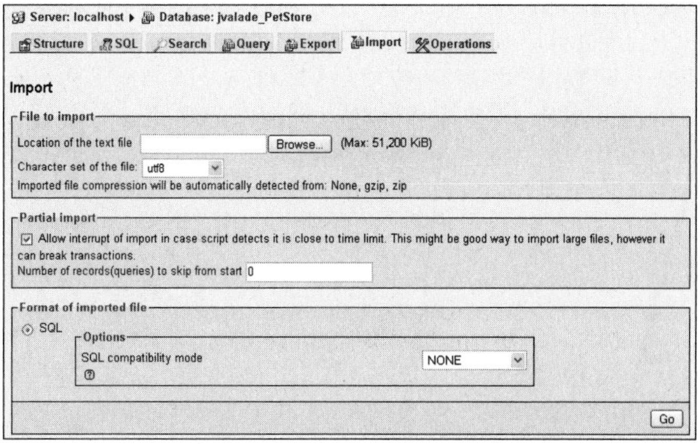

Figure 5-7:
The
phpMyAdmin
Import page.

In some cases, you may want to replace only part of the database. For instance, the backup file created in the previous section contains two tables: Member and Login. If only the Login table is damaged, you want to replace only the Login table.

Your database is now restored with all the data that was in it at the time the copy was made. If the data has changed since the copy was made, the changes are lost. For instance, if more data was added after the backup copy was made, the new data is not restored. If you know the changes that were made, you can make them manually in the restored database.

You can control which data is replaced by editing the backup file. Because the backup is a text file, you can edit it with any text editor. Remove any SQL queries that you do not want to execute. For instance, if you do not want to restore the Member table, only the Login table, remove all the SQL queries from the file that CREATE or INSERT INTO the Member table.

Part III
PHP

"Give him air! Give him air! He'll be okay. He's just been exposed to some raw PHP code. It must have accidently flashed across his screen from the server."

In this part . . .

In Part III, you find out how to use PHP for your Web database application. Here are some of the topics described:

- ✔ Adding PHP to HTML files
- ✔ PHP features that are useful for building a dynamic Web database application
- ✔ Using PHP features
- ✔ Using forms to collect information from users
- ✔ Showing information from a database in a Web page
- ✔ Storing data in a database
- ✔ Moving information from one Web page to the next

You find out everything you need to know to write PHP programs.

Chapter 6

General PHP

*P*rograms are the application part of your Web database application. Programs perform the tasks: Programs create and display Web pages, accept and process information from users, store information in the database, get information out of the database, and perform any other necessary tasks.

PHP, the language that you use to write your programs, is a scripting language designed for use on the Web. It has features to aid you in programming the tasks needed by dynamic Web applications.

In this chapter, I describe the general rules for writing PHP programs — the rules that apply to all PHP statements. Consider these rules similar to general grammar and punctuation rules. In the remaining chapters in Part III, you find out about specific PHP statements and features and how to write PHP programs to perform specific tasks.

Adding a PHP Section to an HTML Page

PHP is a partner to HTML, enabling HTML to do things it can't do on its own. For example, HTML can display Web pages, and HTML has features that allow you to format those Web pages. HTML also allows you to display graphics in your Web pages and to play music files. But HTML alone does not allow you to interact with the person viewing the Web page.

HTML is almost interactive. That is, HTML forms allow users to type information that the Web page is designed to collect; however, you can't access that information without using a language other than HTML. PHP processes form information and allows other interactive tasks as well.

HTML tags are used to make PHP language statements part of HTML scripts. The file is named with a .php extension. (The PHP administrator can define other extensions, such as .phtml or .php5, but .php is the most common. In this book, I assume .php is the extension for PHP programs.) The PHP language statements are enclosed in PHP tags with the following form:

```
<?php       ?>
```

Sometimes you can use a shorter version of the PHP tags. You can try using `<?` and `?>` without the php. If short tags are enabled, you can save a little typing. However, if you use short tags, your programs will not run if they're moved to another Web host where PHP short tags are not activated.

PHP processes all statements between the two PHP tags. After the PHP section is processed, it's discarded. Or if the PHP statements produce output, the PHP section is replaced by the output. The browser doesn't see the PHP section — the browser sees only its output, if there is any. For more on this process, see the sidebar, "How the Web server processes PHP files."

As an example, I'll start with an HTML program that displays Hello World! in the browser window, shown in Listing 6-1. (It's a tradition that the first program you write in any language is the Hello World program. You might have written a Hello World program when you first learned HTML.)

Listing 6-1: The Hello World HTML Program

```
<html>
<head><title>Hello World Program</title></head>
<body>
   <p>Hello World!</p>
</body>
</html>
```

If you point your browser at this HTML program, you see a Web page that displays

```
Hello World!
```

How the Web server processes PHP files

When a browser is pointed to a regular HTML file with an `.html` or `.htm` extension, the Web server sends the file, as-is, to the browser. The browser processes the file and displays the Web page described by the HTML tags in the file. When a browser is pointed to a PHP file (with a `.php` extension), the Web server looks for PHP sections in the file and processes them instead of just sending them as-is to the browser. The Web server processes the PHP file as follows:

1. The Web server starts scanning the file in HTML mode. It assumes the statements are HTML and sends them to the browser without any processing.

2. The Web server continues in HTML mode until it encounters a PHP opening tag (`<?php`).

3. When it encounters a PHP opening tag, the Web server switches to PHP mode. This is sometimes called *escaping from HTML*. The Web server then assumes that all statements are PHP statements and executes the PHP statements. If there is output, the output is sent by the server to the browser.

4. The Web server continues in PHP mode until it encounters a PHP closing tag (`?>`).

5. When the Web server encounters a PHP closing tag, it returns to HTML mode. It resumes scanning, and the cycle continues from Step 1.

Listing 6-2 shows a PHP program that does the same thing — it displays `Hello World!` in a browser window.

Listing 6-2: The Hello World PHP Program

```
<html>
<head><title>Hello World Program</title></head>
<body>
<?php
   echo "<p>Hello World!</p>"
?>
</body>
</html>
```

If you point your browser at this program, it displays the same Web page as the HTML program in Listing 6-1.

Don't look at the file directly with your browser. That is, don't choose File⇨Open⇨Browse from your browser menu to navigate to the file and click it. You must open the file by typing its URL, as I discuss in Chapter 2. If you see the PHP code displayed in the browser window instead of the output that you expect, you might not have typed the URL.

In this PHP program, the PHP section is

```
<?php
  echo "<p>Hello World!</p>"
?>
```

The PHP tags enclose only one statement — an echo statement. The echo statement is a PHP statement that you'll use frequently. It simply outputs the text that is included between the double quotes.

There is no rule that says you must enter the PHP on separate lines. You could just as well include the PHP in the file on a single line, like this:

```
<?php echo "<p>Hello World!</p>" ?>
```

When the PHP section is processed, it is replaced with the output. In this case, the output is

```
<p>Hello World!</p>
```

If you replace the PHP section in Listing 6-2 with the preceding output, the program now looks exactly like the HTML program in Listing 6-1. If you point your browser at either program, you see the same Web page. If you look at the source code that the browser sees (in the browser, choose View⇨Source), you see the same source code listing for both programs.

Writing PHP Statements

The PHP section that you add to your HTML file consists of a series of PHP statements. Each PHP statement is an instruction to PHP to do something. In the Hello World program shown in Listing 6-2, the PHP section contains only one simple PHP statement. The echo statement instructs PHP to output the text between the double quotes.

PHP statements end with a semicolon (;). PHP does not notice white space or the ends of lines. It continues reading a statement until it encounters a semicolon or the PHP closing tag, no matter how many lines the statement spans. Leaving out the semicolon is a common error, resulting in an error message that looks something like this:

```
Parse error: expecting `','' or `';'' in /hello.php on
              line 6
```

Notice that the error message gives you the line number where it encountered problems. This information helps you locate the error in your program. This error message probably means that the semicolon was omitted at the end of line 5.

I recommend writing your PHP programs with an editor that uses line numbers. If your editor doesn't let you specify which line you want to go to, you have to count the lines manually from the top of the file every time that you receive an error message. You can find information about many editors, including descriptions and reviews, at www.php-editors.com.

Sometimes groups of statements are combined into a *block*. A block is enclosed by curly braces, { and }. The statements in a block execute together. A common use of a block is as a *conditional block,* in which statements are executed only when certain conditions are true. For instance, you might want your program to do the following:

```
if (the sky is blue)
{
  put leash on dragon;
  take dragon for a walk in the park;
}
```

These statements are enclosed in curly braces to ensure that they execute as a block. If the sky is blue, both put leash on dragon and take dragon for a walk in the park are executed. If the sky is not blue, neither statement is executed (no leash; no walk).

PHP statements that use blocks, such as if statements (which I explain in Chapter 7), are *complex statements.* PHP reads the entire complex statement, not stopping at the first semicolon that it encounters. PHP knows to expect one or more blocks and looks for the ending curly brace of the last block in complex statements. Notice that there is a semicolon before the ending brace. This semicolon is required, but no semicolon is required after the ending curly brace.

If you wanted to, you could write the entire PHP section in one long line, as long as you separated statements with semicolons and enclosed blocks with curly braces. However, a program written this way would be impossible for people to read. Therefore, you should put statements on separate lines, except for occasional, really short statements.

Notice that the statements inside the block are indented. Indenting is not necessary for PHP. Nevertheless, you should indent the statements in a block so that people reading the script can tell more easily where a block begins and ends.

In general, PHP doesn't care whether the statement keywords are in uppercase or lowercase. Echo, echo, ECHO, and eCHo are all the same to PHP.

Error messages and warnings

PHP tries to be helpful when problems arise. It provides error messages and warnings as follows:

- **Parse error:** A parse error is a syntax error that PHP finds when it scans the script before executing it. A parse error is a fatal error, preventing the script from running at all. A parse error looks similar to the following:

  Parse error: `parse error, error, in c:\test\test.php on line 6`

  Often, you receive this error message because you've forgotten a semicolon, a parenthesis, or a curly brace. The error provides more information when possible. For instance, `error might be unexpected T_ECHO, expecting ',' or ';'` means that PHP found an `echo` statement where it was expecting a comma or a semicolon, which probably means you forgot the semicolon at the end of the previous line.

- **Error message:** You receive this message when PHP encounters a serious error during the execution of the program that prevents it from continuing to run. The message contains as much information as possible to help you identify the problem.

- **Warning message:** You receive this message when the program sees a problem but the problem isn't serious enough to prevent the program from running. Warning messages do not mean that the program can't run; the program does continue to run. Rather, warning messages tell you that PHP believes that something is probably wrong. You should identify the source of the warning and then decide whether it needs to be fixed. It usually does.

- **Notice:** You receive a notice when PHP sees a condition that might be an error or might be perfectly okay. Notices, like warnings, do not cause the script to stop running. Notices are much less likely than warnings to indicate serious problems. Notices just tell you that you are doing something unusual and to take a second look at what you're doing to be sure that you really want to do it.

  One common reason why you might receive a notice is if you're echoing variables that don't exist. Here's an example of what you might see in that instance:

  Notice: `Undefined variable: age in ` **testing.php** ` on line ` **9**

- **Strict:** Strict messages, added in PHP 5, warn about language that is poor coding practice or has been replaced by better code.

All types of messages indicate the filename causing the problem and the line number where the problem was encountered.

You can specify which types of error messages you want displayed in the Web page. In general, when you are developing a program, you want to see all messages, but when the program is published on your Web site, you do not want any messages to be displayed to the user.

To change the error-message level for your Web site to show more or fewer messages, you must change your PHP settings. Appendix B describes how to change PHP settings. On your local computer, you edit your `php.ini` file, which contains a section that explains the error-message setting (`error_reporting`), error-message levels, and how to set them. Some possible settings are

```
error_reporting = E_ALL | E_STRICT
error_reporting = 0
error_reporting = E_ALL & ~ E_NOTICE
```

The first setting is best, because it displays everything. It displays E_ALL, which is all errors, warnings, and notices except strict, and E_STRICT, which displays strict messages. The second setting displays no error messages. The third setting displays all error and warning messages, but not notices or stricts. After changing the error_reporting settings, save the edited php. ini file and restart your Web server.

If you're using a local php.ini file on your Web host, just add a statement, like one of the preceding statements, to your local php.ini file.

If you don't have access to php.ini, you can add a statement to a program that sets the error reporting level for that program only. Add the following statement at the beginning of the program:

```
error_reporting(errorSetting);
```

For example, to see all errors except stricts, use the following:

```
error_reporting(E_ALL);
```

You may want to put this statement in the top of your scripts when you run them on your Web host. Then, when your programs are working perfectly and your Web site is ready for visitors, you can remove the statement from the scripts.

In addition, PHP provides a setting that determines whether errors are displayed on the Web page at all. This setting in your php.ini file is:

```
display_errors = On
```

You can change this to Off in a php.ini file or add the following statement to the top of your script:

```
ini_set("display_errors","Off");
```

Using PHP Variables

Variables are containers used to hold information. A variable has a name, and information is stored in the variable. For instance, you might name a variable $age and store the number 12 in it. After information is stored in a variable, it can be used later in the program. One of the most common uses for variables is to hold the information that a user types into a form.

Naming a variable

When you're naming a variable, keep the following rules in mind:

- ✔ All variable names have a dollar sign ($) in front of them. This tells PHP that it is a variable name.
- ✔ Variable names can be any length.
- ✔ Variable names can include letters, numbers, and underscores only.
- ✔ Variable names must begin with a letter or an underscore. They cannot begin with a number.
- ✔ Uppercase and lowercase letters are not the same. For example, $firstname and $Firstname are not the same variable. If you store information in $firstname, for example, you can't access that information by using the variable name $firstName.

When you name variables, use names that make it clear what information is in the variable. Using variable names like $var1, $var2, $A, or $B does not contribute to the clarity of the program. Although PHP doesn't care what you name the variable and won't get mixed up, people trying to follow the program will have a hard time keeping track of which variable holds what information. Variable names like $firstName, $age, and $orderTotal are much more descriptive and helpful.

Creating and assigning values to variables

Variables can hold either numbers or strings of characters. You store information in variables by using a single equal sign (=). For instance, the following four PHP statements assign information to variables:

```
$age = 12;
$price = 2.55;
$number = -2;
$name = "Goliath Smith";
```

Notice that the character string is enclosed in quotes, but the numbers are not. I provide details about using numbers and characters later in this chapter, in the "Working with Numbers" and "Working with Character Strings" sections.

You can now use any of these variable names in an echo statement. For instance, if you use the following PHP statement in a PHP section:

```
echo $age;
```

the output is 12. If you include the following line in an HTML file:

```
<p>Your age is <?php echo $age ?>.
```

the output on the Web page is

```
Your age is 12.
```

Whenever you put information into a variable that did not exist before, you create that variable. For instance, suppose you use the following PHP statement:

```
$firstname = "George";
```

If this statement is the first time that you've mentioned the variable $first name, this statement creates the variable and sets it to "George". If you have a previous statement setting $firstname to "Mary", this statement changes the value of $firstname to "George".

You can also remove information from a variable. For example, the following statement takes information out of the variable $age:

```
$age = "";
```

The variable $age exists but does not contain a value. It does not mean that $age is set to 0 (zero) because 0 is a value. It means that $age does not store any information. It contains a string of length 0.

You can go even further and uncreate the variable by using this statement:

```
unset($age);
```

After this statement is executed, the variable $age no longer exists.

A variable keeps its information for the entire program, not just for a single PHP section. If a variable is set to "yes" at the beginning of a file, it still holds "yes" at the end of the page. For instance, suppose your file has the following statements:

```
<p>Hello World!</p>
<?php
    $age = 15;
    $name = "Harry";
?>
<p>Hello World again!</p>
<?php
    echo $name;
?>
```

The echo statement in the second PHP section displays Harry. The Web page resulting from these statements is

```
Hello World!

Hello World again!

Harry
```

Dealing with notices *error message/warning*

If you use a statement that includes a variable that does not exist, you might get a notice. It depends on the error-message level that PHP is set to. Remember that notices aren't the same as error messages. With a notice, the program continues to run. A notice simply tells you that you're doing something unusual and to take a second look at what you're doing. (See the sidebar, "Error messages and warnings.") For instance, suppose you use the following statements:

```
unset($age);
echo $age;
$age2 = $age;
```

You might see two notices: one for the second statement and one for the third statement. The notices will look something like this:

```
Notice: Undefined variable: age in testing.php on line 9
```

Suppose that you definitely want to use these statements. The program works exactly the way you want it to. The only problems are the unsightly notices. You can prevent notices in a program by inserting an at sign (@) at the point where the notice would be issued. For instance, you can prevent the notices generated by the preceding statements if you change the statements to this:

```
unset($age);
echo @$age;
$age2 = @$age;
```

Using PHP Constants

PHP constants are similar to variables. Constants are given a name, and a value is stored in them. However, constants are constant; that is, they can't be changed by the program. After you set the value for a constant, it stays the same. If you used a constant for age and set it to 29, for example, it can't be changed. Wouldn't that be nice — 29 forever?

Constants are used when a value is needed several places in the program and doesn't change during the program. The value is set in a constant at the start of the program. By using a constant throughout the program, instead of a variable, you make sure that the value won't get changed accidentally. By giving it a meaningful name, you know what the information is instantly. And by setting a constant once at the start of the program (instead of using the value throughout the program), you can change the value in one place if it needs changing, instead of hunting for it in many places in the program to change it.

For instance, you might set one constant that's the company name and another constant that's the company address and use them wherever needed. Then, if the company moves, you could just change the value in the company address at the start of the program instead of having to find every place in your program that echoed the company name to change it.

You can set a constant by using the define statement. The format is

```
define("constantname","constantvalue");
```

For instance, to set a constant with the company name, use the following statement:

```
define("COMPANY","ABC Pet Store");
```

Use the constant in your program wherever you need your company name:

```
echo COMPANY;
```

When you echo a constant, you can't enclose it in quotes. If you do, it echoes the constant name, instead of the value. You can echo it without anything, as shown in the preceding example, or enclosed with parentheses.

You can use any name for a constant that you can use for a variable. Constant names are not preceded by a dollar sign ($). By convention, constants are given names that are all uppercase, so you can easily spot constants, but PHP itself doesn't care what you name a constant. You can store either a string or a number in it. The following statement is perfectly okay with PHP:

```
define("AGE",29);
```

Just don't expect Mother Nature to believe it.

Working with Numbers

PHP allows you to do arithmetic operations on numbers. You indicate arithmetic operations with two numbers and an arithmetic operator. For instance, one operator is the plus (+) sign, so you can indicate an arithmetic operation like this:

```
1 + 2
```

You can also perform arithmetic operations with variables that contain numbers, as follows:

```
$n1 = 1;
$n2 = 2;
$sum = $n1 + $n2;
```

Table 6-1 shows the arithmetic operators that you can use.

Table 6-1	Arithmetic Operators
Operator	*Description*
+	Add two numbers.
–	Subtract the second number from the first number.
*	Multiply two numbers.
/	Divide the first number by the second number.
%	Find the remainder when the first number is divided by the second number. This is called *modulus.* For instance, in $a = 13 % 4, $a is set to 1.

You can do several arithmetic operations at once. For instance, the following statement performs three operations:

```
$result = 1 + 2 * 4 + 1;
```

The order in which the arithmetic is performed is important. You can get different results depending on which operation is performed first. PHP does multiplication and division first, followed by addition and subtraction. If other considerations are equal, PHP goes from left to right. Consequently, the preceding statement sets $result to 10, in the following order:

```
$result = 1 + 2 * 4 + 1    (first it does the multiplication)
$result = 1 + 8 + 1        (next it does the leftmost addition)
$result = 9 + 1            (next it does the remaining addition)
$result = 10
```

You can change the order in which the arithmetic is performed by using parentheses. The arithmetic inside the parentheses is performed first. For instance, you can write the previous statement with parentheses like this:

```
$result = (1 + 2) * 4 + 1;
```

This statement sets $result to 13, in the following order:

```
$result = (1 + 2) * 4 + 1    (first it does the math in the parentheses)
$result = 3 * 4 + 1          (next it does the multiplication)
$result = 12 + 1             (next it does the addition)
$result = 13
```

On the better-safe-than-sorry principle, it's best to use parentheses whenever more than one answer is possible.

Often, the numbers that you work with are dollar amounts, such as product prices. You want your customers to see prices in the proper format on Web pages. In other words, dollar amounts should always have two decimal places. However, PHP stores and displays numbers in the most efficient format. If the number is 10.00, it is displayed as 10. To put numbers into the proper format for dollars, you can use sprintf. The following statement formats a number into a dollar amount:

```
$newvariablename = sprintf("%01.2f", $oldvariablename);
```

This statement reformats the number in $oldvariablename and stores it in the new format in $newvariablename. For example, the following statements display money in the correct format:

```
$price = 25;
$f_price = sprintf("%01.2f",$price);
echo "$f_price<br />";
```

You see the following on the Web page:

```
25.00
```

sprintf can do more than format decimal places. For more information on using sprintf to format values, see Chapter 13.

If you want commas to separate thousands in your number, you can use number_format. The following statement creates a dollar format with commas:

```
$price = 25000;
$f_price = number_format($price,2);
echo "$f_price";
```

You see the following on the Web page:

```
25,000.00
```

The 2 in the `number_format` statement sets the format to two decimal places. You can use any number to get any number of decimal places.

Working with Character Strings

A *character string* is a series of characters. Characters are letters, numbers, and punctuation. When a number is used as a character, it's just a stored character, the same as a letter. It can't be used in arithmetic. For instance, a phone number is stored as a character string because it needs to be only stored — not added or multiplied.

When you store a character string in a variable, you tell PHP where the string begins and ends by using double quotes or single quotes. For instance, the following two statements are the same:

```
$string = "Hello World!";
$string = 'Hello World!';
```

Suppose that you wanted to store a string as follows:

```
$string = 'It is Tom's house';
echo $string;
```

These statements won't work because when PHP sees the ' (single quote) after `Tom`, it thinks that this is the end of the string, and it displays the following:

```
It is Tom
```

You need to tell PHP to interpret the single quote (') as an apostrophe instead of as the end of the string. You can do this by using a backslash (\) in front of the single quote. The backslash tells PHP that the single quote does not have any special meaning; it's just an apostrophe. This is *escaping* the character. Use the following statements to display the entire string:

```
$string = 'It is Tom\'s house';
echo $string;
```

Similarly, when you enclose a string in double quotes, you must also use a backslash in front of any double quotes in the string.

Single-quoted strings versus double-quoted strings

Single-quoted and double-quoted strings are handled differently. Single-quoted strings are stored literally, with the exception of \ ', which is stored as an apostrophe. In double-quoted strings, variables and some special characters are evaluated before the string is stored. Here are the most important differences in the use of double or single quotes in code:

- **Handling variables:** If you enclose a variable in double quotes, PHP uses the value of the variable. However, if you enclose a variable in single quotes, PHP uses the literal variable name. For example, if you use the following statements:

```
$age = 12;
$result1 = "$age";
$result2 = '$age';
echo $result1;
echo "<br />";
echo $result2;
```

the output is

```
12
$age
```

- **Starting a new line:** The special characters \n tell PHP to start a new line. When you use double quotes, PHP starts a new line at \n, but with single quotes, \n is a literal string. For instance, when using the following statements:

```
$string1 = "String in \ndouble quotes";
$string2 = 'String in \nsingle quotes';
```

string1 outputs as

```
String in
double quotes
```

and string2 outputs as

```
String in \nsingle quotes
```

- **Inserting a tab:** The special characters \t tell PHP to insert a tab. When you use double quotes, PHP inserts a tab at \t, but with single quotes, \t is a literal string. For instance, when using the following statements:

```
$string1 = "String in \tdouble quotes";
$string2 = 'String in \tsingle quotes';
```

string1 outputs as

```
String in      double quotes
```

and string2 outputs as

```
String in \tsingle quotes
```

The quotes that enclose the entire string determine the treatment of variables and special characters, even if other sets of quotes are inside the string. For example, look at the following statements:

```
$number = 10;
$string1 = "There are '$number' people in line.";
$string2 = 'There are "$number" people waiting.';
echo $string1."<br>\n";
echo $string2;
```

The output is as follows:

```
There are '10' people in line.
There are "$number" people waiting.
```

Joining strings

You can join strings, a process called *concatenation,* by using a dot (.). For instance, you can join strings with the following statements:

```
$string1 = 'Hello';
$string2 = 'World!';
$stringall = $string1.$string2;
echo $stringall;
```

The echo statement outputs

```
HelloWorld!
```

Notice that no space appears between Hello and World. That's because no spaces are included in the two strings that are joined. You can add a space between the words by using the following concatenation statement rather than the earlier statement:

```
$stringall = $string1." ".$string2;
```

You can use .= to add characters to an existing string. For example, you can use the following statements in place of the preceding statements:

```
$stringall = "Hello";
$stringall .= " World!";
echo $stringall;
```

The echo statement outputs this:

```
Hello World!
```

You can also take strings apart. You can separate them at a given character or look for a substring in a string. You use functions to perform these and other operations on a string. I explain functions in Chapter 7.

Working with Dates and Times

Dates and times can be important elements in a Web database application. PHP has the ability to recognize dates and times and handle them differently than plain character strings. Dates and times are stored by the computer in a format called a *timestamp*. However, this is not a format in which you or I would want to see the date. PHP converts dates from your notation into a timestamp that the computer understands and from a timestamp into a format familiar to people. PHP handles dates and times by using built-in functions.

The timestamp format is a Unix Timestamp, which is an integer that is the number of seconds from January 1, 1970, 00:00:00 GMT (Greenwich Mean Time) to the time represented by the timestamp. This format makes it easy to calculate the time between two dates — just subtract one timestamp from the other.

Setting local time

The current time is a tricky concept on the Web. The current time is the time stored in the server where PHP is running. If you're using a Web hosting company, you probably don't even know where your Web hosting company maintains the servers that house your Web site. In addition, the visitors that visit your Web site might be anywhere in the world. Consequently, you rarely want to display the current time on your Web site. Even the date can be different if your Web server and the visitor are enough time zones apart.

If you have a reason to want to display the current time in a specific location, you do that by including the following statement in your script:

```
date_default_timezone_set(timezone);
```

where *timezone* is a code for the time zone that you want to use. For example, you might use

```
date_default_timezone_set("America/Los_Angeles")
```

You can find a list of the time zone codes in Appendix H of the PHP online documentation at www.php.net/manual/en/timezones.america.php.

On your local computer, if you're using PHP 5.1 or later, you probably need to set a default time zone. If no default time zone is set, PHP guesses, which sometimes results in GMT. In addition, PHP displays a message advising you to set your local time zone.

You can set your time zone in the `php.ini` file:

1. **Open `php.ini` in a text editor.**
2. **Scroll down to the section headed [Date].**
3. **Find the setting `date.timezone =`.**
4. **If the line begins with a semicolon (;), remove the semicolon.**
5. **Add a time zone code after the equal sign.**

You can see which time zone is currently your default time zone by using the following:

```
$def = date_default_timezone_get()
echo $def;
```

Formatting a date

The function that you will use most often is `date`, which converts a date or time from the timestamp format into a format that you specify. The general format is

```
$mydate = date("format",$timestamp);
```

`$timestamp` is a variable with a timestamp stored in it. You previously stored the timestamp in the variable, using a PHP function as I describe later in this section. If `$timestamp` is not included, the current time is obtained from the operating system and used. Thus, you can get today's date with the following:

```
$today = date("Y/m/d");
```

If today is August 10, 2009, this statement returns

```
2009/08/10
```

The *format* is a string that specifies the date format that you want stored in the variable. For instance, the format `"y-m-d"` returns 09-08-10, and `"M.d.Y"` returns Aug.10.2009. Table 6-2 lists some of the symbols that you can use in the format string. (For a complete list of symbols, see the documentation at `www.php.net/manual/en/function.date.php`.) You can separate the parts of the date with a hyphen (-), a dot (.), a forward slash (/), or a space.

Table 6-2	Date Format Symbols	
Symbol	*Meaning*	*Example*
F	Month in text, not abbreviated	January
M	Month in text, abbreviated	Jan
m	Month in numbers with leading zeros	02, 12
n	Month in numbers without leading zeros	1, 12
d	Day of the month; two digits with leading zeros	01, 14
j	Day of the month without leading zeros	3, 30
l	Day of the week in text, not abbreviated	Friday
D	Day of the week in text, abbreviated	Fri
w	Day of the week in numbers	From 0 (Sunday) to 6 (Saturday)
Y	Year in four digits	2002
y	Year in two digits	02
g	Hour between 0 and 12 without leading zeros	2, 10
G	Hour between 0 and 24 without leading zeros	2, 15
h	Hour between 0 and 12 with leading zeros	01, 10
H	Hour between 0 and 24 with leading zeros	00, 23
i	Minutes	00, 59
s	Seconds	00, 59
a	am or pm in lowercase	am, pm
A	AM or PM in uppercase	AM, PM

Storing a timestamp in a variable

You can assign a timestamp with the current date and time to a variable with the following statements:

```
$today = time();
```

Another way to store a current timestamp is with the statement

```
$today = strtotime("today");
```

You can store specific timestamps by using `strtotime` with various key-words and abbreviations that are similar to English. For instance, you can create a timestamp for January 15, 2009, as follows:

```
$importantDate = strtotime("January 15 2009");
```

`strtotime` recognizes the following words and abbreviations:

- **Month names:** Twelve month names and abbreviations
- **Days of the week:** Seven days and some abbreviations
- **Time units:** year, month, fortnight, week, day, hour, minute, second, am, pm
- **Some useful English words:** ago, now, last, next, this, tomorrow, yesterday
- **Plus and minus:** + or -
- **All numbers**
- **Time zones:** For example, gmt (Greenwich Mean Time), pdt (Pacific Daylight Time), and akst (Alaska Standard Time)

You can combine the words and abbreviations in a wide variety of ways. The following statements are all valid:

```
$importantDate = strtotime("tomorrow"); #24 hours from now
$importantDate = strtotime("now + 24 hours");
$importantDate = strtotime("last saturday");
$importantDate = strtotime("8pm + 3 days");
$importantDate = strtotime("2 weeks ago"); # current time
$importantDate = strtotime("next year gmt");
$importantDate = strtotime("this 4am");    # 4 AM today
```

If you want to know how long ago `$importantDate` was, you can subtract it from `$today`. For instance:

```
$timeSpan = $today - $importantDate;
```

This statement gives you the number of seconds between the important date and today. Or use the statement

```
$timeSpan =(($today - $importantDate)/60)/60
```

to find out the number of hours since the important date.

Using dates with MySQL

Often you want to store a date in your MySQL database. For instance, you might want to store the date when a customer made an order or the time when a member logged in. MySQL also recognizes dates and times and handles them differently than plain character strings. However, MySQL also handles them differently than PHP. To use dates and times in your application, you need to understand both how PHP handles dates (which I describe in the previous few sections) and how MySQL handles dates.

I discuss the DATE and DATETIME data types for MySQL in detail in Chapter 3. The following is a summary:

- ✔ DATE: MySQL DATE columns expect dates with the year first, the month second, and the day last. The year can be yyyy or yy. The month can be mm or m. The day can be dd or d. The parts of the date can be separated by a hyphen (-), a forward slash (/), a dot (.), or a space.

- ✔ DATETIME: MySQL DATETIME columns expect both the date and the time. The date is formatted as I describe in the preceding bullet. The date is followed by the time in the format hh:mm:ss.

Dates and times must be formatted in the correct MySQL format to store them in your database. PHP functions can be used for formatting. For instance, you can format today's date into a MySQL format with this statement:

```
$today = date("Y-m-d");
```

You can format a specific date by using the statement

```
$importantDate = date("Y.m.d",strtotime("Jan 15 2009"));
```

You can then store the formatted date in a database with an SQL query like this:

```
UPDATE Member SET createDate="$today"
```

In some cases, MySQL date functions are easier to use than PHP statements to manipulate dates. For example, MySQL provides a function named DATEDIFF that computes the number of days between two dates, as follows:

```
DATEDIFF(date1,date2)
```

The function returns the number of days from *date2* to *date1*. For example, to determine the number of days between a date in a table and the current date, you can use the following:

```
SELECT DATEDIFF(NOW(),Birth_date) FROM Customer
```

NOW() is a MySQL function that returns the current date and time, and Birth_date is the name of a column in the Customer table.

You can also use the function to return the number of days between dates that you provide, as follows:

```
SELECT DATEDIFF('2009-1-15','1997-12-30')
```

MySQL provides many useful functions. All the date/time functions are described at http://dev.mysql.com/doc/refman/5.1/en/date-and-time-functions.html.

Comparing Values

In programs, you often use *conditional statements*. That is, if something is true, your program does one thing, but if something is not true, your program does something different. Here are two examples of conditional statements:

```
if user is a child
    show toy catalog
if user is not a child
    show electronics catalog
```

To know which conditions exist, the program must ask questions. Your program then performs tasks based on the answers. Some questions (conditions) that you might want to ask — and the actions that you might want taken — are

✔ Is the customer a child? If so, display a toy catalog.

✔ Which product has more sales? Display the most popular one first.

✔ Did the customer enter the correct password? If so, display the Members Only Web page.

✔ Does the customer live in Ohio? If so, display the map to the Ohio store location.

To ask a question in a program, you form a statement that compares values. The program tests the statement and determines whether the statement is true or false. For instance, you can state the preceding questions as

- ✔ The customer is less than 13 years of age. True or false? If true, display the toy catalog.
- ✔ Product 1 sales are higher than Product 2 sales. True or false? If true, display Product 1 first; if false, display Product 2 first.
- ✔ The customer's password is `secret`. True or false? If true, show the Members Only Web page.
- ✔ The customer lives in Ohio. True or false? If true, display a map to the Ohio store location.

Comparisons can be quite simple. For instance, is the first value larger than the second value? Or smaller? Or equal to? But sometimes you need to look at character strings to see whether they have certain characteristics instead of looking at their exact values. For instance, you might want to identify strings that begin with *S* or strings that look like phone numbers. For this type of comparison, you compare a string to a pattern, which I describe in the section "Matching character strings to patterns," later in this chapter.

Making simple comparisons

Simple comparisons compare one value to another value. PHP offers several ways to compare values. Table 6-3 shows the comparisons that are available.

Table 6-3	Comparing Values
Comparison	*Description*
==	Are the two values equal?
>	Is the first value larger than the second value?
>=	Is the first value larger than or equal to the second value?
<	Is the first value smaller than the second value?
<=	Is the first value smaller than or equal to the second value?
!=	Are the two values not equal to each other?
<>	Are the two values not equal to each other?

You can compare both numbers and strings. Strings are compared alphabetically, with all uppercase characters coming before any lowercase characters. For instance, *SS* comes before *Sa.* Characters that are punctuation also have an order, and one character can be found to be larger than another character. However, comparing a comma to a period doesn't have much practical value.

Strings are compared based on their ASCII (American Standard Code for Information Interchange) code. In the ASCII character set, each character is assigned an ASCII code that corresponds to a decimal number between 0 and 127. For instance, the number that represents the comma is 44. The period corresponds to 46. Therefore, if a period and a comma are compared, the period is seen as larger.

Comparisons are often used to execute statements only under certain conditions. For instance, in the following example, the block of statements is executed only when the comparison $weather == "raining" is true:

```
if ( $weather == "raining" )
{
    put up umbrella;
    cancel picnic;
}
```

PHP checks the variable $weather to see whether it is equal to "raining". If it is, PHP executes the two statements. If $weather is not equal to "raining", PHP does not execute either of the two statements.

The comparison sign is two equal signs (==). One of the most common mistakes is to use a single equal sign for a comparison. A single equal sign puts the value into the variable. Thus, a statement like if ($weather = "raining") would set $weather to raining rather than check whether it already equaled raining and would thus always be true.

For example, here's a solution to the programming problem presented at the beginning of this section. The problem is

```
if user is a child
    show toy catalog
if user is not a child
    show electronics catalog
```

To determine whether a customer is an adult, you compare the customer's age with the age when the customer is considered to be an adult. You need to decide at what age a customer would stop being interested in toy catalogs and start being more interested in electronic catalogs. Suppose you decide that 13 seems like the right age. You then ask whether the customer is younger than 13 by comparing the customer's age to 13. If the age is less than 13, show the toy catalog; if the age is 13 or over, show the electronics catalog. These comparisons would have the following format:

```
$age < 13      (is the customer's age less than 13?)
$age >= 13     (is the customer's age greater than or equal to 13?)
```

One way to program the conditional actions is to use the following statements:

```
if ($age < 13)
    $status = "child";
if ($age >= 13)
    $status = "adult";
```

These statements instruct PHP to compare the customer's age to 13. In the first statement, if the customer's age is less than 13, the customer's status is set to "child". In the second statement, if the customer's age is greater than or equal to 13, the customer's status is set to "adult". You then show the toy catalog to customers whose status is child and show the electronic catalog to those whose status is adult. Although you can write these if statements in a more efficient way, these statements do work. A full description of conditional statements is provided in Chapter 7.

Matching character strings to patterns

Sometimes you need to compare character strings to see whether they fit certain characteristics rather than match exact values. For instance, you might want to identify strings that begin with *S* or strings that have numbers in them. For this type of comparison, you compare the string to a pattern. These patterns are *regular expressions,* often called *regex.*

You've probably used some form of pattern matching in the past. When you use an asterisk (*) as a wildcard when searching for files (dir s*.doc or ls s*.txt), you are pattern matching. For instance, c*.txt is a pattern. Any string that begins with a c and ends with the string .txt, with any characters in between the c and the .txt, matches the pattern. The strings cow. txt, c3333.txt, and c3c4.txt all match the pattern. Using regular expressions is just a more complicated variation of using wildcards.

The most common use for pattern matching on Web pages is to check the input from a form. If the information doesn't make sense, it's probably not something that you want to store in your database. For instance, if the user types a name into a form, you can check whether it seems like a real name by matching patterns. You know that a name consists mainly of letters and spaces. Other valid characters might be a hyphen (-) — for example, in the name *Smith-Kline* — and a single quote (') — for example, O'Hara. You can check the name by setting up a pattern that's a string containing only letters, spaces, hyphens, and single quotes and then matching the name to the pattern. If the name doesn't match — that is, if it contains characters not in the pattern, such as numerals or a question mark (?) — it's not a real name.

Patterns consist of literal characters and special characters. *Literal characters* are normal characters, with no other special meaning. A *c* is a *c* with no meaning other than it's one of the 26 letters in the English alphabet. Special characters have special meaning in the pattern, such as the asterisk (*) when used as a wildcard. Table 6-4 shows the special characters used in patterns.

Table 6-4	Special Characters Used in Patterns			
Character	**Meaning**	**Example**	**Match**	**Not a Match**
^	Beginning of line	^c	cat	my cat
$	End of line	c$	tic	stick
.	Any single character	. .	Any string that contains at least two characters	a, I
?	Preceding character is optional	mea?n	mean, men	moan
( )	Groups literal characters into a string that must be matched exactly	m(ea)n	mean	men, mn
[ ]	Encloses a set of optional literal characters	m[ea]n	men, man	mean, mn
–	Represents all the characters between two characters	m[a-c]n	man, mbn, mcn	mdn, mun, maan
+	One or more of the preceding items	door[1-3]+	door111, door131	door, door55
*	Zero or more of the preceding items	door[1-3]*	door, door311	door4, door445
{ , }	The starting and ending numbers of a range of repetitions	a{2,5}	aa, aaaaa	a, xx3
\	The following character is literal	m*n	m*n	men, mean
(| |)	A set of alternate strings	(Tom|Tommy)	Tom, Tommy	Thomas, To

Literal and special characters are combined to make patterns — sometimes long, complicated patterns. A string is compared to the pattern, and if it matches, the comparison is true. Some example patterns follow, with a breakdown of the pattern and some sample matching and nonmatching strings:

✔ `^[A-Z].*` — **Strings that begin with an uppercase letter**

  - `^[A-Z]` — Uppercase letter at the beginning of the string

  - `.*` — A string of characters that is one or more characters long

Strings that match:

  - Play it again, Sam

  - I

Strings that do not match:

  - play it again, Sam

  - i

✔ `Dear (son|daughter)` — **Two alternative strings**

  - `Dear` — Literal characters

  - `(son|daughter)` — Either son or daughter

Strings that match:

  - Dear son

  - My Dear daughter

Strings that do not match:

  - Dear Goliath

  - son

✔ `^[0-9]{5}(\-[0-9]{4})?$` — **Any zip code**

  - `^[0-9]{5}` — Any string of five numbers

  - `\-` — A literal

  - `[0-9]{4}` — A string of numbers that is four characters long

  - `( )?` — Groups the last two parts of the pattern and makes them optional

Strings that match:

  - 90001

  - 90002–4323

Strings that do not match:

  - 9001

  - 12–4321

✔ `^.+@.+\.com$` — **Any string with @ embedded that ends in** `.com`

- `^.+` — Any string of one or more characters at the beginning
- `@` — A literal @ (at sign); @ is not a special character
- `.+` — Any string of one or more characters
- `\.` — A literal dot
- `com$` — A literal string `com` at the end of the string

A string that matches:

- mary@hercompany.com

Strings that do not match:

- mary@hercompany.net
- @mary.com

You can compare a string to a pattern by using `ereg`. The general format is

```
ereg("pattern", string);
```

Either `pattern` or `string` can be a literal, as follows:

```
ereg("[0-9]*","1234");
```

or can be stored in variables, as follows:

```
ereg($pattern, $string);
```

To use `ereg` to check the name that a user typed in a form, compare the name to a pattern as follows:

```
ereg("^[A-Za-z' -]+$", $name)
```

The pattern in this statement does the following:

✔ **Uses ^ and $ to signify the beginning and end of the string.** This means all the characters in the string must match the pattern.

✔ **Encloses all the literal characters allowed in the string in [ ].** No other characters are allowed. The allowed characters are uppercase and lowercase letters, an apostrophe ('), a blank space, and a hyphen (-).

You can specify a range of characters using a hyphen within the [ ]. When you do that, as in A-Z in the example, the hyphen does not represent a literal character. Because you want the hyphen included as a literal character that's allowed in your string, you need to add a hyphen that is not between any two other characters. In this case, the hyphen is included at the end of the list of literal characters.

✔ **Follows the list of literal characters in the [ ] with a +.** The plus sign means that the string can contain any number of the characters inside the [ ] but must contain at least one character.

Joining Comparisons with and/or/xor

Sometimes one comparison is sufficient to check for a condition, but often you need to ask more than one question. For instance, suppose that your company offers catalogs for different products in different languages. You need to know which product the customer wants to see *and* which language he or she needs to see it in. This is the general format for a series of comparisons:

```
comparison and|or|xor comparison and|or|xor comparison and|or|xor ...
```

Comparisons are connected by one of the three following words:

✔ and: Both comparisons are true.

✔ or: One comparison or both comparisons are true.

✔ xor: One of the comparisons is true, but both comparisons are not true.

Table 6-5 shows some examples of multiple comparisons.

Table 6-5	Multiple Comparisons
Condition	**Is True If**
`$customer == "Smith" or` `$customer == "Jones"`	The customer is named Smith or Jones.
`$customer == "Smith" and` `$custState =="OR"`	The customer is named Smith, and the customer lives in Oregon.
`$customer == "Smith" or` `$custState == "OR"`	The customer is named Smith, or the customer lives in Oregon, or both.
`$customer == "Smith" or` `$custState == "OR"`	The customer is named Smith, or the customer lives in Oregon — but not both.
`$customer != "Smith" and` `$custAge < 13`	The customer is named anything except Smith and is under 13 years of age.

You can string together as many comparisons as necessary. The comparisons that use and are tested first, the comparisons that use xor are tested next, and the comparisons that use or are tested last. For instance, the following is a condition that includes three comparisons:

```
$age == 200 or $age == 300 and $name == "Goliath"
```

If the customer's name is Goliath and he is 300 years old, this statement is true. The statement is also true if the customer is 200 years old, regardless of what his name is. This condition is not true if the customer is 300 years old but his name is not Goliath. You get these results because the program checks the condition as follows:

1. The and is compared.

   The program checks $age to see whether it equals 300, and it checks $name to see whether it equals Goliath. If both match, the condition is true, and the program does not need to check or. If only one or neither of the variables equal the designated value, the testing continues.

2. The or is compared.

   The program checks $age to see whether it equals 200. If it does, the condition is true. If it does not, the condition is false.

You can change the order in which comparisons are made by using parentheses. The word inside the parentheses is evaluated first. For instance, you can rewrite the previous statement with parentheses as follows:

```
( $age == 200 or $age == 300 ) and $name == "Goliath"
```

The parentheses change the order in which the conditions are checked. Now the or is checked first. This condition is true if the customer's name is Goliath and he is either 200 or 300 years old. You get these results because the program checks the condition as follows:

1. The or is compared.

   The program checks $age to see whether it equals either 200 or 300. If it does, this part of the condition is true. However, the comparison on the other side of the and must also be true, so the testing continues.

2. The and is compared.

   The program checks $name to see whether it equals Goliath. If it does, the condition is true. If it does not, the condition is false.

Use parentheses liberally, even when you believe you know the order of the comparisons. Unnecessary parentheses can't hurt, but comparisons that have unexpected results can.

If you're familiar with other languages, such as C, you may have used || (for or) and && (for and) in place of the words. The || and && work in PHP as well. The statement $a < $b && $c > $b is just as valid as the statement $a < $b and $c > $b. The || is checked before or; the && is checked before and.

Adding Comments to Your Program

Comments are notes embedded in the program itself. Adding comments in your programs that describe their purpose and what they do is essential. It's important for the lottery factor — that is, if you win the lottery and run off to a life of luxury on the French Riviera, someone else will have to finish the application. The new person needs to know what your program is supposed to do and how it does it. Actually, comments benefit you as well. You might need to revise the program next year when the details are long buried in your mind under more recent projects.

Use comments liberally. PHP ignores comments; comments are for humans. You can embed comments in your program anywhere as long as you tell PHP that they are comments. The format for comments is

```
/*  comment text
more comment text  */
```

Your comments can be as long or as short as you need. When PHP sees code that indicates the start of a comment (/*), it ignores everything until it sees the code that indicates the end of a comment (*/).

One possible format for comments at the start of each program is as follows:

```
/*  name:         catalog.php
    description:  Program that displays descriptions of
                  products. The descriptions are stored
                  in a database. The product descriptions
                  are selected from the database based on
                  the category the user entered into a
                  form.
    written by:   Lola Designer
    created:      2/1/09
    modified:     3/15/09
*/
```

You should use comments throughout the program to describe what the program does. Comments are particularly important when the program statements are complicated. Use comments such as the following frequently:

```
/* Get the information from the database */
/* Check whether the customer is over 18 years old */
/* Add shipping charges to the order total */
```

PHP also has a short comment format. You can specify that a single line is a comment by using the pound sign (#) or two forward slashes (//) in the following manner:

```
# This is comment line 1
// This is comment line 2
```

All text from the # or // to the end of the line is a comment. You can also use # or // in the middle of a line to signal the beginning of a comment. PHP will ignore everything from the # or // to the end of the line. This technique is useful for commenting a particular statement, as in the following example:

```
$average = $orderTotal/$nItems  // compute average price
```

Sometimes you want to emphasize a comment. The following format makes a comment very noticeable:

```
#####################################
##   Double-Check This Section      ##
#####################################
```

PHP comments are not included in the HTML code that's sent to the user's browser. The user does not see these comments.

Use comments as often as necessary in the script to make it clear. However, using too many comments is a mistake. Don't comment every line or everything you do in the script. If your script is too full of comments, the important comments can get lost in the maze. Use comments to label sections and to explain unusual or complicated code — not obvious code.

Chapter 7

PHP Building Blocks for Programs

*P*HP programs are a series of instructions in a file named with an extension that tells the Web server to look for PHP sections in the file. (The extension is usually .php or .phtml, but it can be anything that the Web server is configured to expect.) PHP begins at the top of the file and executes each instruction, in order, as it comes to it. Instructions are the building blocks of PHP programs.

The basic building blocks are simple *statements* — a single instruction followed by a semicolon. A simple program consists of a series of simple statements. For example, the Hello World program in Chapter 6 is a simple program. However, the programs that make up a Web database application aren't that simple. They're dynamic and interact with both the user and the database. Consequently, the programs require more complex building blocks.

Here are some common programming tasks that require complex building blocks:

✔ **Storing groups of related values together:** You often have related information, such as the description, picture, and price of a product or a list of customers. Storing this information as a group that you can access under one name is efficient and useful. This PHP feature is an *array*.

✔ **Setting up statements that execute only when certain conditions are met:** Programs frequently need to do this. For instance, you may want to display a toy catalog to a child and an electronics catalog to an adult.

This type of statement is a *conditional statement.* The PHP conditional statements are the if statement and the case statement.

✔ **Setting up a block of statements that is repeated:** You frequently need to repeat statements. For instance, you may want to create a list of all your customers. To do that, you might use two statements: one that gets the customer row from the database and a second one that stores the customer name in a list. You would need to repeat these two statements for every row in the customer database. The feature that enables you to do this is a *loop.* Three types of loops are for loops, while loops, and do..while loops.

✔ **Writing blocks of statements that can be reused many times:** Many tasks are performed in more than one part of the application. For instance, you might want to retrieve product information from the database and display it numerous times in an application. Getting and displaying the information might require several statements. Writing a block of statements that displays the product information and using this block repeatedly is much more efficient than writing the statements over again every time you need to display the product information. PHP allows you to reuse statement blocks by creating a *function.*

In this chapter, you find out how to use the building blocks of PHP programs. I describe the most frequently used simple statements and the most useful complex statements and variables. You find out how to construct the building blocks and what they're used for. Then in Chapter 8, you find out how to use these building blocks to move data in and out of a database.

Useful Simple Statements

A *simple statement* is a single instruction followed by a semicolon (;). Here are some useful simple statements used in PHP programs:

✔ echo statement: Produces output that browsers handle as HTML

✔ Assignment statement: Assigns values to variables

✔ Increment statement: Increases or decreases numbers in variables

✔ exit statement: Stops the execution of your program

✔ Function call: Uses stored blocks of statements at any location in a program

I discuss these simple statements and when to use them in the following sections.

Using echo statements

You use echo statements to produce output. The output from an echo statement is sent to the user's browser, which handles the output as HTML.

The general format of an echo statement is

```
echo outputitem,outputitem,outputitem,...
```

where the following rules apply:

- ✔ An *outputitem* can be a number, a string, or a variable. A string must be enclosed in quotes. The difference between double and single quotes is explained in Chapter 6.
- ✔ List as many *outputitem*s as you need, separated by commas.

Table 7-1 shows some echo statements and their output. For the purposes of the table, assume that $string1 is set to Hello and $string2 is set to World!.

Table 7-1	echo Statements
echo Statement	*Output*
echo "Hello";	Hello
echo 123;	123
echo "Hello","World!";	HelloWorld!
echo Hello World!;	Not valid; results in an error message
echo "Hello World!";	Hello World!
echo 'Hello World!';	Hello World!
echo $string1;	Hello
echo $string1,$string2;	HelloWorld!
echo "$string1 $string2";	Hello World!
echo "Hello ",$string2;	Hello World!
echo "Hello"," ",$string2;	Hello World!
echo '$string1',"$string2";	$string1World!

Double quotes and single quotes have different effects on variables. When you use single quotes, variable names are echoed as-is. When you use double quotes, variable names are replaced by the variable values.

You can separate variable names with curly braces ({ }). For instance, the following statements

```
$pet = "bird";
echo "The $petcage has arrived.";
```

will not output `bird` as the `$pet` variable. In other words, the output will not be `The birdcage has arrived`. Rather, PHP looks for the variable `$petcage` and won't be able to find it. You can echo the correct output by using curly braces to separate the `$pet` variable:

```
$pet = "bird";
echo "The {$pet}cage has arrived.";
```

The preceding statement will output

```
The birdcage has arrived.
```

echo statements output a line of text that is sent to a browser. The browser considers the text to be HTML and handles it that way. Therefore, you need to make sure that your output is valid HTML code that describes the Web page that you want the user to see.

When you want to display a Web page (or part of a Web page) by using PHP, you need to consider three stages in producing the Web page:

✔ **The PHP program:** PHP echo statements that you write.

✔ **The HTML source code:** The source code for the Web page that you see when you choose View➪Source in your browser. The *source code* is the output from the echo statements.

✔ **The Web page:** The Web page that your users see. The Web page results from the HTML source code.

The echo statements send exactly what you echo to the browser — no more, no less. If you don't echo any HTML tags, none are sent.

PHP allows some special characters that format output, but they aren't HTML tags. The PHP special characters affect only the output from the echo statement — not the display on the Web page. For instance, if you want to start a new line in the PHP output, you must include a special character (\n) that tells PHP to start a new line. However, this special character just starts a new line in the output; it does *not* send an HTML tag to start a new line on the Web page. Table 7-2 shows examples of the three stages.

Table 7-2	Stages of Web Page Delivery	
echo Statement	*HTML Source Code*	*Web Page Display*
echo "Hello World!";	Hello World!	Hello World!
echo "Hello World!"; echo "Here I am!";	Hello World! Here I am!	Hello World!Here I am!
echo "Hello World!\n"; echo "Here I am!";	Hello World! Here I am	Hello World!Here I am!
echo "Hello World!"; echo " "; echo "Here I am!";	Hello World! Here I am!"	Hello World! Here I am!
echo "Hello"; echo " World! \n"; echo "Here I am!";	Hello World! Here I am!"	Hello World! Here I am!

Table 7-2 summarizes the differences between the stages in creating a Web page with PHP. To look at these differences more closely, consider the following two echo statements:

```
echo "Line 1";
echo "Line 2";
```

If you put these lines in a program, you might *expect* the Web page to display

```
Line 1
Line 2
```

However, this is *not* the output that you would get. The Web page would display this:

```
Line 1Line 2
```

If you look at the source code for the Web page, you see exactly what is sent to the browser, which is this:

```
Line 1Line 2
```

Notice that the line that is output and sent to the browser contains exactly the characters that you echoed — no more, no less. The character strings that you echoed did not contain any spaces, so no spaces appear between the lines. Also notice that the two lines are echoed on the same line. If you want a new line to start, you have to send a signal indicating the start of a new line. To signal that a new line starts here in PHP, echo the special character \n. Change the echo statements to the following:

```
echo "line 1\n";
echo "line 2";
```

Now you get what you want, right? Well, no. Now you see the following on the Web page:

```
line 1 line 2
```

If you look at the source code, you see this:

```
line 1
line 2
```

So, the \n did its job: It started a new line in the output. However, HTML displays the output on the Web page as one line. If you want HTML to display two lines, you must use a tag, such as the <br> tag. So, change the PHP end-of-line special character to an HTML tag, as follows:

```
echo "line 1<br />";
echo "line 2";
```

Now you see what you want on the Web page:

```
line 1
line 2
```

If you look at the source code for this output, you see this:

```
line 1<br />line 2
```

Use \n liberally. Otherwise, your HTML source code will have some really long lines. For instance, if you echo a long form, the whole thing might be one long line in the source code, even though it looks fine in the Web page. Use \n to break the HTML source code into reasonable lines. It's much easier to examine and troubleshoot the source code if it's not a mile-long line.

Using assignment statements

Assignment statements are statements that assign values to variables. The variable name is listed to the left of the equal sign; the value to be assigned to the variable is listed to the right of the equal sign. Here is the general format:

```
$variablename = value;
```

The *value* can be a single value or a combination of values, including values in variables. A variable can hold numbers or characters but not both at the same time. Therefore, a value cannot be a combination of numbers and characters. The following are valid assignment statements:

```
$number = 2;
$number = 2+1;
$number = (2 - 1) * (4 * 5) -17;
$number2 = $number + 3;
$string = "Hello World";
$string2 = $string." again!";
```

If you combine numbers and strings in a value, you won't get an error message; you'll just get unexpected results. For instance, the following statements combine numbers and strings:

```
$number = 2;
$string = "Hello";
$combined = $number + $string;
$combined2 = $number.$string;
echo $combined;
echo <br />;
echo $combined2;
```

The output of these statements is

```
2          ($string is evaluated as 0)
2Hello     ($number is evaluated as a character)
```

Using increment statements

Often a variable is used as a `counter`. For instance, suppose you want to be sure that everyone sees your company logo, so you display it three times. You set a variable to 0. Each time that you display the logo, you add 1 to the variable. When the value of the variable reaches 3, you know that it's time to stop showing the logo. The following statements show the use of a `counter`:

```
$counter=0;
$counter = $counter + 1;
echo $counter;
```

These statements would output 1. Because counters are used so often, PHP provides shortcuts. The following statements have the same effect as the preceding statements:

```
$counter=0;
$counter++;
echo $counter;
```

This echo statement also outputs 1 because ++ adds 1 to the current value of $counter. Or you can use the following statement, which subtracts 1 from the current value of $counter.

```
$counter--;
```

Sometimes you may want to do a different arithmetic operation. You can use any of the following shortcuts:

evil

```
$counter+=2;
$counter-=3;
$counter*=2;
$counter/=3;
```

These statements add 2 to $counter, subtract 3 from $counter, multiply $counter by 2, and divide $counter by 3, respectively.

Using exit

Sometimes you want the program to stop executing — just stop at some point in the middle of the program. For instance, if the program encounters an error, often you want it to stop rather than continue with more statements. The exit statement stops the program. No more statements are executed after the exit statement. The format of an exit statement is

```
exit("message");
```

The *message* is a message that is output when the program exits. For instance, you might use the statement

```
exit("The program is exiting");
```

evil

You can also stop the program with the die statement, as follows:

```
die("The program is dying");
```

The die statement is the same as the exit statement. Sometimes it's just more fun to say *die*.

Using function calls

Functions are blocks of statements that perform certain specified tasks. You can think of functions as mini-programs or subprograms. The block of statements is stored under a function name, and you can execute the block of statements any place you want by *calling* the function by its name. (For details on how to use functions, check out the section "Using Functions," later in this chapter.)

You can call a function by listing its name followed by parentheses, like this:

```
functionname();
```

For instance, you might have a function that gets all the names of customers who reside in a certain state from the database and displays the names in a list in the format *last name, first name*. You write the statements that do these tasks and store them as a function under the name get_names. Then when you call the function, you need to specify which state. You can use the following statement at any location in your program to get the list of customer names from the given state, which in this case is California:

```
get_names('CA');
```

The value 'CA' is *passed* to the function so it knows which state you're specifying. You can pass more than one value.

PHP provides many built-in functions. For example, in Chapter 6, I discuss a built-in function called unset. You can uncreate a variable named $testvar with this function call:

```
unset($testvar);
```

Using PHP Arrays

Arrays are complex variables. An *array* stores a group of values under a single variable name. An array is useful for storing related values. For instance, you can store information about a shirt (such as size, color, and cost) in a single array named $shirtinfo. Information in an array can be handled, accessed, and modified easily. For instance, PHP has several methods for sorting an array. The following sections give you the lowdown on arrays.

Creating arrays

The simplest way to create an array is to assign a value to a variable with square brackets ([ ]) at the end of its name. For instance, assuming that you have not referenced $pets at any earlier point in the program, the following statement creates an array called $pets:

```
$pets[1] = "dragon";
```

At this point, the array named $pets has been created and has only one value: dragon. Next, you use the following statements:

```
$pets[2] = "unicorn";
$pets[3] = "tiger";
```

Now the array $pets contains three values: dragon, unicorn, and tiger.

An array can be viewed as a list of *key/value pairs.* To get a particular value, you specify the *key* in the brackets. In the preceding array, the keys are numbers — 1, 2, and 3. However, you can also use words for keys. For instance, the following statements create an array of state capitals:

```
$capitals['CA'] = "Sacramento";
$capitals['TX'] = "Austin";
$capitals['OR'] = "Salem";
```

You can use shortcuts rather than write separate assignment statements for each number. One shortcut uses the following statements:

```
$pets[] = "dragon";
$pets[] = "unicorn";
$pets[] = "tiger";
```

When you create an array using this shortcut, the values are automatically assigned keys that are serial numbers, starting with the number 0. For example, the following statement

```
echo "$pets[0]";
```

outputs dragon.

The first value in an array with a numbered index is 0 unless you deliberately set it to a different number. One common mistake when working with arrays is to think of the first number as 1 rather than 0.

An even better shortcut is to use the following statement:

```
$pets = array( "dragon","unicorn","tiger");
```

This statement creates the same array as the preceding shortcut. It assigns numbers as keys, starting with 0. You can use a similar statement to create arrays with words as keys. For example, the following statement creates the array of state capitals:

```
$capitals = array( "CA" => "Sacramento", "TX" => "Austin",
                   "OR" => "Salem" );
```

Viewing arrays

You can echo an array value like this:

```
echo $capitals['TX'];
```

If you include the array value in a longer echo statement enclosed by double quotes, you may need to enclose the array value name in curly braces:

```
echo "The capital of Texas is {$capitals['TX']}<br />";
```

You can see the structure and values of any array by using a print_r or a var_dump statement. To display the $capitals array, use one of the following statements:

```
print_r($capitals);

var_dump($capitals);
```

This print_r statement provides the following output:

```
Array
(                   9.  see page 174
    [CA] => Sacramento            [4] is index
    [TX] => Austin
    [OR] => Salem
)
```

The var_dump statement provides the following output:

```
array(3) {
   ["CA"]=>
   string(10) "Sacramento"
   ["TX"]=>
   string(6) "Austin"
   ["OR"]=>
   string(5) "Salem"
}
```

The print_r output shows the key and the value for each element in the array. The var_dump output shows the data type, as well as the keys and values.

When you display the output from print_r or var_dump on a Web page, it displays with HTML, which means that it displays in one long line. To see the output on the Web in the useful format that I describe here, send HTML tags that tell the browser to display the text as received, without changing it, by using the following statements:

```
echo "<pre>";
var_dump($capitals);
echo "</pre>";
```

Removing values from arrays

Sometimes you need to completely remove a value from an array. For example, suppose you have the following array:

```
$pets = array( "dragon", "unicorn", "tiger",
               "scorpion", "parrot" );
```

This array has five values. Now you decide that you no longer want to carry scorpions in your pet store, so you use the following statement to try to remove scorpion from the array:

```
$pets[3] = "";
```

Although this statement sets $pets[3] to an empty string, it does not remove the string from the array. You still have an array with five values, with one of the five values being empty. To totally remove the item from the array, you need to unset it with the following statement:

```
unset($pets[3]);
```

Now your array has only four values in it. $pets[3] is totally removed. The array now consists of four elements:

```
$pets[0] = dragon
$pets[1] = unicorn
$pets[2] = tiger
$pets[4] = parrot
```

Sorting arrays

One of the most useful features of arrays is that PHP can sort them for you. PHP originally stores array elements in the order in which you create them. Often, you want to change this order when you display an array. For example, you may want to display the array in alphabetical order by value or by key.

PHP can sort arrays in a variety of ways. To sort an array that has numbers as keys, use a sort statement as follows:

```
sort($pets);
```

This statement sorts by the values and assigns new keys that are the appropriate numbers. When the values are strings, the values are sorted with numbers first, uppercase letters next, and lowercase letters last. When the values are numbers, the values are sorted in numerical order. Sorting an array with mixed values — some strings, some numeric — is not recommended because the sort can produce unexpected results.

Consider the `$pets` array created in the preceding section:

```
$pets[0] = "dragon";
$pets[1] = "unicorn";
$pets[2] = "tiger";
```

After the following `sort` statement

```
sort($pets);
```

the array becomes

```
$pets[0] = "dragon";
$pets[1] = "tiger";
$pets[2] = "unicorn";
```

If you use `sort()` to sort an array with words as keys, the keys are changed to numbers, and the word keys are thrown away.

To sort arrays that have words for keys, use the `asort` statement. This statement sorts the capitals by value but keeps the original key for each value instead of assigning a number key. For instance, consider the state capitals array created in the preceding section:

```
$capitals['CA'] = "Sacramento";
$capitals['TX'] = "Austin";
$capitals['OR'] = "Salem";
```

After the following `sort` statement

```
asort($capitals);
```

the array becomes

```
$capitals['TX'] = "Austin";
$capitals['CA'] = "Sacramento";
$capitals['OR'] = "Salem";
```

Notice that the keys stayed with the value when the elements were reordered. Now the elements are in alphabetical order, and the correct state key is still with the appropriate state capital. If the keys had been numbers, the numbers would now be in a different order. For example, if the original array was

```
$capitals[1] = "Sacramento";
$capitals[2] = "Austin";
$capitals[3] = "Salem";
```

after an `asort` statement, the new array would be

```
$capitals[2] = Austin
$capitals[1] = Sacramento
$capitals[3] = Salem
```

It's unlikely that you want to use `asort` on an array with numbers as a key.

Several other `sort` statements sort in other ways. Table 7-3 lists all the available `sort` statements.

Table 7-3	Ways You Can Sort Arrays
Sort Statement	**What It Does**
`sort($arrayname)`	Sorts by value; assigns new numbers as the keys
`asort($arrayname)`	Sorts by value; keeps the same key
`rsort($arrayname)`	Sorts by value in reverse order; assigns new numbers as the keys
`arsort($arrayname)`	Sorts by value in reverse order; keeps the same key
`ksort($arrayname)`	Sorts by key
`krsort($arrayname)`	Sorts by key in reverse order
`usort($arrayname, functionname)`	Sorts by a function (see "Using Functions," later in this chapter)

Getting values from arrays

You can retrieve any individual value in an array by accessing it directly. Here's an example:

```
$CAcapital = $capitals['CA'];
echo $CAcapital ;
```

The output from these statements is

```
Sacramento
```

If you use an array element that doesn't exist in a statement, a notice is displayed. (Read about notices in Chapter 6.) For example, suppose that you use the following statement:

```
$CAcapital = $capitals['CAx'];
```

If the array $capitals exists but no element has the key CAx, you see the following notice:

Notice: Undefined index: CAx in **d:\testarray.php** on line **9**

A notice doesn't cause the script to stop. Statements after the notice continue to execute. But because no value has been put into $CAcapital, any subsequent echo statements echo a blank space. You can prevent the notice from being displayed by using the @ symbol:

```
@$CAcapital = $capitals['CAx'];
```

You can get several values at once from an array using the list statement or all the values from an array by using the extract statement.

The list statement gets values from an array and puts them into variables. The following statements include a list statement:

```
$shirtInfo = array ("blue", "large", 12.00);
list($firstvalue,$secondvalue) = $shirtInfo;
echo $firstvalue,"<br />";
echo $secondvalue,"<br />";
```

The first line creates the $shirtInfo array. The second line sets up two variables named $firstvalue and $secondvalue and copies the first two values in $shirtInfo into the two new variables, as if you had used the two statements

```
$firstvalue=$shirtInfo[0];
$secondvalue=$shirtInfo[1];
```

The third value in $shirtInfo is not copied into a variable because the list statement includes only two variables. The output from the echo statements is

```
blue
large
```

You can retrieve all the values from an array with words as keys using `extract`. Each value is copied into a variable named for the key. For instance, suppose you defined the `$shirtinfo` array with words for keys, as follows:

```
$shirtInfo = array ( "color"=>"blue", "size"=>"large",
                     "cost"=>12.00);
```

The following statements get all the information from `$shirtInfo` and echo it:

```
extract($shirtInfo);
echo "size is $size; color is $color; cost is $cost";
```

The output for these statements is

```
size is large; color is blue; cost is 12;
```

Walking through an array

You'll often want to do something to every value in an array. You might want to echo each value, store each value in the database, or add 6 to each value in the array. In technical talk, walking through each and every value in an array, in order, is *iteration*. It is also sometimes called *traversing*. Here are two ways to walk through an array:

- ✔ **Manually:** Move a pointer from one array value to another
- ✔ **Using** `foreach`**:** Automatically walk through the array, from beginning to end, one value at a time

Manually walking through an array

You can walk through an array manually by using a pointer. To do this, think of your array as a list. Imagine a pointer pointing to a value in the list. The pointer stays on a value until you move it. After you move it, it stays there until you move it again. You can move the pointer with the following instructions:

- ✔ `current($arrayname)`: Refers to the value currently under the pointer; does not move the pointer
- ✔ `next($arrayname)`: Moves the pointer to the value after the current value

✔ previous ($*arrayname*): Moves the pointer to the value before the current pointer location

✔ end ($*arrayname*): Moves the pointer to the last value in the array

✔ reset ($*arrayname*): Moves the pointer to the first value in the array

The following statements manually walk through an array containing state capitals:

```
$value = current ($capitals);
echo "$value<br />";
$value = next ($capitals);
echo "$value<br />";
$value = next ($capitals);
echo "$value<br />";
```

Unless you moved the pointer previously, the pointer is located at the first element when you start walking through the array. If you think that the array pointer may have been moved earlier in the script or if your output from the array seems to start somewhere in the middle, use the reset statement before you start walking, as follows:

```
reset($capitals);
```

When using this method to walk through an array, you need an assignment statement and an echo statement for every value in the array — for each of the 50 states. The output is a list of all the state capitals.

This method gives you flexibility. You can move through the array in any manner — not just one value at a time. You can move backwards, go directly to the end, skip every other value by using two next statements in a row, or whatever method is useful. However, if you want to go through the array from beginning to end, one value at a time, PHP provides foreach, which does exactly what you need much more efficiently. foreach is described in the next section.

Using foreach to walk through an array

foreach walks through the array one value at a time. The current key and value of the array can be used in the block of statements each time the block executes. The general format is

```
foreach( $arrayname as $keyname => $valuename )
{
    block of statements;
}
```

Fill in the following information:

- ✔ *arrayname*: The name of the array that you're walking through.
- ✔ *keyname*: The name of the variable where you want to store the key. *keyname* is optional. If you leave out $*keyname* =>, only the value is put into a variable that can be used in the block of statements.
- ✔ *valuename*: The name of the variable where you want to store the value.

For instance, the following foreach statement walks through the sample array of state capitals and echoes a list:

```
$capitals = array("CA" => "Sacramento", "TX" => "Austin",
                   "OR" => "Salem" );
ksort($capitals);
foreach( $capitals as $state => $city )
{
    echo "$city, $state<br />";
}
```

The preceding statements give the following Web page output:

```
Sacramento, CA
Salem, OR
Austin, TX
```

You can use the following line in place of the foreach line in the previous statements:

```
foreach( $capitals as $city )
```

When using this foreach statement, only the city is available for output. You would then use the following echo statement:

```
echo "$city<br />";
```

The output with these changes is

```
Sacramento
Salem
Austin
```

When foreach starts walking through an array, it moves the pointer to the beginning of the array. You don't need to reset an array before walking through it with foreach.

Multidimensional arrays

In the earlier sections of this chapter, I describe arrays that are a single list of key/value pairs. However, on some occasions, you might want to store values with more than one key. For instance, suppose you want to store these product prices together in one variable:

- ✔ shirt, 20.00
- ✔ pants, 22.50
- ✔ blanket, 25.00
- ✔ bedspread, 50.00
- ✔ lamp, 44.00
- ✔ rug, 75.00

You can store these products in an array as follows:

```
$productPrices['shirt'] = 20.00;
$productPrices['pants'] = 22.50;
$productPrices['blanket'] = 25.00;
$productPrices['bedspread'] = 50.00;
$productPrices['lamp'] = 44.00;
$productPrices['rug'] = 75.00;
```

Your program can easily look through this array whenever it needs to know a price. But suppose that you have 3,000 products. Your program would need to look through 3,000 products to find the one with *shirt* or *rug* as the key.

Notice that the list of products and prices includes a wide variety of products that can be classified into groups: clothing, linens, and furniture. If you classify the products, the program would need to look through only one classification to find the correct price. Classifying the products would be much more efficient. You can classify the products by putting the costs in a multidimensional array as follows:

```
$productPrices['clothing']['shirt'] = 20.00;
$productPrices['clothing']['pants'] = 22.50;
$productPrices['linens']['blanket'] = 25.00;
$productPrices['linens']['bedspread'] = 50.00;
$productPrices['furniture']['lamp'] = 44.00;
$productPrices['furniture']['rug'] = 75.00;
```

This kind of array is a *multidimensional* array because it's like an array of arrays. Figure 7-1 shows the structure of $productPrices as an array of arrays. The figure shows that $productPrices has three key/value pairs. The keys are clothing, linens, and furniture. The value for each key is an array with two key/value pairs. For instance, the value for the key clothing is an array with the two key/value pairs: shirt/20.00 and pants/22.50.

$productPrices	key	value	
		key	value
	clothing	shirt	20.00
		pants	22.50
	linens	blanket	25.00
		bedspread	50.00
	furniture	lamp	44.00
		rug	75.00

Figure 7-1:
An array of
arrays.

$productPrices is a two-dimensional array. PHP can also understand multidimensional arrays that are four, five, six, or more levels deep. However, my head starts to hurt if I try to comprehend an array that is more than three levels deep. The possibility of confusion increases when the number of dimensions increases.

You can get values from a multidimensional array by using the same procedures that you use with a one-dimensional array. For instance, you can access a value directly with this statement:

```
$shirtPrice = $productPrices['clothing']['shirt'];
```

You can also echo the value:

```
echo $productPrices['clothing']['shirt'];
```

However, if you combine the value within double quotes, you need to use curly braces to enclose the variable name. The $ that begins the variable name must follow the { immediately, without a space, as follows:

```
echo "The price of a shirt is
            \${$productPrices['clothing']['shirt']}";
```

Notice the backslash (\\) in front of the first dollar sign ($). The backslash tells PHP that $ is a literal dollar sign and not the beginning of a variable name. The output is

```
The price of a shirt is $20
```

You can walk through a multidimensional array by using `foreach` statements (described in the preceding section). You need a `foreach` statement for each array. One `foreach` statement is inside the other `foreach` statement. Putting statements inside other statements is called *nesting*.

Because a two-dimensional array, such as `$productPrices`, contains two arrays, it takes two `foreach` statements to walk through it. The following statements get the values from the multidimensional array and output them in an HTML table:

```
echo "<table border='1'>";
foreach( $productPrices as $category )
{
    foreach( $category as $product => $price )
    {
      $f_price = sprintf("%01.2f", $price);
      echo "<tr><td>$product:</td>
              <td>\$$f_price</td></tr>";
    }
}
echo "</table>";
```

Figure 7-2 shows the Web page produced with these PHP statements.

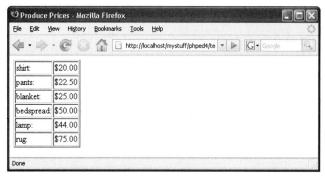

Figure 7-2:
The Web page output for the multidimensional array.

Here's how the program interprets these statements:

1. Outputs the `table` tag.

2. Gets the first key/value pair in the `$productPrices` array and stores the value in the variable `$category`. The value is an array.

3. Gets the first key/value pair in the `$category` array. Stores the key in `$product` and stores the value in `$price`.

4. Formats the value in `$price` into the correct format for money.

5. Echoes one table row for the product and its price.

6. Goes to the next key/value pair in the `$category` array.

7. Formats the price and echoes the next table row for the product and its price.

8. Because there are no more key/value pairs in `$category`, the inner `foreach` statement ends.

9. Goes to the next key/value pair in the outer `foreach` statement. Puts the next value in `$category`, which is an array.

10. Repeats Steps 2–9 until the last key/value pair in the last `$category` array is reached. The inner `foreach` statement ends. The outer `foreach` statement ends.

11. Outputs the `/table` tag to end the table.

In other words, the outer `foreach` starts with the first key/value pair in the array. The key is `clothing`, and the value of this pair is an array that is put into the variable `$category`. The inner `foreach` then walks through the array in `$category`. When it reaches the last key/value pair in `$category`, it ends. The program is then back in the outer loop, which goes on to the second key/value pair . . . and so on until the outer `foreach` reaches the end of the array.

Useful Conditional Statements

A *conditional statement* executes a block of statements only when certain conditions are met. Here are two useful types of conditional statements:

✓ `if` **statement:** Sets up a condition and tests it. If the condition is true, a block of statements is executed.

✓ `switch` **statement:** Sets up a list of alternative conditions. Tests for the true condition and executes the appropriate block of statements.

I describe these statements in more detail in the following two sections.

Using if statements

An `if` statement asks whether certain conditions exist. A block of statements executes depending on which conditions are met. The general format of an `if` conditional statement is

```
if( condition ... )
{
   block of statements
}
elseif( condition ... )
{
   block of statements
}
else
{
   block of statements
}
```

The `if` statement consists of three sections:

✔ **if:** This section is required. It tests a condition.

- *If condition is true:* The block of statements is executed. After the statements are executed, the program moves to the next instruction following the conditional statement; if the conditional statement contains any `elseif` or `else` sections, the program skips over them.

- *If condition is not true:* The block of statements is not executed. The program skips to the next instruction, which can be an `elseif`, an `else`, or the next instruction after the `if` conditional statement.

✔ **elseif:** This section is optional. It tests a condition. You can use more than one `elseif` section if you want.

- *If condition is true:* The block of statements is executed. After executing the block of statements, the program goes to the next instruction following the conditional statement; if the `if` statement contains any additional `elseif` sections or an `else` section, the program skips over them.

- *If condition is not true:* The block of statements is not executed. The program skips to the next instruction, which can be an `elseif`, an `else`, or the next instruction after the `if` conditional statement.

✔ **else:** This section is optional. Only one `else` section is allowed. This section does not test a condition; rather, it executes the block of statements. If the program has entered this section, it means that the `if` section and all the `elseif` sections are not true.

Each section of the `if` conditional statement tests a condition that consists of one or more comparisons. A comparison asks a question that can be true or false. Some conditions are

```
$a == 1;
$a < $b
$c != "Hello"
```

The first comparison asks whether `$a` is equal to 1; the second comparison asks whether `$a` is smaller than `$b`; the third comparison asks whether `$c` is not equal to `"Hello"`. You can use two or more comparisons in a condition by connecting the comparisons with `and`, `or`, or `xor`. I discuss comparing values and using more than one comparison in detail in Chapter 6.

The following example uses all three sections of the `if` conditional statement. Suppose that you have German, French, Italian, and English versions of your product catalog. You want your program to display the correct language version, based on where the customer lives. The following statements set a variable to the correct catalog version (depending on the country where the customer lives) and set a message in the correct language. You can then display a message in the appropriate language.

```
if($country == "Germany" )
{
    $version = "German";
    $message = "Sie sehen unseren Katalog auf Deutsch";
}
elseif($country == „France" )
{
    $version = „French";
    $message = "Vous verrez notre catalogue en francais";
}
elseif($country == „Italy" )
{
    $version = „Italian";
    $message = „Vedrete il nostro catalogo in Italiano";
}
else
{
    $version = „English";
    $message = „You will see our catalog in English";
}
echo "$message<br />";
```

The if conditional statement proceeds as follows:

1. Compares the variable $country to "Germany".

   If they're the same, $version is set to "German", $message is set in German, and the program skips to echo. If $country does *not* equal Germany, $version and $message are *not* set, and the program skips to the first elseif section.

2. Compares the variable $country to "France".

   If they're the same, $version and $message are set, and the program skips to the echo statement. If $country does *not* equal France, $version and $message are *not* set, and the program skips to the second elseif section.

3. Compares the variable $country to "Italy".

   If they're the same, $version is set to "Italian", and the program skips to the echo statement. If $country does *not* equal Italy, $version and $message are *not* set, and the program skips to the else section.

4. $version is set to English, and $message is set in English.

   The program continues to the echo statement.

Notice that only the message is echoed in this example. However, the variable $version is stored because the version is useful information that can be used later in the program.

When the block to be executed by any section of the if conditional statement contains only one statement, the curly braces are not needed. For instance, if the preceding example had only one statement in the blocks

```
if($country == "France")
{
    $version = "French";
}
```

you could write it as follows:

```
if($country == "France" )
    $version = "French";
```

This shortcut can save some typing, but it can lead to confusion when you use several if statements.

You can have an if conditional statement inside another if conditional statement. Putting one statement inside another is *nesting*. For instance, suppose that you need to contact all your customers who live in Idaho. You plan to send e-mail to those who have an e-mail address and send a letter to those who don't have an e-mail address. You can identify the groups of customers by using the following nested `if` statements:

```
if( $custState == "ID" )
{
   if( $EmailAdd != "" )
   {
      $contactMethod = "email";
   }
   else
   {
      $contactMethod = "letter";
   }
}
else
{
   $contactMethod = "none needed";
}
```

These statements first check to see whether the customer lives in Idaho. If the customer does live in Idaho, the program tests for an e-mail address. If the e-mail address is not blank, the contact method is set to `email`. If the e-mail address is blank, the contact method is `letter`. If the customer does not live in Idaho, the `else` section sets the contact method to indicate that the customer won't be contacted at all.

Using switch statements

For most situations, the `if` conditional statement works best. Sometimes, however, you have a list of conditions and want to execute different statements for each of the conditions. For instance, suppose that your program computes sales tax. How do you handle the different state sales tax rates? The `switch` statement was designed for such situations.

The `switch` statement tests the value of one variable and executes the block of statements for the matching value of the variable. The general format is

```
switch ( $variablename )
{
   case value :
      block of statements;
      break;
   case value :
      block of statements;
      break;
   ...
   default:
      block of statements;
      break;
}
```

The switch statement tests the value of $variablename$. The program then skips to the case section for that value and executes statements until it reaches a break statement or the end of the switch statement. If there is no case section for the value of $variablename$, the program executes the default section. You can use as many case sections as you need. The default section is optional. If you use a default section, it's customary to put the default section at the end, but it can go anywhere.

The following statements set the sales tax rate for different states:

```
switch ( $custState )
{
   case "OR" :
      $salestaxrate = 0;
      break;
   case "CA" :
      $salestaxrate = 1.0;
      break;
   default:
      $salestaxrate = .5;
      break;
}
$salestax = $orderTotalCost * $salestaxrate;
```

In this case, the tax rate for Oregon is 0, the tax rate for California is 100 percent, and the tax rate for all the other states is 50 percent. The switch statement looks at the value of $custState and skips to the section that matches the value. For instance, if $custState is TX, the program executes the default section and sets $salestaxrate to .5. After the switch statement, the program computes $salestax at .5 times the cost of the order.

The break statements are essential in the case section. If a case section does not include a break statement, the program does *not* stop executing at the end of the case section. The program continues executing statements past the end of the case section, on to the next case section, and continues until it reaches a break statement in a later case section or the end of the switch statement.

The last case section in a switch statement doesn't actually require a break statement. You can leave it out, but it's a good idea to include it for clarity.

Using Loops

Loops, which are used frequently in programs, set up a block of statements that repeat. Sometimes, the loop repeats a specified number of times. For instance, a loop to echo all the state capitals needs to repeat 50 times.

Sometimes, the loop repeats until a certain condition exists. For instance, a loop that displays product information for all the products needs to repeat until it has displayed all the products, regardless of how many products there are. Here are three types of loops:

- **Basic `for` loop:** Sets up a counter; repeats a block of statements until the counter reaches a specified number

- **`while` loop:** Sets up a condition; checks the condition; and if it's true, repeats a block of statements

- **`do..while` loop:** Sets up a condition; executes a block of statements; checks the condition; if the condition is true, repeats the block of statements

I describe each of these loops in detail in the following few sections.

Using for loops

The most basic `for` loops are based on a counter. You set the beginning value for the counter, set the ending value, and set how the counter is incremented. The general format is

```
for(startingvalue;endingcondition;increment)
{
    block of statements;
}
```

Fill in the following values:

- *startingvalue*: A statement that sets up a variable to be your counter and sets it to your starting value. For instance, the statement $i=1; sets $i as the counter variable and sets it equal to 1. Frequently, the counter variable is started at 0 or 1. The starting value can be a combination of numbers (2 + 2) or a variable.

- *endingcondition*: A statement that sets your ending value. As long as this statement is true, the block of statements keeps repeating. When this statement is not true, the loop ends. For instance, the statement $i<10; sets the ending value for the loop to 10. When $i is equal to 10, the statement is no longer true (because $i is no longer less than 10), and the loop stops repeating. The statement can include variables, such as $i<$size;.

- *increment*: A statement that increments your counter. For instance, the statement $i++; adds 1 to your counter at the end of each block of statements. You can use other increment statements, such as $I+=1; or $i--;.

The basic `for` loop sets up a variable — for example, a variable called `$i`, — that is a counter. This variable has a value during each loop. The variable `$i` can be used in the block of statements that is repeating. For instance, the following simple loop displays `Hello World!` three times:

```
for($i=1;$i<=3;$i++)
{
   echo "$i. Hello World!<br />";
}
```

PHP doesn't care whether the statements in the block are indented. However, indenting the blocks makes it much easier for you to understand the program.

The output from these statements is

```
1. Hello World!
2. Hello World!
3. Hello World!
```

`for` loops are particularly useful for looping through an array. Suppose that you have an array of customer names and want to display them all. You can do this easily with a loop:

```
for($i=0;$i<100;$i++)
{
   echo "$customerNames[$i]<br />";
}
```

The output displays a Web page with a list of all customer names, one on each line. In this case, you know that you have 100 customer names. But suppose that you don't know how many customers are in this list. You can ask PHP how many values are in the array and use that value in your `for` loop. For example, you can use the following statements:

```
for($i=0;$i<sizeof($customerNames);$i++)
{
   echo "$customerNames[$i]<br />";
}
```

Notice that the ending value is `sizeof($customerNames)`. This statement finds out the number of values in the array and uses that number. That way, your loop repeats exactly the number of times that there are values in the array.

The first value in an array with a numbered index is 0 unless you deliberately set it to a different number. One common mistake when working with arrays is to think of the first number as 1 rather than 0.

Using while loops

A while loop continues repeating as long as certain conditions are true. The loop works as follows:

1. You set up a condition.

2. The condition is tested at the top of each loop.

3. If the condition is true, the loop repeats. If the condition is not true, the loop stops.

The general format of a while loop is

```
while( condition )
{
    block of statements
}
```

A *condition* is any expression that can be found to be true or false. Comparisons, such as the following, are often used as conditions. (For detailed information on using comparisons, see Chapter 6.)

```
$test <= 10
$test1 == $test2
$a == "yes" and $b != "yes"
$name != "Smith"
```

As long as the condition is found to be true, the loop repeats. When the condition tests false, the loop stops. The following statements set up a while loop that looks through an array for a customer named Smith:

```
$customers = array( "Huang", "Smith", "Jones" );
$testvar = "no";
$k = 0;
while( $testvar != "yes" )
{
   if($customers[$k] == "Smith" )
   {
     $testvar = "yes";
     echo "Smith<br />";
   }
   else
   {
     echo "$customers[$k], not Smith<br />";
   }
   $k++;
}
```

These statements display the following on a Web page:

```
Huang, not Smith
Smith
```

The program executes the previous statements as follows:

1. Sets the variables before starting the loop.

   $customers (an array with three values), $testvar (a test variable set to "no"), and $k (a counter variable set to 0).

2. Starts the loop by testing whether $testvar != "yes" is true.

   Because $testvar is set to "no", the statement is true, so the loop continues.

3. Tests the if statement.

   Is $customers[$k] == "Smith" true? At this point, $k is 0, so the program checks $customers[0]. Because $customers[0] is "Huang", the statement is not true. The statements in the if block are not executed, so the program skips to the else statement.

4. Executes the statement in the else block.

   The else block outputs the line "Huang, not Smith". This is the first line of the output.

5. Adds 1 to $k, which now becomes equal to 1.

6. Reaches the bottom of the loop.

7. Goes to the top of the loop.

8. Tests the condition again.

   Is $testvar != "yes" true? Because $testvar has not been changed and is still set to "no", it is true, so the loop continues.

9. Tests the if statement.

   Is $customers[$k] == "Smith" true? At this point, $k is 1, so the program checks $customers[1]. Because $customers[1] is "Smith", the statement is true. So the loop enters the if block.

10. Executes the statements in the if block.

    Sets $testvar to "yes". Outputs "Smith". This is the second line of the output.

11. Adds 1 to $k which now becomes equal to 2.

12. Reaches the bottom of the loop.

13. Goes to the top of the loop.

14. Tests the condition again.

> Is $testvar != "yes" true? Because $testvar has been changed and is now set to "yes", it is *not* true. The loop stops.

It's possible to write a while loop that is infinite — that is, a loop in which the condition is always true. If the condition never becomes false, the loop never ends. For a discussion of infinite loops, see the "Infinite loops" section, later in this chapter.

Using do..while loops

A do..while loop is similar to a while loop. A do..while loop continues repeating as long as certain conditions are true. You set up a condition. The condition is tested at the bottom of each loop. If the condition is true, the loop repeats. When the condition is not true, the loop stops.

The general format for a do..while loop is

```
do
{
    block of statements
} while( condition );
```

The following statements set up a loop that looks for the customer named Smith. This program does the same thing as a program in the preceding section using a while loop:

```
$customers = array( "Huang", "Smith", "Jones" );
$testvar = "no";
$k = 0;
do
{
   if ($customers[$k] == "Smith" )
   {
     $testvar = "yes";
     echo "Smith<br />";
   }
   else
   {
     echo "$customers[$k], not Smith<br />";
   }
   $k++;
} while ( $testvar != "yes" );
```

The output of these statements in a browser is

```
Huang, not Smith
Smith
```

This is the same output shown for the while loop example. The difference between a while loop and a do..while loop is where the condition is checked. In a while loop, the condition is checked at the top of the loop. Therefore, the loop never executes if the condition is never true. In the do.. while loop, the condition is checked at the bottom of the loop. Therefore, the loop always executes at least once even if the condition is never true.

For instance, in the preceding loop that checks for the name Smith, suppose the original condition is set to yes, instead of no, by using this statement:

```
$testvar = "yes";
```

The condition would test false from the beginning. It would never be true. In a while loop, there would be no output. The statement block would never run. However, in a do..while loop, the statement block would run once before the condition was tested. Thus, the while loop would produce no output, but the do..while loop would produce the following output:

```
Huang, not Smith
```

The do..while loop produces one line of output before the condition is tested. It does not produce the second line of output because the condition tests false.

Infinite loops

You can easily set up loops so that they never stop. These are *infinite loops*. They repeat forever. However, seldom does anyone create an infinite loop intentionally. It's usually a mistake in the programming. For instance, a slight change to the program that sets up a while loop can make it into an infinite loop.

Here's the program shown in the "Using while loops" section, earlier in this chapter:

```
$customers = array ( "Huang", "Smith", "Jones" );
$testvar = "no";
$k = 0;
while ( $testvar != "yes" )
{
  if ($customers[$k] == "Smith" )
  {
    $testvar = "yes";
    echo "Smith<br />";
  }
  else
  {
    echo "$customers[$k], not Smith<br />";
  }
  $k++;
}
```

Here's the program with a slight change:

```
$customers = array ( "Huang", "Smith", "Jones" );
$testvar = "no";
while ( $testvar != "yes" )
{
   $k = 0;
   if ($customers[$k] == "Smith" )
   {
     $testvar = "yes";
     echo "Smith<br />";
   }
   else
   {
     echo "$customers[$k], not Smith<br />";
   }
   $k++;
}
```

The small change is moving the statement $k = 0; from outside the loop to inside the loop. This small change makes it into an endless loop. The output of this changed program is

```
Huang, not Smith
Huang, not Smith
Huang, not Smith
Huang, not Smith
. . .
```

This loop repeats forever. Every time the loop runs, it resets $k to 0. Then it gets $customers[0] and echoes it. At the end of the loop, $k is incremented to 1. However, when the loop starts again, $k is set back to 0. Consequently, only the first value in the array, Huang, is ever read. The loop never gets to the name Smith, and $testvar is never set to "yes". The loop is endless.

Don't be embarrassed if you write an infinite loop. I guarantee that the best programming guru in the world has written many infinite loops. It's not a big deal. If you're testing a program and get output in your Web page repeating endlessly, it will stop by itself in a short time. The default time is 30 seconds, but the timeout period may have been changed by the PHP administrator. You can also click the Stop button on your browser to stop the display in your browser. Then you can figure out why the loop is repeating endlessly and fix it.

A common mistake that can result in an infinite loop is using a single equal sign (=) when you mean a double equal sign (==). The single equal sign stores a value in a variable; the double equal sign tests whether two values are equal. If you write the following condition with a single equal sign:

```
while ($testvar = "yes")
```

it is always true. The condition simply sets $testvar equal to "yes". This is not a question that can be false. What you probably meant to write is this:

```
while ($testvar == "yes")
```

This is a question asking whether $testvar is equal to "yes", which can be answered either true or false.

You can bulletproof your programs against this error by changing the condition to "yes" == $testvar. It's less logical to read but protects against the single-equal-sign problem. If you use a single equal sign instead of a double equal sign in this condition, you get an error, and your program fails to run.

Another common mistake is to leave out the statement that increments the counter. For instance, in the program earlier in this section, if you leave out the statement $k++;, $k is always 0, and the result is an infinite loop.

Breaking out of a loop

Sometimes you want your program to break out of a loop. PHP provides two statements for this purpose:

- ✔ break: Breaks completely out of a loop and continues with the program statements after the loop.
- ✔ continue: Skips to the end of the loop where the condition is tested. If the condition tests positive, the program continues from the top of the loop.

break and continue are usually used in a conditional statement. break, in particular, is used most often in switch statements, as I discuss earlier in the chapter.

The following two sets of statements show the difference between continue and break. The first statements use the break statement:

```
$counter = 0;
while( $counter < 5 )
{
  $counter++;
  if( $counter == 3 )
  {
      echo "break<br />";
      break;
  }
  echo "End of while loop: counter=$counter<br />";
}
echo "After the break loop<br />";
```

The following statements use the `continue` statement:

```
$counter = 0;
while( $counter < 5 )
{
   $counter++;
   if( $counter == 3 )
   {
       echo "continue<br />";
       continue;
   }
   echo "End of while loop: counter=$counter<br />";
}
echo "After the continue loop<br />";
```

These statements build two loops that are the same, except the first uses `break` and the second uses `continue`. The output from the first set of statements that uses the `break` statement displays in your browser as follows:

```
End of while loop: counter=1
End of while loop: counter=2
break
After the break loop
```

The output from the second set of statements, with the `continue` statement, is

```
End of while loop: counter=1
End of while loop: counter=2
continue
End of while loop: counter=4
End of while loop: counter=5
After the continue loop
```

The first loop ends at the `break` statement. It stops looping and jumps immediately to the statement after the loop. The second loop does not end at the `continue` statement. It just stops the third repeat of the loop and jumps back up to the top of the loop. It then finishes the loop, with the fourth and fifth repeats, before it goes to the statement after the loop.

One use for `break` statements is insurance against infinite loops. The following statements inside a loop can stop it at a reasonable point:

```
$test4infinity++;
if( $test4infinity > 100 )
{
    break;
}
```

If you're sure that your loop should never repeat more than 100 times, these statements will stop the loop if it becomes endless. Use whatever number seems reasonable for the loop that you're building.

Using Functions

Applications often perform the same task at different points in the program or in different programs. For instance, your application might display the company logo on several Web pages or in different parts of the program. Suppose that you use the following statements to display the company logo:

```
echo "<div style='float: left'>
      <hr style='width: 50'>","\n";
echo "<img src='/images/logo.jpg' width='50'
         height='50' />","\n";
echo "<hr style='width: 50' /></div>","\n";
```

You can create a function that contains the preceding statements and name it `display_logo`. Then whenever the program needs to display the logo, you can just call the function `display_logo` with a simple function call, as follows:

```
display_logo();
```

Notice the parentheses after the function name. These are required in a function call because they tell PHP that this is a function.

Using a function offers several advantages:

- ✔ **Less typing:** You have to type the statements only once — in the function. Forever after, you just use the function call and never have to type the statements again.

- ✔ **Easier to read:** The line `display_logo()` is much easier for a person to understand at a glance.

- ✔ **Fewer errors:** After you have written your function and fixed all its problems, it runs correctly wherever you use it.

- ✔ **Easier to change:** If you decide to change how the task is performed, you need to change it in only one place. You just change the function instead of finding all the different places in your program where you performed the task and changing the code in all those places. For instance, suppose that you changed the name of the graphics file that holds the company logo. You just change the filename in one place — the function — and it works correctly everywhere.

You can create a function by putting the code into a function block. The general format is

```
function functionname()
{
    block of statements;
    return;
}
```

For instance, you create the function to display the company logo with the following statements:

```
function display_logo()
{
    echo "<div style='float: left'>
            <hr style='width: 50'>","\n";
    echo "<img src='/images/logo.jpg' width='50'
              height='50' />","\n";
    echo "<hr style='width: 50' /></div>","\n";
    return;
}
```

The `return` statement stops the function and returns to the main program. The `return` statement at the end of the function is not required, but it makes the function easier to understand. It's often used for a conditional end to a function.

Suppose that your function displays an electronics catalog. You might use the following statement at the beginning of the function:

```
if ( $age < 13 )
    return;
```

If the customer's age is less than 13, the function stops, and the electronics catalog isn't displayed.

You can put functions anywhere in the program, but the usual practice is to put all the functions at the beginning or the end of the program file. Functions that you plan to use in more than one program can be in a separate file. Each program accesses the functions from the external file. For more on organizing applications into files and accessing separate files, see Chapter 10.

Notice that the sample function is quite simple. It doesn't use variables, and it doesn't share any information with the main program. It just performs an independent task when called. You can use variables in functions and pass information between the function and the main program as long as you know the rules and limitations. The remaining sections in this chapter explain how to use variables and pass values.

Using variables in functions

You can create and use variables that are local to the function. That is, you can create and use a variable inside your function. However, the variable isn't available outside the function; it's not available to the main program. You can make the variable available at any location in the program by using a special statement called global. For instance, the following function creates a variable:

```
function format_name()
{
   $first_name = "Goliath";
   $last_name = "Smith";
   $name = $last_name.", ".$first_name;
   return;
}
format_name();
echo "$name";
```

this value is still available after return

These statements produce no output. In the echo statement, $name doesn't contain any value. The variable $name was created inside the function, so it doesn't exist outside the function.

To create a variable inside a function that does exist outside the function, you use the global statement. The following statements contain the same function with a global statement added:

```
function format_name()
{
   $first_name = "Goliath";
   $last_name = "Smith";
   global $name;
   $name = $last_name.", ".$first_name;
   return;
}
format_name();
echo "$name";
```

The program now echoes this:

```
Smith, Goliath
```

The `global` statement makes the variable available at any location in the program. You must make the variable global before you can use it. If the `global` statement follows the `$name` assignment statement, the program does not produce any output.

The same rules apply when you're using a variable created in the main program. You can't use a variable in a function that was created outside the function unless the variable is global, as shown in the following statements:

```
$first_name = "Goliath";
$last_name = "Smith";
function format_name()
{
    global $first_name, $last_name;
    $name = $last_name.", ".$first_name;
    echo "$name";
    return;
}
format_name();
```

← Function is executed to set variables for further access

If you don't use the `global` statement, `$last_name` and `$first_name` inside the function are different variables, created when you name them. They have no values. The program would produce no output without the `global` statement.

Passing values between a function and the main program

You can pass values into the function and receive values from the function. For instance, you might write a function to add the correct sales tax to an order. The function would need to know the cost of the order and which state the customer resides in. The function would need to send back the amount of the sales tax.

Passing values to a function

You can pass values to a function by putting the values between the parentheses when you call the function, as follows:

```
functionname(value,value,...);
```

Of course, the variables can't just show up. The function must be expecting them. The function statement includes variable names for the values that it's expecting, as follows:

```
function functionname($varname1,$varname2,...)
{
    statements
    return;
}
```

For example, the following function computes the sales tax:

```
function compute_salestax($amount,$custState)
{
  switch ( $custState )
  {
    case "OR" :
      $salestaxrate = 0;
      break;
    case "CA" :
      $salestaxrate = 1.0;
      break;
    default:
      $salestaxrate = .5;
      break;
  }
  $salestax = $amount * $salestaxrate;
  echo "$salestax<br />";
  return;
}
$cost = 2000.00;
$custState = "CA";
compute_salestax($cost,$custState);
```

The first line shows that the function expects two values, as follows:

```
function compute_salestax($amount,$custState)
```

The last line is the function call, which passes two values to the function compute_salestax, as it expects. The amount of the order and the state in which the customer resides are passed. The output from this program is 2000 because the tax rate for California is 100 percent.

You can pass as many values as you need to. Values can be variables or values, including computed values. The following function calls are valid:

```
compute_salestax(2000,"CA");
compute_salestax(2*1000,"");
compute_salestax(2000,"C"."A");
```

Values can be passed in an array. The function receives the variable as an array. For instance, the following statements pass an array:

```
$arrayofnumbers = array( 100, 200);
addnumbers($arrayofnumbers);
```

The function receives the entire array. For instance, suppose the function starts with the following statement:

```
function addnumbers($numbers)
```

The variable $numbers is an array. The function can include statements such as

```
$total = $numbers[0] + $numbers[1];
```

The values passed are passed by position. That is, the first value in the list that you pass is used as the first value in the list that the function expects, the second is used for the second, and so forth. If your values aren't in the same order, the function uses the wrong value when performing the task. For instance, for compute_salestax, you might call compute_salestax passing values in the wrong order:

```
compute_salestax($custState,$orderCost);
```

The function uses the state as the cost of the order, which it sets to 0 because the value passed is a string. It sets the state to the number in $orderCost, which wouldn't match any of its categories. The output would be 0.

If you don't send enough values, the function sets the missing value to an empty string for a string variable or to 0 for a number. If you send too many values, the function ignores the extra values.

If you pass the wrong number of values to a function, you might get a warning message, depending on the error message level that PHP is set to:

```
Warning: Missing argument 2 for compute_salestax() in /
         test7.php on line 5
```

For an explanation of warning messages, check out Chapter 6.

You can set default values to be used when a value isn't passed. The defaults are set when you write the function by assigning a default value for the value(s) that it is expecting, as follows:

```
function add_2_numbers($num1=1,$num2=1)
{
   $total = $num1 + $num2;
   echo $total;
   return;
}
```

If one or both values are not passed, the function uses the assigned defaults. But if a value is passed, it is used instead of the default. For example, you could use one of the following calls:

```
add_2_numbers(2,2);
add_2_numbers(2);
add_2_numbers();
```

The results, in consecutive order, are as follows:

```
$total = 4
$total = 3
$total = 2
```

Getting a value from a function

When you call a function, you can pass values as described in the previous section. The function can also pass a value back to the program that called it, using the `return` statement. The program can store the value in a variable or use the value directly, such as using it in a conditional statement. The `return` statement also returns control to the main program; that is, it stops the function.

The general format of the return statement is

```
return value;
```

For instance, in the tax program from the preceding section, I echo the sales tax by using the following statements:

```
$salestax = $amount * $salestaxrate;
echo "$salestax<br />";
```

I could return the sales tax to the main program, rather than echoing it, by using the following statement:

```
$salestax = $amount * $salestaxrate;
return $salestax;
```

In fact, I could use a shortcut and send it back to the main program with one statement:

```
return $amount * $salestaxrate;
```

The return statement sends the salestax back to the main program and ends the function. The main program can use the value in any of the usual ways. The following statements use the function call in valid ways:

```
$salestax = compute_salestax($cost,$custState);
```

```
$totalcost = $cost + compute_salestax($cost,$custState);
```

```
if( compute_salestax($cost,$custState) > 100000.00 )
       $echo "Thank you very, very, very much";
```

```
foreach($customerOrder as $amount)
{
   $total = $amount +
                compute_salestax($amount,$custState);
   echo "Your total is $total";
}
```

A return statement can return only one value. However, the value returned can be an array, so you can actually return many values from a function.

You can use return statements in a conditional statement to return different values for different conditions. For example, the following function returns one of two different strings:

```
function compare_values($value1,$value2)
{
   if($value1 < $value2)
   {
      return "less than";
   }
   else
   {
      return "not less than";
   }
}
```

Although the function contains two `return` statements, only one is going to be executed, depending on the values in `$value1` and `$value2`.

Using built-in functions

PHP's many built-in functions are one reason why PHP is so powerful and useful for Web pages. The functions included with PHP are normal functions. They are no different than functions that you create yourself. It's just that PHP already did all the work for you.

I discuss some of the built-in functions in this chapter and the earlier chapters. For example, see Chapter 6 for more on the functions `unset` and `number_format`. Some useful functions for interacting with your MySQL database are discussed in Chapter 8. Other useful functions are listed in Part V.

And all the functions are listed and described in the PHP documentation on the PHP Web site at `www.php.net/docs.php`.

Chapter 8

Data In, Data Out

● ●

● ●

*P*HP and MySQL work well together. This dynamic partnership is what makes PHP and MySQL so attractive for Web database application development. Whether you have a database full of information that you want to make available to users (such as a product catalog) or a database waiting to be filled up by users (for example, a membership database), PHP and MySQL work together to implement your application.

One of PHP's strongest features is its ability to interact with databases. It provides functions that make communicating with MySQL extremely simple. You use PHP functions to send SQL queries to the database. You don't need to know the details of communicating with MySQL; PHP handles the details. You only need to know the SQL queries and how to use the PHP functions.

In previous chapters, I describe the tools that you use to build your Web database application. You find out how to build SQL queries in Chapter 4 and how to construct and use the building blocks of the PHP language in Chapters 6 and 7. In this chapter, you find out how to use these tools for the specific tasks that a Web database application needs to perform.

PHP and MySQL Functions

You use built-in PHP functions to interact with MySQL. These functions connect to the MySQL server, select the correct database, send SQL queries, and perform other communication with MySQL databases. You don't need to know the details of interacting with the database because PHP handles all the details. You need to know only how to use the functions.

As of PHP 5, PHP offers two sets of functions for communicating with MySQL: one set of functions (the mysqli functions) for use with MySQL 4.1 or later and another set of functions (the mysql functions) for use with MySQL 4.0 and earlier versions. Most Web hosts offer MySQL 5.0 or 5.1. If they offer only earlier versions of MySQL, you might want to contact the folks in tech support to see when they're going to provide a more recent version of MySQL.

If you're using PHP 5 on your Web host, the mysqli functions should be available. If only the mysql functions are available, contact tech support at your Web host and ask someone to activate the mysqli functions. There is no reason to continue to use mysql functions when using PHP 5 or later.

On your local computer, if you installed your software using XAMPP, as suggested in this book and described in Appendix A, you have PHP 5 running on your computer and both the mysql and mysqli functions are available. You can change to PHP 4 using the XAMPP main page, but there should be no reason to do this. Unless you need to work on an existing Web site, written in PHP 4, you should not use PHP 4, which is now obsolete and no longer updated by the PHP developers. For learning PHP and developing any new Web site, you should use PHP 5, or PHP 6 when it is released.

If you're using PHP 4 for some reason, the mysqli functions are not available. Instead, you use the mysql functions, even with later versions of MySQL. The mysql functions can communicate with the later versions of MySQL, but they cannot access some of the new features added in the later versions of MySQL. The mysql functions are activated automatically in PHP 4.

Throughout the book, my examples and programs use MySQL 5.1 and use the mysqli functions to communicate with MySQL. The PHP functions for use with MySQL 5.1 have the following general format:

```
mysqli_function(value,value,...);
```

The i in the function name stands for *improved* (MySQL Improved). The second part of the function name is specific to the function, usually a word that describes what the function does. In addition, the function requires one or more values to be passed, specifying things such as the database connection or the data location. Following are two of the functions discussed in this chapter:

```
mysqli_connect(connection information);
mysqli_query($cxn,"SQL statement");
```

If you're using PHP 4 or are communicating with MySQL 4.0 or earlier, the corresponding mysql functions are

```
mysql_connect(connection information);
mysql_query("SQL statement");
```

The functionality and syntax of the functions are similar but not identical for all functions. If you need to use the mysql functions rather than the mysqli functions, you need to edit the programs in this book, replacing the mysqli functions with mysql functions. Table 8-1 shows the equivalent mysql functions and their syntax.

Table 8-1	Syntax for mysql and mysqli Functions
mysqli Function	*mysql Function*
mysqli_connect($host, $user,$passwd,$dbname)	mysql_connect($host,$user,$passwd) followed by mysql_select_db($dbname)
mysqli_errno($cxn)	mysql_errno() or mysql_errno($cxn)
mysqli_error($cxn)	mysql_error() or mysql_error($cxn)
mysqli_fetch_array ($result)	mysql_fetch_array($result)
mysqli_fetch_assoc ($result)	mysql_fetch_assoc($result)
mysqli_fetch_row ($result)	mysql_fetch_row($result)
mysqli_insert_id($cxn)	mysql_insert_id($cxn)
mysqli_num_rows ($result)	mysql_num_rows($result)
mysqli_query($cxn,$sql)	mysql_query($sql) or mysql_query($sql,$cxn)
mysqli_select_db($cxn,$dbname)	mysql_select_db($dbname)
mysqli_real_escape_string($cxn,$data)	mysql_real_escape_string($data)

Making a Connection

Before you can store any data or get any data, you need to connect to the database. The database might be on the same computer with your PHP programs, or it might be on a different computer. You don't need to know the details of connecting to the database because PHP handles all the details. All you need to know is the name and location of the database. Think of a database connection in the same way that you think of a telephone connection. You don't need to know the details about how the connection is made — that is, how your words move from your telephone to another telephone. You need to know only the area code and phone number. The phone company handles the details.

After connecting to the database, you send SQL queries to the MySQL database by using a PHP function designed for this purpose. You can send as many queries as you need. The connection remains open until you close it or the program ends. Similarly, in a telephone conversation, the connection remains open until you terminate it by hanging up the phone.

Connecting to the MySQL server

The first step in communicating with your MySQL database is connecting to the MySQL server. To connect to the server, you need to know the name of the computer where the database is located, the name of your MySQL account, and the password to your MySQL account. To open the connection, use the `mysqli_connect` function as follows:

```
$cxn=mysqli_connect("host","acct","password","dbname")
     or  die ("message");
```

Fill in the following information:

- ✔ *host*: The name of the computer where MySQL is installed. On your local computer, it's `localhost`. Your Web host provides you with this information, which may be `localhost` or may be another name. If you're developing on a company computer, your IT staff provides you with this name. If this information is blank (`" "`), PHP assumes `localhost`.

- ✔ *acct*: The name of any valid MySQL account. (I discuss MySQL accounts in detail in Chapter 5.)

- ✔ *password*: The password for the MySQL account specified by *acct*. If the MySQL account does not require a password, don't type anything between the quotes: `" "`.

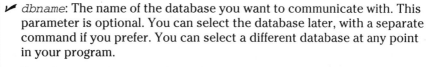

✔ *dbname*: The name of the database you want to communicate with. This parameter is optional. You can select the database later, with a separate command if you prefer. You can select a different database at any point in your program.

If you're using the mysql functions, you cannot select the database in the connect function. You must use a separate function — mysql_select_db — to select the database.

✔ *message*: The message sent to the browser if the connection fails. The connection fails if the computer or network is down or the MySQL server isn't running. It also may fail if the information provided isn't correct — for example, if the password contains a typo.

You might want to use a descriptive *message* during development, such as Couldn't connect to server, but use a more general message suitable for customers after the application is in use, such as The Pet Catalog is not available at the moment. Please try again later.

The *host* includes a port number that is needed for the connection. Almost always, the port number is 3306. On rare occasions, the MySQL administrator needs to set up MySQL to connect on a different port. In these cases, the port number is required for the connection. The port number is specified as *hostname:portnumber*. For instance, you might use localhost:8808.

With these statements, mysqli_connect attempts to open a connection to the named computer, using the account name and password provided. If the connection fails, the program stops running at this point and sends *message* to the browser.

The following statement connects to the MySQL server on the local computer by using a MySQL account named catalog that does not require a password:

```
$cxn = mysqli_connect("localhost","catalog",
                      "","PetCatalog)
    or  die ("Couldn't connect to server.");
```

For security reasons, it's a good idea to store the connection information in variables and use the variables in the connection statement, as follows:

```
$host="localhost";
$user="catalog";
$passwd="";
$dbname = "PetCatalog";
$cxn = mysqli_connect($host,$user,$passwd,$dbname)
    or  die ("Couldn't connect to server.");
```

For even more security, you can put the assignment statements for the connection information in a separate file in a hidden location so that the account name and password aren't even in the program. I explain how to do this in Chapter 10.

The variable `$cxn` contains information that identifies the connection. You can have more than one connection open at a time by using more than one variable name. A connection remains open until you close it or until the program ends. You close a connection as follows:

```
mysqli_close($connectionname);
```

For instance, to close the connection in the preceding example, use this statement:

```
mysqli_close($cxn);
```

Handling MySQL errors

You use the `mysqli` functions of the PHP language, such as `mysqli_connect` and `mysqli_query`, to interact with the MySQL database. If one of these functions fails to execute correctly, a MySQL error message is returned with information about the problem. However, this error message isn't sent to the browser unless the program deliberately sends it. The MySQL error message is returned by its own function, `mysqli_error($csn)`. To see the MySQL error message, which contains extra information about the error, you need to include the `mysqli_error` function in your script.

Here are the three usual ways to call the `mysqli` functions:

✔ **Calling the function without error handling:** The function is called without any statements that provide error messages. For instance, the `mysqli_connect` function can be called as follows:

```
$cxn = mysqli_connect($host,$user,$password,$dbname);
```

If this statement fails (for instance, the account isn't valid), the connection is not made, but the remaining statements in the program continue to execute. In most cases, this isn't useful because some of the statements in the rest of the program might depend on having an open connection, such as getting or storing data in the database.

✔ **Calling the function with a `die` statement:** The function is called with a `die` statement that sends a message to the browser. For instance, the `mysqli_connect` function can be called as follows:

```
$cxn = mysqli_connect($host,$user,$password,$dbname)
    or die ("Couldn't connect to server");
```

If this statement fails, the connection is not made, and the `die` statement is executed. The `die` statement stops the program and sends the message to the browser. If the connection can't be established, no more statements are executed. You can put any message that you want in the `die` statement.

✔ **Calling the function in an `if` statement:** The function is called by using an `if` statement that executes a block of statements if the connection fails. For instance, the `mysqli_connect` function can be called as follows:

```
if (!$cxn = mysqli_connect($host,$user,$password,
$dbname))
{
        $message = mysqli_error($cxn);
        echo "$message";
        die();
}
```

If this statement fails, the statements in the `if` block are executed. The `mysqli_error` function returns the MySQL error message and saves it in the variable `$message`. The error message is then echoed. The `die` statement ends the program so that no more statements are executed. Notice the ! (exclamation point) in the `if` statement. ! means "not". In other words, the `if` statement is true if the assignment statement is not true.

The type of error handling you want to include in your program depends on what you expect to happen in the program. When you're developing the program, you expect some errors to happen. Therefore, during development, you probably want error handling that's more descriptive, such as the third method in the preceding list. For instance, suppose that you're using an account called `root` to access your database and that you make a typo as in the following statements:

```
$host = "localhost";
$user = "rot";
$password = "";
if (!$cxn = mysqli_connect($host,$user,$password))
    {
        $message = mysqli_error($cxn);
        echo "$message";
        die();
    }
```

Because you typed `"rot"` instead of `"root"`, you would see an error message similar to the following one:

```
Access denied for user: 'rot@localhost' (Using password: NO)
```

This error message has the information that you need to figure out what the problem is; it shows your account name with the typo. However, after your program is running and customers are using it, you probably don't want your users to see a technical error message like the preceding one. Instead, you probably want to use the second method with a general statement in the `die` message, such as `The Pet Catalog is not available at the moment. Please try again later.`

Selecting the right database

If you don't select the database with the connect function, you can select the database using the `mysqli_select_db` function. You can also use this function to select a different database at any time in your program. The format is

```
mysqli_select_db($connectionname,"databasename")
       or die ("message");
```

Fill in the following information:

- *connectionname*: The variable that contains the connection information.

- *databasename*: The name of the database.

- *message*: The message that is sent to the browser if the database can't be selected. The selection might fail because the database can't be found, which is usually the result of a typo in the database name.

For instance, you can select the database `PetCatalog` with the following statement:

```
mysqli_select_db($cxn,"PetCatalog")
       or die ("Couldn't select database.");
```

If `mysqli_select_db` is unable to select the database, the program stops running at this point, and the message `Couldn't select database.` is sent to the browser.

For security reasons, it's a good idea to store the database name in a variable and use the variable in the connection statement, as follows:

```
$dbname = "PetCatalog";
mysql_select_db($cxn,$dbname)
       or die ("Couldn't select database.");
```

For more security, you can put the assignment statement for the database name in a separate file in a hidden location — as suggested for the assignment statements for the connection information — so that the database name isn't in the program. I explain how to do this in Chapter 10.

The database stays selected until you select a different database. To select a different database, just use a new `mysqli_select_db` function statement.

Sending SQL queries

After you have an open connection to the MySQL server and PHP knows which database you want to interact with, you send your SQL query. The *query* is a request to the MySQL server to store some data, update some data, or retrieve some data. (See Chapter 4 for more on the SQL language and how to build SQL queries.)

To interact with the database, put your SQL query into a variable and send it to the MySQL server by using the function `mysqli_query`, as in the following example:

```
$query = "SELECT * FROM Pet";
$result = mysqli_query($cxn,$query)
     or    die ("Couldn't execute query.");
```

The query is executed on the currently selected database for the specified connection.

The variable `$result` holds information on the result of executing the query. The information depends on whether or not the query gets information from the database:

> ✔ **For queries that don't get any data:** The variable `$result` contains information on whether the query executed successfully. If it's successful, `$result` is set to `TRUE`; if it's not successful, `$result` is set to `FALSE`. Some queries that don't return data are `INSERT` and `UPDATE`.

> ✔ **For queries that return data:** The variable `$result` contains a result identifier that identifies where the returned data is located, not the returned data itself. Some queries that do return data are `SELECT` and `SHOW`.

Beginning with MySQL 4.1, if you use PHP 5 and the `mysqli` functions, you can send multiple queries to the server at once, separated by semicolons. You use the `mysqli_multiple_query` function for this purpose. However, sending more than one query at once can make your program less secure. Use multiple queries seldom and carefully. See the MySQL online manual for information on how to use multiple queries: `http://us2.php.net/manual/en/mysqli.multi-query.php`.

The use of single and double quotes can be a little confusing when assigning the query string to `$query`. You're actually using quotes on two levels: the quotes needed to assign the string to `$query` and the quotes that are part of the SQL language query itself. The following rules can help you avoid any problems with quotes:

white box testing:
s w QA
needs to
know how
to design
test cases
for different
errors,
the code
show to all
to handle
all cases

✔ Use double quotes at the beginning and end of the string.

✔ Use single quotes before and after variable names.

✔ Use single quotes before and after literal values.

The following are examples of assigning query strings:

```
$query = "SELECT firstName FROM Member";
$query = "SELECT firstName FROM Member WHERE lastName='Smith'";
$query = "UPDATE Member SET lastName='$last_name'";
```

The query string itself does not include a semicolon (;), so don't put a semi-colon inside the final quote. The only semicolon is at the very end; this is the PHP semicolon that ends the statement.

Getting Information from a Database

Getting information from a database is a common task for Web database applications. Here are two common uses for information from the database:

✔ **Use the information to conditionally execute statements.** For instance, you might get the state of residence from the Member Directory and send different messages to members who live in different states.

✔ **Display the information in a Web page.** For instance, you might want to display product information from your database.

To use the database information in a program, you need to put the information in variables. Then you can use the variables in conditional statements, echo statements, or other statements. Getting information from a database is a two-step process:

1. You build a SELECT query and send the query to the database. When the query is executed, the selected data is stored in a temporary location.

2. You move the data from the temporary location into variables and use it in your program.

Sending a SELECT query

You use the SELECT query to get data from the database. SELECT queries are written in the SQL language. (I discuss the SELECT query in detail in Chapter 4.)

To get data from the database, build the SELECT query that you need, storing it in a variable, and then send the query to the database. The following statements select all the information from the Pet table in the PetCatalog database:

```
$query = "SELECT * FROM Pet";
$result = mysqli_query($cxn,$query)
    or    die ("Couldn't execute query.");
```

The mysqli_query function gets the data requested by the SELECT query and stores it in a temporary location. You can think of this data as being stored in a table, similar to a MySQL table, with the information in rows and columns.

The function returns a result identifier that contains the information needed to find the temporary location where the data is stored. In the preceding statements, the result identifier is put into the variable $result. If the function fails (because, for example, the query is incorrect), $result contains false.

The next step after executing the function is to move the data from its temporary location into variables that can be used in the program.

Getting and using the data

You use the mysqli_fetch_assoc function or the mysqli_fetch_row function to get the data from the temporary location. The mysqli_fetch_assoc function returns the data in an associative array; mysqli_fetch_row returns the data in a numeric array. Occasionally, you might need to fetch the data in both an associative and a numeric array, which you can do with mysqli_fetch_array.

The functions get one row of data from the temporary location. The temporary data table might contain only one row of data or, more likely, your SELECT query resulted in more than one row of data. If you need to fetch more than one row of data from the temporary location, you use the mysqli_fetch_assoc or mysqli_fetch_row function in a loop.

Getting one row of data

To move the data from its temporary location and put it into variables that you can use in your program, you use the PHP function mysqli_fetch_assoc or mysql_fetch_row. The general format for these functions is

```
$row = mysqli_fetch_assoc($resultidentifier);
```

This statement gets one row from the data table in the temporary location and puts it in an array variable called $row. *resultidentifier* is the variable that points to the temporary location of the results.

The mysql_fetch_assoc function gets one row of data from the temporary location. In some cases, one row is all you selected. For instance, to check the password entered by a user, you only need to get the user's password from the database and compare it with the password that the user entered. The following statements check a password:

```
$userEntry = "secret";    // password user entered in form
$query = "SELECT password FROM Member
                 WHERE loginName='gsmith'";
$result = mysqli_query($cxn,$query)
      or   die ("Couldn't execute query.");
$row = mysqli_fetch_assoc($result);
if ( $userEntry == $row['password'] )
{
    echo "Login accepted <br />";
    statements that display Members Only Web pages
}
else
{
    echo "Invalid password";
    statements that allow user to try another password
}
```

Note the following points about the preceding statements:

✔ The SELECT query requests only one field (password) from one row (row for gsmith).

✔ The mysqli_fetch_assoc function returns an array called $row with column names as keys.

✔ The if statement uses two equal signs (==) to compare the password that the user typed in ($userEntry) with the password obtained from the database ($row['password']) to see whether they are the same.

✔ If the comparison is true, the passwords match, and the if block (which displays the Members Only Web pages) is executed.

✔ If the comparison is not true, the user did not enter a password that matches the password stored in the database, and the else block is executed. The user sees an error message stating that the password is not correct and is returned to the login Web page.

PHP provides a convenient shortcut for using the variables retrieved with the mysqli_fetch_assoc function. You can use the extract function, which splits the array into variables that have the same name as the key. For instance, you can use the extract function to rewrite the previous statements that test the password. Here's how:

```
$userEntry = "secret"; #password entered in a form
$query = "SELECT password FROM Member
                WHERE loginName='gsmith'";
$result = mysqli_query($cxn,$query)
    or    die ("Couldn't execute query.");
$row = mysqli_fetch_assoc($result);
extract($row);
if ( $userEntry == $password )
{
    echo "Login accepted<br />";
    statements that display Members Only Web pages
}
else
{
    echo "Invalid password<br>";
    statements that allow user to try another password
}
```

The extract function took the information from $row['password'], created
a variable named with the array key (in this case, password) and stored the
information in the new variable called $password.

Using a loop to get all the rows of data

If you selected more than one row of data, use a loop to get all the rows from
the temporary location. The statements in the loop block get one row of data
and process it. The loop repeats until all rows have been retrieved. You can
use a while loop or a for loop to retrieve this information. (while loops
and for loops are explained in Chapter 7.)

The most common way to process the information is to use a while loop as
follows:

```
while($row = mysqli_fetch_assoc($result))
{
    block of statements
}
```

This loop repeats until it has fetched the last row from $result. If you just
want to echo all the data, for example, you would use a loop similar to the
following:

```
while($row = mysqli_fetch_assoc($result))
{
    extract($row);
    echo "$petType: $petName<br />";
}
```

Now, take a look at an example of how to get information for the Pet Catalog
application. Assume the Pet Catalog has a table called Pet with four columns:
petName, petType, petDescription, and price. Table 8-2 shows a sample
set of data in the Pet table.

Table 8-2		Sample Data in Pet Table	
petName	*petType*	*petDescription*	*price*
Unicorn	Horse	Spiral horn centered in forehead	10000
Pegasus	Horse	Flying; wings sprouting from back	15000
Pony	Horse	Very small; half the size of standard horse	500
Asian dragon	Dragon	Serpentine body	30000
Medieval dragon	Dragon	Lizard-like body	30000
Lion	Cat	Large; maned	2000
Gryphon	Cat	Lion body; eagle head; wings	25000

The petDisplay.php program in Listing 8-1 selects all the horses from the Pet table and displays the information in an HTML table in the Web page. The variable $pettype contains information that a user typed into a form.

Listing 8-1: Displaying Items from the Pet Catalog

```php
<?php
/* Program: petDisplay.php
 * Desc:    Displays all pets in selected category.
 */
?>
<html>
<head><title>Pet Catalog</title></head>
<body>
<?php
  $user="catalog";
  $host="localhost";
  $password="";
  $database = "PetCatalog";
  $cxn = mysqli_connect($host,$user,$password,$database)
        or die ("couldn't connect to server");
  $pettype = "horse";   //horse was typed in a form by user
  $query = "SELECT * FROM Pet WHERE petType='$pettype'";
  $result = mysqli_query($cxn,$query)
          or die ("Couldn't execute query.");

  /* Display results in a table */
  $pettype = ucfirst($pettype)."s";
  echo "<h1>$pettype</h1>\n";
  echo "<table cellspacing='15'>\n";
  echo "<tr><td colspan='3'><hr /></td></tr>\n";
  while($row = mysqli_fetch_assoc($result))
```

```
    {
        extract($row);
        $f_price = number_format($price,2);
        echo "<tr>\n
            <td>$petName</td>\n
            <td>$petDescription</td>\n
            <td style='text-align: right'>\$$f_price</td>\n
            </tr>\n";
        echo "<tr><td colspan='3'><hr /></td></tr>\n";
    }
    echo "</table>\n";
?>
</body></html>
```

Figure 8-1 shows the Web page displayed by the program in Listing 8-1. The Web page shows the `Pet` items for the `petType horse`, with the display formatted in an HTML table.

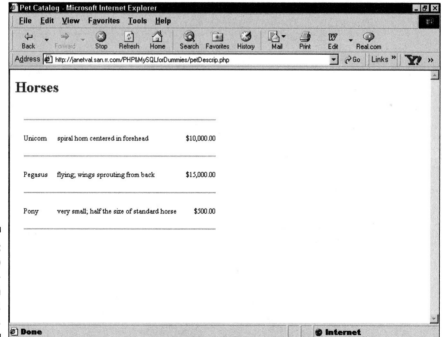

Figure 8-1:
The Web page resulting from petDisplay. php.

The program in Listing 8-1 uses a `while` loop to get all the rows from the temporary location. In some cases, you might need to use a `for` loop. For instance, if you need to use a number in your loop, a `for` loop is more useful than a `while` loop. To use a `for` loop, you need to know how many rows of data were selected. You can find out how many rows are in temporary storage by using the PHP function `mysqli_num_rows`:

```
$nrows = mysqli_num_rows($result);
```

The variable `$nrows` contains the number of rows in the temporary storage location. By using this number, you can build a `for` loop to get all the rows:

```
for($i=0;$i<$nrows;$i++)
{
    $row = mysqli_fetch_assoc($result))
    block of statements;
}
```

For instance, the program in Listing 8-1 displays the `Pet` items of the type horse. Suppose that you want to number each item. Listing 8-2, the `pet DescripFor.php` program, displays a numbered list with a `for` loop.

Listing 8-2: Displaying a Numbered List of Items from the Pet Catalog

```php
<?php
/* Program: petDescripFor.php
 * Desc:    Displays a numbered list of all pets in
 *          selected category.
 */
?>
<html>
<head><title>Pet Catalog</title></head>
<body>
<?php
  $user="catalog";
  $host="localhost";
  $password="";
  $database = "PetCatalog";
  $cxn = mysqli_connect($host,$user,$password,$database)
         or die ("Couldn't connect to server");
  $pettype = "horse";   //horse was typed in a form by user
  $query = "SELECT * FROM Pet WHERE petType='$pettype'";
  $result = mysqli_query($cxn,$query)
            or die ("Couldn't execute query.");
  $nrows = mysqli_num_rows($result);

  /* Display results in a table */
  echo "<h1>Horses</h1>";
  echo "<table cellspacing='15'>";
  echo "<tr><td colspan='4'><hr /></td></tr>";
  for ($i=0;$i<$nrows;$i++)
```

```
   {
      $n = $i + 1;   #add 1 so numbers don't start with 0
      $row = mysqli_fetch_assoc($result);
      extract($row);
      $f_price = number_format($price,2);
       echo "<tr>\n
             <td>$n.</td>\n
             <td>$petName</td>\n
             <td>$petDescription</td>\n
             <td style='text-align: right'>\$$f_price</td>\n
             </tr>\n";
      echo "<tr><td colspan='4'><hr></td></tr>\n";
   }
   echo "</table>\n";
?>
</body></html>
```

Figure 8-2 shows the Web page that results from using the for loop in this program. Notice that a number appears before the listing for each Pet item on this Web page.

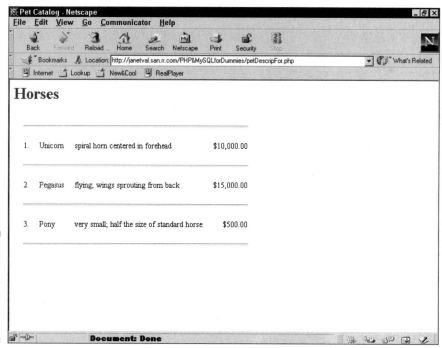

Figure 8-2:
The Web page resulting from petDescrip For.php.

Using functions to get data

In most applications, you get data from the database. Often you get the data in more than one location in your program or more than one program in your application. *Functions* — blocks of statements that perform specified tasks — are designed for such situations. (I explain functions in detail in Chapter 7.)

A function to get data from the database can be really useful. Whenever the program needs to get data, you call the function. Functions not only save you a lot of typing but also make the program easier for you to follow. For example, consider a product catalog, such as the Pet Catalog. You'll need to get information about a specific product many times. You can write a function that gets the data and then use that function whenever you need data.

Listing 8-3 for program getdata.php shows how to use a function to get data. The function in Listing 8-3 will get the information for any single pet in the Pet Catalog. The pet information is put into an array, and the array is returned to the main program. The main program can then use the information any way that it wants. In this case, it echoes the pet information to a Web page.

Listing 8-3: Using a Function to Get Data from a Database

```php
<?php
/* Program: getdata.php
 * Desc:    Gets data from a database using a function
 */
?>
<html>
<head><title>Pet Catalog</title></head>
<body>
<?php

  $petInfo = getPetInfo("Unicorn");        //call function

  $f_price = number_format($petInfo['price'],2);
  echo "<p><b>{$petInfo['petName']}</b><br />\n
       Description: {$petInfo['petDescription']}<br />\n
       Price: \${$petInfo['price']}\n"
?>
</body></html>

<?php
function getPetInfo($petName)
```

```
{
    $user="catalog";
    $host="localhost";
    $password="";
    $dbname = "PetCatalog";
    $cxn = mysqli_connect($host,$user,$password,$dbname)
            or die ("Couldn't connect to server");
    $query = "SELECT * FROM Pet WHERE petName='$petName'";
    $result = mysqli_query($cxn,$query)
            or die ("Couldn't execute query.");
    return mysqli_fetch_assoc($result);
}
?>
```

The Web page displays

Unicorn
```
Description: spiral horn centered in forehead
Price: $10,000.00
```

Note the following about the program in Listing 8-3:

✔ The program is easier to read with the function call than it would be if all the statements in the function were in the main program.

✔ The function call sends the string `"Unicorn"`. In most cases, the function call uses a variable name.

✔ The program creates the variable `$petInfo` to receive the data from the function. `$petInfo` is an array because the information stored in it is an array.

The preceding function is very simple: It returns one row of the results as an array. But functions can be more complex. The preceding section provides a program to get all the pets of a specified type. The program `getPets.php` in Listing 8-4 uses a function for the same purpose. The function returns a multi-dimensional array with the pet data for all the pets of the specified type.

Listing 8-4: Using a Function to Display a Numbered List of Pets

```
<?php
/* Program: getPets.php
 * Desc:     Displays list of items from a database.
 */
?>
```

(continued)

Listing 8-4 *(continued)*

```php
<html>
<head><title>Pet Catalog</title></head>
<body>
<?php
  $type = "Horse";
  $petInfo = getPetsOfType($type);        //call function

  /* Display results in a table */
  echo "<h1>{$type}s</h1>\n";
  echo "<table cellspacing='15'>\n";
  echo "<tr><td colspan='4'><hr /></td></tr>\n";
  for($i=1;$i<=sizeof($petInfo);$i++)
  {
     $f_price = number_format($petInfo[$i]['price'],2);
     echo "<tr>\n
          <td>$i.</td>\n
          <td>{$petInfo[$i]['petName']}</td>\n
          <td>{$petInfo[$i]['petDescription']}</td>\n
          <td style='text-align: right'>\$$f_price</td>\n
          </tr>\n";
     echo "<tr><td colspan='4'><hr /></td></tr>\n";
  }
  echo "</table>\n";
?>
</body></html>

<?php
function getPetsOfType($petType)
{
  $user="catalog";
  $host="localhost";
  $passwd="";
  $cxn = mysqli_connect($host,$user,$passwd,"PetCatalog")
        or die("Couldn't connect to server");
  $query = "SELECT * FROM Pet WHERE petType='$petType'";
  $result = mysqli_query($cxn,$query)
            or die("Couldn't execute query.");

  $j = 1;
  while($row=mysqli_fetch_assoc($result))
  {
    foreach($row as $colname => $value)
    {
       $array_multi[$j][$colname] = $value;
    }
    $j++;
  }
  return $array_multi;
}
?>
```

The program in Listing 8-4 proceeds as follows:

1. It calls the function `getPetsOfType`.

   It passes `"horse"` in a variable `$type` containing the type of pet. It also sets up `$petInfo` to receive the data returned by the function.

2. The function connects to the database and selects the database `PetCatalog`.

3. The function sends a query to get all the rows with `$petType` in the `petType` column.

   `$petType` is passed to the function in the function call. The data is stored in a table in a temporary location. The variable `$result` identifies the location of the temporary table.

4. It sets up a counter.

   `$j` is a counter that is incremented in each loop. It starts at 1 before the loop.

5. It starts a `while` loop.

   The function attempts to get a row from the temporary data table and is successful. If there were no rows to get in the temporary location, the `while` loop would end.

6. It starts a `foreach` loop.

   The loop walks through the row, processing each field.

7. It stores values in a multidimensional array.

   `$array_multi` is a multidimensional array. Its first key is a number, which is set by the counter. Because this is the first time through the `while` loop, the counter — `$j` — is now equal to 1. All the fields in the row are stored in `$array_multi` with the column name as the key. (I explain multidimensional arrays in detail in Chapter 7.)

8. It increments the counter.

   `$j` is incremented by 1.

9. It reaches the end of the `while` loop.

10. It returns to the top of the `while` loop.

11. It repeats Steps 5–10 for every row in the results.

12. It returns `$array_multi` to the main program.

    `$array_multi` contains all the data for all the selected rows.

13. `$petInfo` receives data from the function.

    All the data is passed. Figure 8-3 shows the structure of `$petInfo` after the function has finished executing.

```
petInfo   [1]   [petName]          =  Unicorn
                [petDescription]   =  spiral horn centered in forehead
                [price]            =  10000

          [2]   [petName]          =  Pegasus
                [petDescription]   =  flying; wings sprouting from back
                [price]            =  15000

          [3]   [petName]          =  Pony
                [petDescription]   =  very small; half the size of a standard horse
                [price]            =  500
```

Figure 8-3:
The struc-
ture of the
multidimen-
sional array
$petInfo.

14. The main program sends Pet Descriptions to the browser in an HTML table.

The appropriate data is inserted from the $petInfo array.

The Web page that results from the program in Listing 8-4 is identical to the Web page shown in Figure 8-2, which is produced by a program that does not use a function. Functions do not produce different output. Any program that you can write that includes a function, you can also write without using a function. Functions just make programming easier.

Getting Information from the User

Many applications are designed to ask questions that users answer by typing information. Sometimes the information is stored in a database; sometimes the information is used in conditional statements to deliver an individual Web page. Some of the most common application tasks that require users to answer questions are

- **Online ordering:** Customers need to select products and enter shipping and payment information.
- **Registering:** Many sites require users to provide some information before they receive certain benefits, such as access to special information or downloadable software.
- **Logging in:** Many sites restrict access to their pages. Users must enter an account name and password before they can see the Web pages.
- **Viewing selected information:** Many sites allow users to specify what information they want to see. For instance, an online catalog might allow users to type the name of the product or select a product category that they want to see.

You ask questions by displaying HTML forms. The user answers the questions by typing information into the form or selecting items from a list. The user then clicks a button to submit the form information. When the form is submitted, the information in the form is passed to a second, separate program, which processes the information.

In the next few sections, I don't tell you about the HTML required to display a form; I assume that you already know HTML. (If you don't know HTML or need a refresher, check out *HTML, XHTML, and CSS All-in-One Desk Reference For Dummies* by Andy Harris and Chris McCulloh; Wiley.) What I do tell you is how to use PHP to display HTML forms and to process the information that users type into the form.

Using HTML forms

HTML forms are very important for interactive Web sites. (If you're unfamiliar with HTML forms, you need to read the forms section of an HTML book.) To display a form with PHP, you can do one of the following:

✔ **Use `echo` statements to echo the HTML for a form.** For example:

```php
<?php
   echo "<form action='processform.php'
            method='POST'>\n
      <input type='text' name='fullname' />\n
      <input type='submit' value='Submit Name' />\n
      </form>\n";
?>
```

✔ **Use plain HTML outside the PHP sections.** For a plain static form, there is no reason to include it in a PHP section. For example:

```php
<?php
   statements in PHP section
?>
<form action="processform.php" method="POST">
   <input type="text" name="fullname" />
   <input type="submit" value="Submit Name" />
</form>
<?php
   statements in PHP section
?>
```

Either of these methods produces the form displayed in Figure 8-4.

Joe Customer fills in the HTML form. He clicks the submit button. You now have the information that you wanted — his name. So where is it? How do you get it?

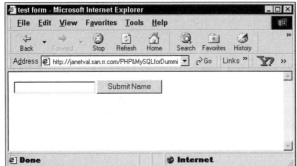

Figure 8-4:
A form
produced
by HTML
statements.

You get the form information by running a program that receives the form information. When the submit button is clicked, PHP automatically runs a program. The `action` parameter in the form tag tells PHP which program to run. For instance, in the preceding program, the parameter `action=processform.php` tells PHP to run the program `processform.php` when the user clicks the submit button. The program `processform.php` can display, store, or otherwise use the form data it receives when the form is submitted.

When the user clicks the submit button, the program specified in the `action` attribute runs, and statements in this program can get the form information from PHP built-in arrays and use the information in PHP statements. The built-in arrays that contain form information are `$_POST`, `$_GET`, and `$_REQUEST`, which are superglobal arrays. When the form uses the `POST` method, the information from the form fields is stored in the `$_POST` array. The `$_GET` array contains the variables passed as part of the URL, including fields passed from a form using the `GET` method. The `$_REQUEST` array contains all the array elements together that are contained in the `$_POST`, `$_GET`, and `$_COOKIES` arrays. Cookies are explained in Chapter 9.

When the form is submitted, the program that runs can get the form information from the appropriate built-in array. In these built-in arrays, each array index is the name of the input field in the form. For instance, if the user typed **Goliath Smith** in the input field shown in Figure 8-4 and clicked the submit button, the program `processform.php` runs and can use an array variable in the following format:

```
$_POST['fullname']
```

Notice that the name typed into the form is available in the `$_POST` array because the form tag specified `method='POST'`. Also, note that the array key is the name given the field in the HTML form with the `name` attribute `name="fullname"`.

The superglobal arrays, including $_POST and $_GET, were introduced in PHP 4.1. Up until that time, form information was passed in old arrays named $HTTP_POST_VARS and $HTTP_GET_VARS. If you're using PHP 4.0 or earlier, you must use the long arrays. Both types of built-in arrays exist up until PHP 5. The long arrays no longer exist in PHP 6. If you're working with some old programs that use the long array names, you need to change the array names from the long names, such as $HTTP_POST_VARS, to the superglobal array names, such as $_POST. In most cases, a search-and-replace in a text editor makes the change with one command per array.

A program that displays all the fields in a form is a useful program for testing a form. You can see what values are passed from the form to be sure that your form is formatted properly and sends the field names and values that you expect. All the fields in a POST type form are displayed by the program in Listing 8-5, named processform.php. When the form shown in Figure 8-4 is submitted, the following program is run.

Listing 8-5: A Script That Displays All the Fields from a Form

```php
<?php
/*  Script name:   processform.php
 *  Description:   Script displays all the information
 *                 passed from a form.
 */
  echo "<html>
        <head><title>Customer Address</title></head>
        <body>";
  foreach ($_POST as $field => $value)
  {
     echo "$field = $value<br />\n";
  }
?>
</body></html>
```

If the user types **Goliath Smith** into the form in Figure 8-4, the following output is displayed:

```
fullname = Goliath Smith
```

The output displays only one line because there is only one field in the form in Figure 8-4.

The program in Listing 8-5 is written to process the form information from any form that uses the POST method. Suppose that you have a slightly more complicated form, such as the program in Listing 8-6, which displays a form with several fields.

Listing 8-6: Displaying a Phone Number Form

```php
<?php
/*  Program name: displayForm
 *  Description:  Script displays a form that asks for
 *                the customer phone number.
 */
$labels = array( "first_name" => "First Name",
                 "middle_name" => "Middle Name",
                 "last_name" => "Last Name",
                 "phone" => "Phone");
?>
<html>
<head>
<title>Customer Phone Number</title>
<style type='text/css'>
<!--
  form { margin: 1.5em 0 0 0; padding: 0; }
  .field { padding-top: .5em; }
  label { font-weight: bold; float: left; width: 20%;
          margin-right: 1em; text-align: right; }
  #submit { margin-left: 35%; padding-top: 1em; }
-->
</style>
</head>

<body>
<h3>Please enter your phone number.</h3>
<form action='processform.php' method='POST'
<?php
  /* Loop that displays the form fields */
  foreach($labels as $field => $label)
  {
    echo "<div class='field'>
            <label for='$field'>$label</label>
              <input type='text' name='$field' id='$field'
                size='65' maxlength='65' /></div>\n";
  }
  echo "<div id='submit'><input type='submit'
                value='Submit Phone Number' />\n";
  echo "</div>\n</form>\n</body>\n</html>";
?>
```

Notice the following in `displayForm.php`, as shown in Listing 8-6:

> ✔ **An array is created that contains the labels used in the form.** The keys
> are the field names. Setting up your fields in an array at the top of the
> program makes it easy to see what fields are displayed in the form and
> to add, remove, or modify fields.

✔ **The script `processform.php` is named as the script that runs when the form is submitted.** The information in the form is sent to `process form.php`, which processes the information.

✔ **The form is formatted with CSS.** If you're not familiar with CSS, check out *HTML, XHTML, and CSS All-in-One Desk Reference For Dummies* by Andy Harris and Chris McCulloh (Wiley).

✔ **The script loops through the `$labels` array with a `foreach` statement.** The HTML code for each field is echoed in the `foreach` block. The appropriate array values are used in the HTML code.

TIP

For security reasons, always include `maxlength` — which defines the number of characters that users are allowed to type into the field — in your HTML statement. Limiting the number of characters helps prevent the bad guys from typing malicious code into your form fields. If the information is stored in a database, set `maxlength` to the same number as the width of the column in the database table.

Figure 8-5 shows the form displayed by the program in Listing 8-6.

Figure 8-5:
A form for entering a customer's phone number.

> 🜲 Customer Phone Number - Mozilla Firefox
> File Edit View Go Bookmarks Tools Help
> ◀ · ▶ · 🜲 🜲 🜲 | http://localhost/P ▾ | 🜲 Go | 🜲
>
> **Please enter your phone number below.**
>
> First Name [   ]
> Middle Name [   ]
> Last Name   [   ]
> Phone   [   ]
>   [Submit Phone Number]
>
> Done

When Goliath Smith fills in the form shown in Figure 8-5 and submits it, the program `processform.php` runs and produces the following output:

```
first_name = Goliath
middle_name =
last_name = Smith
phone = 555-5555
```

In `processform.php`, all elements of the `$_POST` built-in array are displayed because both of the forms shown in this section used the POST method, as do most forms.

Making forms dynamic

PHP brings new capabilities to HTML forms. Because you can use variables in PHP forms, your forms can now be dynamic. Here are the major capabilities that PHP brings to forms:

✔ Using variables to display information in input text fields
✔ Using variables to build dynamic lists for users to select from
✔ Using variables to build dynamic lists of radio buttons
✔ Using variables to build dynamic lists of check boxes

Displaying dynamic information in form fields

When you display a form on a Web page, you can put information into the fields rather than just displaying a blank field. For example, if most of your customers live in the United States, you might automatically enter **US** in the country field when you ask customers for their address. If the customer does indeed live in the United States, you've saved the customer some typing. And if the customer doesn't live in the United States, he or she can just replace *US* with the appropriate country. Also, the text automatically entered into the field doesn't have any typos — well, unless you included some yourself.

To display a text field that contains information, you use the following format for the input field HTML statements:

```
<input type="text" name="country" value="US" />
```

Using PHP, you can use a variable to display this information with either of the following statements:

```
<input type="text" name="country"
       value="<?php echo $country ?>" />
```

```
echo "<input type='text' name='country'
       value='$country' />";
```

The first example creates an input field in an HTML section, using a short PHP section for the value only. The second example creates an input field by using an `echo` statement inside a PHP section. If you're using a long form with only an occasional variable, using the first format is more efficient. If your form uses many variables, it's more efficient to use the second format.

If you have user information stored in a database, you might want to display the information from the database in the form fields. For instance, you might show the information to the user so that he or she can make any needed changes. Or you might display the shipping address for the customer's last online order so that he or she doesn't need to retype the address. Listing 8-7 shows the program `displayAddress.php`, which displays a form with information from the database. This form is similar to the form shown in Figure 8-5, except that this form has information in it (retrieved from the database) and the fields in the form in Figure 8-5 are blank.

Listing 8-7: Displaying an HTML Form with Information

```
<?php
/*  Program name: displayAddress
 *  Description:   Script displays a form with address
 *                 information obtained from the database.
 */

  $labels = array( "firstName"=>"First Name:",
                   "lastName"=>"Last Name:",
                   "street"=>"Street Address:",
                   "city"=>"City:",
                   "state"=>"State:",
                   "zip"=>"Zipcode:");
  $user="admin";
  $host="localhost";
  $password="";
  $database = "MemberDirectory";
  $loginName = "gsmith";      // user login name

  $cxn = mysqli_connect($host,$user,$password,$database)
         or die ("couldn't connect to server");
  $query = "SELECT * FROM Member
                    WHERE loginName='$loginName'";
  $result = mysqli_query($cxn,$query)
            or die ("Couldn't execute query.");
  $row = mysqli_fetch_assoc($result);
?>

<html>
<head>
<title>Customer Phone Number</title>
<style type='text/css'>
<!--
  form { margin: 1.5em 0 0 0; padding: 0; }
  .field { padding-top: .5em; }
  label { font-weight: bold; float: left; width: 20%;
          margin-right: 1em; text-align: right; }
  #submit { margin-left: 35%; padding-top: 1em; }
-->
</style>
</head>
```

(continued)

Listing 8-7 *(continued)*

```php
<body>
<?php
  echo "<div style='text-align: center'>
        <h1>Address for $loginName</h1>\n";
  echo "<p style='font-size: large; font-weight: bold'>
          Please check the information below and change
          any information that is incorrect.</p>
          <hr /></div>\n";
  echo "<form action='processAddress.php' method='POST'>";
  foreach($labels as $field => $label)
  {
    echo "<div class='field'>
          <label for='$field'>$label</label>
            <input type='text' name='$field' id='$field'
            value='$row[$field]' size='65'
            maxlength='65' /></div>\n";
  }
  echo "<div id='submit'><input type='submit'
          value='Submit Address' />\n";
  echo "</div>\n</form>\n</body>\n</html>";
?>
```

Notice the following in the program in Listing 8-7:

- ✔ **The form statement transfers the action to the program process Address.php.** This program processes the information in the form and updates the database with any information that the user changed. This is a program that you write yourself. Checking data in a form and saving information in the database are discussed later in this chapter in the sections "Checking the information" and "Putting Information into a Database," respectively.

- ✔ **Each input field in the form is given a name.** The information in the input field is stored in a variable that has the same name as the input field.

- ✔ **The program gives the field names in the form the same names as the columns in the database.** This simplifies moving information between the database and the form, so you don't have to transfer information from one variable to another.

- ✔ **The values from the database are displayed in the form fields with the value parameter in the input field statement.** The value parameter displays the appropriate value from the array $row, which contains data from the database.

For security reasons, always include maxlength in your HTML statement. maxlength defines the number of characters that a user is allowed to type into the field. If the information is going to be stored in a database, set maxlength to the same number as the width of the column in the database table.

Figure 8-6 shows the Web page resulting from the program in Listing 8-7. The information in the form is the information stored in the database.

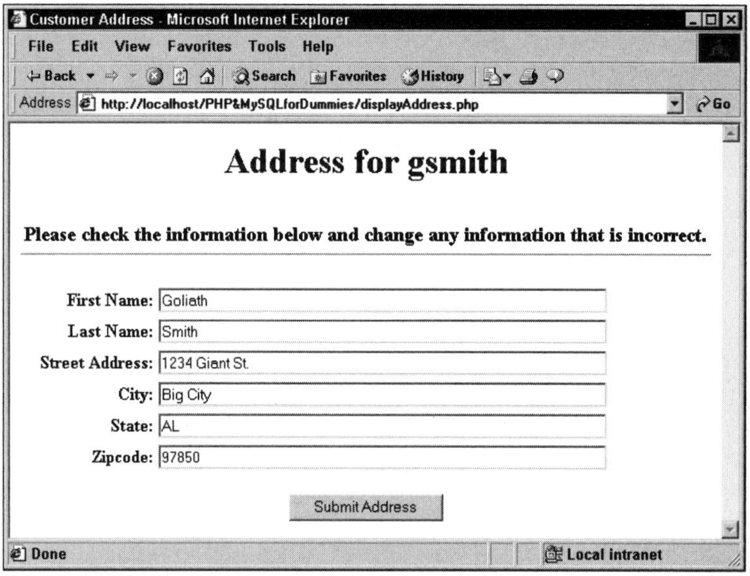

Figure 8-6:
A form showing the user's address.

Building selection lists

One type of field that you can use in an HTML form is a *selection list.* Instead of typing into a field, your users select from a list. For instance, in a product catalog, you might provide a list of categories from which users select what they want to view. Or the form for users' addresses might include a list of states that users can select. Or users might enter a date by selecting a month, day, and year from a list.

Use selection lists whenever feasible. When the user selects an item from a list, you can be sure that the item is accurate, with no misspellings, odd characters, or other problems introduced by users' typing errors.

An HTML selection list for the categories in the Pet Catalog is formatted as follows:

```
<form action="processform.php" method="POST">
  <select name="petType">
    <option value="horse">horse</option>
    <option value="cat" selected="selected">cat</option>
    <option value="dragon">dragon</option>
  </select>
  <input type="submit" value="Select Type of Pet" />
</form>
```

Figure 8-7 shows the selection list that these HTML statements produce. Notice that *cat* is the choice that is selected when the field is first displayed. You determine this default selection by including `selected="selected"` in the option tag.

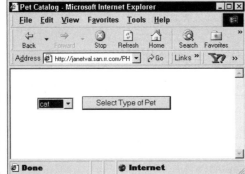

Figure 8-7:
A selection field for the Pet Catalog.

When the user clicks the arrow on the select drop-down list box, the entire list drops down, as shown in Figure 8-8, and the user can select any item in the list. Notice that *cat* is selected until the user selects a different item.

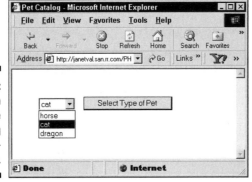

Figure 8-8:
A selection field for the Pet Catalog with a drop-down list.

When using PHP, your options can be variables. This capability allows you to build dynamic selection lists. For instance, you must maintain the static list of pet categories shown in the preceding example. If you add a new pet category, you must add an `option` tag manually. However, with PHP variables, you can build the list dynamically from the categories in the database. When you add a new category to the database, the new category is automatically added to your selection list without your having to change the PHP program. Listing 8-8 for the program `buildSelect.php` builds a selection list of pet categories from the database.

Listing 8-8: Building a Selection List

```php
<?php
/*  Program name: buildSelect.php
 *  Description:   Program builds a selection list
 *                 from the database.
 */
  $user="admin";
  $host="localhost";
  $password="";
  $database = "PetCatalog";
  $cxn = mysqli_connect($host,$user,$password,$database)
        or die ("couldn't connect to server");
  $query = "SELECT DISTINCT petType FROM Pet ORDER BY petType";
  $result = mysqli_query($cxn,$query)
            or die ("Couldn't execute query.");
?>
<html>
<head><title>Pet Types</title></head>

<body>
<form action='processform.php' method='POST'>
  <select name='petType'>
<?php
   while($row = mysqli_fetch_assoc($result))
   {
     extract($row);
     echo "<option value='$petType'>$petType</option>\n";
   }
?>
  </select>
  <input type='submit' value='Select Type of Pet' />
</form></body></html>
```

Notice the following in the program in Listing 8-8:

- ✔ **Using DISTINCT in the query:** DISTINCT causes the query to get each pet type only once. Without DISTINCT, the query would return each pet type several times if it appeared several times in the database.

- ✔ **Using ORDER BY in the query:** The pet types are sorted alphabetically.

- ✔ **echo statements before the loop:** The form and select tags are echoed before the while loop starts because they are echoed only once.

- ✔ **echo statements in the loop:** The option tags are echoed in the loop — one for each pet type in the database. No item is marked as selected, so the first item in the list is selected automatically.

- ✔ **echo statements after the loop:** The end form and select tags are echoed after the loop because they are echoed only once.

The selection list produced by this program is initially the same as the selection list shown in Figure 8-7, with cat selected. However, cat is selected in this program because it's the first item in the list — not because it's specifically selected as it is in the HTML tags that produce Figure 8-7. The drop-down list produced by this program is in alphabetical order, as shown in Figure 8-9.

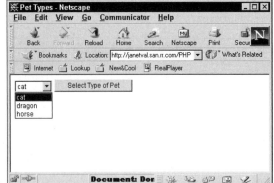

Figure 8-9:
A selection field for the Pet Catalog produced by the program buildSelect. php.

You can use PHP variables also to set up which option is selected when the selection box is displayed. For instance, suppose that you want the user to select a date from month, day, and year selection lists. You believe that most people will select today's date, so you want today's date to be selected by default when the box is displayed. Listing 8-9 shows the program date Select.php, which displays a form for selecting a date and selects today's date automatically.

Listing 8-9: Building a Date Selection List

```php
<?php
/*  Program name: dateSelect.php
 *  Description:   Program displays a selection list that
 *                 customers can use to select a date.
 */
$monthName = array(1 => "January", "February", "March",
                    . "April", "May", "June", "July",
                    . "August", "September", "October",
                    . "November", "December");
$today = time();                    //stores today's date
$f_today = date("M-d-Y",$today);    //formats today's date

echo "<html>
      <head><title>Select a date</title></head>
      <body>
      <div style = 'text-align: center'>\n";
```

```php
/* display today's date */
echo "<h3>Today is $f_today</h3><hr />\n";

/* create form containing date selection list */
echo "<form action='processform.php' method='POST'>\n";

/* build selection list for the month */
$todayMO = date("n",$today);   //get the month from $today
echo "<select name='dateMO'>\n";
for($n=1;$n<=12;$n++)
{
  echo "<option value=$n\n";
  if($todayMO == $n)
  {
    echo " selected='selected'";
  }
  echo " > $monthName[$n]\n";
}
echo "</select>\n";

/* build selection list for the day */
$todayDay= date("d",$today);     //get the day from $today
echo "<select name='dateDay'>\n";
for($n=1;$n<=31;$n++)
{
  echo " <option value=$n";
  if($todayDay == $n )
  {
    echo " selected='selected'";
  }
  echo " > $n\n";
}
echo "</select>\n";

/* build selection list for the year */
$startYr = date("Y", $today);  //get the year from $today
echo "<select name='dateYr'>\n";
for($n=$startYr;$n<=$startYr+3;$n++)
{
  echo " <option value=$n";
  if($startYr == $n )
  {
    echo " selected='selected'";
  }
  echo " > $n\n";
}
echo "</select>\n";
?>
</form></body></html>
```

The Web page produced by the program in Listing 8-9 is shown in Figure 8-10. The date appears above the form so that you can see that the select list shows the correct date. The selection list for the month shows all 12 months when it drops down. The selection list for the day shows 31 days when it drops down. The selection list for year shows four years.

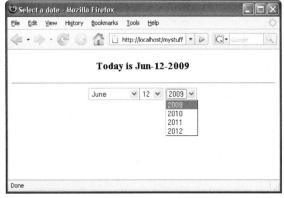

Figure 8-10:
A selection field for the date with today's date selected.

The program in Listing 8-9 produces the Web page in Figure 8-10 by following these steps:

1. Creates an array containing the names of the months.

   The keys for the array are the numbers. The first month, January, starts with the key 1 so that the keys of the array match the numbers of the months.

2. Creates variables containing the current date.

   $today contains the date in a system format and is used in the form. $f-today is a formatted date that is used to display the date in the Web page.

3. Displays the current date at the top of the Web page.

   The current date is displayed so you can compare it with the selected options in the drop-down lists.

4. Builds the selection field for the month:

   i. Creates a variable containing today's month.

   ii. Echoes the select tag, which should be echoed only once.

   iii. Starts a for loop that repeats 12 times.

      iv. Inside the loop, echoes the `option` tag by using the first value from the `$monthName` array.

      v. If the number of the month being processed is equal to the number of the current month, adds the selected attribute to the `option` tag.

      vi. Repeats the loop 11 more times.

      vii. Echoes the closing `select` tag for the selection field, which should be echoed only once.

5. Builds the selection field for the day.

   Uses the procedure described in Step 4 for the month. However, only numbers are used for this selection list. The loop repeats 31 times.

6. Builds the selection field for the year:

      i. Creates the variable `$startYr`, containing today's year.

      ii. Echoes the `select` tag, which should be echoed only once.

      iii. Starts a `for` loop. The starting value for the loop is `$startYr`. The ending value for the loop is `$startYr+3`.

      iv. Inside the loop, echoes the `option` tag, using the starting value of the `for` loop, which is today's year.

      v. If the number of the year being processed is equal to the number of the current year, adds the selected attribute to the option tag.

      vi. Repeats the loop until the ending value equals `$startYr+3`.

      vii. Echoes the closing `select` tag for the selection field, which should be echoed only once.

7. Echoes the ending tag for the form.

Building lists of radio buttons

You might want to use radio buttons instead of selection lists. For instance, you can display a list of radio buttons for your Pet Catalog and have users select the button for the pet category that they're interested in.

The format for radio buttons in a form is

```
<input type="radio" name="name" value="value" />
```

You can build a dynamic list of radio buttons representing all the pet types in your database in the same manner that you build a dynamic selection list in the preceding section. Listing 8-10 shows the program `buildRadio.php`, which creates a list of radio buttons based on pet types.

Listing 8-10: Building a List of Radio Buttons

```php
<?php
/*  Program name: buildRadio.php
 *  Description:   Program displays a list of radio
 *                 buttons from database info.
 */
$user="catalog";
$host="localhost";
$password="";
$database = "PetCatalog";
$cxn = mysqli_connect($host,$user,$password,$database)
       or die ("Couldn't connect to server");
$query = "SELECT DISTINCT petType FROM Pet
               ORDER BY petType";
$result = mysqli_query($cxn,$query)
          or die ("Couldn't execute query.");
?>
<html>
<head><title>Pet Types</title></head>
<body>
<div style='margin-left: .5in; margin-top: .5in'>
  <p style='font-weight: bold'>
     Which type of pet are you interested in?</p>
  <p>Please choose one type of pet from the
     following list:</p>
<form action='processform.php' method='POST'>
<?php
 while($row = mysqli_fetch_assoc($result))
 {
     extract($row);
     echo "<input type='radio' name='interest'
                   value='$petType' />$petType<br />\n";
 }
?>
<p><input type='submit' value='Select Type of Pet' /></p>
</form></div></body></html>
```

This program is similar to the program in Listing 8-9. The Web page produced by this program is shown in Figure 8-11.

Building lists of check boxes

You might want to use check boxes in your form. Check boxes are different from selection lists and radio buttons because they allow users to select more than one option. For instance, if you display a list of pet categories with check boxes, a user can select two or three or more pet categories. The program buildCheckbox.php in Listing 8-11 creates a list of check boxes.

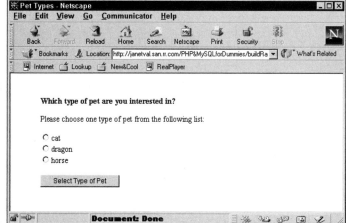

Figure 8-11:
A list of
radio
buttons
produced by
the program
in build
Radio.php.

Listing 8-11: Building a List of Check Boxes

```php
<?php
/*  Program name: buildCheckbox.php
 *  Description:  Program displays a list of
 *               check boxes from database info.
 */
$user="catalog";
$host="localhost";
$password="";
$database = "PetCatalog";
$cxn = mysqli_connect($host,$user,$password,$database)
        or die ("couldn't connect to server");
$query = "SELECT DISTINCT petType FROM Pet
                ORDER BY petType";
$result = mysqli_query($cxn,$query)
        or die ("Couldn't execute query.");
?>

<html>
<head><title>Pet Types</title></head>
<body>
<div style='margin-left: .5in; margin-top: .5in'>
  <p style='font-weight: bold'>
     Which type of pet are you interested in?</p>
  <p>Choose as many types of pets as you want:</p>
  <form action='processform.php' method='POST'>
<?php
   while($row = mysqli_fetch_assoc($result))
   {
```

(continued)

Listing 8-11 *(continued)*

```
        extract($row);
        echo "<input type='checkbox'
                    name='interest[$petType]'
                    value='$petType' />$petType<br />\n";
    }
    echo "<p><input type='submit'
                    value='Select Type of Pet' />\n";
?>
</form></div></body></html>
```

This program is similar to the program in Listing 8-10, which builds a list of radio buttons. However, notice that the input field uses an array $interest as the name for the field. This is because more than one check box can be selected. This program creates an element in the array with a key/value pair for each check box that's selected. For instance, if the user selects both *horse* and *dragon,* the following array is created:

```
$interest[horse]=horse
$interest[dragon]=dragon
```

The program that processes the form has the selections available in the POST array, as follows:

```
$_POST['interest']['horse']
$_POST['interest']['dragon']
```

Figure 8-12 shows the Web page produced by buildCheckbox.php.

Figure 8-12:
A list of
check boxes
produced
by the
program in
buildCheck
box.php.

Using the information from the form

As I discuss earlier in this section, Joe Customer fills in an HTML form, selecting from lists and typing information into text fields. He clicks the submit button. In the `form` tag, you tell PHP which program to run when the submit button is clicked. You do this by including `action="programname"` in the `form` tag. For instance, in most of the example listings in this chapter, I use `action="processform.php"`. When the user clicks the submit button, the program runs and receives the information from the form. Handling form information is one of PHP's best features. You don't need to worry about the form data — just get it from one of the built-in arrays and use it.

The form data is available in the processing program in arrays, such as `$_POST` or `$_GET`. The key for the array element is the name of the input field in the form. For instance, if you echo the following field in your form

```
echo "<input type='text' name='firstName' />";
```

the processing program can use the variable `$_POST[firstName]`, which contains the text that the user typed into the field. The information that the user selects from selection drop-down lists or radio buttons is similarly available for use. For instance, if your form includes the following list of radio buttons

```
echo "<input type='radio' name='interest'
         value='dog' />dog\n";
echo "<input type='radio' name='interest'
         value='cat' />cat\n";
```

you can access the variable `$_POST[interest]`, which contains either `dog` or `cat`, depending on what the user selected.

You handle check boxes in a slightly different way because the user can select more than one check box. As shown earlier in Listing 8-11, the data from a list of check boxes can be stored in an array so that all the check boxes are available. For instance, if your form includes the following list of check boxes

```
echo "<input type='checkbox' name='interest[dog]'
         value='dog' />dog\n";
echo "<input type='checkbox' name='interest[cat]'
         value='cat' />cat\n";
```

you can access the data by using the multidimensional variable `$_POST[interest]`, which contains the following:

```
$_POST[interest][dog] = dog
$_POST[interest][cat] = cat
```

In some cases, you might want to access all the fields in the form. Perhaps you want to check them all to make sure that the user didn't leave any fields blank. As shown in the program processform.php, earlier in this chapter (see Listing 8-5), you can use foreach to walk through the $_POST or $_GET built-in array. Most of the sample programs and statements in this book use the POST method. The keys are the field names. See the sidebar "Post versus get" for more on the two methods.

For instance, suppose your program includes the following statements to display a form:

```
echo "<form action='processform.php' method='POST'>\n";
echo "<input type='text' name='lname'
        value='Smith' /><br />\n";
echo "<input type='radio' name='interest'
        value='dog' />dog\n";
echo "<input type='radio' name='interest'
        value='cat' />cat\n";
echo "<input type='hidden' name='hidvar' value='3' />\n";
echo "<br />
      <input type='submit' value='Select Type of Pet' />
      </form>\n";
```

The program processform.php contains the following statements, which lists all the variables received from the form:

```
foreach($_POST as $field => $value)
{
    echo "$field, $value<br />";
}
```

The output from the foreach loop is

```
lname, Smith
interest, dog
hidvar, 3
```

The output shows three variables with these three values for the following reasons:

- ✔ **The user didn't change the text in the text field.** The value "Smith" that the program displayed is still the text in the text field.

- ✔ **The user selected the radio button for dog.** The user can select only one radio button.

- ✔ **The program passed a hidden field named hidvar.** The program sets the value for hidden fields. The user can't affect the hidden fields.

Post versus get

You use one of two methods to submit form information. The methods pass the form data differently and have different advantages and disadvantages.

✔ **get method:** The form data is passed by adding it to the URL that calls the form-processing program. For instance, the URL might look like this:

```
processform.php?
lname=Smith&
fname=Goliath
```

The advantages of this method are simplicity and speed. The disadvantages are that less data can be passed and that the information is displayed in the browser,

which can be a security problem in some situations.

✔ **post method:** The form data is passed as a package in a separate communication with the processing program. The advantages of this method are unlimited information passing and security of the data. The disadvantages are the additional overhead and slower speed.

In PHP programs, the get and post methods are equally easy to use. Therefore, when using PHP, it's almost always better to use the post method because you have the advantages of the post method (unlimited data passing, better security) without its main disadvantage (more difficult to use).

Checking the information

Joe Customer fills in an HTML form, selecting from lists and typing information into text fields. He clicks the submit button. You now have all the information that you wanted. Well, maybe. Joe might have typed information that contains a typo. Or he might have typed nonsense. Or he might even have typed malicious information that can cause problems for you or other people using your Web site. Before you use Joe's information or store it in your database, you want to check it to make sure it's the information you asked for. Checking the data is *validating* the data.

Validating the data includes the following:

✔ **Checking for empty fields:** You can require users to enter information in a field. If the field is blank, the user is told that the information is required, and the form is displayed again so the user can type the missing information.

✔ **Checking the format of the information:** You can check the information to see that it is in the correct format. For instance, *ab3&*xx* is clearly not a valid zip code.

Checking for empty fields

When you create a form, you can decide which fields are required and which are optional. Your decision is implemented in the PHP program. You check the fields that require information. If a required field is blank, you send a message to the user, indicating that the field is required, and you then re-display the form.

The general procedure to check for empty fields is

```
if(empty($last_name))
{
    echo "You did not enter your last name.
          Last name is required.<br />\n";
    display the form;
    exit();
}
echo "<p>Welcome to the Members Only club.
      You may select from the menu below.<br /></p>\n";
display the menu;
```

Notice the `exit` statement, which ends the `if` block. Without the `exit` statement, the program would continue to the statements after the `if` statement. In other words, without the `exit` statement, the program would display the form and then continue to echo the welcome statement and the menu as well.

In many cases, you want to check all the fields in the form. You can do this by looping through the array `$_POST`. The following statements check the array for any empty fields:

```
foreach($_POST as $value)
{
    if(empty($value))
    {
      echo "You have not filled in all the fields<br />\n";
      display the form;
      exit();
    }
}
echo "Welcome";
```

When you redisplay the Web form, make sure that it contains the information that the user already typed. If users have to retype correct information, they are likely to get frustrated and leave your Web site.

In some cases, you might require the user to fill in most but not all fields. For instance, you might request a fax number in the form or provide a field for a middle name, but you don't really mean to restrict registration on your Web site to users with middle names and faxes. In this case, you can make an exception for fields that are not required, as follows:

```
foreach($_POST as $field => $value)
{
  if( $field != "fax" and $field != "middle_name" )
  {
    if(empty($value))
    {
      echo "A required field is empty.<br />\n";
      display the form;
      exit();
    }
  }
}
echo "Welcome";
```

Notice that the outside `if` conditional statement is true only if the field is not the fax field and is not the middle name field. For those two fields, the program doesn't reach the inside `if` statement, which checks for blank fields.

In most cases, the program should create two arrays: one that contains the names of the fields that are inappropriately blank and one that contains the data that is correct, so you can display or store it. The need for an array of correct data becomes clearer later in this section, when I discuss checking the format of data and cleaning data.

In some cases, you might want to tell the user exactly which fields need to be filled in. The `checkBlank.php` program in Listing 8-12 processes the form produced by the program `displayForm`, shown in Listing 8-6, which has four fields: `first_name`, `middle_name`, `last_name`, and `phone`. All the fields are required except `middle_name`.

To use the program in Listing 8-12, first edit the `displayForm` program, shown in Listing 8-6, so that `checkBlank.php` is shown in the `action` attribute in the `form` tag. Replace `processform.php` with `checkBlank.php`, as follows:

```
<form action='checkBlank.php' method='POST'>
```

Then run the `displayForm.php` program, fill in the form, and click the submit button, which runs the `checkBlank.php` program.

Listing 8-12: Checking for Blank Fields

```
<?php
/*  Program name: checkBlank.php
 *  Description:  Program checks all the form fields for
 *               blank fields.
 */
?>
```

(continued)

Listing 8-12 *(continued)*

```html
<html>
<head>
<title>Customer Phone Number</title>
<style type='text/css'>
<!--
   form { margin: 1.5em 0 0 0; padding: 0; }
   .field { padding-top: .5em; }
   label { font-weight: bold; float: left; width: 20%;
           margin-right: 1em; text-align: right; }
   #submit { margin-left: 35%; padding-top: 1em; }
-->
</style>
</head>

<body>
<?php
   /* set up array with all the fields */
   $labels = array( "first_name" => "First Name",
                    "middle_name" => "Middle Name",
                    "last_name" => "Last Name",
                    "phone" => "Phone");
   /* check each field except middle name for
      blank fields */
   foreach($_POST as $field => $value)
   {
     if($field != "middle_name")
     {
       if(empty($value))
       {
          $blank_array[] = $field;
       }
     }
   }
   /* if any fields were blank, display error message and
      redisplay form */
   if(@sizeof($blank_array) > 0) //blank fields are found
   {
     echo "<p><b>You didn't fill in one or more required
              fields. You must enter:</b><br />\n";
     /* display list of missing information */
     foreach($blank_array as $value)
     {
       echo "   {$labels[$value]}<br />\n";
     }
     echo "</p>";
     /* redisplay form */
     echo "<form action='$_SERVER[PHP_SELF]'
              method='POST'>\n";
     foreach($labels as $field => $label)
     {
```

```
        $good_data[$field]=strip_tags(trim($_POST[$field]));
        echo "<div class='field'>
            <label for='$field'>$label</label>
                <input type='text' name='$field'
                        id='$field' size='65'
                        maxlength='65'
                        value='$good_data[$field]' />\n
            </div>\n";
    }
    echo "<div id='submit'><input type='submit'
                value='Submit Phone Number' />\n";
    echo "</div>\n</form>\n</body>\n</html>";
    exit();
    }
    echo "All required fields contain information";
?>
```

To check for blanks, the program does the following:

1. Sets up an array of field labels.

   These labels are used as labels in the form to display the list of missing information and to display the form.

2. Loops through all the variables passed from the form, checking for blanks.

   The variables are in the array $_POST. The field middle_name is not checked for blanks because it is not a required field. Any blank fields are added to an array of blank fields, $blank_array.

3. Checks whether any blank fields were found.

   Checks the number of items in $blank_array.

4. If zero blank fields were found, jumps to the message; all required fields contain information.

5. If one or more blank fields were found:

   i. Displays an error message. This message explains to the user that some required information is missing.

   ii. Displays a list of missing information. Loops through $blank_array and displays the label(s).

   iii. Creates an array of good data. The data is cleaned so it can be safely displayed in the form.

   iv. Redisplays the form. Because the form includes variable names in the value attribute, the information that the user previously entered is retrieved from $good_data and displayed.

   v. Exits. Stops after the form displays. The user must click the submit button to continue.

Remember, programs that process forms use the information from the form. If you run them by themselves, they don't have any information passed from the form and don't run correctly. These programs are intended to run when the user clicks the submit button for a form.

Don't forget the `exit` statement. Without the `exit` statement, the program would continue and would display the welcome message after displaying the form.

Figure 8-13 shows the Web page that results if the user didn't enter a first or a middle name. Notice that the list of missing information doesn't include Middle Name because Middle Name is not required. Also, notice that the information the user originally typed into the form is still displayed in the form fields.

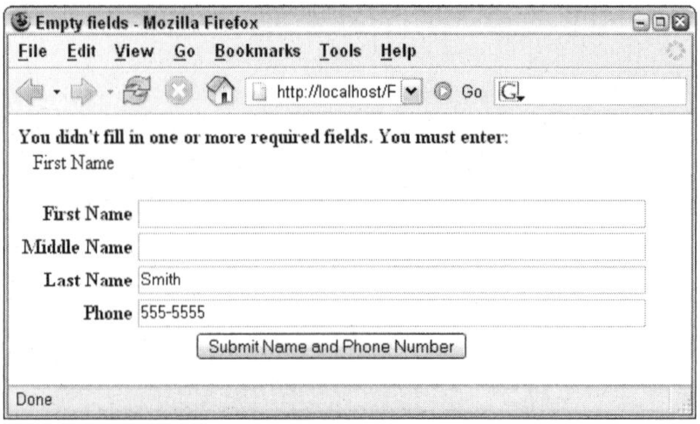

Figure 8-13:
The result of process-ing a form with missing information.

Checking the format of the information

Whenever users must type information in a form, you can expect a certain number of typos. You can detect some of these errors when the form is sub-mitted, point out the error(s) to the user, and then request that he or she retype the information. For instance, if the user types **8899776** in the zip code field, you know this is not correct. This information is too long to be a zip code and too short to be a zip+4 code.

You also need to protect yourself from malicious users — users who might want to damage your Web site or your database or steal information from you or your users. You don't want users to enter HTML tags into a form field — something that might have unexpected results when sent to a browser. A par-ticularly dangerous tag would be a script tag that allows a user to enter a program into a form field.

If you check each field for its expected format, you can catch typos and prevent most malicious content. However, checking information is a balancing act. You want to catch as much incorrect data as possible, but you don't want to block any legitimate information. For instance, when you check a phone number, you might limit it to numbers. The problem with this check is that it would screen out legitimate phone numbers in the form 555-5555 or (888) 555-5555. So you also need to allow hyphens (-), parentheses ( ), and spaces. You might limit the field to a length of 14 characters, including parentheses, spaces, and hyphens, but this screens out overseas numbers or numbers that include an extension. The bottom line: You need to think carefully about what information you want to accept or screen out for any field.

You can check field information by using *regular expressions,* which are patterns. You compare the information in the field against the pattern to see whether it matches. If it doesn't match, the information in the field is incorrect, and the user must type it over. (See Chapter 6 for more on regular expressions.)

In general, these are the statements that you use to check fields:

```
if(!preg_match("pattern",$variablename) )
{
    echo error message;
    redisplay form;
    exit();
}
echo "Welcome";
```

Notice that the condition in the if statement is negative. That is, the ! (exclamation mark) means "not". So, the if statement actually says this: If the variable does *not* match the pattern, execute the if block.

For example, suppose that you want to check an input field that contains the user's last name. You can expect names to contain letters, not numbers, and possibly apostrophe and hyphen characters (as in *O'Hara* and *Smith-Jones*) and also spaces (as in *Van Dyke*). Also, it's difficult to imagine a name longer than 50 characters. Thus, you can use the following statements to check a name:

```
if(!preg_match("/^[A-Za-z' -]{1,50}$/",$last_name)
{
    echo error message;
    redisplay form;
    exit();
}
echo "Welcome";
```

WARNING!

If you want to list a hyphen (–) as part of a set of allowable characters that are surrounded by square brackets ([ ]), you must list the hyphen at the beginning or at the end of the list. Otherwise, if you put it between two characters, the program interprets it as the range between the two characters, such as *A–Z*.

You also need to check multiple-choice fields. Although multiple choice prevents honest users from entering mistakes, it doesn't prevent clever users with malicious intentions from entering unexpected data into the fields. You can check multiple-choice fields for acceptable output with the following type of `regex`:

```
if(!preg_match("/(male|female)/",$gender)
```

If the field contains anything except the value `male` or the value `female`, the `if` block executes.

In the preceding section, you find out how to check every form field to ensure that it isn't blank. In addition, you probably also want to check all the fields that have data to be sure the data is in an acceptable format. You can check the format by making a few simple changes to the program shown earlier in Listing 8-12. Listing 8-13 shows the modified program, called `checkAll.php`.

The program in Listing 8-13, like the program in Listing 8-12, processes data submitted from the form produced by the `displayForm` program in Listing 8-6. To use the program in Listing 8-13, first edit the `displayForm` program, shown in Listing 8-6, so that `checkAll.php` is shown in the `action` attribute in the form tag. Replace `processform.php` with `checkAll.php`, as follows:

```
<form action='checkAll.php' method='POST'>
```

Then run the `displayForm.php` program, fill in the form, and click the submit button, which runs the `checkAll.php` program.

Listing 8-13: Checking All the Data in Form Fields

```
<?php
/*  Program name: checkAll.php*  Description:   Program
 *               checks all the form fields for
 *               blank fields and incorrect format.
 */
?>
<html>
<head>
<title>Customer Phone Number</title>
<style type='text/css'>
<!--
```

```
  form { margin: 1.5em 0 0 0; padding: 0; }
  .field { padding-top: .5em; }
  label { font-weight: bold; float: left; width: 20%;
          margin-right: 1em; text-align: right; }
  #submit { margin-left: 35%; padding-top: 1em; }
-->
</style>
</head>
<body>
<?php
  /* set up array containing all the fields */
  $labels = array ( "first_name" => "First Name",
                    "middle_name" => "Middle Name",
                    "last_name" => "Last Name",
                    "phone" => "Phone");
  foreach ($_POST as $field => $value)
  {
    /* check each field except middle name for blank
       fields */
    if(empty($value))
    {
       if($field != "middle_name")
       {
           $blank_array[] = $field;
       }
    }
    /* check names for invalid formats. */
    elseif($field == "first_name" or $field ==
           "middle_name" or $field == "last_name" )
    {
        if(!preg_match("/^[A-Za-z' -]{1,50}$/",$_
           POST[$field]) )
        {
            $bad_format[] = $field;
        }
    }
    /* check phone for invalid format. */
    elseif($field == "phone")
    {
      if(!preg_match("/^[0-9]( -]{7,20}
         (([xX]|(ext)|(ex))?[ -]?[0-9]{1,7})?$/",$value))
      {
            $bad_format[] = $field;
      }
    }
  }
  /* if any fields are not okay, display error message
     and form */
  if(@sizeof($blank_array) >0 or @sizeof($bad_format) > 0)
  {
```

(continued)

Listing 8-13 *(continued)*

```php
    if(@sizeof($blank_array) > 0)
    {
        /* display message for missing information */
        echo "<p><b>You didn't fill in one or more
                required fields.
                You must enter:</b><br />\n";
        /* display list of missing information */
        foreach($blank_array as $value)
        {
          echo "   {$labels[$value]}
                <br />\n";
        }
echo "</p>\n";
    }
    if(@sizeof($bad_format) > 0)
    {
        /* display message for bad information */
        echo "<p><b>One or more fields have information
                that appears to be incorrect.
                Correct the format for:</b><br />\n";
        /* display list of bad information */
        foreach($bad_format as $value)
        {
            echo "   {$labels[$value]}
                <br />\n";
        }
        echo "</p>\n";
    }
    /* redisplay form */
    echo "<form action='$_SERVER[PHP_SELF]'
            method='POST'>";
    foreach($labels as $field => $label)
    {
      $clean_data[$field] =
          strip_tags(trim($_POST[$field]));
        echo "<div class='field'>
            <label for='$field'>$label</label>
              <input type='text' name='$field'
                id='$field'
                size='65' maxlength='65'
                value='$clean_data[$field]' /></div>\n";
    }
    echo "<div id='submit'><input type='submit'
            value='Submit Phone Number' />\n";
    echo "</div>\n</form>\n</body>\n</html>";
    exit();
  }
  /* if data is good */
  echo "<p>All data is good</p></body></html>";
?>
```

Here are the differences between this program and the program in Listing 8-12:

- ✔ **This program creates two arrays for problem data.** It creates $blank_
  array, as did the previous program. But this program also creates
  $bad_format for fields that contain information that isn't in an accept-
  able format.

- ✔ **This program loops through $bad_format to create a separate list of
  problem data.** If any fields are blank, it creates one error message and a
  list of problem fields, as did the previous program. If any fields are in an
  unacceptable format, this program also creates a second error message
  and a list of problem fields.

The Web page in Figure 8-14 results when the user accidentally types his or her
first name into the Middle Name field and also types nonsense for his or her
phone number. Notice that two error messages appear, showing that the First
Name field is blank and that the Phone field contains incorrect information.

Figure 8-14:
The result
of process-
ing a form
with both
missing and
incorrect
information.

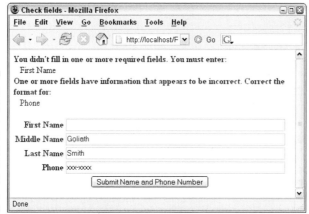

Giving users a choice with multiple submit buttons

You can use more than one submit button in a form. For instance, in a
customer order form, you might use a button that reads *Submit Order* and
another button that reads *Cancel Order.* However, you can list only one program in the action=programname part of your form tag, meaning that the
two buttons run the same program. PHP solves this problem. By using PHP,
you can process the form differently, depending on which button the user
clicks. The program in Listing 8-14 displays a form with two buttons.

Listing 8-14: Displaying a Form with Two Submit Buttons

```php
<?php
/*  Program name: displayTwoButtons.php
 *  Description:  Program displays a form with two
 *                buttons.
 */
?>
<html>
<head><title>Two Buttons</title></head>
<body>
<?php
echo "<form action='processTwoButtons.php' method='POST'>
        Last Name: <input type='text' name='last_name'
                                maxlength='50' /><br />
        <input type='submit' name='display_button'
                value='Show Address' />
        <input type='submit' name='display_button'
                value='Show Phone Number' />
    </form>";
?>
</body></html>
```

Notice that the submit button fields have a name: `display_button`. The fields each have a different value. Whichever button the user clicks sets the value for `$display_button`. The program `processTwoButtons.php` in Listing 8-15 processes the preceding form.

Listing 8-15: Processing Two Submit Buttons

```php
<?php
/*  Program name: processTwoButtons.php
 *  Description:  Program displays different information
 *                depending on which submit button was
 *                pushed.
 */
?>
<html>
<head><title>Member Address or Phone Number</title></head>
<body>
<?php
  $user="admin";
  $host="localhost";
  $password="";
  $database = "MemberDirectory";
  $cxn = mysqli_connect($host,$user,$password,$database)
        or die ("Couldn't connect to server");
  if($_POST['display_button'] == "Show Address")
  {
```

```
        $query = "SELECT street,city,state,zip FROM Member
                    WHERE lastName='$_POST[last_name]'";
        $result = mysqli_query($cxn,$query)
                    or die ("Couldn't execute query.");
        $row = mysqli_fetch_assoc($result);
        extract($row);
        echo "$street<br />$city, $state  $zip<br />";
    }
    else
    {
        $query = "SELECT phone FROM Member
                    WHERE lastName='$_POST[last_name]'";
        $result = mysqli_query($cxn,$query)
                    or die ("Couldn't execute query.");
        $row = mysqli_fetch_assoc($result);
        echo "Phone: {$row['phone']}";
    }
?>
</body></html>
```

The program executes different statements, depending on which button is clicked. If the user clicks the button for the address, the program outputs the address for the name submitted in the form; if the user clicks the Show Phone Number button, the program outputs the phone number.

Putting Information into a Database

Your application probably needs to store data in your database. For example, your database might store information that a user typed into a form for your use — a Member Directory is an example of this. Or your database might store data temporarily during the application. Either way, you store data by sending SQL queries to MySQL. (I explain SQL queries in detail in Chapter 4.)

Preparing the data

You need to prepare the data before storing it in the database. Preparing the data includes the following:

✔ Putting the data into variables

✔ Making sure that the data is in the format expected by the database

✔ Cleaning the data

✔ Escaping the data

Putting the data into variables

You store the data by sending it to the database in an SQL query. You add the data to the query by including the variable names in the query. Most of the data that you want to store is typed by the user into a form. As I discuss earlier in this chapter, PHP stores the form data in a built-in array, with the name of the form field as the array key. You just use the PHP built-in array elements in the query. Occasionally, you'll want to store information that you generate yourself, such as today's date or a customer order number. You just need to assign this data to a variable so that you can include it in a query.

Using the correct format

When you design your database, you set the data type for each column. The data that you want to store must match the data type of the column that you want to store it in. For instance, if the column expects a data type integer, the data sent must be numbers. Or if the column expects data that's a date, the data that you send must be in a format that MySQL recognizes as a date. If you send incorrectly formatted data, MySQL still stores the data, but it might not store the value that you expected. Here's a rundown of how MySQL stores data for the most frequently used data types:

✔ CHAR or VARCHAR: Stores strings. MySQL stores pretty much any data sent to a character column, including numbers and dates, as strings. When you created the column, you specified a length. For example, if you specified CHAR(20), only 20 characters can be stored. If you send a string longer than 20 characters, only the first 20 characters are stored. The remaining characters are dropped.

Set the maxlength for any text input fields in a form to the same length as the column width in the database where the data will be stored. That way, the user can't enter any more characters than the database can store.

✔ INT or DECIMAL: Stores numbers. MySQL tries to interpret any data sent to a number column as a number, whether or not it makes sense. For instance, it might interpret a date as a number, and you could end up with a number like 2001.00. If MySQL is unable to interpret the data sent as a number, it stores 0 (zero) in the column.

✔ DATE: Stores dates. MySQL expects dates as numbers, with the year first, month second, and day last. The year can be two or four digits (2009 or 09). The date can be a string of numbers, or each part can be separated by a hyphen (-), a period (.), or a forward slash (/). Some valid date formats are 20091203, 980103, 2009-3-2, and 2000.10.01. If MySQL cannot interpret the data sent as a date, it stores the date as 0000-00-00.

✔ ENUM: Stores only the values that you allowed when you created the column. If you send data that is not allowed, MySQL stores a 0.

In many cases, the data is collected in a form and stored in the database as is. For instance, users type their names in a form, and the program stores them. However, in some cases, the data needs to be changed before you store it. For instance, if a user enters a date into a form in three separate selection lists for month, day, and year (as I describe in the section, "Building selection lists," earlier in this chapter), the values in the three fields must be put together into one variable. The following statements put the fields together:

```
$expDate = $_POST['expYear']."-";
$expDate .= $_POST['expMonth']."-";
$expDate .= $_POST['expDay'];
```

Another case in which you might want to change the data before storing it is when you're storing phone numbers. Users enter phone numbers in a variety of formats, using parentheses, dashes, dots, or spaces. Rather than storing these varied formats in your database, you might just store the numbers. Then when you retrieve a phone number from the database, you can format the number however you want before you display it. The following statement removes characters from the string:

```
$phone = preg_replace("/[ )(.-]/","",$_POST['phone']);
```

The function `preg_replace` uses regular expressions to search for a pattern. The first string passed is the regular expression to match. If any part of the string matches the pattern, it is replaced by the second string. In this case, the regular expression is `[ )(.-]`, which means any one of the characters in the square brackets. The second string is `""`, which is a string with nothing in it. Therefore, any spaces, parentheses, dots, or hyphens in the string (characters that you might consider valid and allow when checking the data) are replaced by nothing.

Cleaning the data

The earlier "Getting Information from the User" section, which describes the use of HTML forms, discusses checking the data in forms. Users can type data into a text field, either accidentally or maliciously, that can cause problems for your application, your database, or your users. Checking the data and accepting only the characters expected for the information requested can prevent many problems. However, you can miss something. Also, in some cases, the information that the user enters needs to allow pretty much anything. For instance, you normally wouldn't allow the characters < and > in a field. However, there might be a situation in which the user needs to enter these characters — perhaps the user needs to enter a technical formula or specification that requires them.

PHP has two functions that can clean the data, thus rendering it harmless:

- ✔ strip_tags: This function removes all text enclosed by < and > from the data. The function looks for an opening < and removes it and everything following it, until the function finds a closing > or reaches the end of the string. You can include specific tags that you want to allow. For instance, the following statement removes all tags from a character string except <b> and <i>:

```
$last_name = strip_tags($last_name, "<b><i>");
```

- ✔ htmlspecialchars: This function changes some special characters with meaning to HTML into an HTML format that allows them to be displayed without any special meaning. The changes are

  - < becomes <

  - > becomes >

  - & becomes &

In this way, the characters < and > can be displayed on a Web page without HTML interpreting them as tags. The following statement changes these special characters:

```
$last_name = htmlspecialchars($last_name);
```

If you're positive that you don't want to allow your users to type any < or > characters into a form field, use strip_tags. However, if you want to allow < or > characters, you can safely store them after they've been processed by htmlspecialchars.

Another function that you should use before storing data in your database is trim. Users often type spaces at the beginning or end of a text field without meaning to. Trim removes any leading or trailing spaces so they don't get stored. Use the following statement to remove these spaces:

```
$last_name = trim($_POST['last_name']);
```

Escaping the data

A user can type information into your form that, when used in your query, changes your query so that it operates differently than you expect. Some of these damaging queries are created by manipulating the quotes in your query. You can protect against this kind of attack, called an *SQL injection,* by escaping any quotes sent in form fields. *Escaping* special characters, such as quotes, means to place a backslash (\) in front of the character. The special character is then treated as any other character, not as a special character with special meaning, rendering the query safe. I discuss escaping characters in Chapter 6.

PHP versions before version 6 provide a feature called *magic quotes* that automatically escapes all strings in the $_POST and $_GET arrays. Single quotes, double quotes, backslashes, and null characters are escaped. This feature, designed to help beginning users, is controlled by the magic_quotes-gpc setting in php.ini and is turned on by default in PHP 4 and PHP 5. In PHP 6, the magic quotes feature is no longer available.

The magic quotes feature is convenient and protects beginning users from SQL injection attacks that they may be unaware of. However, all $_POST and $_GET data is escaped, even if it isn't going to be stored in a database. This unnecessary escaping is inefficient. In addition, if you just display the form data or use it in an e-mail, the backslashes in front of the quotes are displayed or added to the e-mail, unless you remove them first.

Most experienced users turn off magic quotes and escape quotes using PHP functions. Even if you use magic quotes in programs you run on PHP 4 or 5, you must modify your programs before they run correctly on PHP 6. You can check whether magic quotes are on or off on your Web site with phpinfo().

If your Web host has magic quotes turned on, you need to turn them off for the programs in this book to run correctly. If your host allows local php.ini files, you can turn off magic quotes by adding the following line to your local php.ini file in the directories where you run scripts:

```
magic_quotes_gpc = Off
```

If you can't use local php.ini files, you may be able to turn off magic quotes in the .htaccess file. You can't turn them off in your PHP script. To turn off magic quotes in the .htaccess file, add the following line to your file:

```
php_flag magic_quotes_gpc = off
```

You may not be able to use this line in your .htaccess file. You may get a system error message after you add this line. If you can't use a local php.ini file and can't add this line to your .htaccess file, you need to contact your Web host to find out how to change this PHP setting. Then, be sure to turn off magic quotes on your local computer in your php.ini file so that the settings are the same for your Web site and your development site.

PHP provides the mysqli_real_escape_string() function (and the mysql_real_escape_string function) to escape form data for use in a MySQL query. The function is used after a connection is made to the MySQL server. The connection is passed to the function, along with the unescaped string, and the function escapes the string with respect to the connection. If magic quotes are on when you use the function, the string is already escaped by magic quotes, resulting in a double escaped string. In this book, all escaping is accomplished using the PHP function `mysqli_real_escape_string`.

If you plan to use your scripts on other computers, it may not be safe to assume that magic quotes are turned on or off. To write portable code, you need to test whether magic quotes are on or off in the script and then use the code that fits the status. You can use the PHP escape functions if magic quotes are turned off or just store the data as if magic quotes is turned on. You can test whether magic quotes is on or off using the `get_magic_quotes_gpc()` function in a conditional statement. The function returns 0 if magic quotes is off and 1 if magic quotes is turned on.

Adding new information

You use the INSERT query (described in Chapter 4) to add new information to the database. INSERT adds a new row to a database table. The general format is

```
$query = "INSERT INTO tablename (col,col,col...)
             VALUES ('var','var','var'...)";
$result = mysqli_query($cxn,$query)
     or die ("Couldn't execute query.");
```

For instance, the statements to store the name and phone number that a user enters in a form are

```
$query = "INSERT INTO Member (lastName,firstName,phone)
        VALUES ('$_POST[lastName]','$_POST[firstName]',
             '$_POST[phone]')";
$result = mysqli_query($query)
        or die ("Couldn't execute query.");
```

You would never insert data directly from the form field in the $_POST array. Always check its format first and clean it, as discussed earlier in this chapter.

Listing 8-16 shows a program that displays a form, and Listing 8-17 lists a program called `savePhone.php` that processes the form in Listing 8-16 and stores a name and a phone number from the form in a database.

Listing 8-16: Displaying a Form

```
<?php
/*  Program name: displayPhone
 *  Description:   Script displays a form that asks for
 *                 the customer phone number.
 */
```

```
$labels = array ( "first_name" => "First Name",
                  "last_name" => "Last Name",
                  "phone" => "Phone");
?>
<html>
<head>
<title>Customer Phone Number</title>
<style type='text/css'>
<!--
   form { margin: 1.5em 0 0 0; padding: 0; }
   .field { padding-top: .5em; }
   label { font-weight: bold; float: left; width: 20%;
           margin-right: 1em; text-align: right; }
   #submit { margin-left: 35%; padding-top: 1em; }
-->
</style>
</head>

<body>
<h3>Please enter your phone number below.</h3>
<form action='savePhone.php' method='POST'>
<?php
   /* Loop that displays the form fields */
   foreach($labels as $field => $label)
   {
     echo "<div class='field'>
            <label for='$field'>$label</label>
            <input type='text' name='$field' id='$field'
              size='65' maxlength='65' /></div>\n";
   }
   echo "<div id='submit'><input type='submit'
                  value='Submit Phone Number' />\n";
   echo "</div>\n</form>\n</body>\n</html>";
?>
```

The displayed form provides three fields: first_name, last_name, and phone.

Listing 8-17: Storing Data from a Form

```
<?php
/*  Program name: savePhone.php
 *  Description:   Program checks all the form fields for
 *                 blank fields and incorrect format. Saves
 *                 the correct fields in a database.
 */
/* set up array of field labels */
$labels = array( "first_name" => "First Name",
                 "last_name" => "Last Name",
                 "phone" => "Phone");
```

(continued)

Listing 8-17 *(continued)*

```
?>
<html>
<head>
<title>Customer Phone Number</title>
<style type='text/css'>
<!--
  form { margin: 1.5em 0 0 0; padding: 0; }
  .field { padding-top: .5em; }
  label { font-weight: bold; float: left; width: 20%;
          margin-right: 1em; text-align: right; }
  #submit { margin-left: 35%; padding-top: 1em; }
-->
</style>
</head>

<body>
<?php
/* Check information from form */
foreach($_POST as $field => $value)
{
  /* check each field for blank fields */
  if(empty($value))
  {
    $blank_array[] = $field;
  }
  /* check format of each field */
  elseif(preg_match("/name/i",$field))
  {
    if(!preg_match("/^[A-Za-z' -]{1,50}$/",$value) )
    {
      $bad_format[] = $field;
    }
  }
  elseif($field == "phone")
  {
    if(!preg_match("/^[0-9]( -]{7,20}(([xX]|(ext)|(ex))?
                   [ -]?[0-9]{1,7})?$/",$value) )
    {
      $bad_format[] = $field;
    }
  }
}
/* if any fields were not okay, display error and form */
if(@sizeof($blank_array) > 0 or @sizeof($bad_format) > 0)
{
  if(@sizeof($blank_array) > 0)
  {
    /* display message for missing information */
    echo "<p><b>You didn't fill in one or more required
             fields. You must enter:</b><br />";
    foreach($blank_array as $value)
    {
```

```
            echo "   {$labels[$value]}<br />";
        }
        echo "</p>";
    }
    if(@sizeof($bad_format) > 0)
    {
        /* display message for bad information */
        echo "<p><b>One or more fields have information that
                appears to be incorrect. Correct the format
                for:</b><br />";
        foreach($bad_format as $value)
        {
            echo "   {$labels[$value]}<br />";
        }
        echo "</p>";
    }
    /* redisplay form */
    echo "<p><hr />";
    echo "<h3>Please enter your phone number below.</h3>";
    echo "<form action='$_SERVER[PHP_SELF]' method='post'>";
    foreach($labels as $field => $label)
    {
        $good_data[$field]=strip_tags(trim($_POST[$field]));
        echo "<div class='field'>
            <label for='$field'>$label</label>
            <input type='text' name='$field' id='$field'
                size='65' maxlength='65'
                value='$good_data[$field]' /></div>\n";
    }
    echo "<div id='submit'><input type='submit'
            value='Submit Phone Number' />\n";
    echo "</div>\n</form>\n</body>\n</html>";
    exit();
}
else    //if data is okay
{
    $user="admin";
    $host="localhost";
    $passwd="";
    $dbnamee = "MemberDirectory";
    $cxn = mysqli_connect($host,$user,$passwd,$dbname)
            or die ("couldn't connect to server");
    foreach($labels as $field => $value)
    {
        $good_data[$field] =
                strip_tags(trim($_POST[$field]));
        if($field == "phone")
        {
            $good_data[$field] =
                preg_replace("/[)( .-]/","",$good_
                data[$field]);
        }
```

Listing 8-17 *(continued)*

```
      $good_data[$field] =
              mysqli_real_escape_string($cxn,
              $good_data[$field]);
   }
   $query = "INSERT INTO Phone (";                    →118
   foreach($good_data as $field => $value)            →119
   {
     $query .= "$field,";
   }
   $query .= ") VALUES (";                            →123
   $query = preg_replace("/,\)/",")",$query);         →124
   foreach($good_data as $field => $value)            →125
   {
     $query .= "'$value',";
   }
   $query .= ")";
   $query = preg_replace("/,\)/",")",$query);
   $result = mysqli_query($cxn,$query)
            or die ("Couldn't execute query. "
                    .mysqli_error($cxn));
   echo "<h4>New Member added to database</h4>";
 }
 ?>
 </body></html>
```

This program builds on the program checkAll.php in Listing 8-13. It checks the data from the form for blank fields and incorrect formats, asking the user to retype the data when it finds a problem. If the data is okay, the program trims the data, cleans it, and stores it in the database.

Notice that the program builds the query that stores the data. It uses the information from the $good_data array to build the query. Here's how it works:

→118   The first part of the SQL query stores the data set in the variable $query.

→119   Starts a foreach loop that adds the field names to the query, using the concatenation assignment statement (.=).

→123   After the loop, line 123 adds the middle part of the SQL INSERT query.

→124   Removes the comma that was inserted after the last field name.

→125   The procedure repeats to add the values to the last part of the query.

Your application might need to store data in several places. A function that stores data from a form can be very useful. The following function stores all the data in a form:

```
function storeForm($formdata,$tablename,$cxn)
{
   if(!is_array($formdata))
   {
     return FALSE;
     exit();
   }
   foreach($formdata as $field => $value)
   {
      $formdata[$field] = trim($formdata[$field]);
      $formdata[$field] = strip_tags($formdata[$field]);
      if($field == "phone")
      {
         $formdata[$field] =
            preg_replace("/[)( .-]/",
               "",$formdata[$field]);
      }
      $field_array[]=$field;
      $value_array[]=$formdata[$field];
   }
   $fields=implode(",",$field_array);
   $values=implode('","',$value_array);
   $query = "INSERT INTO $tablename ($fields)
                 VALUES (\"$values\")";
   if($result = mysqli_query($cxn,$query))
      return TRUE;
   else
      return FALSE;
}
```

The function returns TRUE if it finishes inserting the data without an error or FALSE if it is unable to insert the data. At the beginning, the function checks that the data passed to it is actually an array. If $formdata isn't an array, the function stops and returns FALSE.

Notice that this function works only if the field names in the form are the same as the column names in the database table. Also notice that this function assumes you're already connected to the MySQL server and have selected the correct database. The database connection is passed to the function.

The following code shows how you can call the function:

```
else    //if data is okay
{
  $user="admin";
  $host="localhost";
  $password="";
  $database = "MemberDirectory";
  $cxn = mysqli_connect($host,$user,$password,$database)
        or die ("couldn't connect to server");
  if(storeForm($good_data,"Phone",$cxn))
      echo "New Member added to database<br>";
  else
      echo "New Member was not added to the database<br>";
}
?>
</body></html>
```

Notice how much easier this program is to read with the majority of the statements in the function. Furthermore, this function works for any form as long as the field names in the form are the same as the column names in the database table. If the function is unable to execute the query, it stops execution at that point and prints the error message `"Couldn't execute query"`. If the query might fail in certain circumstances, you need to take these into consideration.

Updating existing information

You update existing information with the UPDATE query, as I describe in Chapter 4. Updating means changing data in the columns of rows that are already in the database — not adding new rows to the database table. The general format is

```
$query = "UPDATE tablename SET col=value WHERE col=value";
$result = mysqli_query($cxn,$query)
        or die ("Couldn't execute query.");
```

For instance, the statements to update the phone number for Goliath Smith are

```
$query = "UPDATE Member SET phone='$_POST[phone]'
            WHERE lastName='$_POST[lastName]'
            AND firstName='$_POST[firstName]'";
$result = mysqli_query($cxn,$query)
        or die ("Couldn't execute query.");
```

If you don't use a WHERE clause in an UPDATE query, the field that is SET is set for all the rows. That is seldom what you want to do.

You would never update data using data directly from the form field in the `$_POST` array. Always check its format first and clean it, as discussed earlier.

Listing 8-18 shows a program called `updatePhone.php`, which updates a phone number in an existing database record. `updatePhone.php` processes data from the same form as `storePhone.php` — the form displayed by `displayPhone.php` listed in Listing 8-16. You just need to change the `form` tag so that the program in the `action` attribute is `updatePhone.php`, as follows:

```
echo "<form action='updatePhone.php' method='POST'>";
```

Listing 8-18: Updating Data

```php
<?php
/*  Program name: updatePhone.php
 *  Description:   Program checks the phone number for
 *                 incorrect format. Updates the phone
 *                 number in the database
 *                 for the specified name.
 */
$labels = array ( "first_name" => "First Name",
                  "last_name" => "Last Name",
                  "phone" => "Phone");
?>
<html>
<head>
<title>Customer Phone Number Update</title>
<style type='text/css'>
<!--
  form { margin: 1.5em 0 0 0; padding: 0; }
  .field { padding-top: .5em; }
  label { font-weight: bold; float: left; width: 20%;
          margin-right: 1em; text-align: right; }
  #submit { margin-left: 35%; padding-top: 1em; }
-->
</style>
</head>

<body>
<?php
/* check each field for blank fields */
foreach($_POST as $field => $value)
{
  if(empty($value))
  {
      $blank_array[] = $field;
  }
}
```

(continued)

Listing 8-18 *(continued)*

```
/* check format of phone number */
if(!preg_match
    ("/^[0-9]( -]{7,20}(([xX]|(ext)|(ex))?
       [ -]?[0-9]{1,7})?$/",
    $_POST['phone']))
{
    $bad_format[] = "phone";
}
/* if any fields were not okay, display error and form */
if(@sizeof($blank_array) > 0 or @sizeof($bad_format) > 0)
{
  if(@sizeof($blank_array) > 0)
  {
    /* display message for missing information */
    echo "<p><b>You didn't fill in one or more required
            fields. You must enter:</b><br />";
    /* display list of missing information */
    foreach($blank_array as $value)
    {
        echo "   {$labels[$value]}<br />";
    }
    echo "</p>";
  }
  if(@sizeof($bad_format) > 0)
  {
    /* display message for bad phone number */
    echo "<p><b>Your phone number appears to be incorrect.
            </b></p>";
  }
  /* redisplay form */
  echo "<p><hr />";
  echo "<h3>Please enter your phone number below.</h3>";
  echo "<form action='$_SERVER[PHP_SELF]' method='post'>";
  foreach($labels as $field => $label)
  {
    $good_data[$field] = strip_tags(trim($_POST[$field]));
    echo "<div class='field'>
            <label for='$field'>$label</label>
              <input type='text' name='$field' id='$field'
              size='65' maxlength='65'
              value='$good_data[$field]' /></div>\n";
  }
  echo "<div id='submit'><input type='submit'
            value='Submit Phone Number' />\n";
  echo "</div>\n</form>\n</body>\n</html>";
  exit();
}
else    //if data is okay
{
```

```
$good_data['phone'] = strip_tags(trim($_POST['phone']));
$good_data['phone'] =
        ereg_replace("[)( .-]","",$good_data['phone']);
$user="admin";
$host="localhost";
$passwd="";
$dbname = "MemberDirectory";
$cxn = mysqli_connect($host,$user,$passwd,$dbname)
        or die ("Couldn't connect to server");
$query = "UPDATE Phone SET phone='$good_data[phone]'
                WHERE last_name='$_POST[last_name]'
                    AND first_name='$_POST[first_name]'";
$result = mysqli_query($cxn,$query)
            or die ("Couldn't execute query: "
                    .mysqli_error($cxn));
if(mysqli_affected_rows($cxn) > 0)
{
    echo "<h3>The phone number for {$_POST['first_name']}
            {$_POST['last_name']} has been updated</h3>";
}
else
    echo "No record updated";
}
?>
</body></html>
```

The program in Listing 8-18, which updates the database, is very similar
to the program in Listing 8-17, which adds new data. Using an UPDATE
query in this program — instead of the INSERT query you used to add new
data — is the major difference. Both programs check the data and then
clean it because both programs store the data in the database.

If you see backslashes (\) in the database after you have inserted or updated
the record, your data was escaped twice. This probably means you have
magic quotes turned on and also used mysqli_real_escape_quotes. Turn
off magic quotes. When your strings are escaped correctly, the escapes make
sure the query is executed correctly, but the escapes are not stored in the
database.

Getting Information in Files

Sometimes you want to receive an entire file of information from a user, such
as user résumés for your job-search Web site or pictures for your photo
album Web site. Or, suppose you're building the catalog from information
supplied by the Sales department. In addition to descriptive text about the
product, you want Sales to provide a picture of the product. You can supply
a form that Sales can use to upload an image file.

Using a form to upload the file

You can display a form that allows a user to upload a file by using an HTML form designed for that purpose. The general format of the form is as follows:

```
<form enctype="multipart/form-data"
        action="processfile.php" method="post">
<input type="hidden" name="MAX_FILE_SIZE" value="30000" />
<input type="file" name="user_file" />
<input type="submit" value="Upload File" />
</form>
```

Notice the following points regarding the form:

- ✔ **The enctype attribute is used in the form tag.** You must set this attribute to multipart/form-data when uploading a file to ensure that the file arrives correctly.

- ✔ **A hidden field is included that sends a value (in bytes) for MAX_FILE_SIZE.** If the user tries to upload a file that is larger than this value, it won't upload. You can set this value as high as 2MB. If you need to upload a file larger than that, you must change the default setting for upload_max_filesize in php.ini to a larger number before sending a value larger than 2MB for MAX_FILE_SIZE in the hidden field.

- ✔ **The input field that uploads the file is of type file.** Notice that the field has a name — user_file — as do other types of fields in a form. The filename that the user enters into the form is sent to the processing program and is available in the built-in array called FILES. I explain the structure and information in FILES in the following section.

When the user submits the form, the file is uploaded to a temporary location. The script that processes the form needs to copy the file to another location because the temporary file is deleted as soon as the script is finished.

Processing the uploaded file

Information about the uploaded file is stored in the PHP built-in array called $_FILES. An array of information is available for each file that was uploaded, resulting in $_FILES being a multidimensional array. As with any other form, you can obtain the information from the array by using the name of the field. The following is the array available from $_FILES for each uploaded file:

```
$_FILES['fieldname']['name']
$_FILES['fieldname']['type']
$_FILES['fieldname']['tmp_name']
$_FILES['fieldname']['size']
```

For example, suppose that you use the following field to upload a file, as shown in the preceding section:

```
<input type="file" name="user_file" />
```

If the user uploads a file named test.txt by using the form, the resulting array that can be used by the processing program looks something like this:

```
$_FILES[user_file][name] = test.txt
$_FILES[user_file][type] = text/plain
$_FILES[user_file][tmp_name] = D:\WINNT\php92C.tmp
$_FILES[user_file][size] = 435
```

In this array, name is the name of the file that was uploaded, type is the type of file, tmp_name is the path/filename of the temporary file, and 435 is the size of the file. Notice that name contains only the filename, but tmp_name includes the path to the file as well as the filename.

If the file is too large to upload, the tmp_name in the array is set to none, and the size is set to 0. The processing program must move the uploaded file from the temporary location to a permanent location. The general format of the statement that moves the file is as follows:

```
move_uploaded_file(path/tempfilename,path/permfilename);
```

The path/tempfilename is available in the built-in array element $_FILES ['fieldname']['tmp_file']. The path/permfilename is the path to the file where you want to store the file. The following statement moves the file uploaded in the input field, given the name user_file, shown earlier in this section:

```
move_uploaded_file($_FILES['user_file']['tmp_name'],
   'c:\data\new_file.txt');
```

The destination directory (in this case, c:\data) must exist before the file can be moved to it. This statement doesn't create the destination directory.

Allowing strangers to load files onto your computer is a security risk; someone might upload malicious files. You want to check the files for as many factors as possible after they're uploaded, using conditional statements to check file characteristics, such as expected file type and size. In some cases, for even more security, it might be a good idea to change the name of the file to something else so that users don't know where their files are or what they're called.

Putting it all together

A complete example script is shown in Listing 8-19. This program displays a form for the user to upload a file, saves the uploaded file, and then displays a message after the file has been successfully uploaded. That is, this program both displays the form and processes the form. This program expects the uploaded file to be an image file and tests to make sure that it's an image file, but any type of file can be uploaded. The HTML code that formats and displays the form is in a separate file — the include file shown in Listing 8-20. A Web page displaying the form is shown in Figure 8-15.

Listing 8-19: Uploading a File with a POST Form

```php
<?php
 /* Script name: uploadFile.php
  * Description: Uploads a file via HTTP with a POST form.
  */
 if(!isset($_POST['Upload']))                                    →5
 {
    include("form_upload.inc");
 }
 else                                                            →9
 {
    if($_FILES['pix']['tmp_name'] == "none")                     →11
    {
      echo "<p style='font-weight: bold'>
        File did not successfully upload. Check the
            file size. File must be less than 500K.</p>";
      include("form_upload.inc");
      exit();
    }
    if(!ereg("image",$_FILES['pix']['type']))                    →19
    {
      echo "<p style='font-weight: bold'>
        File is not a picture. Please try another
            file.</p>";
      include("form_upload.inc");
      exit();
    }
    else                                                         →27
    {
      $destination='c:\data'."\\".$_FILES['pix']['name'];
      $temp_file = $_FILES['pix']['tmp_name'];
      move_uploaded_file($temp_file,$destination);
      echo "<p style='font-weight: bold'>
        The file has successfully uploaded:
            {$_FILES['pix']['name']}
            ({$_FILES['pix']['size']})</p>";
    }
 }
?>
```

Here's how Listing 8-19 works:

→**5**   This line is an `if` statement that tests whether the form has been submitted. If not, you can display the form by including the file containing the form code. The `include` file is shown in Listing 8-20.

→**9**   This line starts an `else` block that executes if the form has been submitted. This block contains the rest of the script and processes the submitted form and uploaded file.

→**11**   This line begins an `if` statement that tests whether the file was successfully uploaded. If not, an error message is displayed, and the form is redisplayed.

→**19**   This line is an `if` statement that tests whether the file is a picture. If not, an error message is displayed, and the form is redisplayed.

→**27**   This line starts an `else` block that executes if the file has been successfully uploaded. The file is moved to its permanent destination, and a message is displayed to tell the user that the file has been uploaded.

Listing 8-20 shows the `include` file used to display the upload form.

Listing 8-20: An Include File That Displays the File Upload Form

```
<!-- Program Name: form_upload.inc
     Description:  Displays a form to upload a file -->
<html>
<head><title>File Upload</title></head>
<body>
<ol><li>Enter the file name of the product picture you
        want to upload or use the browse button
        to navigate to the picture file.</li>
    <li>When the path to the picture file shows in the
        text field, click the Upload Picture
        button.</li>
</ol>
<div align="center"><hr />
<form enctype="multipart/form-data"
        action="uploadFile.php" method="POST">
  <input type="hidden" name="MAX_FILE_SIZE"
        value="500000" />
  <input type="file" name="pix" size="60" />
  <p><input type="submit" name="Upload"
        value="Upload Picture" />
</form>
</div></body></html>
```

Notice that the `include` file contains no PHP code — just HTML code.

The form that allows users to select a file to upload is shown in Figure 8-15. The form has a text field for inputting a filename and a Browse button that enables the user to navigate to the file and select it.

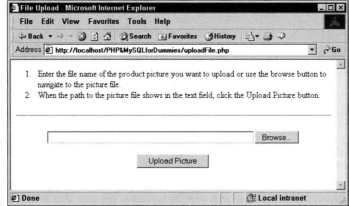

Figure 8-15:
A form that allows users to upload an image file.

Chapter 9

Moving Information from One Web Page to the Next

*M*ost Web sites consist of more than one Web page. This includes the static Web pages that you may have developed in the past. With static Web pages, users click a link in one Web page, and a new Web page appears in their browser. When users move from page to page this way, no information is transferred from the first page to the second. Each new page that is sent to the user's browser is independent of any other pages the user may have seen previously.

With dynamic Web pages, you may need to transfer information from one page to the next. If you're an advanced HTML developer, you may have experience with limited methods for transferring information from one page to the next using HTML forms and CGI (Common Gateway Interface) or cookies. However, PHP is a more powerful method for passing information from Web page to Web page.

Moving Your User from One Page to Another

When using only HTML, you provide links so that a visitor can go from one page to another in your Web site. When using PHP, you have three options for moving your user from one page to the next:

- ✔ **Links:** You can echo the HTML tags that display a link. The general format of an HTML statement that displays a link is

  ```
  <a href="newpage.php">Text user sees as a link</a>
  ```

  When users click the link, the program `newpage.php` is sent to their browsers. This method is used extensively in HTML Web pages. You're likely familiar with creating links from your HTML experience, but if you need a refresher, find out more about links in any HTML book, such as *HTML 4 For Dummies Quick Reference,* 2nd Edition, by Deborah S. Ray and Eric J. Ray (Wiley).

- ✔ **Form submit buttons:** You can use an HTML form with one or more submit buttons. When the user clicks a submit button, the program in the `form` tag runs and sends a new Web page to the user's browser. You can create a form with no fields — only a submit button — but the user must click the submit button to move to the next page. I discuss forms and submit buttons thoroughly in Chapter 8.

- ✔ **The `header` function:** You can send a message to the Web server with the PHP header function that tells the server to send a new page. When using this method, you can display a new page in the user's browser without the user having to click a link or a button.

You can use the PHP `header` function to send a new page to the user's browser. The program uses a header statement and displays the new Web page without needing any user action. When the `header` statement is executed, the new page is displayed. The format of the header function that requests a new page is

```
header("Location: URL");
```

The file located at URL is sent to the user's browser. Either of the following statements are valid `header` statements:

```
header("Location: newpage.php");
header("Location: http://company.com/cat/catalog.php");
```

TECHNICAL STUFF

URLs

A *URL* (Uniform Resource Locator) is an address on the Web. Every Web page has its own URL or address. The URL is used by the Web server to find the Web page and send it to a browser.

The format of a URL is

```
HTTP://servername:portnumber/
    path#target?string=string
```

Here's a breakdown of the parts that make up the URL:

✔ `HTTP://servername`: This part tells the server that the address is a Web site and gives the name of the computer where the Web site is located. Other types of transfer can be specified, such as FTP (File Transfer Protocol), but these aren't related to the subject of this book. If this part of the URL is left out, the Web server assumes that the computer is the same computer that the URL is typed on. Valid choices for this part might be `HTTP://amazon.com` or `HTTP://localhost`. *Note:* HTTP doesn't have to be in uppercase letters.

✔ `:portnumber`: The Web server exchanges information with the Internet at a particular port on the computer. Most of the time, the Web server is set up to communicate via port 80. If the port number isn't specified, port 80 is assumed. In some unusual circumstances, a Web server may use a different port number, in which case the port number must be specified. The most common reason for using a different port number is to set up a test Web site on another port that's available only to developers and testers, not customers. When the

site is ready for customers, it is made available on port 80.

✔ `path`: This is the path to the file, which follows the rules of any path. The root of the path is the main Web site directory. If the path points to a directory, rather than a file, the Web server searches for a default filename, such as `default.html` or `index.html`. The person who administers the Web site sets the default filename. The path `/catalog/show.php` indicates a directory called `catalog` in the main Web site directory and a file named `show.php`. The path `catalog/show.php` indicates a directory called `catalog` in the current directory.

✔ `#target`: An HTML tag defines a target. This part of the URL displays a Web page at the location where the target tag is located. For instance, if the tag `<a name="target"></a>` is in the middle of the file somewhere, the Web page will be displayed at the tag rather than at the top of the file.

✔ `?string=string`: The question mark allows information to be attached to the end of the URL. The information in forms that use the `get` method is passed at the end of the URL in the format `fieldname=value`. You can add information to the end of a URL to pass it to another page. PHP automatically gets information from the URL and puts it into built-in arrays. You can pass more than one `string=string` pair by separating each pair with an ampersand (`&`): for example, `?state=CA&city=home`.

Statements that must come before output

Some PHP statements can only be used before sending any output. `header` statements, `setcookie` statements, and `session` functions, all described in this chapter, must all come before any output is sent. If you use one of these statements after sending output, you may see the following message:

```
Cannot add header information - headers already sent
```

The message also provides the name of the file and indicates which line sent the previous output. Or you might not see a message at all; the new page might just not appear. (Whether you see an error message depends on what error message level is set in PHP; see Chapter 6 for details.) The following statements will fail because the `header` message is not the first output:

```
<body>
<?php
   header("Location: http://company.com");
?>
</body>
```

One line of HTML code is sent before the `header` statement. The following statements will work, although they don't make much sense:

```
<?php
   header("Location: http://company.com");
?>
<body>
</body>
```

The following statements will fail:

```
 <?php
   header("Location: http://company.com");
?>
<html>
```

The reason why these statements fail isn't easy to see, but if you look closely, you'll notice a single blank space before the opening PHP tag. This blank space is output to the browser, although the resulting Web page looks empty. Therefore, the `header` statement fails because there is output before it. This is a common mistake and difficult to spot.

The `header` function has a major limitation, however. You must use the `header` statement only *before* you send any other output. You cannot send a message requesting a new page in the middle of a program after you have echoed some output to the Web page. See the sidebar "Statements that must come before output" for a discussion.

In spite of its limitation, the `header` function can be useful. You can have as many PHP statements as you want before the `header` function as long as they don't send output. Therefore, the following statements will work:

```php
<?php
   if($customer_age < 13)
   {
      header("Location: ToyCatalog.php");
   }
   else
   {
      header("Location: ElectronicsCatalog.php");
   }
?>
```

These statements run a program that displays a toy catalog if the customer's age is less than 13 but run a program that displays an electronics catalog if the customer's age is 13 or older.

Moving Information from Page to Page

HTML pages are independent from one another. When a user clicks a link, the Web server sends a new page to the user's browser, but the Web server doesn't know anything about the previous page. For static HTML pages, this process works fine. However, many dynamic applications need information to pass from page to page. For instance, you might want to store a user's name and refer to that person by name on another Web page.

Dynamic Web applications often consist of many pages and expect the user to view several different pages. The period beginning when a user views the first page and ending when a user leaves the Web site is a *session*. Often you want information to be available for a complete session. The following are examples of sessions that necessitate sharing information among pages:

- **Restricting access to a Web site:** Suppose that your Web site is restricted and users log in with a password to access the site. You don't want users to have to log in on every page. You want them to log in once and then be able to see all the pages that they want. You want users to bring information with them to each page showing that they have logged in and are authorized to view the page.

- **Providing Web pages based on the browser:** Because browsers interpret some HTML features differently, you might want to provide different versions of your Web pages for different browsers. You want to check the user's browser when the user views the first page and then deliver all the other pages based on the user's browser type and version.

With PHP, you can move information from page to page by using any of the following methods:

- **Adding information to the URL:** You can add certain information to the end of the URL of the new page, and PHP puts the information into built-in arrays that you can use in the new page. This method is most appropriate when you need to pass only a small amount of information.

- **Storing information via cookies:** You can store *cookies* — small amounts of information containing `variable=value` pairs — on the user's computer. After the cookie is stored, you can get it from any Web page. However, users can refuse to accept cookies. Therefore, this method works only in environments where you know for sure that the user has cookies turned on.

- **Passing information using HTML forms:** You can pass information to a specific program by using a `form` tag. When the user clicks the submit button, the information in the form is sent to the next program. This method is useful when you need to collect information from users.

- **Using PHP session functions:** Beginning with PHP 4, PHP functions are available that set up a user session and store session information on the server; this information can be accessed from any Web page. This method is useful when you expect users to view many pages in a session.

Adding information to the URL

A simple way to move information from one page to the next is to add the information to the URL. Put the information in the following format:

```
variable=value
```

The `variable` is a variable name, but do not use a dollar sign ($) in it. The `value` is the value to be stored in the variable. You can add the `variable=value` pair anywhere that you use a URL. You signal the start of the information with a question mark (?). The following statements are all valid ways of passing information in the URL:

```
<form action="nextpage.php?state=CA" method="POST">
```

```
<a href="nextpage.php?state=CA">go to next page</a>
```

```
header("Location: nextpage.php?state=CA");
```

You can add several `variable=value` pairs, separating them with ampersands (`&`) as follows:

```
<form action="next.php?state=CA&city=home" method="POST">
```

Here are two reasons why you might not want to pass information in the URL:

✓ **Security:** The URL is shown in the address line of the browser, which means that the information that you attach to the URL is also shown. If the information needs to be secure, you don't want it shown so publicly. For example, if you're moving a password from one page to the next, you probably don't want to pass it in the URL. Also, the URL can be book-marked by the user. There may be reasons why you don't want your users to save the information that you add to the URL.

✓ **Length of the string:** There is a limit on the length of the URL. The limit differs for various browsers and browser versions, but there's always a limit. Therefore, if you're passing a lot of information, you may not have room for it in the URL.

Adding information to the URL is useful for quick, simple data transfer. For instance, suppose that you want to provide a Web page where users can update their phone numbers. You want the form to behave as follows:

1. When the user first displays the form, the phone number from the data-base is shown in the form so that the user can see what number is currently stored in the database.

2. When the user submits the form, the program checks the phone number to see whether the field is blank or whether the field is in a format that couldn't possibly be a phone number.

3. If the phone number checks out okay, it's stored in the database.

4. If the phone number is blank or has bad data, the program redisplays the form. However, this time you don't want to show the data from the database. Instead, you want to show the bad data that the user typed and submitted in the form field.

The `changePhone.php` program in Listing 9-1 shows how to use the URL to determine whether this is the first showing of the form or a later showing. The program displays the phone number for the user's login name and allows the user to change the phone number.

Listing 9-1: Displaying a Phone Number in a Form

```php
<?php
/*  Program name: changePhone.php
 *  Description:  Displays a phone number retrieved
 *                from the database and allows the user
 *                to change the phone number.
 */
?>
<html>
<head><title>Change phone number</title></head>
<body>
<?php
  $host="localhost";
  $user="admin";
  $password="";
  $database="MemberDirectory";
  $loginName = "gsmith";  // passed from previous page
  $cxn = mysqli_connect($host,$user,$password,$database)
        or die ("couldn't connect to server");

  if(@$_GET['first'] == "no")                               →19
  {
    $phone = trim($_POST['phone']);                         →21
    if(!ereg("^[0-9]( -]{7,20}$",$phone) or $phone=="")
    {
      echo "<h3 style='text-align: center'> Phone
          number does not appear to be valid.</h3>";
      display_form($loginName,$phone);                      →26
    }
    else // phone number is okay                            →28
    {
      $query = "UPDATE Member SET phone='$phone'
                      WHERE loginName='$loginName'";
      $result = mysqli_query($cxn,$query)
              or die ("Couldn't execute query.");
      echo "<h3>Phone number has been updated.</h3>";
      exit();
    }
  }
  else // first time form is displayed                      →38
  {
    $query = "SELECT phone FROM Member
            WHERE loginName='$loginName'";
    $result = mysqli_query($cxn,$query)
            or die ("Couldn't execute query.");
    $row = mysqli_fetch_row($result);
    $phone = $row[0];
    display_form($loginName,$phone);                        →45
  }
```

```
function display_form($loginName,$phone)                    →48
{
  echo "<div style='text-align: center'>";
  echo "<form action='$_SERVER[PHP_SELF]?first=no'          →51
          method='POST'>
        <h4>Please check the phone number below
          and correct it if necessary.</h4><hr />
        <p><b>$loginName</b>
          <input type='text' name='phone'
          maxlength='20' value='$phone'></p>
        <p><input type='submit'
          value='Submit phone number'></p>
      </form>";
  echo "</div>";
}
?>
</body></html>
```

Notice the following key points about this program:

✔ **The same program displays and processes the form.** The name of this program is changePhone.php. The form tag on line 51 includes action='$_SERVER[PHP_SELF], meaning that when the user clicks the submit button, the same program runs again.

✔ **Information is added to the URL.** The form tag on line 51 includes action='$_SERVER[PHP_SELF]?first=no'. When the user clicks the submit button and changePhone.php runs the second time, a variable $first is passed with the value "no".

✔ **The value that was passed for first in the built-in $_GET array is checked at the beginning of the program on line 19.** This code checks whether this is the first time the program has run.

✔ **If $_GET[first] equals "no", the phone number is checked.** $_GET[first] equals no only if the form is being submitted. $_GET[first] does not equal no if this is the first time through the program.

  • If the phone number is not okay, an error message is printed, and the form is redisplayed. This block of code starts on line 22.

  • If the phone number is okay, it's stored in the database, and the program ends. This block of code starts on line 28.

✔ **If $_GET[first] does *not* equal "no", the phone number is retrieved from the database.** In other words, if $_GET[first] doesn't equal no, it *is* the first time that the program has run. The program should get the phone number from the database. This block of code starts on line 38.

✔ **The program includes a function that displays the form.** The function is defined beginning on line 48. Whenever the form needs to be displayed, the function is called (lines 26 and 45).

The form displayed by the program in Listing 9-1 is shown in Figure 9-1. This shows what the Web page looks like the first time it's displayed. The URL in the browser address field doesn't have any added information.

Figure 9-1:
HTML form
to update
a phone
number.

Figure 9-2 shows the results when a user types a nonsense phone number in the form in Figure 9-1 and clicks the submit button. Notice that the URL in the browser address field now has `?first=no` added to the end of it.

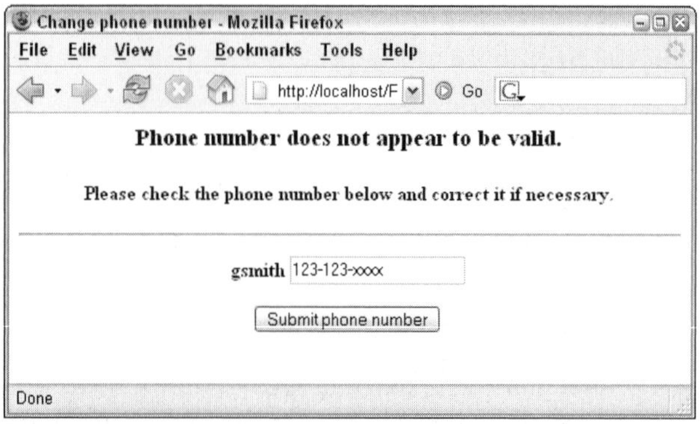

Figure 9-2:
HTML form
when a user
submits a
nonsense
phone
number.

Storing information via cookies

You can store information as cookies. *Cookies* are small amounts of information containing `variable=value` pairs, similar to the pairs that you can add to a URL. The user's browser stores cookies on the user's computer. Your application can then get the cookie from any Web page. Why these are called cookies is one of life's great mysteries. Perhaps they're called cookies because they seem at first glance to be a wonderful thing, but on closer examination, you realize that they aren't that good for you. For some people in some situations, cookies aren't helpful at all.

At first glance, cookies seem to solve the entire problem of moving data from page to page. Just stash a cookie on the user's computer and get it whenever you need it. In fact, the cookie can be stored so that it remains there after the user leaves your site and is still available when the user enters your Web site again a month later. Problem solved! Well, not exactly. Cookies are not under your control: They're under the user's control. The user can delete the cookie at any time. In fact, users can set their browsers to refuse to allow any cookies. And many users do refuse cookies or routinely delete them. Many users aren't comfortable with the whole idea of a stranger storing things on their computers, especially files that remain after they leave the stranger's Web site. It's an understandable attitude. However, it definitely limits the usefulness of cookies. If your application depends on cookies and the user has turned off cookies, your application won't work for that user.

Cookies were originally designed for storing small amounts of information for short periods of time. Unless you specifically set the cookie to last a longer period of time, the cookie disappears when the user closes his or her browser. Although cookies are useful in some situations, you're unlikely to need them for your Web database application for the following reasons:

- ✔ **Users may set their browsers to refuse cookies.** Unless you know for sure that all your users will have cookies turned on or you can request that they turn on cookies (and expect them to follow your request), cookies are a problem. If your application depends on cookies, it won't run if cookies are turned off.

- ✔ **PHP has features that work better than cookies.** Beginning with PHP 4, PHP includes functions that create sessions and store information that's available for the entire session. The session feature is more reliable and much easier to use than cookies for making information available to all the Web pages in a session. Sessions don't work for long-term storage of information, but MySQL databases can be used for that.

- ✔ **You can store data in your database.** Your application includes a database where you can store and retrieve data, which is usually a better solution than a cookie. Users can't delete the data in your database unexpectedly. Because you're using a database in this application, you can use it for any data storage needed, especially long-term data storage. Cookies are more useful for applications that don't make use of a database.

You store cookies by using the setcookie function. The general format is

```
setcookie("variable","value");
```

The *variable* is the variable name, but do not include the dollar sign ($). This statement stores the information only until the user leaves your Web site. For instance, the following statement

```
setcookie("state","CA");
```

stores CA in a cookie variable named state. After you set the cookie, the information is available to your other PHP programs in the element of a built-in array as $_COOKIE[state]. You don't need to do anything to get the information from the cookie. PHP does this automatically. The cookie is not available in the program where it's set. The user must go to another page or redisplay the current page before the cookie information can be used.

If you're using a version of PHP earlier than PHP 4.1, you must get the data from the long array called $HTTP_COOKIE_VARS. However, long arrays are no longer available in PHP 6. To run old scripts in PHP 6, you must change the array name in your code from $HTTP_COOKIE_VARS to $_COOKIE.

If you want the information stored in a cookie to remain in a file on the user's computer after the user leaves your Web site, set your cookie with an expiration time, as follows:

```
setcookie("variable","value",expiretime);
```

The *expiretime* value sets the time when the cookie expires. *expiretime* is usually set by using the time or mktime function, as follows:

- ✔ time: This function returns the current time in a format that the computer can understand. You use the time function plus a number of seconds to set the expiration time of the cookie, as follows:

```
setcookie("state","CA",time()+3600); //expires in 1
        hour
setcookie("Name",$Name,time()+(3*86400)) // exp in 3
        days
```

- ✔ mktime: This function returns a date and time in a format that the computer can understand. You must provide the desired date and time in the following order: hour, minute, second, month, day, and year. If any value is not included, the current value is used. You use the mktime function to set the expiration time of the cookie, as follows:

```
setcookie("state","CA",mktime(3,0,0,4,1,2009));
    //expires at 3:00 AM on April 1, 2009.
setcookie("state","CA",mktime(12,0,0,,,));
    //expires at noon today
```

You can remove a cookie by setting its value to nothing. Either of the following statements removes the cookie:

```
setcookie("name");
setcookie("name","");
```

The `setcookie` function has a major limitation. The `setcookie` function can only be used *before* any other output is sent. You *cannot* set a cookie in the middle of a program after you've echoed output to the Web page. See the sidebar "Statements that must come before output" elsewhere in this chapter.

Passing information with HTML forms

The most common way to pass information from one page to another is with HTML forms. An HTML form is displayed with a submit button. When the user clicks the submit button, the information in the form fields is passed to the program designated in the `form` tag. The general format is

```
<form action="processform.php" method="POST">
    tags for one or more fields
    <input type="submit" value="string">
</form>
```

The most common use of a form is to collect information from users (which I discuss in detail in Chapter 8). However, forms can also be used to pass other types of information using *hidden fields* — fields that are not displayed in the form. In fact, you can create a form that has only hidden fields. You always need a submit button, and the new page doesn't display until the user clicks the submit button, but you don't need to include any fields for the user to fill in.

For instance, the following statements pass the user's preferred background color to the next page when the user clicks a button named Next Page:

```
<?php
  $color="blue"; //passed to this program via a user form
  echo "<form action='nextpage.php' method='POST'>
        <input type='hidden' name='color' value='$color'>
        <input type='submit' value='Next Page'>
        </form>\n";
?>
```

The Web page shows a submit button labeled Next Page, but it doesn't ask the user for any information. When the user clicks the button, `nextpage.php` runs and can use the array element `$_POST[color]`, which contains `"blue"`.

Using PHP Sessions

A *session* is the time that a user spends at your Web site. Users can view many Web pages between the time they enter your site and leave it. Often you want information to follow the user around your site so that it's available on every page. PHP, beginning with version 4.0, provides a way to do this.

Understanding how PHP sessions work

PHP enables you to set up a session on one Web page and save variables as session variables. Then you can open the session in any other page, and the session variables are available for your use in the built-in array $_SESSION. To do this, PHP does the following:

1. Assigns a session ID number.

   The number is a long, nonsense number that is unique for the user and that no one could possibly guess. The session ID is stored in a PHP system variable named PHPSESSID.

2. Stores session variables in a file on the server.

   Your Web host provides a place to store your session file; you don't need to know where it is. On your local computer, the file is named with the session ID number in \tmp on Unix and Linux or in the session data directory in the main PHP directory in Windows.

   On your local computer, you can change the location where the session files are stored by changing the setting for session.save_path in php.ini. Change the path to the location where you want to store the files.

3. Passes the session ID number to every page.

   If the user has cookies turned on, PHP passes the session ID using cookies. If the user has cookies turned off, PHP passes the session ID in the URL for links or in a hidden variable for forms that use the post method.

4. Gets the variables from the session file for each new session page.

   Whenever a user opens a new page that's part of the session, PHP gets the variables from the file, using the session ID number that was passed from the old page, and puts them into the built-in array $_SESSION. You can use the array elements with the variable name as the key, and they have the value that you assigned in the previous page.

If users have cookies turned off, sessions do not work unless `trans-sid` is turned on. You find out how to turn `trans-sid` on and off later, in the "Using PHP session variables" section.

Opening sessions

You should open a session on each Web page. Open the session with the `session_start` function, as follows:

```
session_start();
```

The function first checks for an existing session ID number. If it finds one, it sets up the `$_SESSION` array. If it doesn't find one, it starts a new session by creating a new session ID number.

Because sessions use cookies if the user has them turned on, `session_start` is subject to the same limitation as cookies. That is, the `session_start` function must be called before any output is sent. For complete details, see the sidebar "Statements that must come before output," elsewhere in this chapter.

Using PHP session variables

When you want to save a variable as a session variable — that is, available to other Web pages that the user might visit — save it in the `$_SESSION` array as follows:

```
$_SESSION['variablename'] = value;
```

The value is then available in `$_SESSION` on other Web pages. For example, you can store the state where the user lives with the following statement:

```
$_SESSION['state'] = "CA";
```

You can then use `$_SESSION['state']` in any other Web page, and it has the value `CA`.

The following two programs show how to use sessions to pass information from one page to the next. The first program, `sessionTest1.php` in Listing 9-2, shows the first page where the session begins. Listing 9-3 shows the program `sessionTest2.php` for the second page in a session.

Listing 9-2: Starting a Session

```php
<?php
  session_start();
?>
<html>
<head><title>Testing Sessions page 1</title></head>
<body>
<?php
  $_SESSION['session_var'] = "testing";
  echo "This is a test of the sessions feature.
       <form action='sessionTest2.php' method='POST'>
       <input type='hidden' name='form_var'
            value='testing'>
       <input type='submit' value='go to next page'>
       </form>";
?>
</body></html>
```

Note that this program sets two variables to be passed to the second page. The session variable session_var is created. In addition, a form is displayed with a hidden variable form_var, which is also passed to the second page when the user presses the submit button. Both variables are set to "testing".

Listing 9-3: The Second Page of a Session

```php
<?php
  session_start();
?>
<html>
<head><title>Testing Sessions page 2</title></head>
<body>
<?php
  echo "session_var = {$_SESSION['session_var']}<br>\n";
  echo "form_var = {$_POST['form_var']}<br>\n";
?>
</body></html>
```

Point your browser at sessionTest1.php and then click the submit button that reads Go to Next Page. You then see the following output from sessionTest2.php:

```
session_var = testing
form_var = testing
```

Because sessions work differently for users with cookies turned on and for users with cookies turned off, you should test the two programs in both conditions. To turn off cookies in your browser, you change the settings for options or preferences.

To disable cookies in Internet Explorer, follow these steps:

1. **Choose Tools⇨Internet Options.**
2. **Click the Privacy tab.**
3. **Move the slider to the higher level, which says "Block All Cookies," and then click OK.**

To disable cookies in Firefox, follow these steps:

1. **Choose Tools⇨Options.**
2. **Click the Privacy tab.**
3. **Deselect the Accept Cookies from Sites option and then click OK.**

If the output from `sessionTest2` shows a blank value for `$session_var` when you turn off cookies in your browser, `trans-sid` probably is not turned on. You can turn on `trans-sid` in your `php.ini` file. Find the following line:

```
session.use_trans_sid = 0
```

Change the 0 to 1 to turn on `trans-sid`. If you can't get this problem fixed, you can still use sessions, but you must pass the session ID number in your programming statements; PHP won't pass the session ID number automatically when cookies are turned off. For details on how to use sessions when `trans-sid` is not turned on, check out the next section.

For PHP 4.1.2 or earlier, `trans-sid` is not available unless it was enabled by using the option `--enable-trans-sid` when PHP was compiled.

Sessions without cookies

Many users turn off cookies in their browsers. PHP checks the user's browser to see whether cookies are allowed and behaves accordingly. If the user's browser allows cookies, PHP does the following:

- ✓ Sets the variable `$PHPSESSID` equal to the session ID number
- ✓ Uses cookies to move `$PHPSESSID` from one page to the next

If the user's browser is set to refuse cookies, PHP does the following:

- ✔ **Sets a constant called SID:** The constant contains a `variable=value` pair that looks like `PHPSESSID=longstringofnumbers`.

- ✔ **Might or might not move the session ID number from one page to the next, depending on whether trans-sid is turned on:** If it's turned on, PHP passes the session ID number; if it's not turned on, PHP does not pass the session ID number.

Turning on `trans-sid` has advantages and disadvantages. The advantages are that sessions work seamlessly even when users turn off cookies and it's much easier to program sessions. The disadvantage is that the session ID number is often passed in the URL. In some situations, the session ID number should not be shown in the browser address. Also, when the session ID number is in the URL, it can be bookmarked by the user. Then, if the user returns to your site by using the bookmark with the session ID number in it, the new session ID number from the current visit can get confused with the old session ID number from the previous visit and possibly cause problems.

Sessions with trans-sid turned on

When `trans-sid` is turned on and the user has cookies turned off, PHP automatically sends the session ID number in the URL or as a hidden form field. If the user moves to the next page by using a link, a `header` function, or a form with the `get` method, the session ID number is added to the URL. If the user moves to the next page by using a form with the `post` method, the session ID number is passed in a hidden field. PHP recognizes `$PHPSESSID` as the session ID number and handles the session without any special programming on your part.

The session ID number is added only to the URLs for pages on your own Web site. If the URL of the next page includes a server name, PHP assumes that the URL is on another Web site and doesn't add the session ID number. For instance, here are two link statements:

```
<a href="newpage.php">
<a href="HTTP://www.company.com/newpage.php">
```

PHP adds the session ID number to the first link, but *not* to the second link.

Sessions without trans-sid turned on

When `trans-sid` is *not* turned on, PHP does *not* send the session ID number to the next page when users have cookies turned off. Rather, you must send the session ID number yourself.

Fortunately, PHP provides a constant that you can use to send the session ID yourself. A *constant* is a variable that contains information that can't be changed. (Constants are described in Chapter 6.) The constant that PHP provides is named `SID` and contains a `variable=value` pair that you can add to the URL, as follows:

```
<a href="nextpage.php?<?php echo SID?>" > next page </a>
```

This link statement adds a question mark (?) and the constant `SID` to the URL. `SID` contains the session ID number formatted as `variable=value`. Therefore, the URL that is sent is

```
<a href = "nextpage.php?PHPSESSID=877c22163d8df9deb342c7333cfe38a7>
   next page </a>
```

For one of several reasons (which I discuss in the section "Adding information to the URL," earlier in this chapter), you may not want the session ID number to appear in the URL shown by the browser. To prevent that, you can send the session ID number in a hidden field in a form that uses the `post` method. First, get the session ID number; then send it in a hidden field. The statements to do this are

```
<?php
   $PHPSESSID = session_id();
   echo "<form action='nextpage.php' method='POST'>
         <input type='hidden' name='PHPSESSID'
                value='$PHPSESSID'>
         <input type='submit' value='Next Page'>
      </form>";
?>
```

These statements do the following:

1. Stores the session ID number in a variable called `$PHPSESSID`.

   Use the function `session_id`, which returns the current session ID number.

2. Sends `$PHPSESSID` in a hidden form field.

On the new page, PHP automatically uses `$PHPSESSID` to get any session variables without any special programming needed from you.

Making sessions private

PHP session functions are ideal for restricted Web sites that require users to log in with a login name and password. Those Web sites undoubtedly have many pages, and you don't want the user to have to log in to each page. PHP sessions can keep track of whether the user has logged in and refuse access to users that aren't logged in. You can use PHP sessions to do the following:

1. Show users a login page.

2. If a user logs in successfully, set and store a session variable.

3. Whenever a user goes to a new page, check the session variable to see whether the user has logged in.

4. If the user has logged in, show the page.

5. If the user has not logged in, bring up the login page.

To check whether a user has logged in, add the following statements to the top of every page:

```php
<?php
  session_start()
  if( @$_SESSION['login'] != "yes" )
  {
    header("Location: loginPage.php");
    exit();
  }
?>
```

In these statements, $_SESSION[login] is a session variable that's set to "yes" when the user logs in. The statements check whether $_SESSION[login] is equal to "yes". If it is not, the user is not logged in and is sent to the login page. If $_SESSION[login] equals "yes", the program proceeds with the rest of the statements on the Web page.

Closing PHP sessions

For restricted sessions that users log in to, you often want users to log out when they're finished. To close a session, use the following statement:

```php
session_destroy();
```

This statement gets rid of all the session variable information stored in the session file. PHP no longer passes the session ID number to the next page. However, the statement does *not* affect the variables currently set on the current page: They still equal the same values. If you want to remove the variables from the current page — as well as prevent them from being passed to the next page — unset them with this statement:

```php
unset($_SESSION);
```

Part IV
Applications

The 5th Wave   By Rich Tennant

"What I'm looking for are dynamic Web applications and content, not Web innuendoes and intent."

In this part . . .

In this part, you find out how to take the planning and getting started information from Part I, the MySQL information from Part II, and the PHP information from Part III and put it all together into a dynamic Web database application. Chapters 11 and 12 present two sample applications, complete with their databases and all their PHP programs.

Chapter 10

Putting It All Together

- -

- -

*T*he previous chapters provide you with the tools you need to build your Web database application. In Part I, you find out how PHP and MySQL work and how to get access to them. In addition, you discover what you need to do to build your application and in what order. In Part II, you find out how to build and use a MySQL database. In Part III, you discover what features PHP has and how to use them. In addition, Part III explains how to show information in a Web page, collect information from users, and store information in a database. Now here, in the first chapter in Part IV, you're ready to put all the pieces together into a complete application. To do this, you need to

✔ Organize the application.

✔ Make sure that the application is secure.

✔ Document the application.

I describe each of these steps in detail.

Organizing the Application

Organizing the application is for your benefit. As far as PHP is concerned, the application could be 8 million PHP statements all on one line of one computer file. PHP doesn't care about lines, indents, or files. However, humans write and maintain the programs for the application, and humans need organization. Applications require two levels of organization:

✔ **The application level:** Most applications need more than one program to deliver complete functionality. You must divide the functions of the application into an organized set of programs.

✔ **The program level:** Most programs perform more than one specific task. You must divide the tasks of the program into sections within the program.

Organizing at the application level

In general, Web database applications consist of one program per Web page. For instance, you might have a program that provides a form to collect information and a program that stores the information in a database and tells the user that the data has been stored.

Another basis for organization is one program per major task. For instance, you might have a program to present the form and a program that stores the data in a database. For Web applications, most major tasks involve sending a Web page. Collecting data from the user requires a Web page for the HTML form; providing product information to customers requires Web pages; and when you store data in a database, you usually want to send a confirmation page to the user that the data was stored.

One program per Web page or one program per major task is not a rule but merely a guideline. The only rule regarding organization is that it must be clear and easy to understand, and that's subjective. Still, the organization of an application such as the Pet Catalog need not be overly complicated. Suppose that the Pet Catalog design calls for the first page to list all the pet types — such as cat, dog, and bird — that the user can select from. Then, after the user selects a type, all the pets in the catalog for that type are shown on the next Web page. A reasonable organization would be two programs: one to show the page of pet types and one to show the pets based on the pet type that was chosen.

Here are a few additional pointers for organizing your programs:

✔ **Choose descriptive names for the programs in your application.** Program names are part of the documentation that makes your application understandable. For instance, useful names for the Pet Catalog programs might be `ShowPetTypes.php` and `ShowPets.php`. It's usual, but not a requirement, to begin program names with an uppercase letter. Case isn't important for program names on Windows computers, but it's important on Unix and Linux computers. Pay attention to the uppercase and lowercase letters so that your programs can run on any computer if needed.

✔ **Put program files into subdirectories with meaningful names.** For instance, put all the graphic files into a directory called `images`. If you have only three files, you may be okay with only one directory, but looking through dozens of files for a specific file can waste a lot of time.

Organizing at the program level

A well-organized individual program is important for the following reasons:

- ✔ **It's easier for you to write.** The better organized your program is, the easier it is for you to read and understand it. You can see what the program is doing and find and correct problems faster.

- ✔ **It's easier for others to understand.** Others may need to understand your program. After you claim that big inheritance and head off to the South Sea Island that you purchased, someone else will have to maintain your application.

- ✔ **It's easier for you to maintain.** No matter how thoroughly you test your application, it's likely to have a problem or two. The better organized your program is, the easier it is for you to find and correct problems, especially later.

- ✔ **It's easier to change.** At some point, you or someone else will need to change the program. The needs of the user may change. The needs of the business may change. The technology may change. The ozone layer may change. Figuring out what the program does and how it does it so that you can change it is much easier if the program is well organized. I guarantee that you won't remember the details; you just need to be able to understand the program.

The following rules will produce well-organized programs. I hesitate to call them *rules* because there can be reasons in a specific environment to break one or more of them — but I strongly recommend that you think carefully before doing so.

- ✔ **Divide the statements into sections for each specific task.** Start each section with a comment describing what the section does. Separate sections from each other by adding blank lines. For instance, for the Pet Catalog, the first program might have three sections for three tasks:

  1. *Echo introductory text, such as the page heading and instructions.* The comment before the section might be /* opening text */. If the program echoes a lot of complicated text and graphics, you might make it into more than one section, such as /* title and logo */ and /* instructions */.

  2. *Get a list of pet types from the database.* If this section is long and complicated, you can divide it into smaller sections, such as a) connect to database; b) execute SELECT query; and c) put data into variables.

  3. *Create a form that displays a selection list of the pet types.* Forms are often long and complicated. It can be useful to have a section for each part of the form.

✔ **Use indents.** Indent blocks in the PHP statements. For instance, indent `if` blocks and `while` blocks as I did in the sample code for this book. If blocks are nested inside other blocks, indent the nested block even further. It's much easier to see where blocks begin and end when they're indented, which in turn makes it easier to understand what the program does. Indenting the HTML statements can also be helpful. For instance, if you indent the lines between the open and close tags for a form or between the `<table>` and `</table>` tags, you can more easily see what the statements are doing.

✔ **Use comments liberally.** Definitely add comments at the beginning that explain what the program does. And add comments for each section. Also, comment any statements that aren't obvious or where you may have done something in an unusual way. If it took you a while to figure out how to do it, it's probably worth commenting. Don't forget short comments on the end of lines; sometimes just a word or two can help.

✔ **Use simple statements.** Sometimes programmers get carried away with the idea of concise code to the detriment of readability. Nesting six function calls inside each other may save some lines and keystrokes, but it also makes the program more difficult to read.

✔ **Reuse blocks of statements.** If you find yourself typing the same ten lines of PHP statements in several places in the program, you can move that block of statements into another file and call it when you need it. One line in your program that reads `getData()` is much easier to read than ten lines that get the data. Not only that, if you need to change something within those lines, you can change it in one external file instead of having to find and change it a dozen different places in your program. You can reuse statements in two ways: functions and `include` statements. Chapter 7 explains how to write and use functions. The following two sections explain the use of functions and `include` statements in program organization.

✔ **Use constants.** If your program uses the same value many times, such as the sales tax for your state, you can define a constant at the beginning of the program with a function that creates a constant called `CA_SALES_TAX` that is `.97` and use it whenever it's needed. Defining a constant that gives the number a name helps anyone reading the program understand what the number is — plus, if you ever need to change it, you have to change it in only one place. Constants are described in detail in Chapter 6.

Using include statements

PHP allows you to put statements into an *external* file — that is, a file separate from your program — and insert the file wherever you want in the program by using an `include` statement. `include` files are useful for storing a block of statements that is repeated. You add an `include` statement wherever you want to use the statements instead of adding the entire block of statements at several locations. It makes your program shorter and easier to read. The format for an `include` statement is

```
include("filename");
```

The file can have any name. I like to use the extension .inc so that I can tell from their names that they are `include` files, not scripts. The statements in the file are included, as-is, at the point where the `include` statement is used.

The statements are included as HTML, not PHP. Therefore, if you want to use PHP statements in your `include` file, you must include PHP tags in the `include` file. Otherwise, all the statements in the `include` file are seen as HTML and output to the Web page as-is.

Here are some ways to use `include` files to organize your programs:

✔ **Put all or most of your HTML into `include` files.** For instance, if your program sends a form to the browser, put the HTML for the form into an external file. When you need to send the form, use an `include` statement. Putting the HTML into an `include` file is a good idea if the form is shown several times. It's even a good idea if the form is shown only once because it makes your program much easier to read. The programs in Chapters 11 and 12 put HTML code for forms into separate files and include the files when the forms are displayed.

✔ **Store the information needed to access the database in a file separate from your program.** Store the variable names in the file as follows:

```php
<?php
  $host="localhost";
  $user="phpuser";
  $password="secret";
?>
```

Notice that this file needs the php tags in it because the `include` statement inserts the file as HTML. Include this file at the top of every program that needs to connect to the database. If any of the information (such as the password) changes, just change the password in the `include` file. You don't need to search through every program file to change the password. For a little added security, use a misleading filename, rather than something obvious like `secret_passwords.inc`.

✔ **Put your functions in `include` files.** You don't need the statements for functions in the program; you can put them in an `include` file. If you have a lot of functions, organize related functions into several `include` files, such as `data_functions.inc` and `form_functions.inc`. Use `include` statements at the top of your programs, reading in the functions that are used in the program.

✔ **Store statements that all the files on your Web site have in common.**
Most Web sites have many Web pages with many elements in common.
For instance, all Web pages start with <html>, <head>, and <body> tags.
If you store the common statements in an include file, you can include
them in every Web page, ensuring that all your pages look alike. For
instance, you might have the following statements in an include file:

```
<html>
<head><title><?php echo $title ?></title></head>
<body topmargin="0">
<p style="text-align: center">
    <img src="logo.gif" width="100" height="200">
<hr color="red" />
```

If you include this file at the top of every program on your Web site, you
save a lot of typing, and you know that all your pages match. In addition,
if you want to change anything about the look of all your pages, you only
have to change it in one place — in the include file.

PHP provides a related statement — the include_once statement. If the
specified file has already been included in a previous statement, the file is not
included again. The format is as follows:

```
include_once("filename");
```

This statement prevents include files with similar variables from overwrit-
ing each other. Use include_once when you include your functions.

You can use a variable name for the filename as follows:

```
include("$filename");
```

For example, you might want to display different messages on different days.
You might store these messages in files that are named for the day on which
the message should appear. For instance, you could have a file named Sun.
inc with the following content

```
<p>Go ahead. Sleep in. No work today.</p>
```

and similar files for all days of the week. You can use the following statements to display the correct message for the current day:

```
$today   = date("D");
include("$today".".inc");
```

After the first statement, $today contains the day of the week, in abbrevia-
tion form. The date statement is discussed in Chapter 6. The second statement includes the correct file, using the day stored in $today. If $today
contains Sun, the statement includes a file called Sun.inc.

Storing include files

You can store your `include` files in the same directories where you store your scripts. The `include` statement finds the `include` file if it is in the same directory. You can also store your `include` files in a separate directory, such as a subdirectory in your main directory, which you name `includes`. If you do this, you need to use the complete path in your `include` statement, such as

```
include("includes/file1.inc");
```

Notice that the path name uses forward slashes. Using backward slashes (\ ) like you use on Windows results in an error message. PHP knows what you mean with the forward slashes.

You can avoid having to use paths by setting up an include directory where PHP looks for any files specified in an `include` statement. You set up an include directory with the configuration setting `include_path`. See Appendix B for a discussion of PHP configuration settings and how to change them.

You can set up the include path in your `php.ini` file. On your local computer or on a Web hosting account that allows you to have a local `php.ini` file, set up an `include_path` in the `php.ini` file. The include path setting has the following general format:

```
include_path = "paths"
```

For example, a common include path is:

```
include_path = ".:/php/includes"
```

This line sets up two directories where PHP looks for include files. The first directory is . (dot), meaning the current directory, followed by the second directory path, which is a directory named `includes` in the current directory. You can specify as many `include` directories as you want, and PHP searches them for the `include` file in the order in which they are listed. The directory paths are separated by a semicolon for Windows and a colon for Unix and Linux.

You can also set up an include path in an `.htaccess` file, with the following directive:

```
php_value   include_path   ".:./includes"
```

If you have trouble with the preceding techniques, you can set the include path in your PHP script, using an `ini_set` statement, such as the following:

```
ini_set("include_path","./includes");
```

The `ini_set` statement sets the include path only for the script that contains the `ini_set` statement. You need to make sure that every script in your Web site that uses an `include` statement also includes an `ini_set` statement to set the include path.

In most cases, you want to store your `include` files in a separate directory and set your include path to the directory. This allows you to use only the filename in your `include` statement, rather than the entire path. Using only the filename in the `include` statement makes the code more flexible and easier to maintain. If you move your `include` files into a different directory or move your script onto another computer, you only need to change the setting for the `include` path so that your program can find it. If you don't have an `include` path, but use full paths instead, any change in the location of the `include` files requires you to find every `include` statement in your scripts and change the path to the new path.

Protecting include files

When you store your `include` files in your main Web site directory, the files are available to your visitors if they know the name. For instance, a visitor might come to your Web site using the URL www.yoursite.com/file1. inc. If she does, she can see what's in your `include` file. If it's just the HTML for your Web page, it's okay, but if the `include` file she looks at is `secret passwords.inc`, which contains the information to access your database, it's much less okay.

The best way to protect `include` files is to store them in a protected directory that can't be accessed by visitors to your Web site. The previous section describes setting up a directory to contain your `include` files and setting a path to the `include` file directory. To protect your `include` files, you need to protect the `include` file directory so that your Web site visitors can't access it.

You can protect a directory from visitors on your Web host by adding an `.htaccess` file to the directory you want to protect (such as includes/ `.htaccess`). You may already have a file named `.htaccess` in your main Web site directory. This new `.htaccess` file is a separate file that goes only in the subdirectory to be protected. Add the following line to your `.htaccess` file:

```
Deny from all.
```

The Deny directive prevents any user from accessing any file in this subdirectory. Only your own script can access the include file.

If you're publishing a Web site on a company computer, ask your IT staff to provide you with access to a directory outside your Web space for your include files. This should be a directory that is not in your main Web site directory, but is somewhere else on the computer where Web site visitors can't access it.

Using functions

Make frequent use of functions to organize your programs. (In Chapter 7, I discuss creating and using functions.) Functions are useful when your program needs to perform the same task at repeated locations in a program or in different programs in the application. After you write a function that does the task and you know it works, you can use it anywhere that you need it.

Look for opportunities to use functions. Your program is much easier to read and understand with a line like this:

```
getMemberData();
```

than with 20 lines of statements that actually get the data. In fact, after you've been writing PHP programs for a while, you will have a stash of functions that you've written for various programs. Very often the program that you're writing can use a function that you wrote for an application two jobs ago. For instance, I often have a need for a list of the states. Rather than include a list of all 50 states every time I need it, I have a function called getState Names() that returns an array that holds the 50 state names in alphabetical order and a function called getStateCodes() that returns an array with all 50 two-letter state codes in the same order.

Use descriptive function names. The function calls in your program should tell you exactly what the functions do. Long names are okay. You don't want to see a line in your program that reads

```
function1();
```

Even a line like the following is less informative than it could be:

```
getData();
```

You want to see a line like this:

```
getAllMemberNames();
```

Keeping It Private

You need to protect your Web database application. People out there may have nefarious designs on your Web site for purposes such as

- ✔ **Stealing stuff:** They hope to find a file sitting around full of valid credit card numbers or the secret formula for eternal youth.

- ✔ **Trashing your Web site:** Some people think this is funny. Some people do it to prove that they can.

- ✔ **Harming your users:** A malicious person can add things to your Web site that harm or steal from the people who visit your site.

This is not a security book. Security is a large, complex issue, and I am not a security expert. Nevertheless, I want to call a few issues to your attention and make some suggestions. The following measures increases the security of your Web site, but if your site handles important, secret information, read some security books and talk to some experts:

- ✔ **Ensure the security of the computer that hosts your Web site.** This is probably not your responsibility, but you want to talk to the people responsible and discuss your security concerns. You'll feel better if you know that someone is worrying about security, such as your Web host.

- ✔ **Don't let the Web server display filenames.** Users don't need to know the names of the files on your Web site.

- ✔ **Hide things.** Store your information so that it can't be easily accessed from the Web.

- ✔ **Don't trust information from users.** Always clean any information that you didn't generate yourself.

- ✔ **Use a secure Web server.** This requires extra work, but it's important if you have top-secret information.

Ensure the security of the computer

First, the computer itself must be secure. The system administrator of the computer is responsible for keeping unauthorized visitors and vandals out of the system. Security measures include such things as firewalls, encryption, password shadowing, and scan detectors. In most cases, the system administrator is not you. If it is, you need to do some serious investigation into security issues. If you're using a Web hosting company, you may want to discuss security with those folks to reassure yourself that they're using sufficient security measures.

Don't let the Web server display filenames

You may have noticed that sometimes you get a list of filenames when you go to a URL in your browser. If you go to a directory (rather than a specific file) and the directory doesn't contain a file with the default filename (such as `index.html`), the Web server may display a list of files for you to select from. You probably don't want your Web server to do this; your site won't be very secure if a visitor can look at any file on your site. On other Web sites, you may have seen an error message that reads

```
Forbidden
You don't have permission to access /secretdirectory on this server.
```

On those sites, the Web server is set so that it doesn't display a list of filenames when the URL points to a directory. Instead, it delivers this error message. This is more secure than listing the filenames. If the filenames are being sent from your Web site, a setting for the Web server needs to be changed.

You can change this setting on your Web host by adding a line to your `.htaccess` file. This should be in the `.htaccess` file in the main directory for your Web site. Add the line:

```
Options -Indexes
```

This line in the `.htaccess` file on your Web site prevents users from seeing the filenames.

If you don't have access to an `.htaccess` file, request that the Web site administrator change this setting.

Hide things

Keep information as private as possible. Of course, the Web pages that you want visitors to see must be stored in your public Web space directory. But not everything needs to be stored there. For instance, you can store `include` files in another location altogether — in a space on the computer that can't be accessed from the Web. Your database certainly isn't stored in your Web space, but it might be even more secure if it was stored on a different computer.

Another way to hide things is to give them misleading names. For instance, the `include` file containing the database variables shouldn't be called `passwords.inc`. A better name might be `UncleHenrysChickenSoup Recipe.inc`. I know this suggestion violates other sections of the book where I promote informative filenames, but this is a special case. Malicious people sometimes do obvious things like typing `www.yoursite.com/passwords.html` into their browser to see what happens.

Don't trust information from users

Malicious users can use the forms in your Web pages to send dangerous text to your Web site. Therefore, never store information from forms directly into a database without checking, cleaning, and escaping it first. Check the information that you receive for reasonable formats and dangerous characters. In particular, you don't want to accept HTML tags, such as `<script>` tags, from forms. By using script tags, a user could enter an actual script — perhaps a malicious one. If you accept the form field without checking it and store it in your database, you could have any number of problems, particularly if the stored script was sent in a Web page to a visitor to your Web site. For more on checking, cleaning, and escaping data from forms, see Chapter 8.

Use a secure Web server

Communication between your Web site and its visitors is not totally secure. When the files on your Web site are sent to the user's browser, someone on the Internet between you and the user can read the contents of these files as they pass by. For most Web sites, this isn't an issue; however, if your site collects or sends credit card numbers or other secret information, use a secure Web server to protect this data.

Secure Web servers use Secure Sockets Layer (SSL) to protect communication sent to and received from browsers. This is similar to the scrambled telephone calls that you hear about in spy movies. The information is *encrypted* (translated into coded strings) before it is sent across the Web. The receiving software decrypts it into its original content. In addition, your Web site uses a certificate that verifies your identity. Using a secure Web server is extra work, but it's necessary for some applications.

You can tell when you're communicating using SSL. The URL begins with *HTTPS,* rather than *HTTP.*

Many Web hosts offer SSL communication for Web site accounts. Check with your Web host for information about using SSL.

Completing Your Documentation

I'm making one last pitch here. Documenting your Web database application is essential. You start with a plan describing what the application is supposed to do. Based on your plan, you create a database design. Keep the plan and the design up-to-date. Often, as a project moves along, changes are made. Make sure that your documentation changes to match the new decisions.

While you design your programs, associate the tasks in the application plan with the programs that you plan to write. List the programs and what each one will do. If the programs are complicated, you may want to include a brief description of how the program will perform its tasks. If this is a team effort, list who is responsible for each program. When you complete your application, you should have the following documents:

- ✔ **Application plan:** Describes what the application is supposed to do, listing the tasks that it will perform

- ✔ **Database design:** Describes the tables and fields in the database

- ✔ **Program design:** Describes how the program(s) will perform the tasks in the application plan

- ✔ **Program comments:** Describe the details of how the individual program works

Pretend that it's five years in the future and you're about to do a major rewrite of your application. What will you need to know about the application to change it? Be sure that you include all the information that you need in your documentation.

Chapter 11

Building an Online Catalog

*O*nline catalogs are everywhere on the Web. Every business that has products for sale uses an online catalog. Some businesses use online catalogs to sell their products online, and some use them to show the quality and worth of their products to the world. Many customers have come to expect businesses to be online and provide information about their products. Customers often begin their search for a product online, researching its availability and cost through the Web.

In this chapter, you find out how to build an online catalog. I chose a pet store catalog for no particular reason except that it sounded like more fun than a catalog of socks or light bulbs. And looking at the pictures for a pet catalog was much more fun than looking at pictures of socks. I introduce the Pet Catalog example in Chapter 3 and use it for many of the examples throughout this book.

In general, all catalogs do the same thing: provide product information to potential customers. The general purpose of the catalog is to make it as easy as possible for customers to see information about the products. In addition, you want to make the products look as attractive as possible so that customers want to purchase them.

Designing the Application

The first step in design is to decide what the application should do. The obvious purpose of the Pet Catalog is to show potential customers information about the pets. A pet store might also want to show information about pet products, such as pet food, cages, fish tanks, and catnip toys . . . but you decide not to include such items in your catalog. The purpose of your online catalog application is to show just pets.

For the customer, displaying the information is the sole function of the catalog. From your perspective, however, the catalog also needs to be maintained; that is, you need to add items to the catalog. So, you must include the task of adding items to the catalog as part of the catalog application. Thus, the application has two distinct functions:

  ✔ Show pets to the customers
  ✔ Add pets to the catalog

Showing pets to the customers

The basic purpose of your online catalog is to let customers look at pets. Customers can't purchase pets online, of course. Sending pets through the mail isn't feasible. But a catalog can showcase pets in a way that motivates customers to rush to the store to buy them.

If your catalog contains only three pets, your catalog can be pretty simple — one page showing the three pets. However, most catalogs have many more items than that. Usually, a catalog opens with a list of the types of products, such as cat, dog, horse, and dragon. Customers select the type of pet they want to see, and the catalog then displays the individual pets of that type. For example, if the customer selects dog, the catalog would then show collies, spaniels, and wolves. Some types of products might have more levels of categories before you see individual products. For instance, furniture might have three levels rather than two. The top level might be the room, such as kitchen or bedroom. The second level might be type, such as chairs or tables. The third level would be the individual products.

The purpose of a catalog is to motivate those who look at it to make a purchase immediately. For the Pet Catalog, pictures are a major factor in motivating customers to make a purchase. Pictures of pets make people go ooooh and aaaah and say, "Isn't he cuuuute!" This generates sales. The main purpose of your Pet Catalog is to show pictures of pets. In addition, the catalog also should show descriptions and prices.

To show the pets to customers, the Pet Catalog will do the following:

1. Show a list of the types of pets and allow the customer to select a type.

2. Show information about the pets that match the selected type. The information includes the description, the price, and a picture of the pet.

Adding pets to the catalog

You can add items to your catalog in several ways, but the easiest way is to use an application designed for the purpose. In many cases, you won't be the person who is adding products to your catalog. One reason for adding maintenance functionality to your catalog application is so someone else can do those boring maintenance tasks. The easier it is to maintain your catalog, the less likely that errors will sneak into it.

An application to add a pet to your catalog should do the following:

1. Prompt the user to enter a pet type for the pet.

    A selection list of possible pet types would eliminate many errors, such as alternative spellings (*dog* and *dogs*) and misspellings. The application also needs to allow the user to add new categories when needed.

2. Prompt the user to enter a name for the pet, such as *collie* or *shark.*

    A selection list of names would help prevent mistakes. The application also needs to allow the user to add new names when needed.

3. Prompt the user to enter the pet information for the new pet.

    The application should clearly specify what information is needed.

4. Store the information in the catalog.

The catalog entry application can check the data for mistakes and enter the data into the correct locations. The person entering the new pet doesn't need to know the inner workings of the catalog.

Building the Database

The catalog itself is a database. It doesn't have to be a database; it's possible to store a catalog as a series of HTML files that contain the product information in HTML tags and display the appropriate file when the customer clicks a link. However, it makes my eyes cross to think of maintaining such a catalog. Imagine the tedium of adding and removing catalog items manually — or finding the right location for each item by searching through many files. Ugh. For these reasons, putting your Pet Catalog in a database is better.

The `PetCatalog` database contains all the information about pets. It uses three tables:

- ✔ `Pet` table
- ✔ `PetType` table
- ✔ `Color` table

The first step in building the Pet Catalog is to build the database. It's pretty much impossible to write programs without a working database to test the programs on. First you design your database; then you build it; then you add the data (or at least some sample data to use while developing the programs).

Building the Pet table

In your design for the Pet Catalog, the main table is the `Pet` table. It contains the information about the individual pets that you sell. The following SQL query creates the `Pet` table:

```
CREATE TABLE Pet (
   petID           INT(5)          SERIAL,
   petName         VARCHAR(25)       NOT NULL,
   petType         VARCHAR(15)       NOT NULL DEFAULT "Misc",
   petDescription  VARCHAR(255),
   price           DECIMAL(9,2),
   pix             CHAR(15)        NOT NULL DEFAULT "na.gif",
 PRIMARY KEY(petID) );
```

Each row of the `Pet` table represents a pet. The columns are as follows:

- ✔ `petID`: A sequence number for the pet. In another catalog, this might be a product number, a serial number, or a number used to order the product. The `petID` column is the primary key, which must be unique. MySQL doesn't allow two rows to be entered with the same `petID`.

  The `CREATE` query defines the `petID` column as `SERIAL` (added in MySQL 4.1). `SERIAL` is a keyword that defines the column in the following ways:

  - `BIGINT`: The data in the field is expected to be a numeric integer, with a range up to 18446744073709551615. The database won't accept a character string in this field.

  - `UNSIGNED`: The integer in the field can't be a negative number.

  - `NOT NULL`: This definition means that this field can't be empty. It must have a value. The primary key must always be `NOT NULL`.

- AUTO-INCREMENT: This definition means that the field isn't automatically filled with a sequential number if you don't provide a specific number. For example, if a row is added with 98 for a petID, the next row is added with 99 for the petID unless you specify a different number. This is a useful way of specifying a column with a unique number, such as a product number or an order number. You can always override the automatic sequence number with a number of your own, but if you don't provide a number, a sequential number is stored.

    Note: If you're using phpMyAdmin to create the database, the keyword SERIAL may not be available. You need to define petID as a BIGINT, UNSIGNED, NOT NULL, and AUTO_INCREMENT, and define it specifically as the primary key.

- petName: The name of the pet, such as lion, collie, or unicorn. The CREATE query defines the petName column in the following ways:

    - VARCHAR(25): This data type defines the field as a variable character string that can be up to 25 characters long. The field is stored in its actual length.

    - NOT NULL: This definition means that this field can't be empty. It must have a value. After all, it wouldn't make much sense to have a pet in the catalog without a name.

    - No default value: If you try to add a new row to the Pet table without a petName, it won't be added. It doesn't make sense to have a default name for a pet.

- petType: The type of pet, such as dog or fish. The CREATE query defines the petType column in the following ways:

    - VARCHAR(15): This data type defines the field as a variable character string that can be up to 15 characters long. The field is stored in its actual length.

    - NOT NULL: This definition means that this field can't be empty. It must have a value. The online catalog application will show categories first and then pets within a category, so a pet with no category will never be shown on the Web page.

    - DEFAULT "Misc": The value "Misc" is stored if you don't provide a value for petType. This ensures that a value is always stored for petType.

- petDescription: A description of the pet. The CREATE query defines petDescription in the following way:

    - VARCHAR(255): This data type defines the field as a variable character string that can be up to 255 characters long. The field is stored in its actual length.

✔ price: The price of the pet. The CREATE query defines price in the following way:

- DECIMAL(9,2): This data type defines the field as a decimal number that can be up to nine digits and has two decimal places. If you store an integer in this field, it's returned with two decimal places, such as 9.00 or 2568.00.

✔ pix: The filename of the picture of the pet. Pictures on a Web site are stored in graphic files with names like dog.jpg, dragon.gif, or cat.png. This field stores the filename for the picture that you want to show for this pet. The CREATE query defines pix in the following ways:

- CHAR(15): The data in this field is expected to be a character string that's 15 characters long. For some applications, the picture files might be in other directories or on other Web sites requiring a longer field, but for this application, the pictures are all in a directory on the Web site and have short names. If the stored string is less than 15 characters, the field is padded so that it always takes up 15 characters of storage.

- NOT NULL: This definition means that this field can't be empty. It must have a value. You need a picture for the pet. When a Web site tries to show a picture that can't be found, it displays an ugly error message in the browser window where the graphic would go. You don't want your catalog to do that, so your database should require a value. In this case, you define a default value so that a value will always be placed in this field.

- DEFAULT "na.gif": The value "na.gif" is stored if you don't provide a value for pix. In this way, a value is always stored for pix. The na.gif file might be a graphic that reads something like: "picture not available".

Notice the following points about this database table design:

✔ **Some fields are CHAR, and some are VARCHAR.** In general, shorter fields should be CHAR because shorter fields don't waste much space. For instance, if your CHAR is 5 characters, the most space that you could possibly waste is 4. However, if your CHAR is 200, you could waste 199. Therefore, short fields can use CHAR with very little wasted space.

✔ **The petID field means different things for different pets.** The petID field assigns a unique number to each pet. However, a unique number isn't necessarily meaningful in all cases. For example, a unique number is meaningful for an individual kitten but not for an individual goldfish.

There are really two kinds of pets. One is the unique pet, such as a puppy or a kitten. After all, the customer buys a specific dog — not just a generic dog. The customer needs to see the picture of the actual animal. On the other hand, some pets are not especially unique, such as a goldfish or a parakeet. When customers purchase a goldfish, they see a tank full of goldfish and point at one. The only real distinguishing characteristic of a goldfish is its color. The customer just needs to see a picture of a generic goldfish, perhaps showing the possible colors — not a picture of the individual fish.

In your catalog, you have both kinds of pets. The catalog might contain several pets with the name *cat* but with different petIDs. The picture would show the individual pet. The catalog also contains pets that aren't individuals but that represent generic pets, such as goldfish. In this case, there's only one entry with the name *goldfish,* with a single petID.

I've used both kinds of pets in this catalog to demonstrate the different kinds of products that you might want to include in a catalog. The unique item catalog might include such products as artwork or vanity license plates. When the unique item is sold, it's removed from the catalog. Most products are more generic, such as clothing or automobiles. Although a picture shows a particular shirt, many identical shirts are available. You can sell the shirt many times without having to remove it from the catalog.

Building the PetType table

You assign each pet a type, such as dog or dragon. The first Web page of the catalog lists the types for the customer to select from. A description of each type is also helpful. You don't want to put the type description in the main Pet table because the description would be the same for all pets with the same category. Repeating information in a table violates good database design.

The PetCatalog database includes a table called PetType that holds the type descriptions. The following SQL query creates the PetType table:

```
CREATE TABLE PetType (
  petType          VARCHAR(15)       NOT NULL,
  typeDescription VARCHAR(255),
  PRIMARY KEY(petType)  );
```

Each row of this table represents a pet type. These are the columns:

✔ petType: The type name. Notice that the petType column is defined the same in the Pet table (which I describe in the preceding section) and in this table. This makes table joining possible and makes matching rows in the tables much easier. However, petType is the primary key in this table but not in the Pet table. The CREATE query defines the pet Type column in the following ways:

- CHAR(15): This data type defines the field as a variable character string that can be up to 15 characters long. The field is stored in its actual length.

- PRIMARY KEY(petType): This definition sets the petType column as the primary key. This is the field that must be unique. MySQL won't allow two rows to be entered with the same petType.

- NOT NULL: This definition means that this field can't be empty. It must have a value. The primary key must always be NOT NULL.

✔ typeDescription: A description of the pet type. The CREATE query defines the typeDescription in the following way:

- VARCHAR(255): The string in this field is expected to be a variable character string that can be up to 255 characters long. The field is stored in its actual length.

Building the Color table

When I discuss building the Pet table (see "Building the Pet table," earlier in this chapter), I discuss the different kinds of pets: pets that are unique (such as puppies) and pets that are not unique (such as goldfish). For unique pets, the customer needs to see a picture of the actual pet. For pets that aren't unique, the customer needs to see only a generic picture.

In some cases, generic pets come in a variety of colors, such as blue parakeets and green parakeets. You might want to show two pictures for parakeets: a picture of a blue parakeet and a picture of a green parakeet. However, because most pets aren't this kind of generic pet, you don't want to add a color column to your main Pet table because it would be blank for most of the rows. Instead, you create a separate table containing only pets that come in more than one color. Then when the catalog application is showing pets, it can check the Color table to see whether there's more than one color available — and if there is, it can show the pictures from the Color table.

The Color table points to pictures of pets when the pets come in different colors so that the catalog can show pictures of all the available colors. The following SQL query creates the Color table:

```
CREATE TABLE Color (
   petName            VARCHAR(25)       NOT NULL,
   petColor           VARCHAR(15)       NOT NULL,
   pix                CHAR(15)          NOT NULL DEFAULT "na.gif",
   PRIMARY KEY(petName,petColor)   );
```

Each row represents a pet type. The columns are as follows:

✔ petName: The name of the pet, such as lion, collie, or Chinese bearded dragon. Notice that the petName column is defined the same in the Pet table and in this table. This makes table joining possible and makes matching rows in the tables much easier. However, the petName is the primary key in this table but not in the Pet table. The CREATE query defines the petName in the following ways:

- VARCHAR(25): This data type defines the field as a variable character string that can be up to 25 characters long. The field is stored in its actual length.

- PRIMARY KEY(petName,petColor): The primary key must be unique. For this table, two columns together are the primary key — this column and the petColor column. MySQL won't allow two rows to be entered with the same petName *and* petColor.

- NOT NULL: This definition means that this field can't be empty. It must have a value. The primary key must always be NOT NULL.

✔ petColor: The color of the pet, such as orange or purple. The CREATE query defines the petColor in the following ways:

- VARCHAR(15): This data type defines the field as a variable character string that can be up to 15 characters long. The field is stored in its actual length.

- PRIMARY KEY(petName,petColor): The primary key must be unique. For this table, two columns together are the primary key — this column and the petName column. MySQL won't allow two rows to be entered with the same petName *and* petColor.

- NOT NULL: This definition means that this field can't be empty. It must have a value. The primary key must always be NOT NULL.

✔ pix: The filename containing the picture of the pet. The CREATE query defines pix in the following ways:

- CHAR(15): This data type defines the field as a character string that's 15 characters long.

- NOT NULL: This definition means that this field can't be empty. It must have a value. You need a picture for the pet. When a Web site tries to show a picture that can't be found, it displays an ugly error message in the browser window where the graphic would go. You don't want your catalog to do that, so your database should require a value. In this case, the CREATE query defines a default value so that a value is always placed in this field.

- DEFAULT "na.gif": The value "na.gif" is stored if you don't provide a value for pix. In this way, a value is always stored for pix. The file na.gif might contain a graphic that reads something like picture not available.

Adding data to the database

You can add the data to the database in many ways. You can use SQL queries to add pets to the database, or you can use the application that I describe in this chapter. My personal favorite during development is to add a few sample items to the catalog by reading the data from a file. Then, whenever my data becomes totally bizarre during development (as a result of programming errors or my weird sense of humor), I can re-create the data in a moment. Just DROP the table, re-create it with the SQL query, and reread the sample data.

For example, the data file for the Pet table might look like this:

```
<TAB>Pekinese<TAB>Dog<TAB>Small, cute, energetic. Good
        alarm system.<TAB>100.00<TAB>peke.jpg
<TAB>House cat<TAB>Cat<TAB>Yellow and white cat. Extremely
        playful. <TAB>20.00<TAB>catyellow.jpg
<TAB>House cat<TAB>Cat<TAB>Black cat. Sleek, shiny. Likes
        children. <TAB>20.00<TAB>catblack.jpg
<TAB>Chinese Bearded Dragon<TAB>Lizard<TAB>Grows up to 2
        feet long. Fascinating to watch. Likes to be
        held.<TAB>100.00<TAB>lizard.jpg
<TAB>Labrador Retriever<TAB>Dog<TAB>Black dog. Large,
        intelligent retriever. Often selected as guide
        dogs for the blind.<TAB>100.00<TAB>lab.jpg
<TAB>Goldfish<TAB>Fish<TAB>Variety of colors. Inexpensive.
        Easy care. Good first pet for small
        children.<TAB>2.00<TAB>goldfish.jpg
<TAB>Shark<TAB>Fish<TAB>Sleek. Powerful. Handle with
        care.<TAB>200.00<TAB>shark.jpg
<TAB>Asian Dragon<TAB>Dragon<TAB>Long and serpentine.
        Often gold or red.<TAB>10000.00<TAB>dragona.jpg
<TAB>Unicorn<TAB>Horse<TAB>Beautiful white steed with
        spiral horn on forehead.<TAB>20000.00<TAB>
        unicorn.jpg
```

These are the data file rules:

- ✔ The <TAB> tags represent real tabs — the kind that you create by pressing the Tab key.

- ✔ Each line represents one pet and must be entered without pressing the Enter or Return key. The lines in the preceding example are shown wrapped to more than one line so that you can see the entire line. However, in the actual file, the data lines are one on each line.

- ✔ A tab appears at the beginning of each line because the first field is not being entered. The first field is the petID, which is entered automatically; you don't need to enter it. However, you do need to use a tab so that MySQL knows there's a blank field at the beginning.

You can then read the data from the file into the database in phpMyAdmin. Reading data from a file is described in Chapter 4. Any time the data table gets odd, you can re-create it and read in the data again.

Designing the Look and Feel

After you know what the application is going to do and what information the database contains, you can design the look and feel of the application. The look and feel includes what the user sees and how the user interacts with the application. Your design should be attractive and easy to use. You can plan this design on paper, indicating what the user sees, perhaps with sketches or with written descriptions. In your design, include the user interaction components, such as buttons or links, and describe their actions. You should include each page of the application in the design. If you're lucky, you know a graphic designer who can develop beautiful Web pages for you. If you're me, you just do your best with a limited amount of graphic know-how.

The Pet Catalog has two look-and-feel designs: one for the catalog that the customer sees, and another, less fancy one for the part of the application that you or whoever is adding pets to the catalog uses.

Showing pets to the customers

The application includes three pages that customers see:

- ✔ **The storefront page:** This is the first page that customers see. It states the name of the business and the purpose of the Web site.

- ✔ **The pet type page:** This page lists all the types of pets and allows customers to select which type of pet they want to see.

- ✔ **The pets page:** This page shows all the pets of the selected type.

Storefront page

The storefront page is the introductory page for the Pet Store. Because most people already know what a pet store is, this page doesn't need to provide much explanation. Figure 11-1 shows the storefront page. The only customer action available on this page is a link that the customer can click to see the Pet Catalog.

Figure 11-1:
The opening
page of the
Pet Store
Web site.

Pet type page

The pet type page lists all the types of pets in the catalog. Each pet type is listed with its description. Figure 11-2 shows the pet type page. Radio buttons appear next to each pet type so that customers can select the type of pet that they want to see.

Pets page

The pets page lists all the pets of the selected type. Each pet is listed with its pet ID, description, picture, and price. The pets page appears in a different format, depending on the information in the catalog database.

Figures 11-3, 11-4, and 11-5 show some possible pets pages.

Figure 11-3 shows a page listing three different dogs from the catalog. Figure 11-4 shows that more than one pet can have the same pet name. Notice that the house cats have different pet ID numbers. Figure 11-5 shows the output when pets are found in the `Color` table, indicating that more than one color is available.

On all these pages, a line at the top reads `Click on any picture to see a larger version`. If the customer clicks the picture, a larger version of the picture is displayed.

Figure 11-4:
This pets page shows three cats with the same pet name.

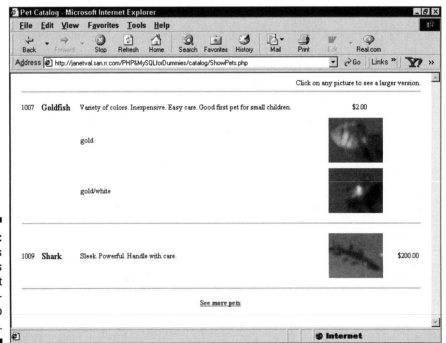

Figure 11-5:
This pets page shows goldfish that are available in two colors.

Adding pets to the catalog

The application includes three pages that customers don't see; these are the pages used to add pets to the Pet Catalog. The three pages work in sequential order to add a single pet:

1. Get pet type page.

   The person adding a pet to the catalog selects the radio button for the pet type. The user can also enter a new pet type.

2. Get pet information page.

   The user selects the radio button for the pet being added and fills in the pet description, price, and picture filename. The user can also enter a new pet name.

3. Receives a feedback page.

   A page is displayed showing the pet information that was added to the catalog.

Get pet type page

The first page gets the pet type for the pet that needs to be added to the catalog. Figure 11-6 shows the get pet type page. Notice that all the pet types currently in the catalog are listed, and a section is provided where the user can enter a new pet type if it's needed.

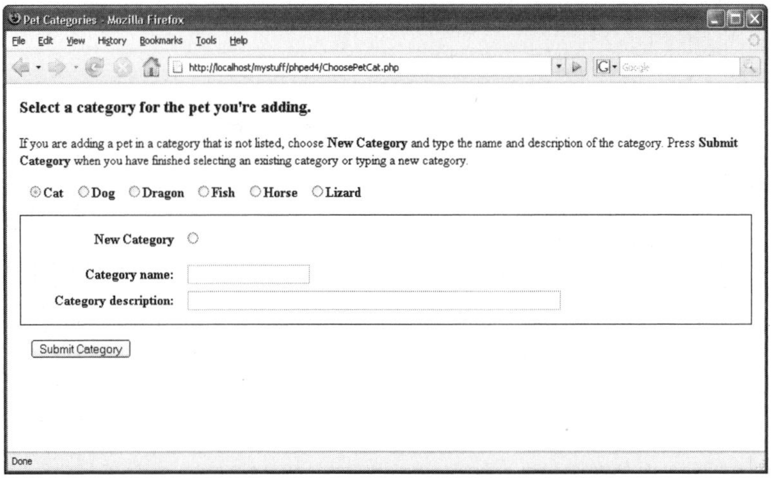

Figure 11-6: The first page for adding a pet to the catalog.

Get pet information page

Figure 11-7 shows the second page. This page lets the user type the information about the pet that goes in the catalog. This page lists all the pet names in the catalog for the selected pet type so that the user can select one. It also provides a section where the user can type a new pet name if needed.

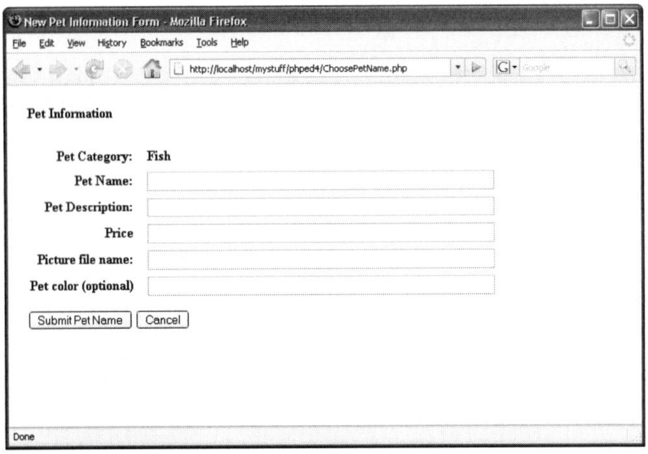

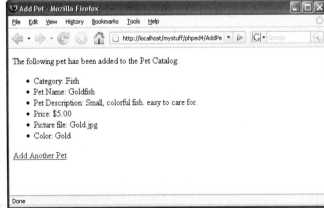

Figure 11-7: The second page asks for the pet name.

Feedback page

When the user submits the pet information, that information is added to the PetCatalog database. Figure 11-8 shows a page that verifies the information that was added to the database. The user can click a link to return to the first page and add another pet.

Figure 11-8: The last page provides feedback.

Get missing information page

The application checks the data to see that the user entered the required information and prompts the user for any information that isn't entered. For instance, if the user selects New Category on the first page, the user must type a category name and description. If the user doesn't type the name or the description, a page is displayed that points out the problem and requests the information. Figure 11-9 shows the page that users see if they forget to type the category name and description.

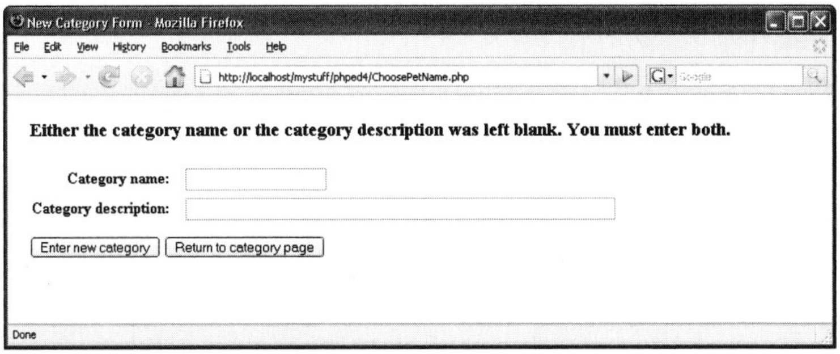

Figure 11-9: This page requests a new category and description.

Writing the Programs

After you know what the pages are going to look like and what they are going to do, you can write the programs. In general, you write a program for each page, although sometimes it makes sense to separate programs into more than one file or to combine programs on a page. (For details on how to organize applications, see Chapter 10.)

As I discuss in Chapter 10, keep the information needed to connect to the database in a separate file and include that file in all the programs that need to access the database. The file should be stored in a secure location and with a misleading name for security reasons. For this application, the following information is stored in a file named `misc.inc`:

```php
<?php
   $user="catalog";
   $host="localhost";
   $password="";
   $database="PetCatalog";
?>
```

The Pet Catalog application has two independent sets of programs: one set to show the Pet Catalog to customers and one set to enter new pets into the catalog.

Showing pets to the customers

The application that shows the Pet Catalog to customers has three basic tasks:

- ✔ Show the storefront page, with a link to the catalog.
- ✔ Show a page where users select the pet type.
- ✔ Show a page with pets of the selected pet type.

Showing the storefront

The storefront page doesn't need any PHP statements. It simply displays a Web page with a link. HTML statements are sufficient to do this. Listing 11-1 shows the HTML file that describes the storefront page.

Listing 11-1:   HTML File for the Storefront Page

```
<?php
  /* Program: PetShopFront.php
   * Desc:    Displays opening page for Pet Store.
   */
?>
<html>
<head><title>Pet Store Front Page</title></head>
<body>
<div style="text-align: center">
  <img src="images/awning-top.gif" alt="awning" />
  <img src="images/Name.gif" alt="Pet Store">
  <p style="margin-top: 40pt">
  <img src="images/lizard-front.jpg" height="186"
       width="280" alt="animal picture" /></p>
  <h2>Looking for a new friend?</h2>
  <p>Check out our
      <a href="PetCatalog.php">Pet Catalog.</a>
  <br /> We may have just what you're looking for.</p>
</div>
</body></html>
```

Notice that the link is to a PHP program called `PetCatalog.php`. When the customer clicks the link, the Pet Catalog program (`PetCatalog.php`) begins.

Showing the pet types

The pet type page (refer to Figure 11-2) shows the customer a list of all the types of pets currently in the catalog. Listing 11-2 shows the program that produces the pet type Web page.

Listing 11-2: Displaying Pet Types

```php
<?php
  /* Program: PetCatalog.php
   * Desc:    Displays a list of pet categories from the
   *          PetType table. Includes descriptions.
   *          Displays radio buttons for user to check.
   */
?>
<html>
<head><title>Pet Types</title></head>
<body>
<?php
  include("misc.inc");                                      →12

  $cxn = mysqli_connect($host,$user,$passwd,$dbname)        →14
        or die ("couldn't connect to server");

  /* Select all categories from PetType table */
  $query = "SELECT * FROM PetType ORDER BY petType";        →18
  $result = mysqli_query($cxn,$query)
            or die ("Couldn't execute query.");             →20

  /* Display text before form */
  echo "<div style='margin-left: .1in'>\n
  <h1 style='text-align: center'>Pet Catalog</h1>\n
  <h2 style='text-align: center'>The following animal
      friends are waiting for you.</h2>\n
  <p style='text-align: center'>Find just what you want
      and hurry in to the store to pick up your
      new friend.</p>
  <h3>Which pet are you interested in?</h3>\n";

  /* Create form containing selection list */
  echo "<form action='ShowPets.php' method='POST'>\n"; →33
  echo "<table cellpadding='5' border='1'>";
  $counter=1;                                               →35
  while($row = mysqli_fetch_assoc($result))                →36
  {
    extract($row)                                           →38
    echo "<tr><td valign='top' width='15%'
                style='font-weight: bold;
                font-size: 1.2em'\n";
    echo "<input type='radio' name='interest'              →42
                value='$petType'\n";                        →43
    if( $counter == 1 )                                     →44
    {
        echo "checked='checked'";
    }
```

(continued)

Listing 11-2 *(continued)*

```
        echo ">$petType</td>";                                    →48
        echo "<td>$typeDescription</td></tr>";                    →49
        $counter++;                                               →50
    }
  echo "</table>";
  echo "<p><input type='submit' value='Select Pet Type'>
        </form></p>\n";                                           →54
?>
</div>
</body></html>
```

Here is a brief explanation of what the following lines do:

→12 The `include` statement brings in a file that contains the information necessary to connect to the database. I call it `misc.inc` because that seems more secure than calling it `passwords.inc`.

→14 Connects to the MySQL server.

→18 A query that selects all the information from the `PetType` table and puts it in alphabetical order based on pet type.

→20 Executes the query on line 18.

→33 The opening tag for a form that holds all the pet types. The action target is `ShowPets.php`, which is the program that shows the pets of the chosen type.

→35 Creates a counter with a starting value of 1. The counter keeps track of how many pet types are found in the database.

→36 Starts a `while` loop that gets the rows containing the pet type and pet description that were selected from the database on lines 19 and 20. The loop executes once for each pet type that was retrieved.

→38 Separates the row into two variables: `$petType` and `$pet Description`.

→42 Lines 42–43 echo a form field tag for a radio button. The value is the value in `$petType`. This statement executes once in each loop, creating a radio button for each pet type. This statement echoes only part of the form field tag.

→44 Starts an `if` block that executes only in the first loop. It echoes the word `"checked='checked'"` as part of the form field. This ensures that one of the radio buttons is selected in the form so that the form can't be submitted with no button selected, which would result in unsightly error messages or warnings. The counter was set up solely for this purpose.

Although adding `"checked='checked'"` to every radio button works in some browsers, it confuses other browsers. However, the extra programming required to add `"checked='checked'"` to only one radio button can prevent potential problems.

→**48**   Echoes the remaining part of the form field tag for the radio button — the part that closes the tag and displays the pet type.

→**49**   Echoes the pet description in a second cell in the table row.

→**50**   Adds 1 to the counter to keep track of the number of times that the loop has executed.

→**53**   Adds the submit button to the form.

→**54**   Closes the form.

When the user selects a radio button and then clicks the submit button, the next program — named `ShowPets.php` in the form tag — runs, showing the pets for the selected pet type.

Showing the pets

The pets page (refer to Figures 11-3, 11-4, and 11-5) shows the customer a list of all the pets of the selected type that are currently in the catalog. Listing 11-3 shows the program that produces the pet Web page.

Listing 11-3:   Displaying a List of Pets

```
<?php
 /* Program: ShowPets.php
  * Desc:    Displays all the pets in a category.
  *          Category is passed in a variable from a
  *          form. The information for each pet is
  *          displayed on a single line, unless the pet
  *          comes in more than one color. If the pet
  *          comes in colors, a single line is displayed
  *          without a picture, and a line for each color,
  *          with pictures, is displayed following the
  *          single line. Small pictures are displayed,
  *          which are links to larger pictures.
  */
?>
<html>
<head><title>Pet Catalog</title></head>
<body>
<?php
 include("misc.inc");

 $cxn = mysqli_connect($host,$user,$passwd,$dbname)
        or die ("couldn't connect to server");
```

(continued)

Listing 11-3 *(continued)*

```
/* Select pets of the given type */
$query = "SELECT * FROM Pet                                          →25
          WHERE petType=\"{$_POST['interest']}\"";  →26
$result = mysqli_query($cxn,$query)
          or die ("Couldn't execute query.");

/* Display results in a table */
echo "<table cellspacing='10' border='0' cellpadding='0'
          width='100%'>";
echo "<tr><td colspan='5' style='text-align: right'>
          Click on any picture to see a larger
              version. <hr /></td></tr>\n";
while($row = mysqli_fetch_assoc($result))                →36
{
  $f_price = number_format($row['price'],2);

  /* check whether pet comes in colors */
  $query = "SELECT * FROM Color
              WHERE petName='{$row['petName']}'";  →42
  $result2 = mysqli_query($cxn,$query)
              or die(mysqli_error($cxn));
  $ncolors = mysqli_num_rows($result2);                →45

  /* display row for each pet */
  echo "<tr>\n";
  echo " <td>{$row['petID']}</td>\n";
  echo " <td style='font-weight: bold;
          font-size: 1.1em'>{$row['petName']}</td>\n";
  echo " <td>{$row['petDescription']}</td>\n";
  /* display picture if pet does not come in colors */
  if( $ncolors <= 1 )                                    →54
  {
     echo "<td><a href='../images/{$row['pix']}'
                       border='0'>
                 <img src='../images/{$row['pix']}'
                  border='0' width='100' height='80' />
                </a></td>\n";
  }
  echo "<td align='center'>\$$f_price</td>\n
        </tr>\n";
  /* display row for each color  */
  if($ncolors > 1 )                                      →65
  {
     while($row2 = mysqli_fetch_assoc($result2))      →67
     {
       echo "<tr><td colspan=2> </td>
                <td>{$row2['petColor']}</td>
                <td><a href='../images/{$row2['pix']}'
                       border='0'>
                  <img src='../images/{$row2['pix']}'
                    border='0' width='100'
```

```
                            height='80' /></a></td>\n";
            }
        }
        echo "<tr><td colspan='5'><hr /></td></tr>\n";
    }
    echo "</table>\n";
    echo "<div style='text-align: center'>
            <a href='PetCatalog.php'>
                <h3>See more pets</h3></a></div>";
?>
</body></html>
```

Many of the tasks in Listing 11-3 are also in most of the programs in this application, such as connecting to the database, creating forms, and executing queries. Because I document these common tasks for Listing 11-2, I don't repeat them here. Following is a brief explanation of what some of the other lines do in the program:

→**25**   Lines 25–26 select all the pets in the catalog that match the chosen type, which was passed in a form from the previous page.

→**36**   Sets up a `while` loop that runs once for each pet selected. The loop creates a line of information for each pet found.

→**42**   Lines 42–45 check whether the pet has any entries in the `Color` table. Notice that the query results are put in `$result2`. They couldn't be put in `$result` because this variable name is already in use. `$ncolors` stores the number of rows found in the `Color` table for the pet. Every pet name is checked for colors when it's processed in the loop.

→**54**   Starts an `if` block that is executed only if zero or one row for the pet was found in the `Color` table. The `if` block displays the picture of the pet. If the program found more than one color for the pet in the `Color` table, the pet is available in more than one color, and the picture shouldn't be shown here. Instead, a picture for each color will be shown in later lines. Refer to Figures 11-3 and 11-4 for pet pages that display the pictures and information on a single row, as in this `if` block.

→**65**   Starts an `if` block that's executed if more than one pet color was found. The `if` block echoes a row for each color found in the `Color` table.

→**67**   Sets up a `while` loop within the `if` block that runs once for each color found in the `Color` table. The loop displays a line, including a picture, for each color. Refer to Figure 11-5 for a pet page that displays separate lines with pictures for each color.

The page has a link to more pets at the bottom. The link points to the previous program that displays the pet types.

Adding pets to the catalog

The application that adds a new pet to the catalog should do the following tasks:

1. Create a form that asks for a pet category.

   The person adding the pet can choose one of the existing pet types or create a new one. To create a new type, the user needs to type a category name and description.

2. If a new type is created, check that the name and description were typed.

3. Create a form that asks for pet information — name, description, price, picture filename, and color.

   The person adding the pet can choose one of the existing pet names for the selected category or create a new name. To create a new pet name, the user needs to type a pet name.

4. If new is selected for the pet name, check that the name was typed in.

5. Store the new pet in the PetCatalog database.

6. Send a feedback page that shows what information was just added to the catalog.

The tasks are performed in three programs:

✔ ChoosePetCat.php: Creates the pet type form (task 1)

✔ ChoosePetName.php: Checks the pet category data and creates the pet information form (tasks 2 and 3)

✔ AddPet.php: Checks the pet name field, stores the new pet in the catalog database, and provides feedback (tasks 4, 5, and 6)

Writing ChoosePetCat

The first program, ChoosePetCat.php, produces a Web page with an HTML form in which the person adding a pet can select a pet type for the pet. ChoosePetCat.php is shown in Listing 11-4.

Listing 11-4:   Selecting a Pet Type

```
<?php
  /* Program: ChoosePetCat.php
   * Desc:    Allows users to select a pet type. All the
   *          existing pet types from the PetType table
   *          are displayed with radio buttons. A section
   *          to enter a new pet type is provided.
   */
?>
```

```
<html>
<head>
 <title>Pet Categories</title>
 <style type='text/css'>
 <!--
   #new { border: thin solid; margin: 1em 0; padding: 1em;
          }
   #radio { padding-bottom: 1em; }
   .field { padding-top: .5em; }
   label { font-weight: bold ; }
   #new label { width: 20%; float: left;
               margin-right: 1em; text-align: right; }
   input { margin-left: 1em; }
   #new input { margin-left: 0 }
   -->
 </style>
</head>

<body style='margin: 1em'>
 <h3>Select a category for the pet you're adding.</h3>
 <p>If you are adding a pet in a category that is not
    listed, choose <b>New Category</b> and type the
    name and description of the category. Press
    <b>Submit Category</b> when you have finished
    selecting an existing category or typing a new
    category.</p>
<?php
 include("misc.inc");
 $cxn = mysqli_connect($host,$user,$passwd,$dbname)
        or die ("couldn't connect to server");
 $query="SELECT petType FROM PetType                    →37
                    ORDER BY petType";                  →38
 $result = mysqli_query($cxn,$query)
           or die ("Couldn't execute query.");

 /* Display form for selecting pet type */
 echo "<form action='ChoosePetName.php'
              method='post'>\n";
 $counter=0;                                            →45
 while($row = mysqli_fetch_assoc($result))              →46
 {
    extract($row);
    echo "<label><input type='radio' name='category'   →49
                        value='$petType'";
         if($counter == 0)                              →51
           {
               echo " checked='checked'";
           }
    echo " />$petType </label>\n";                      →55
    $counter++;                                         →56
 }
```

(continued)

Listing 11-4 *(continued)*

```
?>
<div id="new">                                                      →59
  <div id="radio">
    <label for="category">New Category</label>
      <input type="radio" name="category" id="category"
             value="new" />
  </div>
  <div class="field">
    <label for="newCat">Category name: </label>
      <input type="text" name="newCat" size="20"
             id="newCat" maxlength="20" /></div>
  <div class="field">
    <label for="newDesc">Category description: </label>
      <input type="text" name="newDesc" id="newDesc"
             size="70%" maxlength="255" /></div>
</div>
<input type='submit' value='Submit Category' />
</form></body></html>
```

Many of the tasks in Listing 11-4, such as connecting to the database, creating forms, and executing queries, are found in most of the programs in this application; refer to Listing 11-2 for an explanation. The following list provides a brief explanation of what the following lines do:

→**37** A query (lines 37 and 38) that selects all the pet types from the PetType table and sorts them in alphabetical order.

→**45** Creates a counter with a starting value of 0. The counter keeps track of how many pet types are found in the database.

→**46** Starts a while loop that executes once for each pet type. The loop creates a list of radio buttons for the pet types, with one button selected. Here are the details of the while loop:

→**49** Echoes a form field tag (lines 49 and 50), including a label tag, for a radio button with the value equal to $petType. This statement executes once in each loop, creating a radio button for each pet type. This statement echoes only the first part of the form field tag.

→**51** An if block that executes only in the first loop. It echoes the attribute "checked='checked'" as part of the form field. This attribute ensures that one of the radio buttons is selected when displayed so that the form can't be submitted with no button selected, which would result in unsightly error messages. The counter was set up solely for this purpose.

Although adding "checked='checked'" to every radio button works in some browsers, it causes problems in other browsers. The extra programming required to add "checked= 'checked'" to only one radio button can prevent problems.

→**55** Echoes the remaining part of the form field tag for the radio button — the part that closes the tag.

→**56** Adds 1 to the counter to keep track of the number of times the loop has executed. This is the last line in the while loop.

→**59** From line 59 to the end of the program, HTML code displays the new category section of the form.

Writing ChoosePetName

The second program, ChoosePetName.php, accepts the data from the form in the first program. It checks the information and asks for missing information. After the pet type information is received correctly, the program creates a form in which a user can select a pet name for the new pet being added to the catalog and type the information for the pet. This program brings in two forms from separate files with include statements — NewCat_form. inc and NewName_form.inc. This program also calls a function that's in an include file. Listing 11-5 shows ChoosePetName.php.

Listing 11-5: Asking the User for the Pet Name

```php
<?php
 /* Program: ChoosePetName.php
  * Desc:    Allows the user to enter the information
  *          for the new pet. If the category is new,
  *          it's entered into the database.
  */
if(@$_POST['newbutton'] == "Return to category page"     →7
   or @$_POST['newbutton'] == "Cancel")
{
   header("Location: ChoosePetCat.php");
}
include("misc.inc");
include("functions.inc");                                 →13
$cxn = mysqli_connect($host,$user,$passwd,$dbname)        →14
      or die ("Couldn't connect to server");
/* If new was selected for pet category, check if
   category name and description were filled in. */
if(trim($_POST['category']) == "new")                     →18
{
  $_POST['category']=trim($_POST['newCat']);              →20
  if(empty($_POST['newCat'])                              →21
        or empty($_POST['newDesc']) )
  {
     include("NewCat_form.inc");                          →24
     exit();                                              →25
  }
  else                                                    →27
  {                                                       →28
```

(continued)

Listing 11-5 *(continued)*

```
    addNewType($_POST['newCat'],$_POST['newDesc'],$cxn);
  }
}                                                                      →31
include("NewName_form.inc");                                           →32
?>
```

Only some of the lines are documented in the following list because many of the tasks in the listing are found in most of the programs in this application. The common tasks are documented for Listing 11-2 and explained in other parts of the book, so I don't repeat them here. Here's a brief explanation of what the following lines do in the program:

→**7**   Starts an `if` statement that checks whether the user clicked the submit button labeled *Cancel* or *Return to category page.* If so, it returns to the first page.

→**13**   Includes the file that defines the function `AddNewType()`, which is used later in this program. The function is shown in Listing 11-8.

→**14**   Creates a connection to the database.

→**18**   Starts an `if` block that executes only if the user selected the radio button for New Category in the form from the previous program. This block checks whether the new category name and description are filled in. If the user forgot to type them, he or she is asked for the pet type name and description again. After the name and description are filled, the program calls a function that adds the new category to the `PetType` table. The following lines describe this `if` block in more detail:

    →**20**   Sets the category name, which currently equals `"new"`, to the new category name.

    →**21**   Starts an `if` block that executes only if the category name or the category description is blank. Because this `if` block is inside the `if` block for a new category, this block executes only if the user selected New Category for pet type but didn't fill in the new category name *and* description.

    →**24**   Creates a form that asks for the category name and description. The HTML for the form is included from a file — `NewCat_form.inc`, which is shown in Listing 11-6. This executes only when the `if` statement on line 21 is true — that is, if the category is new and the category name and/or description is blank.

    →**25**   Stops the program after displaying the form on line 24. The program can't proceed until the category name and description are typed. This block repeats until a category name and description are filled.

→**27** Starts an `else` block that executes only if both the category name and description are filled in. Because this block is inside the `if` block for the new radio button, this block executes when the user selected `new` and filled in the new category name and description.

→**29** Calls a function that adds the new category to the `PetType` table.

→**31** This line ends the `if` block. If the user selected one of the existing pet types, the statements between line 17 and this line did not execute.

→**32** Creates the form where the user can enter information about the new pet. A file is included that contains the code for the form, shown in Listing 11-7.

This program brings in three files using `include` statements. Listings 11-6, 11-7, and 11-8 show the three files that are included: `NewCat_form.inc`, `NewName_form.inc`, and `functions.inc`.

In Listing 11-5, line 24 includes a form that requests the user to enter a pet category name and description. This form is only displayed if the user did not type this information on the first page, which is displayed by the program in Listing 11-4. The program `ChoosePatName.php` checks whether the information was entered on the first page, and if it wasn't, it displays the form in Listing 11-6 (shown earlier in Figure 11-9).

Listing 11-6:   HTML Code That Creates New Pet Type Form

```php
<?php
  /* Program: NewCat_form.inc
   * Desc:    Displays a form to collect a category name
   *          and description.
   */
?>
<html>
<head>
<title>New Category Form</title>
<style type='text/css'>
 <!--
  .field { padding-top: .5em; }
  label { font-weight: bold; float: left; width: 18%;
          margin-right: 1em; text-align: right; }
 -->
</style>
</head>
<body style="padding: 1em">
<h3>Either the category name or the category description
    was left blank. You must enter both.</h3>
```

(continued)

Listing 11-6 *(continued)*

```
<form action=<?php echo "$_SERVER[PHP_SELF]" ?>
            method="post">
  <div class="field">
    <label for="newCat">Category name: </label>
      <input type="text" name="newCat" id="newCat"
        size="20" maxlength="20"
        value="<?php echo $_POST['newCat'] ?>" /></div>
  <div class="field">
      <label for="newDesc">Category description: </label>
      <input type="text" name="newDesc" id="newDesc"
        value="<?php echo $_POST['newDesc'] ?>"
        size="70%" maxlength="255" /></div>
  <input type="hidden" name="category" value="new">
  <p><input type="submit" name="newbutton"
        value="Enter new category">
      <input type="submit" name="newbutton"
        value="Return to category page">
</form></body></html>
```

This program is almost all HTML code. Note the following points:

✔ **This form is created only when the user selects the radio button for New Category on the pet type Web page but does not type the pet type name or description.** This form is displayed to give the user a second chance to type the name or description and continues to redisplay until the user enters the required information.

✔ **Most of the file is HTML, with only two small PHP sections that echo values for the two fields.**

✔ **The form returns to the program that generated it for processing.** It's processed in the same manner as the form that was sent from the first page. The field names are the same and are checked again to see whether they are blank.

✔ **A hidden field is included that sends $category with a value of "new".** If this form didn't send $category, the program that processes it — the same program that generated it — wouldn't know that the pet type was new and wouldn't execute the if block that should be executed when a new category is selected.

The program in Listing 11-5, on line 32, includes a file that creates a form where the user can enter information about the pet. Listing 11-7 shows the code for this form. The Web page it displays is shown in Figure 11-7.

Listing 11-7:   HTML File That Creates the Pet Information Form

```php
<?php
/*  Program name: NewName_form.inc
 *  Description:  Script displays a form that asks for
 *                the new pet information.
 */
$labels = array("petName" => "Pet Name: ",
                "petDescription" => "Pet Description: ",
                "price" => "Price",
                "pix" => "Picture file name: ",
                "petColor" => "Pet color (optional)");
if(isset($_POST['category']))                                   →11
{
    $category = $_POST['category'];
}
else
{
    $category = $_POST['newCat'];
}
?>
<html>
<head>
 <title>New Pet Information Form</title>
 <style type='text/css'>
  <!--
    form { margin: 1em; padding: 0; }
    .field { padding-top: .5em; }
    label { font-weight: bold; float: left; width: 18%;
            margin-right: 1em; text-align: right; }
    #submit { margin-top: 1em; )
  -->
 </style>
</head>

<body>
<form action="AddPet.php" method="post">
<?php
 echo "<h4>Pet Information</h4>";                               →37
 echo "<div class='field'> <label>Pet Category:</label>
                          <b>$category</b></div>\n";
 foreach($labels as $field => $label)
 {
   echo "<div class='field'>
          <label for='$field'>$label</label>
          <input type='text' name='$field' id='$field'
            size='65' maxlength='65'
            value='".@$$field."' /></div>\n";
 }
?>
```

(continued)

Listing 11-7 *(continued)*

```
<div id="submit">
 <input type='hidden' name='newCat'
            value='<?php echo $category ?>' />
 <input type='submit' value='Submit Pet Name' />
 <input type='submit' name='newbutton' value='Cancel' />
</div> </form></body></html>
```

The code defines the form where users can enter the pet information. Note
the following points:

✔ **An if statement, staring on line 11, sets the variable $category to
the name of the current category.** The category element in the $_POST
array may contain the value "new", instead of a category name.

✔ **The first line in the form cannot be changed.** The first line displays
the current category. The form does not allow the user to change this
value. The remaining fields in the form allow the user to enter the name,
description, and other information for the new pet.

✔ **The array $labels contains the information for the form fields.** The
foreach loop echoes the fields. This array does not contain the first
field, which contains the category, because it's displayed differently so it
can't be changed.

✔ **A hidden field passed the category value.** Because the first field is not
a normal field, the category is not passed in the $_POST array. A hidden
field is required to pass it.

In addition to form files, the ChoosePetName.php program in Listing 11-5
(earlier in the chapter) calls a function. The function is stored in a file named
functions.inc and is included in the beginning of the program. Listing 11-8
shows the function.

Listing 11-8: Function addNewType()

```
<?php
 /* Function addNewType
  * Desc    Adds a new pet type and description to the
  *         PetType table. Checks for the new pet type
  *         first and does not add it to the table if
  *         it is already there.
  */
function addNewType($petType,$typeDescription,$cxn)
{
  /* Check whether new category is in PetType table.
     If it is not in table, add it to table. */
  $query = "SELECT petType FROM PetType
                       WHERE petType='$petType'";
```

```
$result = mysqli_query($cxn,$query) or
        die("Couldn't execute select query");
$ntype = mysqli_num_rows($result); //
if ($ntype < 1)    // if new type is not in table
{
  $petType = ucfirst(strip_tags(trim($petType)));
  $typeDescription =
      ucfirst(strip_tags(trim($typeDescription)));
  $petType = mysqli_real_escape_string($cxn,$petType);
  $typeDescription =
      mysqli_real_escape_string($cxn,$typeDescription);

  $query="INSERT INTO PetType (petType,typeDescription)
            VALUES ('$petType','$typeDescription')";
  $result = mysqli_query($cxn,$query)
            or die("Couldn't execute insert query");
}
return;
}
?>
```

The function checks whether the pet type is already in the `PetType` table. If it isn't, the function cleans the data and adds it to the table.

Writing AddPet

The last program, `AddPet.php`, accepts the data from the form in the second program. If new was selected for the pet name, the program checks to see that a new name was typed and prompts for it again if it was left blank. After the pet name is filled in, the program stores the pet information from the previous page. Notice that it doesn't check the other information because the other information is optional. This program, as in Listing 11-5, brings in some of the HTML forms and tables from two separate files by using an `include` statement. Listing 11-9 shows `AddPet.php`.

Listing 11-9: Adding a New Pet to the Catalog

```
<?php
 /* Program: AddPet.php
  * Desc:    Adds new pet to the database. A confirmation
  *          page is sent to the user.
  */
if (@$_POST['newbutton'] == "Cancel")                    →6
{
  header("Location: ChoosePetCat.php");
}
include("misc.inc");
$cxn = mysqli_connect($host,$user,$passwd,$dbname)       →11
      or die ("Couldn't connect to server");
```

(continued)

Listing 11-9 *(continued)*

```
foreach($_POST as $field => $value)                           →13
{
  if(empty($value))                                           →15
  {
    if($field == "petName" or $field == "petDescription")
    {
      $blank_array[] = $field;
    }
  }
  else                                                        →22
  {
    if($field != "category")
    {
      if(!preg_match("/^[A-Za-z0-9., _-]+$/",$value))
      {
        $error_array[] = $field;
      }
      if($field == "newCat")
      {
        $clean_data['petType']=trim(strip_tags($value));
      }
      else
      {
        $clean_data[$field] = trim(strip_tags($value));
      }
    }
  }
}                                                             →40
if(@sizeof($blank_array)>0 or @sizeof($error_array)>0)        →41
{
  if(@sizeof($blank_array) > 0)
  {
    echo "<p><b>You must enter both pet name and
                pet description</b></p>\n";
  }
  if(@sizeof($error_array) > 0)
  {
    echo "<p><b>The following fields have incorrect
            information. Only letters, numbers, spaces,
            underscores, and hyphens are allowed:</b><br
            />\n";
    foreach($error_array as $value)
    {
      echo "  $value<br />\n";
    }
  }
  extract($clean_data);
  include("NewName_form.inc");
  exit();
}
```

```
foreach($clean_data as $field => $value)                      →62
{
   if(!empty($value) and $field != "petColor")                →64
   {
      $fields_form[$field] =
         ucfirst(strtolower(strip_tags(trim($value))));
      $fields_form[$field] =
            mysqli_real_escape_string($cxn,
               $fields_form[$field]);
      if($field == "price")                                   →71
      {
         $fields_form[$field] =
               (float) $fields_form[$field];
      }
   }
   if(!empty($_POST['petColor']))                             →77
   {
      $petColor = strip_tags(trim($_POST['petColor']));
      $petColor = ucfirst(strtolower($petColor));
      $petColor =
            mysqli_real_escape_string($cxn,$petColor);
   }
}                                                             →84
?>
<html>
<head><title>Add Pet</title></head>
<body>
<?php
 $field_array = array_keys($fields_form);                     →90
 $fields=implode(",",$field_array);                           →91
 $query = "INSERT INTO Pet ($fields) VALUES (";               →92
 foreach($fields_form as $field => $value)                    →93
 {
   if($field == "price")
   {
      $query .= "$value ,";
   }
   else
   {
      $query .= "'$value' ,";
   }
 }                                                            →103
$query .= ") ";                                               →104
$query = preg_replace("/,\)/",")",$query);                    →105
$result = mysqli_query($cxn,$query)                           →106
     or die ("Couldn't execute query");
$petID = mysqli_insert_id($cxn);                              →108
$query = "SELECT * from Pet WHERE petID='$petID'";            →109
$result = mysqli_query($cxn,$query)
      or die ("Couldn't execute query.");
```

(continued)

Listing 11-9 *(continued)*

```php
$row = mysqli_fetch_assoc($result);
extract($row);
echo "The following pet has been added to the
        Pet Catalog:<br />
        <ul>
          <li>Category: $petType</li>
          <li>Pet Name: $petName</li>
          <li>Pet Description: $petDescription</li>
          <li>Price: \$$price</li>
          <li>Picture file: $pix</li>\n";
if (@$petColor != "")                                      →122
{
    $query = "SELECT petName FROM Color
                WHERE petName='$petName'
                AND petColor='$petColor'";
    $result = mysqli_query($cxn,$query)
            or die("Couldn't execute query.");
    $num = mysqli_num_rows($result);
    if ($num < 1)
    {
      $query = "INSERT INTO Color (petName,petColor,pix)
              VALUES ('$petName','$petColor','$pix')";
      $result = mysqli_query($cxn,$query)
              or die("Couldn't execute query.".mysqli_
          error($cxn));
      echo "<li>Color: $petColor</li>\n";
    }
 }
 echo "</ul>\n";
 echo "<a href='ChoosePetCat.php'>Add Another Pet</a>\n";
?>
</body></html>
```

I document only some of the lines in the following list because many of the most common tasks, such as connecting to the database, have been documented for the previous programs in this chapter. Here's an explanation of what the following lines do in the program:

→6   Checks whether the user clicked the Cancel button. If so, returns to the first page.

→11   Connects to the database.

→13   Starts a `foreach` block that walks through the new pet information submitted on the previous Web page. This block checks and cleans the data. The following line numbers describe the processing in detail:

→15 Starts an `if` block that checks whether `petName` or `pet Description` are empty. If empty, the field name is added to the array `$blank_array`.

→**22** Starts an else block that checks for invalid format in the form fields. The field names that contain invalid data are added to the array $error_array. Data that is okay is cleaned and added to the array $clean_data.

→**40** The end of the foreach loop that checks the data.

→**41** Starts an if block that executes if any blank fields or invalid data was found. The block displays error messages for the blank or invalid data and then displays the form again so the user can enter the correct information. Line 59 redisplays the form, and line 60 stops the program.

→**62** Starts a foreach statement that loops through the $clean_data array. The program does not reach this line until all the required fields are filled and all the data is valid. This loop creates arrays that are used to create an INSERT query to store the new pat in the database. The following lines describe the processing in detail:

→**64** Starts an if block that executes if the field is not blank and if the field is not petColor. The if block creates an array $fields_form that contains the information needed to create the INSERT statement for the Pet table. Because petColor is not stored in the Pet table, it isn't included in this array.

→**71** Starts an if statement that processes price separately. Price must be stored as a number. The MySQL defines price as a decimal number, so MySQL doesn't accept a string in the INSERT query. In this block, price is stored as a number by telling PHP to store the value as a float, which means a decimal number.

→**77** Starts an if block that processes petColor separately, without putting it into the $fields_form array.

→**84** End of the foreach statement that started on line 62.

→**90** Creates an array $field-array of the fields stored in $fields_form.

→**91** Creates a string $fields which contains all of the field names in $fields_form, separated by commas.

→**92** Creates a string $query with the beginning of the INSERT query. It includes the string $fields created on line 91.

→**93** Begins a foreach statement that loops through $fields_form. The foreach block adds the values to the INSERT query. The value for price must be added separately because it can't have quotes around it. If it has quotes around the value, MySQL sees it as a string, not a number, and doesn't accept it as a valid value for the price field in the Pet table.

→**103** Ends the `foreach` loop.

→**104** Finished the `INSERT` query.

→**105** Removes an extra comma from the `INSERT` query.

→**106** Executes the `INSERT` query.

→**108** Stores the Pet ID field that was automatically entered by MySQL when the `INSERT` query was executed. `PetID` contains the ID number.

→**109** Lines 109 to the end of the program send the feedback page to the user. The information for the new pet is retrieved from the database and displayed on the Web page. If a pet color was entered, the `if` block that starts on line 122 executes. The pet name and color are stored in the Color table. And the output line for the color is added to the feedback page.

At the end of the feedback page, this program adds a link to the first page so that the user can add another new pet to the catalog if desired.

Chapter 12

Building a Members Only Web Site

Many Web sites require users to log in. Sometimes users can't view any Web pages without entering a password, while sometimes just part of the Web site requires a login. Here are some reasons why you might want to require a user login:

✔ **The information is secret.** You don't want anyone except a few authorized people to see the information. Or perhaps only your own employees should see the information.

✔ **The information or service is for sale.** The information or service that your Web site provides is your product, and you want to charge people for it. For instance, you might have a corner on some survey data that researchers are willing to pay for. For example, AAA Automobile Club offers some of its information for free, but you have to be a member to see its hotel ratings.

✔ **You can provide better service.** If you know who your customers are or have some of their information, you can make their interaction with your Web site easier. For instance, if you have an account with Barnes and Noble or the Gap and log in to its site, it uses your stored shipping address, and you don't have to type it again.

✔ **You can find out more about your customers.** Marketing would like to know who is looking at your Web site. A list of customers with addresses and phone numbers and perhaps some likes and dislikes is useful. If your Web site offers some attractive features, customers may be willing to provide some information to access your site.

Typically, a login requires the user to enter a user ID and a password. Often, users can create their own accounts on the Web site, choosing their own user IDs and passwords. Sometimes users can maintain their accounts — for example, change their passwords or phone numbers — online.

In Chapter 11, you find out how to build an online catalog for your Pet Store Web site. Now, you want to add a section to your Web site for Members Only. You plan to offer discounts, a newsletter, a database of pet information, and more in the Members Only section. You hope that customers will see the section as so valuable that they'll be willing to provide their addresses and phone numbers to get a member account that lets them use the services in the restricted section. In this chapter, you build a login section for the Pet Store.

Designing the Application

The first step in design is to decide what the application should do. Its basic function is to gather customer information and store it in a database. It offers customers access to valuable information and services to motivate them to provide information for the database. Because state secrets or credit card numbers aren't at risk, you should make it as easy as possible for customers to set up and access their accounts.

The application that provides access to the Members Only section of the Pet Store should do the following:

✔ **Provide a means for customers to set up their own accounts with member IDs and passwords.** This includes collecting from the customer the information that's required to become a member.

✔ **Provide a page where customers type their member ID and password and then check whether they are valid.** If so, the customer enters the Members Only section. If not, the customer can try another login.

✔ **Show the pages in the Members Only section to anyone who is logged in.**

✔ **Refuse to show the pages in the Members Only section to anyone who is *not* logged in.**

✔ **Keep track of member logins.** By doing this, you know who logs in and how often.

Building the Database

The database is the core and purpose of this application. It holds the customer information that's the goal of the Members Only section and the Member ID and password that allow the user to log in to the Members Only section.

The Members Only application database contains two tables:

- ✔ Member table
- ✔ Login table

The first step in building the login application is to build the database. It's pretty much impossible to write programs without a working database to test the programs on. First design your database, then build it, and then add some sample data for use while developing the programs.

Building the Member table

In your design for the login application, the main table is the Member table. It holds all the information entered by the customer, including the customer's personal information (name, address, and so on) and the Member ID and password. The following SQL query creates the Member table:

```
CREATE TABLE Member (
    loginName       VARCHAR(20)    NOT NULL,
    createDate      DATE           NOT NULL,
    password        VARCHAR(255)   NOT NULL,
    lastName        VARCHAR(50),
    firstName       VARCHAR(40),
    street          VARCHAR(50),
    city            VARCHAR(50),
    state           CHAR(2),
    zip             CHAR(10),
    email           VARCHAR(50),
    phone           VARCHAR(15),
    fax             VARCHAR(15),
PRIMARY KEY(loginName) );
```

Each row represents a member. The columns are

- ✔ loginName: A Member ID for the member to use when logging in. The customer chooses and types the login name. The CREATE query defines the loginName in the following ways:

  - VARCHAR(20): This statement defines the field as a variable character string that can be up to 20 characters long. The field is stored in its actual length.

  - PRIMARY KEY(loginName): The primary key identifies the row and must be unique. MySQL doesn't allow two rows to be entered with the same loginName.

  - NOT NULL: This definition means that this field can't be empty. It must have a value. The primary key must always be NOT NULL.

✔ createDate: The date when the row was added to the database — that is, the date when the customer created the account. The query defines createDate as

- DATE: This is a string that's treated as a date. Dates are displayed in the format YYYY-MM-DD. They can be entered in that format or a similar format, such as YY/M/D or YYYYMMDD.

- NOT NULL: This definition means this field can't be empty. It must have a value. Because the program, not the user, creates the date and stores it, this field won't ever be blank.

✔ password: A password for the member to use when logging in. The customer chooses and types the password. The CREATE query defines the password in the following ways:

- VARCHAR(255): This statement defines the field as a variable character string that can be up to 255 characters long. The field is stored in its actual length. You don't expect the password to be 255 characters long. In fact, you expect it to be pretty short. However, you intend to use the MySQL md5 function to encrypt it rather than store it in plain view. After it's encrypted, the string will be longer, so you're allowing room for the longer string.

- NOT NULL: This statement means that this field can't be empty. It must have a value. You're not going to allow an empty password in this application.

✔ lastName: The customer's last name, as typed by the customer. The CREATE query defines the field as

- VARCHAR(50): This data type defines the field as a variable character string that can be up to 50 characters long. The field is stored in its actual length.

✔ firstName: The customer's first name, as typed by the customer. The CREATE query defines the field as

- VARCHAR(40): This data type defines the field as a variable character string that can be up to 40 characters long. The field is stored in its actual length.

✔ street: The customer's street address, as typed by the customer. The CREATE query defines the field as

- VARCHAR(50): This data type defines the field as a variable character string that can be up to 50 characters long. The field is stored in its actual length.

✔ city: The city in the customer's address, as typed by the customer. The CREATE query defines the field as

- VARCHAR(50): This data type defines the field as a variable character string that can be up to 50 characters long. The field is stored in its actual length.

✔ `state`: The state in the customer's address. The string is the two-letter state code. The customer selects the data from a drop-down list containing all the states. The CREATE query defines the field as

- `CHAR(2)`: This data type defines the field as a character string that's 2 characters long. The field always take up 2 characters of storage.

✔ `zip`: The zip code that the customer types. The CREATE query defines the field as

- `CHAR(10)`: This data type defines the field as a character string that's 10 characters long. The field always takes up 10 characters of storage, with padding if the actual string stored is less than ten characters. The field is long enough to hold a zip+4 code, such as 12345–1234.

✔ `email`: The e-mail address that the customer types. The CREATE query defines the field as

- `VARCHAR(50)`: This data type defines the field as a variable character string that can be up to 50 characters long. The field is stored in its actual length.

✔ `phone`: The phone number that the customer types. The CREATE query defines the field as

- `CHAR(15)`: This data type defines the field as a character string that's 15 characters long. The field always takes up 15 characters of storage, with padding if the actual string stored is less than 15 characters.

✔ `fax`: The fax number that the customer types. The CREATE query defines the field as

- `CHAR(15)`: This data type defines the field as a character string that's 15 characters long. The field always takes up 15 characters of storage, with padding if the actual string stored is less than 15 characters.

Building the Login table

The Login table keeps track of member logins by recording the date and time every time a member logs in. Because each member has multiple logins, the login data requires its own table. The CREATE query that builds the Login table is

```
CREATE TABLE Login (
  loginName      VARCHAR(20) NOT NULL,
  loginTime      DATETIME    NOT NULL,
PRIMARY KEY(loginName,loginTime) );
```

The Login table has only two columns, as follows:

✔ loginName: The Member ID that the customer uses to log in with. The loginName is the connection between the Member table (which I describe in the preceding section) and this table. Notice that the loginName column is defined the same in the Member table and in this table. This makes table joining possible and makes matching rows in the tables much easier. The CREATE query defines the loginName in the following ways:

  • VARCHAR(20): This statement defines the field as a variable character string that can be up to 20 characters long. The field is stored in its actual length.

  • PRIMARY KEY(loginName,loginTime): The primary key identifies the row and must be unique. For this table, two columns together are the primary key. MySQL won't allow two rows to be entered with the same loginName *and* loginDate.

  • NOT NULL: This definition means that this field can't be empty. It must have a value. The primary key must always be NOT NULL.

✔ loginTime: The date and time when the member logged in. This field uses both the date and time because the field needs to be unique. It's unlikely that two users would log in at the same second at the Pet Store Web site. However, in some busy Web sites, two users might log in during the same second. At such a site, you might have to create a sequential login number to be the unique primary key for the site. The CREATE query defines the loginTime in the following ways:

  • DATETIME: This is a string that's treated as a date and time. The string is displayed in the format YYYY-MM-DD HH:MM:SS.

  • PRIMARY KEY(loginName,loginTime): The primary key identifies the row and must be unique. For this table, two columns together are the primary key. MySQL won't allow two rows to be entered with the same loginName *and* loginDate.

  • NOT NULL: This definition means that this field can't be empty. It must have a value. The primary key must always be NOT NULL.

Adding data to the database

This database is intended to hold data entered by customers — not by you. It's empty when the application is first made available to customers until customers add data. However, to test the programs while you write them, you need to have at least a few members in the database. You need a few Member IDs and passwords to test the login program. You can add some fake members for testing — by using an INSERT SQL query — and remove them when you're ready to go live with your Members Only application.

Designing the Look and Feel

After you know what the application is going to do and what information you want to get from customers and store in the database, you can design the look and feel. The look and feel includes what the user sees and how the user interacts with the application. Your design should be attractive and easy to use. You can create your design on paper, indicating what the user sees, perhaps with sketches or with written descriptions. You should also show the user interaction components, such as buttons or links, and describe their actions. Include each page of the application in the design.

The Pet Store Members Only application has three pages that are part of the login procedures. In addition, the application includes all the pages that are part of the Members Only section, such as the page that shows the special discounts and the pages that provide discussions of pet care. In this chapter, you build only the pages that are part of the login procedure. You don't build the pages that are part of the Members Only section, but I do discuss what needs to be included in them to protect them from viewing by nonmembers.

The login application includes three pages, plus the group of pages that make up the Members Only section, as follows:

- **Storefront page:** The first page that a customer sees. It provides the name of the business and the purpose of the Web site. In Chapter 11, I introduce a storefront page; in this chapter, you modify the page to provide access to the Members Only section.

- **Login page:** Allows the customer to either log in or create a new member account. It displays a form for the customer to fill in to get a new account.

- **New Member Welcome page:** Welcomes the new users by name, letting them know that their accounts have been created. Provides any information that they need to know. Provides a button so that users can continue to the Members Only section or return to the main page.

- **Members Only section:** A group of Web pages that contain the content of the Members Only section.

Storefront page

The *storefront page* is the introductory page for the Pet Store. Because most people know what a pet store is, the page doesn't need to provide much explanation. Figure 12-1 shows the storefront page. Two customer actions are available on this page: a link that the customer can click to see the Pet Catalog and a link to the Members Only section.

Figure 12-1:
The opening
page of the
Pet Store
Web site.

Login page

The login page, shown in Figure 12-2, allows the customer to log in or create a new member account. It includes the form that customers need to fill out to get a member account. This page has two submit buttons: one to log in with an existing member account and one to create a new member account.

Figure 12-2:
The page
where
customers
log in or
create a
new
member
account.

If a customer makes a mistake on the login page, either in the login section or the new member section, the form is displayed again with an error message. For instance, suppose that a customer makes an error when typing her e-mail address: She forgot to type the .com at the end of the e-mail address. Figure 12-3 shows the screen that she sees after she submits the form with the mistake in it. Notice the error message printed right above the form.

When members successfully log in with a valid Member ID and password, they go to the first page of the Members Only section. When new members successfully submit a form with information that looks reasonable, they go to a New Member Welcome page (see the next section). In addition, an e-mail message is sent to the new member with the following contents:

```
A new Member Account has been set up for you. Your new
Member ID and password are:

gsmith
secret

We appreciate your interest in Pet Store at PetStore.com.

If you have any questions or problems, email
webmaster@petstore.com
```

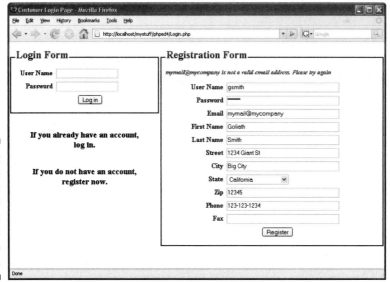

Figure 12-3:
Page showing a message resulting from a mistake in the form.

This e-mail message contains the customer's password. I think that it's helpful to both the customers and the business to provide customers with a hard copy of their passwords. Customers *will* forget their passwords. It seems to be one of the rules. An e-mail message with the password might help a customer when he forgets it, saving both him and you some trouble. Of course, e-mail messages aren't necessarily secure, so sending passwords via e-mail isn't a good idea for some accounts, such as an online bank account. But, for this Pet Store application, with only unauthorized discounts and pet care information at risk, sending the password via e-mail is a reasonable risk.

New Member Welcome page

The New Member Welcome page greets the customer and offers useful information. The customer sees that the account has been created and can then enter the Members Only section immediately. Figure 12-4 shows a welcome page.

Figure 12-4:
A page welcoming new members.

Members Only section

One or more Web pages make up the contents of the Members Only section. Whatever the content is, the pages are no different than any other Web pages or PHP programs, except for some PHP statements in the beginning of each file that prevent nonmembers from viewing the pages.

Writing the Programs

After you know what the pages are going to look like and what they are going to do, you can write the programs. In general, you create a program for each page, although sometimes it makes sense to separate programs into more than one file or to combine programs on a page. (See Chapter 10 for details on how to organize applications.)

As I discuss in Chapter 10, keep the information needed to connect to the database in a separate file and include it in the programs that need to access the database. Store the file in a secure location, with a misleading name. For this application, the following information is stored in a file named dogs.inc:

```php
<?php
  $user="admin";
  $host="localhost";
  $password="";
  $database="MemberDirectory";
?>
```

The member login application has several basic tasks:

1. Show the storefront page.

   This provides a link to the login page.

2. Show a page where customers can fill in a Member ID and a password to log in.

3. Check the Member ID and the password that the customer types against the Member ID and password stored in the database.

   If the ID and password are okay, the customer enters the Members Only section. If the ID and/or password are not okay, the customer is returned to the login page.

4. Show a page where customers can fill in the information needed to obtain a member account.

5. Check the information the customer typed for blank fields or incorrect formats.

   If bad information is found, show the form again so that the customer can correct the information.

6. When good information is entered, add the new member to the database.

7. Show a welcoming page to the new member.

The tasks are performed in three programs:

- ✔ PetShopFront.php: Shows the storefront page (task 1).
- ✔ Login.php: Performs both the login and create new member account tasks (Steps 2–6).
- ✔ New_member.php: Shows the page that welcomes the new member (task 7).

Writing PetShopFront

The storefront page doesn't need any PHP statements. It simply displays a Web page with two links — one link to the Pet Catalog and one link to the Members Only section of the Web site. HTML statements are sufficient to do this. Listing 12-1 shows the HTML file that describes the storefront page.

Listing 12-1:   HTML File for the Storefront Page

```
<?php
  /* Program: PetShopFrontMembers.php
   * Desc:     Displays opening page for Pet Store.
   */
?>
<html>
<head>
<title>Pet Store Front Page</title>
<style type='text/css'>
 <!--
                            #banner { text-align: center; }
        #main { text-align: center; position: relative;}
 .first {padding-top: 3em;}
        #rightcol { background-color: black; color: white;
            link: white; position: absolute; top: 0;
            right: 0; width: 18%;}
                        #rightcol ul { text-align: left;}
                        #last { padding-bottom: 3em; };
 -->
</style>
</head>
<body>
<div id="banner">
    <img src="images/awning-top.gif" alt="awning" />
    <img src="images/Name.gif" alt="Pet Store" />
</div>
<div id="main">
  <p class="first">
  <img src="images/lizard-front.jpg"
      alt="lizard picture"
      height="186" width="280" /></p>
  <h2>Looking for a new friend?</h2>
```

```
    <p>Check out our
      <a href="PetCatalog.php">Pet Catalog.</a>
      <br /> We may have just what you're looking for.</p>

    <div id="rightcol">
      <p class="first">
      <b>Looking for <br />more?</b></p>
      <ul>
        <li>special deals?</li>
        <li>pet information?</li>
        <li>good conversation?</li>
      </ul>
      <p>Try the
        <br /><a href="login.php"
                style="color: white">Members Only</a>
        <br />section <br />of our store</></p>
      <p id="last"><b>It's free!</b></p>
    </div>
  </div>
</body></html>
```

Notice the link to the login PHP program. When the customer clicks the link, the login page appears.

Writing Login

The login page (refer to Figure 12-2) is produced by the program Login. php, shown in Listing 12-2. The program uses a switch to create two sections: one for the login and one for creating a new account. The program creates a session that's opened in all the Members Only Web pages. The login form itself isn't included in this program; it's in a separate file, login_form.inc, and is called into the program, using include statements, when the form is needed.

Listing 12-2:   Logging In to the Members Only Section

```
<?php
/* Program: Login_reg.php
 * Desc:    Main application script for the User Login
 *          application. It provides two options:
 *          (1) login using an existing username and
 *          (2) register a new username.
 */
session_start();                                          →8
switch (@$_POST['Button'])                                →9
```

(continued)

Listing 12-2: *(continued)*

```
{
  case "Log in":                                              →11
    include("dogs.inc");                                      →12
    $cxn = mysqli_connect($host,$user,$passwd,$dbname)
           or die("Query died: connect");
    $sql = "SELECT loginName FROM Member                      →15
             WHERE loginName='$_POST[fusername]'";
    $result = mysqli_query($cxn,$sql)
              or die("Query died: fusername");
    $num = mysqli_num_rows($result);                          →19
    if($num > 0)  //login name was found                      →20
    {
      $sql = "SELECT loginName FROM Member                    →22
              WHERE loginName='$_POST[fusername]'
              AND password=md5('$_POST[fpassword]')";
      $result2 = mysqli_query($cxn,$sql)                      →25
                 or die("Query died: fpassword");
      $num2 = mysqli_num_rows($result2);                      →27
      if($num2 > 0)  //password matches                       →28
      {
        $_SESSION['auth']="yes";                              →30
        $_SESSION['logname'] = $_POST['fusername'];
        $sql = "INSERT INTO Login (loginName,loginTime)
                VALUES ('$_SESSION[logname]',NOW())";
        $result = mysqli_query($cxn,$sql)
                  or die("Query died: insert");
        header("Location: SecretPage.php");
      }                                                       →37
      else  // password does not match                        →38

        $message_1="The Login Name, '$_POST[fusername]'
                  exists, but you have not entered the
                  correct password! Please try again.";
        $fusername=strip_tags(trim($_POST['fusername']));
        include("login_form.inc");                            →44
      }
    }                                                         →46
    else  // login name not found                             →47
    {
      $message_1 = "The User Name you entered does not
                    exist! Please try again.";
      include("login_form.inc");
    }
  break;                                                      →53

  case "Register":                                            →55
  /* Check for blanks */
    foreach($_POST as $field => $value)                       →57
    {
      if($field != "fax")                                     →59
      {
        if(empty($value))                                     →61
```

```
      {
        $blanks[] = $field;
      }
      else
      {
        $good_data[$field] = strip_tags(trim($value));
      }
    }
  }
  if(isset($blanks))                                    →71
  {
    $message_2 = "The following fields are blank.
          Please enter the required information:  ";
    foreach($blanks as $value)
    {
      $message_2 .="$value, ";
    }
    extract($good_data);
    include("login_form.inc");
    exit();
  }
/* validate data */
  foreach($_POST as $field => $value)                   →84
  {
    if(!empty($value))                                  →86
    {
      if(preg_match("/name/i",$field) and
         !preg_match("/user/i",$field) and
         !preg_match("/log/i",$field))
      {
        if (!preg_match("/^[A-Za-z' -]{1,50}$/",$value))
        {
          $errors[] = "$value is not a valid name. ";
        }
      }
      if(preg_match("/street/i",$field) or
          preg_match("/addr/i",$field) or
          preg_match("/city/i",$field))
      {
        if(!preg_match("/^[A-Za-z0-9.,' -]{1,50}$/",
                        $value))
        {
          $errors[] = "$value is not a valid address
                        or city.";
        }
      }
      if(preg_match("/state/i",$field))
      {
        if(!preg_match("/^[A-Z][A-Z]$/",$value))
        {
```

(continued)

Listing 12-2: *(continued)*

```
          $errors[] = "$value is not valid state code.";
        }
      }
      if(preg_match("/email/i",$field))
      {
        if(!preg_match("/^.+@.+\\..+$/",$value))
        {
          $errors[]="$value is not a valid email addr.";
        }
      }
      if(preg_match("/zip/i",$field))
      {
        if(!preg_match("/^[0-9]{5}(\-[0-9]{4})?$/",
            $value))
        {
          $errors[] = "$value is not a valid zipcode. ";
        }
      }
      if(preg_match("/phone/i",$field) or
          preg_match("/fax/i",$field))
      {
        if(!preg_match("/^[0-9](xX -]{7,20}$/",$value))
        {
          $errors[]="$value is not a valid phone no.";
        }
      }
    } // end if not empty
  }
  foreach($_POST as $field => $value)              →140
  {
    $$field = strip_tags(trim($value));
  }
  if(@is_array($errors))                           →144
  {
    $message_2 = "";
    foreach($errors as $value)
    {
      $message_2 .= $value." Please try again<br />";
    }
    include("login_form.inc");
    exit();
  } // end if errors are found                     →153

  /* check to see if username already exists */    →155
  include("dogs.inc");                             →156
  $cxn = mysqli_connect($host,$user,$passwd,$dbname)
          or die("Couldn't connect to server");
  $sql = "SELECT loginName FROM Member
          WHERE loginName='$loginName'";
```

```
        $result = mysqli_query($cxn,$sql)
                   or die("Query died: loginName.");
        $num = mysqli_num_rows($result);
        if($num > 0)                                            →164
        {
          $message_2 = "$loginName already used. Select
                          another User Name.";
          include("login_form.inc");
          exit();
        } // end if username already exists               →170
        else // Add new member to database
        {
          $sql = "INSERT INTO Member (loginName,createDate,
                    password,firstName,lastName,street,city,
                    state,zip,phone,fax,email) VALUES
                    ('$loginName',NOW(),md5('$password'),
                     '$firstName','$lastName','$street','$city',
                     '$state','$zip','$phone','$fax','$email')";
          mysqli_query($cxn,$sql);                        →179
          $_SESSION['auth']="yes";                        →180
          $_SESSION['logname'] = $loginName;              →181
          /* send email to new Customer */
          $emess = "You have successfully registered. ";
          $emess .= "Your new user name and password are: ";
          $emess .= "\n\n\t$loginName\n\t";
          $emess .= "$password\n\n";
          $emess .= "We appreciate your interest. \n\n";
          $emess .= "If you have any questions or problems,";
          $emess .= " email service@ourstore.com";
          $subj = "Your new customer registration";
         # $mailsend=mail("$email","$subj","$emess");     →191
          header("Location: SecretPage.php");             →192
        }                                                 →193
      break;

      default:                                            →196
        include("login_form.inc");
    }
?>
```

The program works like this:

→**8**   Starts a session. The session has to be started at the beginning of
           the program, even though the user hasn't logged in yet.

→**9**   Starts a `switch` statement. The `switch` statement contains
           three sections, based on the value passed for the submit button
           in the form, obtained from the built-in array `$_POST`. The first
           section runs when the value passed for the button is `"Log in"`;

the second section runs when the value passed for `button` is `Register`; and the third section is the default that runs if no value is passed for `button`. The third section just displays the login page and runs only when the customer first links to the login page.

→**11** Starts the `case` block for the login section — the section that runs when the customer logs in. The login section of the form sends the button value `Log in`, which causes this section of the `switch` statement to run.

→**12** Reads in the file that sets the variables needed to connect to the database. The file is called `dogs.inc`, which is a misleading name that seems more secure than calling the file `mypasswords.inc`.

→**13** Lines 13 and 14 connect to MySQL and select the database.

→**15** Lines 15–18 look in the database table `Member` for a row with the username typed by the customer.

→**19** Checks to see whether a row was found with a `loginName` field containing the Member ID typed by the customer. `$num` equals `0` or `1`, depending on whether the row was found.

→**20** Starts an `if` block that executes if the Member ID was found. This means the user submitted a Member ID that is in the database. This block then checks to see whether the password submitted by the user is correct for the given Member ID. This block is documented in more detail in the following list:

    →**22** Lines 22–24 create a query that looks for a row with both the Member ID and the password submitted by the customer. Notice that the password submitted in the form (`$fpassword`) is encrypted by using the MySQL function `md5()`. Passwords in the database are encrypted, so the password you're trying to match must also be encrypted, or it won't match.

    →**25** Lines 25–27 execute the query and check whether a match was found. `$num2` equals `1` or `0`, depending on whether a row with both the Member ID and the password is found.

    →**28** Starts an `if` block that executes if the password is correct. This is a successful login. Lines 30–37 are executed, performing the following tasks: 1) The two session variables, `auth` and `logname`, are stored in the `SESSION` array. 2) A row for the login is entered into the Login table. 3) The first page of the Members Only section is sent to the member.

    →**38** Starts an `else` block that executes if the password is not correct. This is an unsuccessful login. Lines 40–44 are executed, performing the following tasks: 1) The appropriate error message is set in `$message`. 2) The login page is displayed again. The login page shows the error message.

Notice that the block starting on line 40 lets the user know when he or she has a real login name but the wrong password. If the security of your data is important, you may want to write this loop differently. Providing that information may be helpful to someone who is trying to break in because now the cracker needs to find only the password. For more security, just have one condition that gives the same error message whenever either the login name or the password is incorrect. In this example, I prefer to provide the information because it is helpful to the legitimate member (who may not remember whether he or she installed an account at all), and I'm not protecting any vital information.

→**46** Ends the block that executes when the Member ID is found in the database.

→**47** Starts an `else` block that executes when the Member ID is *not* found in the database. This block creates the appropriate error message and shows the login page again, which includes the error message.

→**53** Ends the `case` block that executes when the customer submits a Member ID and password to log in. The login block extends from line 11 to this line.

→**55** Starts the `case` block that executes when the customer fills out the form to get a new member account. The form includes a submit button with a value of "Register", causing the program to jump to this section of the `switch` statement.

→**57** Starts a `foreach` loop that loops through every field in the new member form. The loop checks for empty required fields. The statements in the loop are documented in more detail in the following list:

  →**59** Checks whether the field is the fax field. The fax field is not required, so it isn't checked to see whether it is blank.

  →**61** Checks whether the field is blank. If it is, the `if` block adds the field name to an array named `$blanks`. If it isn't blank, the `else` block cleans the data and adds it to the array `$good_data`.

→**71** Starts an `if` statement that executes if any blank fields were found. The `if` block creates an error message and redisplays the login form, including the error message. The form redisplays with the data from the array `$good_data` in the fields.

→**84** Starts a `foreach` loop that loops through every field in the new member form. The loop checks the field contents for invalid formats. The program doesn't reach this loop until all the required fields contain some data. The nonrequired fields that are blank are not checked (line 86).

This loop contains a series of `if` blocks that check the fields for the correct format. The `if` block tests the content of the field against a regular expression. If the field content is not valid, an information error message is added to an array named `$errors`.

→**140**   Starts a `foreach` loop that cleans the data in the `$_POST` array and stores it in a variable named with the field name. For example, the data in `$_POST['firstName']` is cleaned and stored in the variable `$firstName`. This is done using a variable variable, which is explained in Chapter 6.

→**144**   Starts an `if` statement that executes when invalid data is found. That is, it executes if the `$errors` array contains at least one element. The `if` block creates an error message and redisplays the form, including the error message, so the user can enter the correct information. The error processing block ends on line 153.

→**155**   Begins the section that processes the field information when it's all correct. The script does not reach this line until all required fields contain data and all the data has been tested and found to be valid.

→**156**   Lines 156–162 create and execute an SQL query to search for a record with the username entered by the user as the chosen username. If a record is found, it means the user has chosen a username that is already in use. Duplicate usernames aren't allowed in the database.

→**164**   Starts an `if` statement that executes if the username already exists. An error message is created and the new member form is redisplayed, with the error message, so that the user can enter a different username.

→**170**   Starts an `else` statement that executes if the username was not found in the database. Lines 173–179 create and execute an SQL query that adds the new member to the database.

→**180**   Lines 180 and 181 store variables in the session. These variables are available to all pages in the user session. The session variables can be tested on every session page to determine whether the user is logged in.

→**183**   Lines 183–191 create and send an e-mail message to the new member, letting the user know that his or her new account was successfully created. Notice that the e-mail message is created in the variable `$emess` over several lines — beginning on line 183, adding text (using `.=`) on each line, and ending on line 189. This format is needed to make it easier for humans to read — not because PHP needs it. In an e-mail message, unlike in HTML content, extra spaces and line ends have an effect. For instance, if I created one long message and used extra spaces for indentation, those spaces would appear in the e-mail. So I set the message on several lines that I can indent for readability in the program. Line 191 uses the PHP function `mail` to send the e-mail message.

→**192**   Sends the first page of the restricted section of the Web site to the user's browser.

→**193**   Ends the `case` statement section for the new member form.

→**196**   Starts the `case` block for the default condition. If neither the Login button nor the Register button was pushed, the program skips to this block. This block executes only the first time this program runs — when the user links to it from the storefront page and has not yet submitted either form. This section has only one statement: a statement that displays the login page.

This program shows the login page in many places, using `include` statements that call the file `login_form.inc`, which contains the HTML that produces the login page. The program `Login.php` does *not* produce any output. All the output is produced by `login_form.inc`. This type of application organization is discussed in Chapter 10. This is a good example of the use of `include` files. Just imagine if the statements in `login_form.inc`, shown in Listing 12-3, were included in the Login program at each place where `login_form` is included. Whew, that would be a mess that only a computer could understand.

Listing 12-3:   File That Creates the Login Page

```php
<?php
 /* File: login_form.inc
  * Desc: Contains the code for a Web page that displays
  *       two HTML forms, side by side. One is a login
  *       form and the second is a registration form.
  */
$fields_1 =    array("fusername"  => "User Name",         →7
                     "fpassword"  => "Password" );
$fields_2 =    array("loginName"  => "User Name",         →9
                     "password"   => "Password",
                     "email"      => "Email",
                     "firstName"  => "First Name",
                     "lastName"   => "Last Name",
                     "street"     => "Street",
                     "city"       => "City",
                     "state"      => "State",
                     "zip"        => "Zip",
                     "phone"      => "Phone",
                     "fax"        => "Fax" );

include("function12.inc");                                →21
?>                                                        →22
```

(continued)

Listing 12-3 *(continued)*

```html
<html><head>
<title>Customer Login Page</title>
<style type='text/css'>
 <!--
   label { font-weight: bold; float: left; width: 27%;
           margin-right: .5em; text-align: right; }
                       fieldset { border: 2px solid #000000 }
   legend { font-weight: bold; font-size: 1.5em;
           margin-bottom: .5em;   }
   h3 { text-align: center; margin: 2em; }
                          #wrapper { margin: 0; padding: 0; }
         #login { position: absolute; left: 0; width: 40%;
           padding: 1em 0; }
         #reg { position: absolute; left: 40%; width: 60%;
           padding: 1em 0; }
                           #field {padding-bottom: .5em;}
   .errors { font-weight: bold; font-style: italic;
           font-size: 90%; color: red; margin-top: 0; }
   -->
 </style>
</head>
<body style="margin: 0">
<div id="wrapper">
   <div id="login">                                      →46
    <form action="<?php echo $_SERVER['PHP_SELF']?>"
         method="post">
      <fieldset><legend>Login Form</legend>
<?php                                                     →50
      if(isset($message_1))                               →51
      {
        echo "<p class='errors'>$message_1</p>\n";
      }
      foreach($fields_1 as $field => $value)              →55
      {
        if(preg_match("/pass/i",$field))
          $type = "password";
        else
          $type = "text";
        echo "<div id='field'>
                <label for='$field'>$value</label>
                <input id='$field' name='$field'
                  type='$type' value='".@$$field."'
                  size='20' maxlength='50' /></div>\n";
      }
?>
      <input type="submit" name="Button"
           style='margin-left: 45%; margin-bottom: .5em'
           value="Log in" />
    </fieldset>
   </form>
```

```
   <h3>If you already have an account, log in.</h3>
   <h3>If you do not have an account, register now.</h3>
</div>                                                    →75

<div id="reg">
<form action="<?php echo $_SERVER['PHP_SELF']?>"
      method="post">
   <fieldset><legend>Registration Form</legend>
<?php
     if(isset($message_2))                                →82
     {
       echo "<p class='errors'>$message_2</p>\n";
     }
     foreach($fields_2 as $field => $value)               →86
     {
       if($field == "state")                              →88
       {
         echo "<div id='field'>
            <label for='$field'>$value</label>
            <select name='state' id='state'>";
            $stateName=getStateName();
            $stateCode=getStateCode();
            for($n=1;$n<=50;$n++)
            {
              $state=$stateName[$n];
              $scode=$stateCode[$n];
              echo "<option value='$scode'";
              if(isset($_POST['state']))
              {
                if($_POST['state'] == $scode)
                {
                  echo " selected='selected'";
                }
              }
              else
              {
                if($n < 2)
                {
                  echo " selected='selected'";
                }
              }
              echo ">$state\n</option>";
            }
            echo "</select></div>";
       }
       else                                               →118
       {
         if(preg_match("/pass/i",$field))
           $type = "password";
```

(continued)

Listing 12-3: *(continued)*

```
        else
            $type = "text";
        echo "<div id='field'>
            <label for='$field'>$value</label>
                <input id='$field' name='$field'
                    type='$type' value='".@$$field."'
                    size='40' maxlength='65' /></
        div>\n";
    }  //end else
  }  // end foreach field
?>
        <input type="submit" name="Button"
            style='margin-left: 45%; margin-bottom: .5em'
            value="Register" />
        </fieldset>
    </form>
  </div>                                                  →137
</div></body></html>
```

The following numbers refer to the line numbers in Listing 12-3:

→**7**   Creates the array that contains the fields in the login form.

→**9**   Creates the array that contains the fields in the registration form.

→**21**   Includes a file that contains the functions used in this program. The file contains the functions getStateName() and getState Code() that are used later in the program.

→**22**   Ends the opening PHP section.

→**46**   Opens the <div> that contains the login form.

→**50**   Opens a new PHP section.

→**51**   Begins an if statement that checks whether an error message exists for the login form. If the message exists, the message is displayed.

→**55**   Starts a foreach statement that loops through the array of fields for the login form and echoes the fields for the form.

→**75**   Closes the <div> that contains the login form.

→**77**   Opens the <div> that contains the registration form.

→**82**   Begins an if statement that checks whether an error message exists for the registration form. If the message exists, the message is displayed.

→**86**   Starts a foreach statement that loops through the array of fields for the login form and echoes the fields for the form.

→**88** Begins an `if` statement that checks whether the field is state. If it is, a drop-down list is created for the customer to select a state. Note that lines 93 and 94 call functions. These functions — my functions, not PHP functions — are included in the program on line 21. The functions create arrays from a list of state names and a list of two-letter state codes. The functions eliminate the need to include the two 50-state lists in the program. The functions can be used repeatedly for many programs. The `function12.inc` file contains the two functions, as follows:

```php
<?php
function getStateCode()
{
  $stateCode = array(1=> "AL" ,
      "AK" ,
      "AZ" ,
      . . .
      "WY" );
  return $stateCode;
}

function getStateName()
{
  $stateName = array(1=> "Alabama",
      "Alaska",
      "Arizona",
      . . .
      "Wyoming" );
  return $stateName;
}
```

A `for` loop then creates 50 options for the select list, using the two state arrays. An `if` statement starting on line 100 determines which option tag should be selected, so that it will be the selected option when the drop-down list is displayed. The `if` statement checks whether a state has been selected, which means that the customer submitted the form. If a state is found in the `$_POST` array, the state is selected. If no state is found in the `$_POST` array, the first state, AL, is selected.

→**118** Begins an `else` statement that executes if the field is not the state field. The `else` block displays a text field for all the fields other than the state field.

→**137** Closes the `<div>` for the registration form.

After running `Login.php`, if the user is successful with a login, the first page of the Members Only section of the Web site is shown. If the user successfully obtains a new user account, the `New_member.php` program runs.

Writing New_member

The New Member Welcome page greets new members by name and provides information about their accounts. Members then have the choice of entering the Members Only section or returning to the main page. Listing 12-4 shows the program that displays the page that new members see.

Listing 12-4:   Welcoming New Members

```php
<?php
 /* Program: New_member.php
  * Desc:    Displays the new member welcome page. Greets
             member by name and gives a choice to enter
  *          restricted section or go back to main page.
  */
 session_start();                                             →7

 if (@$_SESSION['auth'] != "yes")                             →9
 {
    header("Location: login.php");
    exit();
 }
 include("dogs.inc");                                         →14
 $cxn = mysqli_connect($host,$user,$passwd,$dbname)
        or die ("Couldn't connect to server.");              →16
 $sql = "SELECT firstName,lastName FROM Member               →17
              WHERE loginName='{$_SESSION['logname']}'";
 $result = mysqli_query($cxn,$sql)
           or die("Couldn't execute query");
 $row = mysqli_fetch_assoc($result);
 extract($row);
 echo "<html>
        <head><title>New Member Welcome</title></head>
        <body>
        <h2 style='margin-top: .7in; text-align: center'>
        Welcome $firstName $lastName</h2>\n";
?>                                                            →28
<p>Your new Member Account lets you enter the Members
Only section of our web site. You'll find special
discounts and bargains, a huge database of animal facts
and stories, advice from experts, advance notification
of new pets for sale, a message board where you can talk
to other Members, and much more.</p>
<p>Your new Member ID and password were emailed to you.
   Store them carefully for future use.</p>
<div style="text-align: center">
<p style="margin-top: .5in; font-weight: bold">
        Glad you could join us!</p>
<form action="member_page.php" method="post">            →40
    <input type="submit"
           value="Enter the Members Only Section">
</form>
```

```
<form action="PetShopFrontMembers.php" method="post">   →44
  <input type="submit" value="Go to Pet Store Main Page">
</form>
</div>
</body></html>
```

Notice the following points about `New_member.php`:

✔ A session starts on line 7. This makes the session variables stored in `Login.php` available to this program.

✔ The program checks whether the customer is logged in, starting on line 9. When the customer successfully logs in or creates a new account in `Login.php`, `$auth` is set to `yes` and stored in the `$_SESSION` array. Therefore, if `$auth` doesn't equal `yes`, the customer isn't logged in. If a customer tries to run the `New_member.php` program without running the `Login.php` program first, `$_SESSION[auth]` won't equal `yes`, and the user is sent to the login page.

✔ The program gets the customer's first and last names from the database, beginning with the database connection statement on line 15.

✔ The query is created, on line 17–18, by using `$_SESSION[logname]` to search for the member's information. The session variable `logname` that contains the Member ID was set in the login program.

✔ The PHP section ends on line 28. The remainder of the program is HTML.

✔ The program uses two different forms to provide two different submit buttons. The form statements on lines 40 and 44 start different programs.

The customer controls what happens next. If the customer clicks the button to return to the main page, the `PetShopFront.php` program runs. If the customer clicks the Members Only Section submit button, the first page of the Members Only section of your Web site is shown.

Writing the Members Only section

The Web pages in the Members Only section are no different than any other Web pages. You just want to restrict them to members who are logged in. To do this, you start a session and check whether they're logged in at the top of every page. The statements for the top of each program are

```
session_start();
if(@$_SESSION['auth'] != "yes")
{
    header("Location: Login.php");
    exit();
}
```

When `session_start` executes, PHP checks for an existing session. If one exists, it sets up the `session` variables. When a user logs in, `$_SESSION[auth]` is set to `yes`. Therefore, if `$_SESSION[auth]` is not set to `yes`, the user is not logged in, and the program takes the user to the login page.

Planning for Growth

The original plan for an application usually includes every wonderful thing that the user might want it to do. Realistically, it's usually important to make the application available to the users as quickly as possible. Consequently, applications usually go public with a subset of the planned functionality. More functionality is added later. That's why it's important to write your application with growth in mind.

Looking at the login application in this chapter, I'm sure you can see many things that could be added to it. Here are some possibilities:

✔ **E-mail a forgotten password.** Users often forget their passwords. Many login applications have a link that users can click to have their passwords e-mailed to them.

✔ **Change the password.** Members might want to change their password. The application could offer a form for password changes.

✔ **Update information.** A member might move or change his phone number or e-mail address. The application could provide a way for members to change their own information.

✔ **Create a member list.** You might want to output a nicely formatted list of all members in the database. This probably is something you want to make available only for yourself. In some situations, however, you might want to make the list available to all members.

You can easily add any of these abilities to the application. For instance, you can add to the login form a *Forgot my password* button that, when clicked, e-mails the password to the e-mail address in the database. The button can run the login program with a section for e-mailing the password or run a different program that e-mails the password. In the same manner, you can add buttons for changing the password or updating customer information. You don't need to wait until an application has all its bells and whistles to let your customers use it. You can write it one step at a time.

Part V
The Part of Tens

The 5th Wave   By Rich Tennant

"What you want to do, is balance the image of the pick-up truck sittin' behind your home page, with a busted washing machine in the foreground."

In this part . . .

The chapters in this part contain hints, tips, and warnings based on my experience. Perhaps they can serve as a shortcut for you on your journey to becoming a confident Web developer. I sincerely hope so.

Chapter 13

Ten Things You Might Want to Do Using PHP Functions

In This Chapter

▶ Finding out about many useful functions

▶ Understanding what functions can do

*O*ne of the strongest aspects of PHP is its many built-in functions. In this chapter, I list the PHP functions that I use most often. Some of them I describe elsewhere in this book, some I mention only in passing, and some I don't mention at all. The PHP language has many hundreds of functions.

For a complete list of PHP functions, see the PHP documentation at www.php. net/manual/en/funcref.php.

Communicate with MySQL

PHP has many functions designed specifically for interacting with MySQL. I describe the following MySQL functions thoroughly in this book:

```
mysqli_connect();      mysqli_fetch_assoc()
mysqli_num_rows();     mysqli_query()
```

The following functions could be useful, but I either don't discuss them or discuss them only briefly:

✔ mysqli_insert_id($cxn): For use with an AUTO-INCREMENT MySQL column. This function gets the last number inserted into the column.

✔ mysqli_select_db($cxn, $database): Selects a database. The currently selected database is changed to the specified database. All succeeding queries are executed on the selected database.

✔ mysqli_fetch_row($result): Gets one row from the temporary results location. The row is put into an array with numbers as keys.

✔ `mysqli_affected_rows($result)`: Returns the number of rows that were affected by a query — for instance, the number of rows deleted or updated.

✔ `mysqli_num_fields($result)`: Returns the number of fields in a result.

✔ `mysqli_field_name($result, N)`: Returns the name of the row indicated by *N*. For instance, `mysqli_field_name($result,1)` returns the name of the second column in the result. The first column is 0.

Send E-Mail

PHP provides a function that sends e-mail from your PHP program. The format is

```
mail(address,subject,message,headers);
```

These are the values that you need to fill in:

✔ *address*: The e-mail address that will receive the message.

✔ *subject*: A string that goes on the subject line of the e-mail message.

✔ *message*: The content that goes inside the e-mail message.

✔ *headers*: A string that sets values for headers. For instance, you might have a *headers* string as follows:

```
"From: member-desk@petstore.com\r\nbcc: mom@hercompany.com"
```

The header would set the From header to the given e-mail address, plus send a blind copy of the e-mail message to mom.

The following is an example of PHP statements that you can use in your script to set up and send an e-mail message:

```
$to = "me@test1.com";
$subj = "Test";
$mess = "This is a test of the mail function";
$headers = bcc:techsupport@mycompany.com\r\n
$mailsend = mail($to,$subj,$mess,$headers);
```

Sometimes you might have a problem with your e-mail. PHP has a configuration setting that must be correct before the mail function can connect to your system e-mail software. Your Web host has the correct settings. On other computers, the default is usually correct, but if your e-mail doesn't seem to be getting to its destination, check the PHP configuration mail setting by looking for the following in the output of `phpinfo()`:

```
Sendmail_path              (on Unix/Linux)
SMTP                       (on Windows)
```

You can change the setting by editing the `php.ini` file. If you're using Windows, look for the following lines:

```
[mail function]
; For Win32 only.
SMTP = localhost

; For Win32 only.
sendmail_from = me@localhost.com
```

The first setting is where you put the name of your outgoing mail server. However you send e-mail — using a LAN at work, a cable modem at home, an ISP via a modem — you send your mail with an SMTP server, which has an address that you need to know.

If you send directly from your computer, you should be able to find the name of the outgoing mail server in your e-mail software. For instance, in Microsoft Outlook Express, choose Tools➪Accounts➪Properties and then click the Servers tab. If you can't find the name of your outgoing mail server, ask your e-mail administrator for the name. If you use an ISP, you can ask the ISP. The name is likely to be in a format similar to the following:

```
mail.ispname.net
```

The second setting is the return address sent with all your e-mail. Change the setting to the e-mail address that you want to use for your return address, as follows:

```
sendmail_from = me@myhome.com
```

If you're using Unix or Linux, looking for these lines in your `php.ini` file:

```
; For Unix only.
;sendmail_path =
```

This default is usually correct. If it doesn't work, talk to your system administrator about the correct path to your outgoing mail server.

Don't forget to remove the semicolon at the beginning of the lines. The semicolon makes the line into a comment, so the setting isn't active until you remove the semicolon.

Use PHP Sessions

The functions to open or close a session follow. I explain these functions in Chapter 9.

```
session_start();        session_destroy()
```

Stop Your Program

Sometimes you just want your program to stop, cease, and desist. Two functions do this: `exit()` and `die()`. Actually, these are two names for the same function, but sometimes it's just more fun to say "die." Both print a message when they stop if you provide one. The format is

```
exit("message string");
```

When `exit` executes, *message string* is output.

Handle Arrays

Arrays are useful in PHP, particularly for getting the results from database functions and for form variables. I explain the following array functions elsewhere in the book, mainly in Chapter 7:

```
array();     extract();     sort();      asort();
rsort();     arsort();      ksort();     krsort();
```

Here are some other useful functions:

- ✔ `array_reverse($varname)`: Returns an array with the values in reverse order.

- ✔ `array_unique($varname)`: Removes duplicate values from an array.

- ✔ `in_array("string", $varname)`: Looks through an array $varname for a string "string".

- ✔ `range(value1, value2)`: Creates an array containing all the values between *value1* and *value2*. For instance, `range('a', 'z')` creates an array containing all the letters between *a* and *z*.

✔ explode("*sep*","*string*"): Creates an array of strings in which each item is a substring of *string*, separated by *sep*. For example, explode (" ",$string) creates an array in which each word in $string is a separate value. This is similar to split in Perl.

✔ implode("*glue*",$array): Creates a string containing all the values in $array with *glue* between them. For instance, implode(", ",$array) creates a string: value1, value2, value3, and so on. This is similar to the join function in Perl.

Many more useful array functions are available. PHP can do almost anything with an array.

Check for Variables

Sometimes you just need to know whether a variable exists. You can use the following functions to test whether a variable is currently set:

```
isset($varname);   // true if variable is set
!isset($varname);  // true if variable is not set
empty($varname);   // true if value is 0 or is not set
```

Format Values

Sometimes you need to format the values in variables. In Chapter 6, I explain how to put numbers into dollar format by using number_format() and sprintf(). In Chapter 6, I also discuss unset(), which removes the values from a variable. In this section, I describe additional capabilities of sprintf().

The function sprintf() allows you to format any string or number, including variable values. The general format is

```
$newvar = sprintf("format",$varname1,$varname2,...);
```

where *format* gives instructions for the format and $*varname* contains the value(s) to be formatted. *format* can contain both literals and instructions for formatting the values in $*varname*. In addition, a *format* containing only literals is valid, such as the following statement:

```
$newvar = sprintf("I have a pet");
```

This statement outputs the literal string. However, you can also add variables, using the following statements:

```
$ndogs = 5;
$ncats = 2;
$newvar = sprintf("I have %s dogs and %s cats",$ndogs,$ncats);
```

The %s is a formatting instruction that tells sprintf to insert the value in the variable as a string. Thus, the output is I have 5 dogs and 2 cats. The % character signals sprintf that a formatting instruction starts here. The formatting instruction has the following format:

```
%pad-width.dectype
```

These are the components of the formatting instructions:

- ✔ %: Signals the start of the formatting instruction.
- ✔ pad: A padding character used to fill out the number when necessary. If you don't specify a character, a space is used. pad can be a space, a 0, or any character preceded by a single quote ('). It's common to pad numbers with 0 — for example, 01 or 0001.
- ✔ -: A symbol meaning to left-justify the characters. If this isn't included, the characters are right-justified.
- ✔ width: The number of characters to use for the value. If the value doesn't fill the width, the padding character is used to pad the value. For instance, if width is 5, pad is 0, and the value is 1, the output is 00001.
- ✔ .dec: The number of decimal places to use for a number.
- ✔ type: The type of value. Use s for most values. Use f for numbers that you want to format with decimal places.

Some possible sprintf statements are

```
sprintf("I have $%03.2f. Does %s have any?",$money,$name);
sprintf("%'.-20s%3.2f",$product,$price);
```

The output of these statements is

```
I have $030.00. Does Tom have any?
Kitten.............. 30.00
```

Compare Strings to Patterns

In earlier chapters in this book, I use regular expressions as patterns to match strings. (I explain regular expressions in Chapter 6.) The following functions use regular expressions to find and sometimes replace patterns in strings:

- ✔ preg_match("*pattern*",$*varname*): Checks whether the *pattern* is found in $*varname*.

- ✔ preg_replace("*pattern*","*string*",$*varname*): Searches for *pattern* in $*varname* and replaces it with *string*.

Find Out about Strings

Sometimes you need to know things about a string, such as its length or whether the first character is an uppercase *O*. PHP offers many functions for checking out your strings:

- ✔ strlen($*varname*): Returns the length of the string.

- ✔ strpos("*string*","*substring*"): Returns the position in *string* where *substring* begins. For instance, strpos("hello","el") returns 1. Remember that the first position for PHP is 0. strrpos() finds the last position in *string* where *substring* begins.

- ✔ substr("*string*",*n1*,*n2*): Returns the substring from *string* that begins at *n1* and is *n2* characters long. For instance, substr("hello",2,2) returns 11.

- ✔ strtr($*varname*,"*str1*","*str2*"): Searches through the string $*varname* for *str1* and replaces it with *str2* every place that it's found.

- ✔ strrev($*varname*): Returns the string with the characters reversed.

Many more string functions exist. See the documentation at www.php.net.

Change the Case of Strings

Changing uppercase letters to lowercase and vice versa is not so easy. Bless PHP for providing functions to do this for you:

- ✔ `strtolower($varname)`: Changes any uppercase letters in the string to lowercase letters

- ✔ `strtoupper($varname)`: Changes any lowercase letters in the string to uppercase letters

- ✔ `ucfirst($varname)`: Changes the first letter in the string to uppercase

- ✔ `ucwords($varname)`: Changes the first letter of each word in the string to uppercase

Ten PHP Gotchas

· ·

· ·

1 guarantee that you will do all the things that I mention in this chapter. It's not possible to write programs without making these mistakes. The trick is to find out how to recognize them; roll your eyes; say, "Not again"; and then correct your mistakes. One error message that you will see many times is

```
Parse error: parse error in c:\test.php on line 7
```

This is PHP's way of saying, "Huh?" It means it doesn't understand something. This message helpfully points to the file and the line number where PHP got confused. Sometimes it points directly at the error, but sometimes PHP's confusion results from an error earlier in the program.

Missing Semicolons

Every PHP statement ends with a semicolon (;). PHP doesn't stop reading a statement until it reaches a semicolon. If you leave out the semicolon at the end of a line, PHP continues reading the statement on the following line. For instance, consider the following statement:

```
$test = 1
echo $test;
```

Of course, the statement doesn't make sense to PHP when it reads the two lines as one statement, so it complains with an error message, such as the annoying

```
Parse error: parse error in c:\test.php on line 2
```

Before you know it, you'll be writing your home address with semicolons at the end of each line.

Not Enough Equal Signs

When you ask whether two values are equal in a comparison statement, you need two equal signs (==). Using one equal sign is a common mistake. It's perfectly reasonable because you've been using one equal sign to mean *equal* since the first grade, when you discovered that 2 + 2 = 4. This is a difficult mistake to recognize because it doesn't cause an error message. It just makes your program do odd things, like infinite loops or if blocks that never execute. I'm continually amazed at how long I can stare at

```
$test = 0;
while ( $test = 0 )
{
    $test++;
}
```

and not see why it's looping endlessly.

Misspelled Variable Names

An incorrectly spelled variable name is another PHP gotcha that doesn't result in an error message, just odd program behavior. If you misspell a variable name, PHP considers it a new variable and does what you ask it to do. Here's another clever way to write an infinite loop:

```
$test = 0;
while ( $test == 0 )
{
    $Test++;
}
```

Remember, to PHP, $test is not the same variable as $Test.

Missing Dollar Signs

A missing dollar sign in a variable name is hard to see, but at least it most likely results in an error message telling you where to look for the problem. It usually results in the old familiar parse error:

```
Parse error: parse error in test.php on line 7
```

Troubling Quotes

You can have too many, too few, or the wrong kind of quotes. You have too many when you put quotes inside of quotes, such as

```
$test = "<table width="100%">";
```

PHP sees the second double quote (") — before 100 — as the ending double quote (") and reads the 1 as an instruction, which makes no sense. *Voilà!* Another parse error. The line must be either

```
$test = "<table width='100%'>";
```

or

```
$test = "<table width=\"100%\">";
```

You have too few quotes when you forget to end a quoted string, such as

```
$test = "<table width='100%'>;
```

PHP continues reading the lines as part of the quoted string until it encounters another double quote ("), which might not occur for several lines. This is one occasion when the parse error pointing to where PHP got confused is not pointing to the actual error. The error occurred some lines previously, when you forgot to end the string.

You have the wrong kind of quotes when you use a single quote (') when you meant a double quote (") or vice versa. The difference between single and double quotes is sometimes important, as I explain in Chapter 6.

Invisible Output

Some statements, such as the header statement, must execute before the program produces any output. If you try to use such statements after sending output, they fail. The following statements will fail because the header message isn't the first output:

```
<html>
<?php
    header("Location: http://company.com");
?>
```

<html> is not in a PHP section and is therefore sent as HTML output. The following statements will work:

```
<?php
    header("Location: http://company.com");
?>
<html>
```

The following statements will fail

```
 <?php
    header("Location: http://company.com");
?>
<html>
```

because there's one single blank space before the opening PHP tag. The blank space is output to the browser, although the resulting Web page looks empty. Therefore, the header statement fails because there is output before it. This is a common mistake and difficult to spot.

Numbered Arrays

PHP believes the first value in an array is numbered zero (0). Of course, humans tend to believe that lists start with the number one (1). This fundamentally different way of viewing lists results in us humans believing an array isn't working correctly when it's working just fine. For instance, consider the following statements:

```
$test = 1;
while( $test <= 3 )
{
    $array[] = $test;
    $test++;
}
echo $array[3];
```

Nothing is displayed by these statements. I leap to the conclusion that there's something wrong with my loop. Actually, it's fine. It just results in the following array:

```
$array[0]=1
$array[1]=2
$array[2]=3
```

And doesn't set anything into $array[3].

Including PHP Statements

When a file is read in using an `include` statement in a PHP section, it seems reasonable to me that the statements in the file will be treated as PHP statements. After all, PHP adds the statements to the program at the point where I include them. However, PHP doesn't see it my way. If a file named `file1.inc` contains the following statements:

```
if( $test == 1 )
   echo "Hi";
```

and I read it in with the following statements in my main program:

```
<?php
$test = 1;
include ("file1.inc");
?>
```

I expect the word `Hi` to appear on the Web page. However, the Web page displays this:

```
if ( $test == 1 ) echo "Hi";
```

Clearly, the file that is included is seen as HTML. To send `Hi` to the Web page, `file1.inc` needs to include PHP tags, as follows:

```
<?php
if( $test == 1 )
   echo "Hi";
?>
```

Missing Mates

Parentheses and curly brackets come in pairs and must be used that way. Opening with a (that has no closing) or a { without a } will result in an error message. One of my favorites is using one closing parenthesis where two are needed, as in the following statement:

```
if( isset($test)
```

This statement needs a closing parenthesis at the end. It's much more difficult to spot that one of your blocks didn't get closed when you have blocks inside blocks inside blocks. For instance, consider the following:

```
while( $test < 3 )
{
if( $test2 != "yes" )
{
if( $test3 > 4 )
{
echo "go";
}
}
```

You can see there are three opening curly brackets and only two closing ones. Imagine that 100 lines of code are inside these blocks. It can be difficult to spot the problem — especially if you think the last closing bracket is closing the `while` loop, but PHP sees it as closing the `if` loop for `$test2`. Somewhere later in your program, PHP might be using a closing bracket to close the `while` loop that you aren't even looking at. It can be difficult to trace the problem in a large program.

Indenting blocks makes it easier to see where closing brackets belong. Also, I often use comments to keep track of where I am, such as

```
while( $test < 3 )
{
   if( $test2 != "yes" )
   {
     if( $test3 > 4 )
     {
         echo "go";
     } // closing if block for $test3
   } // closing if block for $test2
} // closing while block
```

Confusing Parentheses and Brackets

I'm not sure whether mistaking parentheses for brackets and vice versa is a problem for everyone or just for me because I refuse to admit that I can't see as well as I used to. Although PHP has no trouble distinguishing between parentheses and curly brackets, my eyes are not so reliable. Especially while staring at a computer screen at the end of a ten-hour programming marathon, I can easily confuse (and {. Using the wrong one gets you a parse error message.

Part VI

Appendixes

The 5th Wave   By Rich Tennant

"We're here to clean the code."

In this part . . .

This part provides instructions for installing and configuring the Web software on your computer. Appendix A provides instructions for installing Apache, PHP, and MySQL with the XAMPP installer. Appendix B provides instructions for configuring PHP on your computer

Appendix A

Installing PHP, MySQL, and Apache from XAMPP

● ●

*Y*ou can install PHP, MySQL, and Apache on your computer by installing an all-in-one package called XAMPP. The XAMPP installation procedure installs recent versions of Apache 2.2, PHP 5, and MySQL 5.1. XAMPP also installs phpMyAdmin and FileZilla.

The XAMPP installation is perfectly appropriate for a development environment on your own computer. You should not use XAMPP to install the software on a Web server that is going to make the Web site available to the public. The XAMPP installation does not install a configuration that's secure enough or located correctly for a public Web site.

XAMPP installs the same software that would be installed if you downloaded and installed the software from each individual Web site. However, the software is installed in different locations. The default location is `c:\xampp` for Windows or `Applications\xampp` for Mac. If you installed each software package individually, they would be in different locations throughout your machine. Consequently, the configuration files for the software are in different locations than where they would be located if you installed them individually, and some documentation might be misleading. Configuring the Web software is explained in Appendix B.

Installing XAMPP on Windows

Follow these steps to install the Web software using the XAMPP installer:

1. **Go to www.apachefriends.org/en/xampp-windows.html.**

2. **Scroll down to the Download section, shown in Figure A-1.**

3. **Click the Installer link under the Basic Package listing to download the installer version.**

   The current downloaded file is named `xampp-win32-1.7.1-installer.exe`. The version number may be different for you as the software is upgraded regularly.

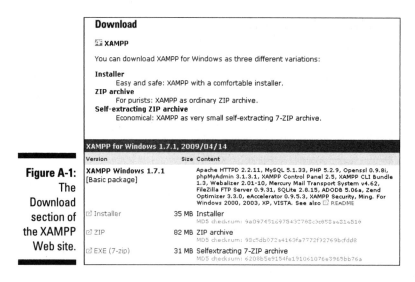

Figure A-1:
The
Download
section of
the XAMPP
Web site.

4. **Save the downloaded file on your hard drive or desktop.**

5. **Navigate to the location where you saved the downloaded XAMPP file and double-click the filename.**

The Setup Wizard starts, as shown in Figure A-2.

6. **Click Next.**

The screen shown in Figure A-3 opens.

Figure A-2:
The
starting
page of
the XAMPP
Setup
Wizard.

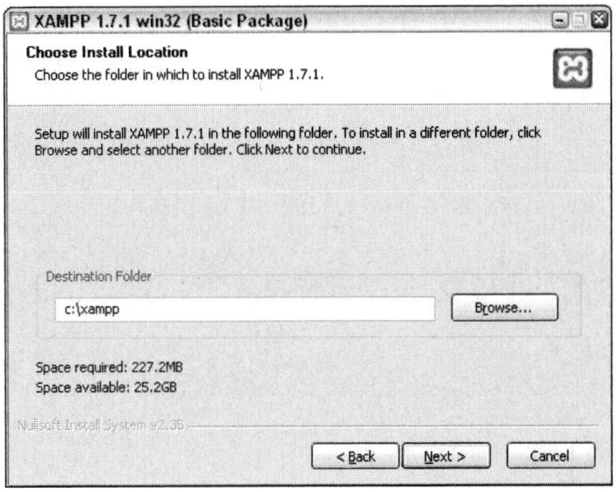

Figure A-3:
The Choose
Install
Location
screen.

7. **Select a location to install XAMPP.**

It's best to accept the default location (c:\xampp) unless you have a really good reason to choose another location. If you're installing on Vista, you cannot install in the Program Files folder because of a protection problem. Also, PHP sometimes has a problem if it's installed in a folder with a space in the path, such as Program Files.

You can click Browse to select another install folder.

8. **When you have chosen the install folder, click Next.**

The XAMPP Options screen appears, as shown in Figure A-4.

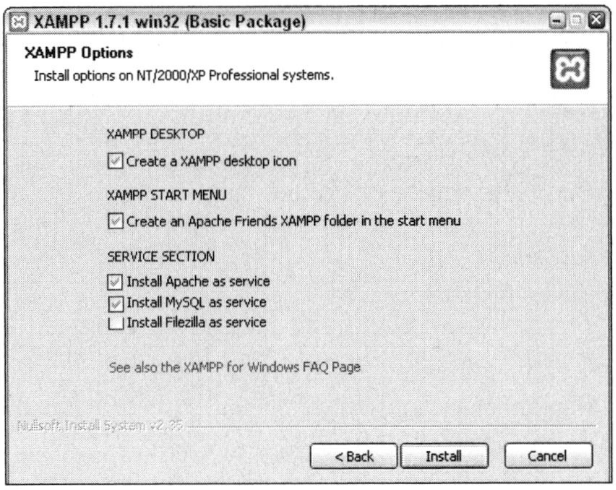

Figure A-4:
The XAMPP
Options
screen.

9. Under SERVICE SECTION, select the Install Apache As Service and the Install MySQL As Service check boxes.

This step installs the tools as Windows services.

10. Click Install.

The Installing screen appears, as shown in Figure A-5.

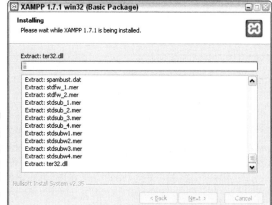

Figure A-5:
The
Installing
screen of
the wizard.

The installation process takes a few minutes to complete. As the installation proceeds, you see various files/components being installed on your system, in the location you specified. A status bar shows the installation progress.

When the installation is complete, the installation complete screen appears, shown in Figure A-6.

Figure A-6:
The XAMPP
installation
complete
screen.

11. **Click Finish.**

The XAMPP installation process may continue with a few additional configuration tasks. Mainly, you just get to watch as things proceed automatically. Sometimes the activity on the screen may stop for a period of time. This is okay. Do not do anything. Just wait. It will continue until it's done.

12. **When a screen asks whether you want the Control Panel to open when the installation finishes, click the Yes button.**

The open Control Panel with Apache and MySQL running is shown in Figure A-7.

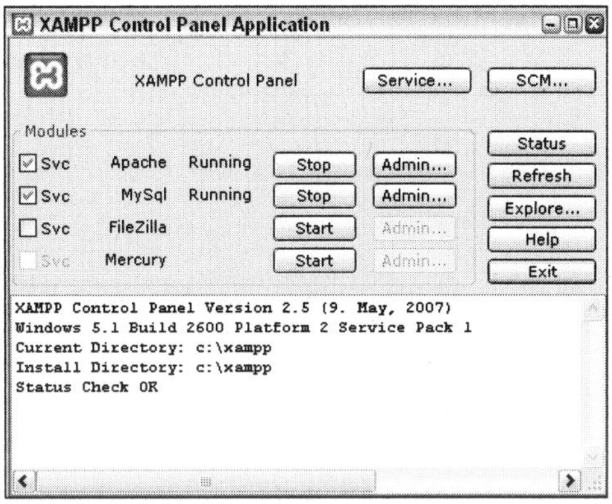

Figure A-7:
The XAMPP
Control
Panel.

In the figure, Apache and MySQL are shown to be running, and the service check box (labeled Svc) is selected, meaning the software is running as a Windows service. This status means your development environment is ready for work.

If the status of Apache and MySQL is Running but the Svc check box is not selected, you can use Apache and MySQL, but they'll stop when your computer is shut down. You'll have to restart them in the XAMPP Control Panel every time you start your computer. It's better to run them as a service so that they'll start automatically whenever your computer starts. To restart Apache and/or MySQL as a service, click Stop to stop the software. Then, select the Svc check box and click Start to restart the software.

You can now close the XAMPP Control Panel. Your software is installed and ready for you to develop your Web database application.

When the Control Panel is running, the orange XAMPP icon is in your system tray. You can click the icon to open the Control Panel. If you don't have the icon in your system tray, you can start the Control Panel by choosing Start➪ All Programs➪Apache Friends➪XAMPP➪XAMPP Control Panel.

If you attempt to start the Control Panel when it's already running, as shown by the icon in your system tray, an error message will be displayed.

Installing XAMPP on Mac

If you're a Mac OS X user, Apache, PHP, and MySQL are already installed on your computer, but not activated.

If you have expertise in its setup, which includes activating the software, accessing hidden and locked files, and editing a configuration file on your own, you can use the pre-installed system. Some setup tips are found at http://foundationphp.com and other sites. You also need to download and install phpMyAdmin on your system separately.

If you prefer, you can use XAMPP. It installs everything in one procedure and is as easy to install as any other software application you're familiar with. However, you need to be sure that the preinstalled software packages are not activated:

1. **Go to your computer's System Preferences and click the Sharing button.**

2. **Make sure that the Web Sharing check box (called Personal Web Sharing in earlier Mac OS X versions) is deselected as shown in Figure A-8.**

   This is very important. If you have this check box selected, the OS's installation of Apache and PHP will interfere with your use of XAMPP.

Figure A-8:
Web
Sharing
panel

3. **Go to www.apachefriends.org/en/xampp-macosx.html.**

4. **Scroll down to the Installation section, shown in Figure A-9.**

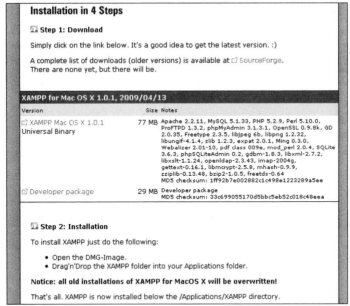

Figure A-9:
The XAMPP
Web page.

5. **Click the first XAMPP Mac OS X link that says Universal Binary below it.**

   Download it to your desktop. (Note that your version may be different than the one in Figure A-9, as the software is updated regularly.)

6. **When the download is complete, the package opens automatically. If it doesn't, double-click it.**

7. **Drag the XAMPP folder to your computer's Applications folder.**

   XAMPP is now installed in the `Applications/xampp` folder.

8. **Double click the XAMPP Control icon in the XAMPP folder in your Applications folder.**

   The open Control Panel is shown in Figure A-10.

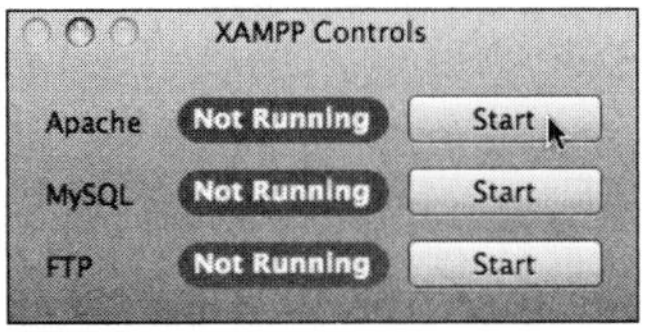

Figure A-10:
The XAMPP
Control
Panel.

In the figure, Apache and MySQL are shown as not running, with a red background on the icon. For your development environment to be ready for work, both must be running.

9. **If Apache and/or MySQL are not running, click Start for each package that isn't running.**

The icon changes to say "Running" with a green background. When both Apache and MySQL are running, your environment is ready for work.

You can now close the XAMPP Control Panel. Your software is installed and ready for you to develop your Web database application.

When the Control Panel is running, its icon is in your Dock. You can click the icon to open the Control Panel.

Using XAMPP

After you complete the XAMPP installation procedure as described in the previous sections, Apache, PHP, and MySQL are ready for you to use.

If it seems like Apache and/or MySQL aren't running correctly, you can open the XAMPP Control Panel to check their status. Sometimes they may not be running, and you can start them. Or, sometimes, stopping and then starting Apache or MySQL can solve a problem.

XAMPP also offers a main page that provides some features that can be useful. The XAMPP main page looks similar to the page shown in Figure A-11.

Figure A-11:
The XAMPP
main page.

To open the XAMPP main page, shown in Figure A-11, open your browser and type **localhost** into the address window. The first time you open XAMPP, you need to choose a language.

The XAMPP main page offers features in a menu down the left side of the page. Some useful features offered are

- ✔ **Status:** Opens a page showing the status of your Web related software.

- ✔ **Documentation:** Provides useful documentation for your Web software.

- ✔ **phpMyAdmin:** Provides a link that opens phpMyAdmin. However, you do not have to open phpMyAdmin through the XAMPP page. You can open phpMyAdmin directly by typing **localhost/phpmyadmin**.

- ✔ **FileZilla FTP:** Provides a link that starts the FileZilla FTP software.

In general, you don't need to use the XAMPP main page very often, if at all. This book doesn't require you to use the page at all. However, it's a good idea to open it once to make sure that everything is working correctly.

Appendix B

Configuring PHP

• •

*T*his appendix assumes that you have the Web software installed.

PHP has many configuration settings that determine how it behaves. I talk about PHP settings at various places throughout the book. For instance, I talk about the PHP error settings when I explain how PHP errors work in Chapter 6. I explain the settings and when they need to be changed in context in the book.

The configuration settings are stored in a text file named php.ini. PHP looks for the file php.ini when it begins and uses the settings it finds. If PHP can't find the file, it uses a set of default settings.

All PHP settings can be changed in the php.ini file. Some settings should always be changed, and some should be changed only in specific circumstances. For example, magic quotes should always be turned off. I explain magic quotes in Chapter 6.

On your own computer, you always have access to the php.ini file and can change the settings yourself. However, a Web host isn't going to allow you access to the general php.ini file, because it controls the settings for all the users on the computer, not just for your site. So, you change any PHP settings on your Web hosting account with a different procedure:

✔ **A local php.ini file:** Some Web hosts allow you to have a local php.ini file that controls: PHP's behavior for your Web site only. If so, you can make any needed changes in this local php.ini file.

✔ **An .htaccess file** You can add directives to your .htaccess file that change PHP settings. Only some settings can be changed this way.

✔ **A statement in the PHP program:** You can add a statement to a PHP program that changes the settings for that program. The new settings only apply to the program it's in, and the old setting is still in place after the script ends. Only some settings can be changed this way.

Notice that only some settings can be changed in an .htaccess file or in a PHP program. You can find a table that shows where PHP settings can be changed at www.php.net/manual/en/ini.list.php. One column in the table is labeled Changeable. The codes in that column define where the setting can be changed, as follows:

✔ PHP_INI_ALL: Can be changed anywhere

✔ PHP_INI_PERDIR: Can be changed in the .htaccess file

✔ PHP_INI_USER: Can be changed temporarily in the PHP program

✔ PHP_INI_SYSTEM: Can be changed only in the php.ini file

Throughout this book, I discuss various settings in context. When I discuss a setting, I discuss how to change it. For example, when I discuss error handling in PHP programs, I discuss the various settings that apply to error handling and how to change them.

Changing Settings in php.ini

You can change all your PHP settings in the php.ini file. You can always edit your own php.ini file with a text editor on your computer. If your Web host allows you a local php.ini on your Web site, you can edit that also with an editor.

In the general php.ini file

Because php.ini is a text file, you can edit it with any text editor. Follow these steps to do so:

1. **Locate the php.ini file that is currently in effect.**

   As explained in Chapter 2, you can see that path to this file in the output from the phpinfo() statement in a PHP program.

2. **Open php.ini in your favorite text editor.**

   The file looks similar to the file shown in Figure B-1.

3. **Scroll down to the setting you want to change.**

   In this example, I am turning magic quotes off. Figure B-2 shows the magic quotes setting that I am going to change.

Figure B-1:
The top of
the php.ini
file.

```
;;;;;;;;;;;
; WARNING ;
;;;;;;;;;;;
; This is the default settings file for new PHP installations.
; By default, PHP installs itself with a configuration suitable for
; development purposes, and *NOT* for production purposes.
; For several security-oriented considerations that should be taken
; before going online with your site, please consult php.ini-recommended
; and http://php.net/manual/en/security.php.


;;;;;;;;;;;;;;;;;;;;;
; About php.ini   ;
;;;;;;;;;;;;;;;;;;;;;
; This file controls many aspects of PHP's behavior.  In order for PHP to
; read it, it must be named 'php.ini'.  PHP looks for it in the current
; working directory, in the path designated by the environment variable
; PHPRC, and in the path that was defined in compile time (in that order).
; Under Windows, the compile-time path is the Windows directory.  The
; path in which the php.ini file is looked for can be overridden using
; the -c argument in command line mode.
;
; The syntax of the file is extremely simple.  Whitespace and Lines
; beginning with a semicolon are silently ignored (as you probably guessed).
; Section headers (e.g. [Foo]) are also silently ignored, even though
; they might mean something in the future.
;
; Directives are specified using the following syntax:
; directive = value
; Directive names are *case sensitive* - foo=bar is different from FOO=bar.
```

4. Change On to Off.

5. Save the changed php.ini file.

6. Restart Apache.

You can open the XAMPP control panel, click Stop, and click Start. Or, you can go into the Services Window, highlight Apache, and click Restart.

Any changes you make to php.ini do not go into effect until you restart Apache.

```
; Magic quotes
;

; Magic quotes for incoming GET/POST/Cookie data.
magic_quotes_gpc = On
```

In a php.ini file on your Web site

If you're allowed a local php.ini file by your Web host, it doesn't need to contain all the settings that are in the general php.ini file. It needs to contain only the settings that you want to change.

In Chapter 2, when testing your setup, you created an empty file named php.ini in your development environment. You can add the settings you want to change to this file.

1. **Open the `php.ini` file in your development site in your favorite text editor.**

   It may be empty or may contain any settings that you previously added to it.

2. **Add the setting you want to change.**

   For instance, to turn off the magic quotes setting, add the following line to the `php.ini` file:

   ```
   magic_quotes_gpc = Off
   ```

3. **Save the `php.ini` file.**

4. **Upload the changed `php.ini` file to your Web site.**

   The changed `php.ini` file replaces the current one, and the setting is changed.

Changing Settings with an .htaccess File

The file named `.htaccess` is an Apache configuration file. Apache reads the file and performs certain tasks based on the directives in the file. You can add directives to the `.htaccess` file that tell Apache to change the configuration settings of PHP. As discussed earlier in this appendix, not all PHP settings can be changed in this file.

The settings in the `.htaccess` file apply to all programs in the directory where the `.htaccess` file resides and in its subdirectories. You can have more than one `.htaccess` file — files with different directives in different directories.

You may or may not already have an `.htaccess` file on your Web site. Some Web hosts use `.htaccess` files on user accounts for their own settings. If there is an `.htaccess` already on your Web site, be careful when you edit it. It may contain directives that are essential to the correct functioning of your Web site.

It's best not to have a copy of the `.htaccess` file in your development environment. The file on your Web site might contain directives that are required on your Web site but cause problems on your local development site, even including disabling your local site.

The directives you use in your `.htaccess` file to change PHP settings are

  ✔ `php_flag`: Used to turn settings on or off.

  ✔ `php_value`: Used to set a value for a setting.

To turn off magic quotes, as shown in the previous section, use the following directive in the .htaccess file:

```
php_flag magic_quotes_gpc Off
```

If you need to set a value for a setting, you use the other directive, such as

```
php_value post_max_size = 10M
```

To change a setting, you just need to edit the .htaccess file to add the new setting. If your Web host provides the ability to edit a file on your Web site, you can edit it there. (The .htaccess file is an exception to my previous statements suggesting you not edit files on your Web site, but only on your development site.)

If you need to edit the .htaccess file on your development site, download the current .htaccess file, add the directive to change the setting, and upload the changed file back to your Web site. Be sure to delete the .htaccess file on your development site after you have uploaded it to your Web site.

Changing Settings with PHP Statements

You can change some PHP settings temporarily with a PHP statement in a program. The setting is changed only while the program is running. When the program finishes, the PHP setting reverts to its previous setting. As mentioned previously, not all PHP settings can be changed in the PHP program.

PHP provides a statement that changes a setting. The general format is

```
ini_set("setting","value");
```

In the previous two sections, I show you how to turn off magic quotes as an example. However, I can't use magic quotes for this example. If you look in the table referenced earlier in this appendix, you'll see that magic_quotes_gpc is shown as PHP_INI_PERDIR. This means that magic quotes cannot be turned off in the program. Magic quotes can be turned off only in the php.ini file or in the .htaccess file.

For this example, I'm turning off errors. When and why you might want to do this is discussed in Chapter 6. To turn off errors, add the following statement at the beginning of a program:

```
ini_set("display_errors","Off");
```

PHP also has some specific statements for certain settings. You can use these instead of the general `ini_set` statement. For example, PHP provides a statement for setting the type of errors you want to display.

It's quite common to want to change which type of errors you display. You might want to use a statement that displays more error messages during development, but you want to display fewer error messages when the Web site goes public. You would rather display error messages in a log file than display them to the general public.

To change the type of errors displayed, temporarily, you use the following statement at the beginning of your program:

```
error_reporting( E_ALL );
```

This statement causes all error messages to be displayed while this program is running, but not for any other program.

Another statement provided by PHP to change a setting is

```
set_time_limit( seconds);
```

This statement sets the amount of time a program can run before PHP decides that something has gone wrong and ends the program.

Index

• N •